“教育部国别和区域研究专项资金资助”（项目批准号：19GBQY011）
结项成果

变革中的埃塞俄比亚：思想的交锋与道路的探索

主　编　翟风杰　Desalegn Amsalu（德萨莱尼·阿姆萨鲁）
副主编　云蔚　潘良　李炜婷

天津大学出版社
TIANJIN UNIVERSITY PRESS

图书在版编目(CIP)数据

变革中的埃塞俄比亚：思想的交锋与道路的探索：汉、英 / 翟风杰, (埃塞) 德萨莱尼・阿姆萨鲁 (Desalegn Amsalu) 主编；云蔚, 潘良, 李炜婷副主编. -- 天津：天津大学出版社, 2022.9

“教育部国别和区域研究专项资金资助”（项目批准号：19GBQY011）结项成果

ISBN 978-7-5618-7306-9

Ⅰ. ①变… Ⅱ. ①翟… ②德… ③云… ④潘… ⑤李… Ⅲ. ①埃塞俄比亚—研究—文集—汉、英 Ⅳ. ①D742.1-53

中国版本图书馆CIP数据核字(2022)第161503号

出版发行	天津大学出版社
地　　址	天津市卫津路92号天津大学内（邮编：300072）
电　　话	发行部：022-27403647
网　　址	www.tjupress.com.cn
印　　刷	北京盛通商印快线网络科技有限公司
经　　销	全国各地新华书店
开　　本	787×1092　1/16
印　　张	20.75
字　　数	674千
版　　次	2022年9月第1版
印　　次	2022年9月第1次
定　　价	59.00元

序言

在众多非洲国家之中,埃塞俄比亚无疑是具特殊性和代表性的国家之一。在地缘政治上,埃塞俄比亚位于非洲之角核心地区,东与吉布提、索马里接壤,南与肯尼亚为邻,西与苏丹和南苏丹交界,北与厄立特里亚相连,在非洲之角地区的和平与安全,尤其是在索马里恐怖主义活动的遏制和亚丁湾的航行安全等方面扮演着重要的角色。

历史上,埃塞俄比亚不仅是撒哈拉以南非洲地区唯一拥有自己的文字体系的文明古国,也是该地区唯一战胜西方殖民者成功捍卫独立主权地位的国家。在过去的三千多年中,埃塞俄比亚人创造了灿烂的文明,并为后人留下了丰富的物质和非物质文化遗产,如拉利贝拉岩石教堂、阿克苏姆方尖碑、吉兹文字、埃塞俄比亚历法等。19 世纪末,孟尼利克二世率领的埃塞俄比亚军队在阿杜瓦战役中击败意大利侵略者,捍卫了埃塞俄比亚的独立,也极大地鼓舞了国际泛非主义运动的发展。

当前,埃塞俄比亚不仅是非洲第二人口大国和经济增长较快的国家之一,还是非洲联盟、联合国非洲经济委员会等重要国际组织的总部所在国,而且已经加入"一带一路"倡议,成为该倡议的重要节点国家,在非洲大陆的区域政治经济格局以及中国和非洲关系大局中都具有显著的战略地位。

和许多受过西方殖民主义和霸权主义侵害的亚非发展中国家一样,埃塞俄比亚的领导人或者说精英阶层一直在探索适合埃塞俄比亚的现代化道路,希望可以借以实现民族和国家的复兴。近代以来,英国、意大利两国曾多次发动对埃塞俄比亚的侵略战争,给埃塞俄比亚人民造成了巨大的伤害。在与西方列强打交道的过程中,埃塞俄比亚的领导人和精英阶层深刻认识到了他们的国家与西方列强的国力差距。为实现埃塞俄比亚的现代化和赶超,海尔·塞拉西皇帝和德格政权曾先后模仿日本和苏联的现代化模式,但最终都以失败告终。

如果说海尔·塞拉西皇帝的改革和德格政府的"科学社会主义"道路是对他国发展道路和模式的复制,那么埃塞俄比亚人民革命民主阵线(简称"埃革阵")已故领导人梅莱斯·泽纳维引领的"革命民主主义"理念和"民主发展型国家"模式则反映了埃塞俄比亚领导人在发展道路探索上的突破。"革命民主主义"理念是梅莱斯·泽纳维将马列主义意识形态与埃革阵执政初期的国际形势及埃塞俄比亚的国情相结合的产物,它一方面反映了梅莱斯·泽纳维在意识形态上向西方自由主义的妥协，另一方面也反映了梅莱斯·泽纳维在道路设计上对埃塞俄比亚国情的分析和思考。作为对"革命民主主义"的补充，"民主发展型国家"模式是梅莱斯·泽纳维借鉴中国、日本、韩国等亚洲国家的发展经验并结合埃塞俄比亚的国情而提出的具有埃塞俄比亚特色的"发展型国家"模式。"革命民主主义"理念和"民主发展型国家"模式集中反映了以梅莱斯·泽纳维为核心的埃革阵领导核心在道路探索上的创新和实践。梅莱斯·泽纳维执政期间（1991—2012），埃塞政局保持了长期的稳定，国民经济也随着经济体制的改革和投资环境的改善而步入快速增长的轨道。在这一时期，埃塞俄比亚显著的经济增长一度被视为非洲经济崛起的标志，但埃革阵在治国理政的理念设计和发展道路探索上忽视了埃塞俄比亚的民族问题和政治体制改革的必要性。提格雷人民解放阵线（简称"提人阵"）对政权的长期垄断导致了埃塞俄比亚族裔民族主义运动的抬头，为梅莱斯·泽纳维去世后提人阵遭到清算埋下了伏笔。

2018 年以来，随着新总理阿比·艾哈迈德·阿里的上台和提人阵的日趋边缘化，埃塞俄比亚国内掀起了关于阿比政府是应该继续走"民主发展型国家"道路，还是应该改弦更张走新自由主义道路的论战。在西方媒体、政客和相关机构明里暗里的支持下，埃塞俄比亚的新自由主义思潮呈现出了前所未有的复苏趋势。阿比上台初期与西方的频繁互动及其改革承诺也引发了外界关于埃塞俄比亚可能走新自由主义道路的猜测。

但阿比领导下的埃塞俄比亚并没有出现完全新自由主义化的趋势。阿比上台后选择了一条相对折中的路线，他拒绝沿着埃革阵的"民主发展型国家"模式继续前行，也没有倒向西方的新自由主义道路，而是创造性地提出了自己的"协同理念"，并致力于将其打造成一个集哲学、政治、经济和文化内涵的本土意识形态框架。该理念强调，个人、族群、国家、资源和观念的有机结合可以带来比他们相互孤立或对抗时大得多的正面效益，是专门针对埃塞俄比亚目前存在的民族冲突、宗教矛盾、意识形态碰撞、利益分配问题等深层次的政治、经济和社会问题而提出的本土理念构想。

"协同理念"的提出反映了阿比作为非洲青年一代领导人探索适合本国国情的发展道路的愿望和决心，是非洲本土创制的又一尝试，在埃塞俄比亚乃至非洲大陆的发展进程中都具有特殊的意义。

翟风杰

2021 年 8 月 25 日

目录

第一部分　道路的探索与国家认同的构建

第二部分 发展与变革中的埃塞俄比亚

第一部分　道路的探索与国家认同的构建

第一部分综述

埃塞俄比亚是“一带一路”倡议的重要节点国家，也是非洲第二人口大国和非洲经济增长较快的国家之一，还是非洲联盟、联合国非洲经济委员会等重要国际组织的总部所在国，在非洲区域政治经济格局以及中国和非洲关系大局中都具有特殊的地位。近年来，受经济发展不平衡、政治和经济体制改革滞后等问题的影响，埃塞俄比亚民族和社会矛盾空前激化，多种社会思潮相互激荡，对该国的政治、经济和安全形势产生了深刻的影响。其中，埃塞俄比亚社会各界关于埃塞俄比亚应继续走“民主发展型国家”道路还是应走新自由主义道路的探讨、族裔民族主义与国家认同之间的矛盾、阿比政府的意识形态倾向性等话题尤其值得关注。

本部分精选中英文学术论文 10 篇，主要涉及埃塞俄比亚“革命民主主义”理念、“民主发展型国家”模式、埃塞俄比亚新自由主义思潮、阿比总理的“协同理念”、埃塞俄比亚的国家认同问题与民族主义思潮等议题。相关选题和内容有助于读者进一步了解埃塞俄比亚主流意识形态的演变趋势以及埃塞俄比亚国家认同问题的现状和历史根源。

阿比·艾哈迈德“协同理念”初探

潘　良　云　蔚　德萨莱尼·阿姆萨鲁（Desalegn Amsalu）①
（天津职业技术师范大学非盟研究中心，天津 300222）

摘要：“协同理念”（“መደመር”或“Medemer”）是埃塞俄比亚（简称“埃塞”）总理阿比·艾哈迈德·阿里（Abiy Ahmed Ali）于 2018 年执政后，以埃塞本土价值观念为内核，以埃塞近代以来的发展经验和教训为借鉴，以团结各民族、维护国家统一和实现国家复兴为目的而构建的本土治国理政思想和理念。“协同理念”的提出反映了阿比作为非洲青年一代领导人探索适合本国国情的发展道路的愿望和决心，是非洲本土创制的又一尝试，在埃塞乃至非洲大陆的发展进程中都具有特殊的意义。本文对阿比“协同理念”的主要内涵进行了梳理，并在此基础上对该理念的意识形态倾向性进行了尝试性的探讨和分析。

关键词：埃塞；协同理念；内涵

自 1974 年封建王朝覆灭后，埃塞先后经历了德格政权（Derg Regime，1974—1991）、埃塞人民革命民主阵线（The Ethiopian People's Revolutionary Democratic Front，简称“埃革阵”，1991—2018）政权和当前的繁荣党（Prosperity Party）政权三个时期，其执政党的指导思想也从门格斯图（Mengism Hale Mariam）的“科学社会主义”转变为梅莱斯·泽纳维（Meles Zenawi）的“革命民主主义”（Revolutionary Democracy）和“民主发展型国家”(Democratic Developmental State) 理念，再到阿比的“协同理念”的转变。与舶来的“科学社会主义”和“革命民主主义”理念有所不同，阿比的“协同理念”强调以埃塞本土传统价值观念为内核构建本土治国理念，具有鲜明的本土创制色彩。

一、埃塞自近代以来的道路探索

埃塞是世界文明古国之一，有着悠久的文化传统。早在公元前 8 世纪左右，该国北部高原地区便形成了早期的国家——达莫特王国（出现于公元前 7—公元前 5 世纪）。公元 1 世纪，阿克苏姆王国（Aksum Kingdom）崛起于现厄立特里亚和埃塞提格雷地区（Tigray）。鼎盛时期的阿克苏姆王国一度横跨红海两岸，控制着东西方贸易的海上通道。公元 4 世纪，基督教传入阿克苏姆王国，并成为阿克苏姆王国的国教。埃塞也因此被视为继亚美尼亚之后第二个正式宣布基督教为国教的国家。此后，直至 1974 年海尔·塞拉西皇帝（Emperor Haile Selassie，1982—1975）遭到废除，埃塞长期处于东正教君主的统治之下。在这一漫长的历史进程中，埃塞东正教信仰逐渐与本土文化元素融合，形成了具有埃塞特色的东正教传统，成

① 埃塞俄比亚亚的斯亚贝巴大学埃塞俄比亚研究院副教授。

为古典埃塞的文化内核。从中世纪(以 13 世纪为开端)到近代(埃塞史学界将 1855 年作为埃塞近代史的开端),埃塞一直以阿比西尼亚王国(Kingdom of Abyssinia)之名为周边地区所熟知。这段时间内,所罗门王朝的统治范围大体上包括现厄立特里亚和埃塞提格雷州大部分地区以及现贡德尔(Gonder)、绍阿(Showa)、沃洛(Wello)等地的部分地区,其人口以闪米特语系的提格雷卜和阿姆哈拉人为主①。

东正教传统作为埃塞国家认同的基石的情况一直维持到近代才开始发生变化。19 世纪末,在约翰内斯四世(Yohannes Ⅳ, 1831—1889)和孟尼利克二世(Menilik Ⅱ, 1844—1913)的武力扩张下,埃塞的版图和人口结构发生了巨大的变化。1879—1904 年,这两位皇帝通过军事征服,先后将现奥罗米亚州、南方各族州、索马利亚州、甘贝拉、本尚古穆等地区纳入埃塞版图②。随着埃塞帝国领土的大幅扩张,埃塞的人口结构,尤其是民族构成和宗教构成发生了根本性的变化,东正教的绝对主导性地位开始动摇,为埃塞国家认同问题的产生埋下了隐患。

为了实现国家的现代化改造,以孟尼利克二世和海尔·塞拉西皇帝为代表的帝国统治者开始将探索发展道路的目光投向了当时先进的工业化国家。由于埃塞和俄国在国情上(双方都是君主制和东正教国家)的相似性,孟尼利克二世长期和沙皇俄国保持着非常密切的合作关系。沙俄不仅在第一次意埃战争中为孟尼利克二世提供了武器支持和军事顾问,而且为埃塞培养了第一批现代军事指挥官。在海尔·塞拉西时期,埃塞的一部分知识分子开始将注意力转向日本,认为日本明治维新的模式更适合埃塞的政体。埃塞历史上第一部宪法便是日本学派知识分子特科勒·哈瓦瑞特(Tekle Hawariat)根据日本的《明治宪法》修改而来的③。海尔·塞拉西的改革试图在不动摇君主地位及封建土地所有制的前提下通过有限的放权和经济、教育等领域改革实现国家的现代化,但这一改革的局限性也决定了其无法从根本上解决埃塞的社会矛盾和问题,也无法改变埃塞帝国走向崩溃的命运。

20 世纪 60 年代,埃塞爆发了反对封建帝制的学生运动。不同于封建统治者,埃塞的学生运动将马克思列宁主义、毛泽东思想引入了埃塞当代政治进程,为 1974 年革命的爆发提供了思想上的武器。在 1974 年的埃塞革命中,以马克思列宁主义、毛泽东思想为指导的学生、知识分子和亚的斯亚贝巴工人阶级(工会)扮演了关键性的角色,赋予了这场革命鲜明的无产阶级革命色彩。但兵变军官组成的委员会④窃取了革命的果实,成为这次革命的最终受益者。德格委员会名义上宣称走社会主义道路,实际上却在门格斯图的主导下走上了彻头彻尾的军事专制统治道路。以门格斯图为首的德格集团长期主导埃塞政权,以至于这个名义上的"社会主义国家"长期没有无产阶级执政党的存在⑤。

1991 年,提格雷人民解放阵线(Tigray People's Liberation Front,简称"提人阵")主导的

① Bahru Zewde, "A History of Modern Ethiopia: 1855-1991", Addis Ababa: Addis Ababa University, 2002, pp.1-26.

② Paul B Henze, *Layers of Time: A History of Ethiopia*, New York: Palgrave, 2000, pp.144-188.

③ Mohammed Girma, "Religion, Politics and the Dilemma of Modernising Ethiopia," *HTS Teologiese Studies/Theological Studies*, 74(1), pp.4-5, retrieved from: https://doi.org/10.4102/hts.v74i1.4878.

④ 1974 年 2 月以来,埃塞多支武装力量的中下层军官先后发动兵变,控制了亚的斯亚贝巴并于 1974 年 6 月组建埃塞国家军队、警察和地方自卫队统筹委员会(Coordinating Committee of the Armed Forces, Police and the Territorial Army),逐步接管国家政权。1974 年 9 月 11 日,该委员会宣布成立埃塞临时军事行政委员会 (Provisional Military Administrative Council),废除海尔·塞拉西皇帝,并宣布成立埃塞临时军政府(Provisional Military Government of Ethiopia),即德格政权(Derg Regime)。

⑤ 1987 年,埃塞工人党(The Workers' Party of Ethiopia)正式成为执政党。

政党联盟埃革阵推翻了门格斯图政权，成为执政党。提人阵成立初期在意识形态领域曾一度推崇中国式的"新民主主义革命"，在军事斗争上也采取"农村包围城市"的战略和游击战术。20 世纪 80 年代初中国实行改革开放政策后，提人阵视中国的改革为走"修正主义"道路并开始在意识形态上转向恩维尔·霍查(Enver Hoxha)的阿尔巴尼亚模式①。20 世纪 80 年代末 90 年代初，随着东欧剧变与苏联的解体，梅莱斯·泽纳维逐渐放弃了原有的马克思列宁主义话语，转而根据国际形势和埃塞国情提出了新的指导思想。梅莱斯·泽纳维认为，占埃塞人口绝大多数的农民阶层构成了埃塞现阶段的社会基础，因此也是埃塞社会发展的根本推动力量。基于这一判断，梅莱斯·泽纳维提出了以广大农民阶层为社会基础，以埃革阵为领导核心，以民主集中制作为党内组织原则，以农业发展带动工业化，推动埃塞实现从以农民为主体的农业社会到以进步资产阶级、中产阶级和工人阶级为社会主体的资本主义社会转型的"革命民主主义"理念。该理念以及 1995 年宪法规定的联邦制、三权分立原则和多党制原则是梅莱斯·泽纳维基于国情和国际形势向西方新自由主义妥协的产物。

在经历了 2001 年的党内政治斗争和 2005 年的大选危机后，梅莱斯·泽纳维深刻意识到埃革阵在意识形态和执政合法性上的薄弱环节，对理念创新及其实践进行了更进一步的探索。"民主发展型国家"开始日益频繁地出现于埃塞的官方话语中，逐渐成为埃塞革命民主主义理念新的补充和埃塞的发展指南。梅莱斯·泽纳维认为，市场机制无法解决发展中国家实现经济增长急需的科技能力积累、社会发展和市场失灵等问题，非洲国家新自由主义尝试的失败表明新自由主义模式在非洲已经成为绝路，而东亚地区国家发展经验表明"发展型国家"模式可以带来经济和社会的快速发展。他认为，"发展型国家"可以同时是一个民主国家，而且笃定"民主发展型国家"模式一定会比其他模式更为有效。因此，他主张非洲国家应考虑将发展模式从新自由主义转向"发展型国家"模式②。梅莱斯·泽纳维执政期间(1991—2012)，埃塞政局保持了长期的稳定，国民经济也随着经济体制和投资环境的改善而日趋步入增长的轨道。但民族联邦制对族裔民族认同的强调和提人阵对政治权利的长期垄断导致了族裔民族主义运动的抬头，为梅莱斯·泽纳维去世后提人阵的逐渐边缘化和埃塞的政治格局演变埋下了伏笔。

从孟尼利克二世到梅莱斯·泽纳维，埃塞的统治者和政治精英在国家的现代化模式上曾先后学习沙俄、日本、苏联以及中国、韩国等亚洲国家的现代化发展模式，但都以失败告终。梅莱斯·泽纳维吸取中国、韩国等亚洲经济体的发展经验而构建的"民主发展型国家"理念在推动经济发展方面取得了前所未有的巨大成效，但在国家认同的构建上存在严重的制度性缺陷，最终导致了埃塞族裔民族主义思潮的兴起和提人阵的下台。埃革阵退出历史舞台后，其执政理念也遭到后来者的否定，道路探索和选择再次成为埃塞的政治精英们不得不面对的新挑战。

---

① Aregawi Berhe, "The Origins of the Tigray People's Liberation Front," *African Affairs,* 2004, 103/413, p.580; Aregawi Berhe, *A Political History of the Tigray People's Liberation Front (*1975-1991*): Revolt, Ideology and Mobilisation in Ethiopia*, Los Angeles, Tsehai Publishers & Distributors, 2009, p. 213.

② Meles Zenawi, *African Development: Dead Ends and New Beginnings (Preliminary Draft)*, retrieved from: https://www.africa-nidea.org/m_zenawi_aug_9_2006.pdf, 20 May 2021.

二、阿比·艾哈迈德·阿里的上台与“协同理念”的提出

2018 年 4 月,在汹涌的奥罗莫和阿姆哈拉族裔民族主义运动的冲击和埃革阵内部权力斗争的双重压力下,埃塞前总理海尔马里亚姆·德萨莱尼(Hailemariam Desalegn)宣布辞职,将权力让渡给具有奥罗莫族和阿姆哈拉族混血背景的阿比·艾哈迈德·阿里。阿比担任总理初期,很多人认为他只是埃革阵为了缓和民族矛盾而推选出来的具有奥罗莫族背景的临时代言人。但事实证明,持有这种想法的人都低估了阿比和奥罗莫民主党的政治动员能力和执政意愿。阿比自上台后很快就提出了强调民族和解的“协同理念”(መደመር),并通过一系列政治动员运动和改革赢得了埃塞人民的支持。作为一个常用的阿姆哈拉语词汇,“መደመር”主要有“加法”“增加”“聚集”等含义。但阿比赋予了该词语更为丰富的内涵,强调个体、组织、民族等社会主体和资源的有机组合可以产生大于它们个体作用之和的增效作用。这一理念最初是阿比总理针对埃塞近年来愈演愈烈的族裔民族主义和认同政治问题而提出的治理理念。区别于埃革阵及其反对党此前提出的多种强调团结一致(Unity)的理念,“协同理念”更强调民族和文化多样性的价值以及这些多样性之间的共存和互动所能产生的协同增效作用。随着阿比及其执政团队对该理念的不断补充和完善,该理念已经日渐成为阿比政府的意识形态框架,具有政治、经济、文化、社会等多领域的广泛内涵。该理念的提出和推广有望深刻影响乃至重塑埃塞在民族和国家认同方面的意识形态,对埃塞的稳定、国家大政方针和发展战略产生深远的影响。

2019 年 1 月,阿比总理在达沃斯论坛上第一次对其提出的“协同理念”进行了较为系统的阐述。他指出,埃塞当前的改革深深扎根于埃塞的“协同理念”,这一理念则主要包括以下三大支柱。

第一,建设一个充满活力的民主体制。阿比认为,建立一个民主和多元化的民主国家需要迅速和果断的行动来增强公民对政府的信任[①]。虽然埃塞经济在过去十年中以年均 10% 的速度快速增长,但埃塞的社会发展在威权主义时期停滞不前,政府的镇压手段严重破坏了自由和民主。因此,他承诺推动多党制的落实,重新审查过去的限制性法律,包括常常用来压制反对意见的《反恐法》和出台新的《公民社会法》等。此前,阿比政府已经释放了 13 000 多名囚犯。提人阵主政时期长期持分裂主义主张的反对派团体——奥罗莫解放阵线和“Ginbot 7”流亡运动也获得了议会的承认并实现了合法化。索马里地区主席阿布迪·穆罕默德·奥马尔(Abdi Mohamoud Omar)也因为其控制下的索马里准军事特警部队(Liyu Police)涉嫌镇压人民而遭到免职。在性别平等方面,阿比的新内阁中有一半是女性,议会任命前外交官萨赫勒-沃克·祖德(Sahel-Wok Zewde)为埃塞历史上的首位女总统。此外,埃塞最高法院和选举委员会的负责人 Meaza Ashenaf 和 Birtukan Mideksa 也均为女性。

第二,保持经济活力。阿比认为,埃塞先前建立的发展模式似乎已经达到极限,新政府必须迅速想出新的战略以拯救埃塞的经济。他指出,作为非洲第二人口大国,埃塞政府需要通过改善教育系统,为公民发挥他们的潜力创造条件。他还强调了赋能妇女和青年的重要

① “A Conversation with Abiy Ahmed, Prime Minister of Ethiopia”, www.weforum.org, retrieved from: https://www.weforum.org/events/world-economic-forum-annual-meeting-2019/sessions/a-conversation-with-abiy-ahmed-prime-minister-of-ethiopia, 22 May 2021.

意义，指出没有妇女和青年的参与，埃塞就无法进入国际市场的中心。因此，要创造一个充满活力的经济环境，埃塞政府需要做到以下几点：为中小企业提供融资便利；放宽创业监管，改善政策环境（包括体制改革、投资法等商业法规的完善等）；使私营部门成为经济的主要组成部分并向国际商业开放（主要举措如出售国有企业的少数股份和重新分配公共开支等）；鼓励公私合营[①]。

第三，坚持区域一体化和对外开放。阿比认为，区域一体化能够减少邻国之间发生冲突的可能性，埃塞将始终坚持对外开放并致力于非洲区域一体化进程，加入自由贸易协定（CFTA），积极参与非洲大陆以及次区域的国际组织，如非盟、东非政府间发展组织（Intergovernmental Authority on Development）、东南非共同市场（Common Market for Easter and Southern Africa）等。他认为，埃塞与厄立特里亚的和解为该地区建立"和平带"创造了机会。此外，埃塞及其邻国可以通过"协同效应"和节约资源的方式来优化其向世界开放的机会。他还进一步主张设立一个能够代表所有伊加特组织国家的单一外交职位，以节省资源，在发展问题上更好地进行区域协调[②]。

三、"协同理念"的主要内涵

2019年10月19日，继获得诺贝尔和平奖之后，埃塞总理阿比·艾哈迈德·阿里在亚的斯亚贝巴发布了《协同理念》[③]一书，书中详细阐述其执政思想和发展理念。阿比认为，埃塞的历史经验表明复制其他国家的发展模式和理念在埃塞是行不通的，只有一个真正内生于埃塞本土文化和传统价值、能够充分考虑埃塞国情特殊性的本土理念或者哲学框架才能解决埃塞的发展问题。"协同理念"就是承此使命而生的一个理念。在这本书中，阿比指出，19世纪以来埃塞一直在借鉴和模仿其他国家的发展模式和意识形态，海尔·塞拉西皇帝学习日本明治维新改革，德格政权复制苏联模式，埃革阵向东亚国家学习"发展型国家"模式，但这些尝试都以失败告终，其根本原因在于这些外来模式并不符合埃塞的特殊国情。因此他认为，埃塞需要一个内生的本土理念或哲学作为国家的思想引领。"协同理念"（或者说"协同哲学"）就是他基于对客观规律的观察和埃塞的传统价值而构建的理念。他指出，"协同"是一个具有广泛适用性的理念，是可以解释政治、经济和社会文化结构与行为的哲学概念，其核心概念即多个行为主体和客体的有机结合可以带来更优的结果，其基本要素为共同目标和愿景[④]。

（一）"协同理念"的哲理内涵

"协同理念"的基本要义可以理解为社会性的个人、团体或者民族为了实现更优的结果而选择接受彼此与相互合作。阿比试图将"协同"的字面含义与人类作为社会性动物的本质联系起来，赋予该词语以哲学层面的新内涵。他在《协同理念》书中指出，人类作为社会

---

① "A Conversation with Abiy Ahmed, Prime Minister of Ethiopia", www.weforum.org, retrieved from: https://www.weforum.org/events/world-economic-forum-annual-meeting-2019/sessions/a-conversation-with-abiy-ahmed-prime-minister-of-ethiopia, 22 May 2021.

② 同①。

③ 阿比·艾哈迈德. 协同理念. 洛杉矶：太阳出版社，2019.

④ 阿比·艾哈迈德. 协同理念. 洛杉矶：太阳出版社，2019, pp.35-48.

性的动物，孤立地生活不是最优的选择。当系统、个人或团体处于相互孤立或者排斥状态，他们便无法通过互动与交流取长补短，所以更容易遭遇挫折和失败。但只要他们走到一起，朝着一个共同的方向努力，他们之间的互动与合作就会产生“1+1>2”的更强的创造力和生产力[①]。

“协同理念”的基本要素是共同目标和愿景。阿比在《协同理念》一书指出，阿杜瓦战役向人们展示了“共同目标”的强大力量，在这场战役中，埃塞的不同民族因为一个共同的目标——保家卫国——紧紧团结在一起，打败了武器装备更为先进的意大利侵略者。目前，埃塞最大的敌人不是其他国家，而是不同民族间的矛盾和经济与社会发展的滞后。在这样一个基本现实中，民族团结和繁荣无疑是埃塞最需要也是最受欢迎的目标和愿景。因此，“协同”是埃塞人民的唯一也是最佳的选择[②]。

（二）“协同理念”的政治内涵

阿比认为埃塞族裔民族主义和公民民族主义之间的矛盾是埃塞探索本土化民主道路的最大障碍，“协同理念”框架可以调解这两种民族主义类型之间的矛盾，使他们成为构建埃塞本土民主道路的砖石而非障碍。阿比认为族裔民族主义和公民民族主义之间并不存在绝对的对立关系。他指出，埃塞的形成是阿比西尼亚军事扩张的结果，这种国家构建模式导致了族裔民族主义的兴起。基于族裔民族主义的民族联邦制是不同族裔民族主义运动相互妥协的结果，但其意识形态基础尤其是对民族文化差异和民族权力的过度强调导致了严重的社会分化和矛盾，对埃塞国家的统一造成了严重的影响[③]。“协同理念”将引导埃塞人重新定义自己的价值观，重建共同的价值，为共同的未来而奋斗。 从这个角度上看，“协同理念”具有显著的泛埃塞公民民族主义倾向。

根据阿比的设想，埃塞要成为一个繁荣、民主的国家，首先需要优先实现以下几个目标。

第一，建设一个自由、独立和称职的公共服务机构体系。阿比认为，缺乏一个行之有效的公共服务机构体系是埃塞历届政权的一个通病，也是这些政权无法长久的重要原因之一。他指出埃塞之所以无法建立自由、独立和称职的政府机构，是因为政府和公共服务机构之间的边界不清晰。在埃塞的官僚机构中，宗族和新宗族形式的效忠关系十分猖獗。结构性腐败和任人唯亲导致公共服务机构已成为基于党派、个人或族裔群体的利益关系而形成的利益群体。这种政治文化腐蚀了执政党的群众基础与执政合法性。因此，埃塞要建立一个繁荣、民主的国家，就必须先建设一个自由、独立和称职的公共服务机构体系[④]。

第二，实现政治领导人从统治者向人民公仆的转变。阿比认为，统治者和领导者在性质上存在本质的区别。统治者惯于使用武力来影响他人，其执政目的是自己的利益。与之相反，领导力应该来自品德和能力。领导者凭借其个人的道德品质和构建共同目标和愿景的能力，吸引他人接受他的思想和主张，自愿为实现这一愿景作出贡献。阿比认为，埃塞需要有能力引导国家走上正确道路的变革型的领导人，而这种变革型的领导人的培养需要一批

① 阿比·艾哈迈德. 协同理念. 洛杉矶：太阳出版社，2019，pp.35-48.
② 同①。
③ 阿比·艾哈迈德. 协同理念. 洛杉矶：太阳出版社，2019，pp.13-14.
④ 阿比·艾哈迈德. 协同理念. 洛杉矶：太阳出版社，2019，pp.126-133.

富有远见的教师队伍，更需要塑造一个尊重品德和能力的政治文化环境①。

第三，基于本土文化和价值观，建构一个健康的政治文化环境。阿比认为，埃塞人有自己独特的政治文化价值观。只是领导人并没有能够充分运用这些价值观来建立一种有弹性的民主文化。相反，人民和政府的每一个解决方案都依赖于外部世界的理念。因此，他的“协同理念”将致力于从本土的价值观和思想中寻求解决本土问题的解决方案②。

（三）“协同理念”的经济内涵

阿比认为，虽然过去28年见证了埃塞的国民经济的快速增长，但这种增长是以严重的收入不平等、两位数的通货膨胀率、生活成本的上升，以及预算赤字、贸易不平衡、储蓄与投资之间的不平衡、债务危机和缺乏外汇储备等宏观经济不平衡为代价的。在阿比看来，目前埃塞在经济发展方面上存在三个短板。

第一，市场的作用没有得到有效发挥。阿比认为，政府对市场的干预过多或太少都会导致市场失衡。埃塞过去的问题在于政府对市场的过度控制。他认为，政府对市场的干预应具有选择性和针对性③。

第二，政府部门在经济领域的领导能力还有待提升。阿比认为，政府领导层的能力不足是埃塞经济体制失败的主要原因。他认为，以前的埃塞政府没能建立一个符合埃塞国情的经济发展模式，也未能制定出可以解决相应经济问题的经济政策。他们所实施的大多数经济政策都是从其他国家的经验中照搬而来的，无法解决现存的经济失衡问题④。

第三，其他部门和经济部门之间缺乏关联。阿比认为，埃塞缺乏一个有利于经济发展的宏观制度环境，其他部门，如教育部门，长期和经济发展脱钩。他还认为，包括政府、大学、私营部门和公民组织等经济生活中的不同主体都应该在建设弹性经济体系方面发挥作用⑤。

针对上述问题，阿比认为，建立基于健康竞争的自由市场体系是建立可持续经济体系的重要解决途径。此外，阿比尤其强调埃塞经济从农业到工业的结构性转变的必要性。他认为，埃塞的农业受土地面积固定、土地肥力恶化和气候变化等问题的制约。在过去20余年中，埃塞一直在贯彻以农业发展带动工业化的思路。但截至目前，埃塞仍然是饥荒易发国家。埃塞的农业部门也没有实现技术改造。因此，阿比认为，埃塞需要重新思考发展政策的导向性，必须将经济发展思路从依赖农业转向工业。他还认为，埃塞的工业发展面临劳动力生产效率低、产业结构不完善、国际贸易竞争较弱、缺乏工艺技术等问题。针对这些问题，他提出了“建设知识型经济”的主张。但他也强调，埃塞不应该成为西方技术的盲目接受者，而应该成为符合埃塞发展需求的技术的创新者⑥。

（四）“协同理念”的外交内涵

阿比在《协同理念》一书中指出，埃塞以往的外交政策并没有出现重大错误，因此埃塞

① 阿比·艾哈迈德. 协同理念. 洛杉矶：太阳出版社，2019，pp.134-143.
② 阿比·艾哈迈德. 协同理念. 洛杉矶：太阳出版社，2019，pp.144-154.
③ 阿比·艾哈迈德. 协同理念. 洛杉矶：太阳出版社，2019，pp.165-196.
④ 同③。
⑤ 同③。
⑥ 阿比·艾哈迈德. 协同理念. 洛杉矶：太阳出版社，2019，pp.216-238.

今后的外交政策不会发生重大转变,但埃塞政府将致力于提高合作水平,优先重视周边国家。因为埃塞是一个内陆国家,邻国是埃塞通向世界其他地方的门户,其港口的准入取决于埃塞与邻国的良好关系。更重要的是,阿比认为,埃塞的和平和安全在很大程度上取决于邻国的和平。因此,埃塞政府将致力于在非洲尤其是东非地区的区域一体化中发挥更加积极的作用[①]。

四、"协同理念"的局限性和挑战

(一)"协同理念"的局限性

"协同理念"是以阿比·艾哈迈德为代表的埃塞新一代政治精英在发展道路探索上一次具有划时代意义的本土创制尝试,具有非凡的意义。但客观而言,"协同理念"还处于理念构建的早期阶段,在民族问题和国家认同构建、本土文化根源的发掘和阐述以及公众参与等方面都存在一定程度的局限性,主要表现在以下几个方面。

第一,解决埃塞的民族矛盾和重塑国家认同是协同理念的初衷,但恰是在这一领域"协同理念"并没有突破性的理论构想和改革方案。尽管阿比曾多次指出埃塞现有民族联邦制的问题,但直至目前,阿比及其执政团队并没有提出明确的联邦制改革方案。在 2021 年 6 月的大选中,相对于反对党要求修改宪法、废除民族联邦制的鲜明主张,繁荣党似乎选择了向族裔民族主义暂时妥协的保守主义立场,倾向于维持现状。

第二,"协同理念"没有就该理念的本土文化根源进行更进一步的挖掘和梳理,导致该理念的内生性遭到了质疑。阿比始终强调"协同理念"植根于埃塞的传统价值观,如埃塞东正教传统和奥罗莫人的盖达制度(Gada System)等,但他并未就此展开进一步的论述。

第三,2019 年《协同理念》一书发布后,部分埃塞学者批评该书只是阿比个人关于埃塞社会问题及其出路的思考,缺乏公众尤其是相关领域的专家、学者和智库的参与,在理论深度上也存在明显的不足,难以引起埃塞各族人民的深层次认同和情感共鸣。在得到社会各界的反馈后,阿比专门为"协同理念"开设了一个专用网站,用于宣传该理念和征集社会各界对该理念的看法和建议[②]。

(二)"协同理念"的挑战

除了上述局限性外,阿比的"协同理念"还存在若干严峻的挑战。

第一,出于对流失选票的担忧,阿比上台以来一直对奥罗莫和阿姆拉哈等主要民族的族裔民族主义思潮过于投鼠忌器,这种对政治现实的妥协导致阿比的繁荣党在 2021 年 6 月的大选中从坚定的泛埃塞俄比亚派转变为主张维持现状的保守派。这与阿比政府对提人阵的铁腕镇压形成了鲜明的对比。这种相互矛盾的立场削弱了阿比"协同理念"的信服力。

第二,来自反对党的猛烈抨击或"抹黑"可能给"协同理念"带来严重的挑战。《协同理念》一书出版后,不少民族主义评论者从宗教角度对阿比的"协同理念"进行了批评和抨击,

---

① 阿比·艾哈迈德. 协同理念. 洛杉矶:太阳出版社,2019,pp.250-267.

② 该网站名称即为"መደመር",网址为:https://medemer.et/。

认为阿比在其执政理念中灌注了大量的五旬节教派的思想。他们认为，阿比的繁荣党之名来源于五旬节教派的“繁荣福音”，而“协同理念”有加法（“+”）之意，恰好是十字架的形状，故而认定阿比正试图用政治手段传播五旬节教派宗教信仰①。阿比的执政理想是否受其宗教信仰的影响我们无从得知，但在民族和宗教认同高度重叠且族裔民族主义思想空前高涨的埃塞，这种言论无疑具有非常大的煽动性。

目前，“协同理念”尚处于理念构建的初期阶段，还存在诸多的不完善之处，且面临着多方面的挑战。但阿比政府已经认识到这些问题和挑战，也在积极创造条件，鼓励社会各界参与该理念的理论构建和完善过程之中。因此，该理念在埃塞落地生根并产生巨大影响的前景依旧可期。

五、“协同理念”的意识形态倾向性

阿比上台后与提人阵的渐行渐远及其本人对埃革阵意识形态的否定一度让国际社会认为阿比政府很可能全盘推翻埃革阵的施政纲领和经济战略，全面投向西方新自由主义的怀抱。在国内外观察者看来，阿比上台以来的举动释放了阿比政府与前任政府在国家发展道路选择上的不同。评论家认为，这些措施体现了他对上届政府的突破。阿比拒绝沿着26年前梅莱斯·泽纳维的“民主发展型道路”前行，因为这条道路受到很多质疑，难以推进，人们期望阿比作为年轻一代领导人能有所突破和创新。阿比在接受《金融时报》采访时曾明确表示，“我的经济模式是资本主义”②。2018年6月，阿比宣布对主要经济部门进行私有化改革，包括完全或部分私有化四个主要的公共企业：埃塞电信、埃塞电力、埃塞航空和埃塞航运与物流服务企业。阿比政府还计划在2020年启动国内证券交易所③。在西方媒体和政客看来，这些举措无一不预示着新自由主义在埃塞的“光明前景”。

但与西方的想象有所不同。阿比政府一面说自己是资本主义者，进行私有化和自由化的改革，与西方保持密切关系，另一面又说从未抛弃“发展型国家”，坚持政府对市场经济的干预。其闪烁其词的官方辞令使人眼花缭乱。在2019年2月的一次采访中，埃塞国家财政部长埃尤布·泰卡林（Eyob Tekalign）称：“国家将继续发挥重要作用。它不会像过去那样做所有事情，但是它将在某些领域发挥领导作用，而‘发展型国家’肯定会继续下去。”④此外，埃塞的金融部门也没有发生重大的结构性变化，外资银行仍然被禁止，国有银行仍然占主导

---

① Worku Burayu, “Prosperity Party's ‘Medemer’ Is Derived from ‘American Prosperity Gospel’” 24, July, 2020, retrieved from: https://kichuu.com/prosperity-partys-medemer-is-derived-from-american-prosperity-gospel/, 25 May 2021; Elias Dawit, “The Prosperity Gospel Comes to Ethiopia”, Agaforum.com, 3 October 2020, retrieved from: http://aigaforum.com/article2020/The-Prosperity-Gospel-Comes-to-Ethiopia.htm, 25 May 2021; Mulubrhan Balehegn, “The Politics and Problems Of Prosperity Party Gospel”, Ethiopian-insight.com, 4 April 2021, retrieved from: https://www.ethiopia-insight.com/2021/04/04/the-politics-and-problems-of-prosperity-party-gospel/, 25 May 2021; René Lefort, “Mind over Matter: Abiy Ahmed's Aim to ‘Pentecostalize Ethiopian politics’”, 24 December, 2020, retrieved from: https://www.ethiopia-insight.com/2020/12/24/mind-over-matter-abiy-ahmeds-aim-to- pentecostalize-ethiopian-politics/, 25 May 2021.

② L Barber，D Pilling, “‘My model is capitalism’: Ethiopia's prime minister plans telecoms privatisation”, 2019, retrieved from: https://www.ft.com/content/433dfa88-36d0-11e9-bb0c-42459962a812, 25 May 2021.

③ 同②。

④ W Davison, “From Meles' ‘Dead End’ to Abiy's ‘New Horizon’”, 2019, retrieved from: https://www.ethiopia-insight.com/2019/06/10/from-meles-dead-end-to-abiys-new-horizon/, 25 May 2021.

地位，中央银行处于政治主导地位，利率较低且资本流出受到控制。阿比政府也没有计划引入私有土地所有权等新自由主义政策[①]。有观察者认为，阿比正在“通过实施足够的新自由主义改革，取得短期收益和增加来自除中国以外的国家的外资。同时，利用中国的长期资助维持国家的主导地位，并在自由民主体制下维持有利于穷人的增长的发展议程”[②]。

随着时间的推移和《协同理念》一书的出版，阿比的意识形态倾向性开始趋于明朗。他在书中否定了埃革阵的“民主发展型国家”模式，同时还对社会主义和自由主义两种意识形态和制度的对立和两者的不足之处进行了分析，并得出了照搬他国的道路和模式是一条不归路的结论，主张埃塞必须以本国的传统价值为源泉，探索和构建适合埃塞国情的发展道路和模式，即他的“协同理念”。

总体来看，阿比上台后选择了一条相对折中的路线，他表面上否定了埃革阵的“民主发展型国家”理念，但也没有完全走西方的新自由主义道路，而是试图将自己的“协同理念”打造成一个集哲学、政治、经济和文化内涵的本土意识形态框架。这个理念的核心就是“1+1>2”的协同增效效应，他相信个人、族群、国家、资源和观念的有机结合可以带来比他们相互孤立或对抗时大得多的正面效益。因此，这个理念强调和而不同、兼容并蓄，是专门针对埃塞目前存在的民族冲突、宗教矛盾、意识形态碰撞、利益分配问题等深层次的政治、经济和社会问题而提出的本土理念构想。

余论

阿比的“协同理念”还只是一个概念雏形，还没有形成一套严谨的理论体系，也尚未提出成熟的国家构建模式和具体的发展主张。但从阿比的初衷和《协同理念》一书的内容来看，阿比的“协同理念”既不是对西方的新自由主义的重新命名，也没有全盘否定“民主发展型国家”模式。相反，该理念呈现出了兼收并蓄的特征，它对国家在经济发展中的角色定位上依旧带着“发展型国家”理念的烙印，同时在部分经济改革举措上也呈现出了明显的新自由主义色彩。对阿比政府而言，本土创制最重要的红利在于它有利于埃塞政府避免在复杂的国际关系格局中站边选队，赋予了埃塞政府更多的政策自主性和容错空间。作为埃塞新一代政治精英的本土创制尝试，“协同理念”在很大程度上反映了非洲新一代国家领导人寻求自主发展道路的愿望和决心。该理念如果在埃塞获得成功，将有望在非洲大陆掀起本土创制的浪潮，对非洲与外部世界的关系乃至国际关系格局产生重大影响。

---

① W Davison, “From Meles’ ‘Dead End’ to Abiy’s ‘New Horizon’”, 2019, retrieved from: https://www.ethiopia-insight.com/2019/06/10/from-meles-dead-end-to-abiys-new-horizon/, 25 May 2021.

② Stephanie Jay, “The New Scramble for Ethiopia”, *Statenow*, 3 June, 2019, retrieved from: https://satenaw.com/the-new-scramble-for-ethiopia/, 25 May 2021.

Major Nationalist Movements and Inclusion of Special Population in Medemer

Zelalem Wondimu①

Abstract: Ethiopia is currently through a historic period of political, economic, and social development. Abiy Ahmed has led the country on an ambitious and transformational endeavor since taking power in April 2018. This owes in part to the 2015 riots, which were sparked by opposition to the disputed Addis Ababa master plan, which planned to expand the city along the Oromia region's borders, displacing thousands of Oromo farmers. Disgruntled Amhara quickly joined them in their quest for more inclusive growth, and the two ethnic groups began to join forces against the EPRDF administration and the political system, which they saw as being dominated by a single political party. Many changes in various developmental domains excite the new Prime Minister. This hope was expressed in his acceptance speech, which symbolized a new idea: UNITY, which triggered the new hope and steered the country away from its downward trajectory. As a result, the prime minister explained his vision and presented his approach to cross-cutting reforms, which he said are profoundly anchored in the Amharic notion of Medemer, with the goal of correcting the country's political crises (meaning synergy, or coming together). The first big fundamental obstacle facing Abiy's government is the radical nationalist threats he is receiving, particularly from Oromo, Amhara, and Tigray radicals. Radical nationalists such as Oromo and Tigray have criticized and rejected the political ideology of "medemer", thinking that Abiy's government is reverting to the previous "Minilik's" rule and they argue that federalism is being supplanted by one ethnic group's supremacy. The Amhara elites, on the other hand, attack his administration, claiming that Abiy's government is increasing "Oromuma" since they believe Abiy is an Oromo. In response to this proposal, Abiy said in an interview with Oromia Broadcast Network that real federalism was missing in Ethiopia and that his government is working hard to restore it, citing Sidama's area as an example of his government's dedication to adopting actual federalism in the country.

The situation is chaotic six months into Abiy's leadership. Since then, a number of high-ranking Amhara Regional State officials have been assassinated in Bahdar, including the Ethiopian Defense Forces' chief, who was killed in Addis Ababa. In addition, Hachalu Hundesa, the most well-known Oromo artist, was slain in Ethiopia's capital, Addis Ababa. Following this

① PhD Student at Department of Special Needs Education, Addis Ababa University.

incident, major political figures such as Jawar Mohamed were imprisoned for more than a year without receiving justice.

Following Hachalu Hundessa's assassination, civilians were killed, displaced, and property was destroyed. The Oromo Federalist Congress (OFC) and Oromo Liberation Front (OLF) withdrew from Ethiopia's election on June 21, 2021, due to arrested political leaders and other factors. The election took place amid a variety of crises, including Covid-19 and the TPLF-federal government fighting. The election results showed that the prosperity party had triumphed. However, there are still uncertainties about how successful he will be in dealing with the new extreme nationalism movements that have resurfaced in the last three years since he arrived at the palace, with the ideology of "medemer" remaining an unsolved question for many political organizations. The inclusion of special populations such as persons with disabilities, internally displaced persons, and refugees in the country's developmental aspects is a critical component of achieving the country's sustainable development goals. In summary, the review looked at how extreme nationalist movements are perceived in the "medemer", what tactics are used to manage heterogeneity in unity, and how scientific studies look at diversity management through the lens of unity, as well as mainstreaming of marginalized groups.

Part One

1.1 The Basic Concept of Nationalism and Diversity in Ethiopia

Although the term "nationalism" has a variety of meanings, it centrally encompasses the attitude that the members of a nation have when they care about their identity as members of that nation and the actions that the members of a nation take in seeking to achieve (or sustain) some form of political sovereignty (Nielsen, 1998).

Since the establishment of modern Ethiopia, those who come to power have made an attempt to address diversity-related issues in a way they thought is best to serve the interest of the country or their political ideology. In relation to issues of diversity, to date, Ethiopia has exercised two broad ideologies of state policy. The first state policy was a unitary system of government which was used until the downfall of the Derg regime in 1991. There were two phases of this system. In the first phase (until the overthrown of the imperial regime), the policy attempted to bring unity without diversity, and resulted in hegemony and suppression. In the second phase (during the Derg regime), the policy recognized diversity but the implementation was far beyond the policy, and thus failed to succeed. The second state policy is a federal system of government that has been used since 1991. It emphasizes and promotes diversity without balancing with unity, and this potentially threatens national unity and leads to tension, conflict and disintegration.

The EPRDF constitution gives every ethnic group an unconditional right to self-determination, including the right to secession. This right is assumed to result in unity in diversity, and the creation of an Ethiopian national identity through the respect for ethnic diversity (Van der Beken, 2008). There are people who consider the right to secession as a conclusion of centuries old ethnic domination in Ethiopia (Nahum, 1997). However, other people argue that it is a signal of disintegration of the historic and multiethnic state of Ethiopia, which endured various ups and downs for three millennia (Haile, 1996). Proponents of ethnic federalism support the system even at the expense of unity because they believe that it is the only means to promote freedom and equality among ethnic groups and check tyranny. On the other hand, opponents argue that ethnic federalism tends to divide people rather than unite them. They expressed their fears about the potential threat of state disintegration because of the division of the country along ethnic lines (Engedayehu, 1993; Gashaw, 1993). Although there may be a few cases where state disintegration lead to relatively more peaceful small states, "dividing states along ethnic lines is not feasible since ethnic groups often cohabit" (Mengisteab, 2001).

Abiy Ahmed, the new chairman of the EPRDF and prime minister since April 2018, championed what he dubbed the "politics of addition", that calls for the unity of Ethiopians from all walks of life and opening up the political space. In his inaugural speech, the Prime Minister proclaimed: "We are Ethiopians while alive and Ethiopia when we die in stark contrast to the previous emphasis of the party-state on group rights and the ethnicization of politics." This emphasis on the unity of Ethiopians and on individual liberty rather than group rights began to appear in the rhetoric of the EPRDF following the peak of more than two years of protests by the Oromo youth, followed by the Amhara and other youth. Despite the Abiy's medemer political philosophy to transform Ethiopia, the major nationalists do not like his ideas of medemer fearing that he is implementing the legacy of Emperor Minilik's and Hailesilasie's. Abiy's interview with Oromia Broadcast Network in his response to this idea depicts that real federalism was absent in Ethiopia and adding that his government is working aggressively to bring up the real federalism taking Sidama's region as an example which has shown his government commitment in practicing the real federalism in the country.

In Ethiopia, there is distressing lack of elite consensus on several key issues ranging from national flag, language (one vs. multiple languages at national level), ownership of the capital city and most importantly the federal structure itself. As a stark departure from the past, in 1995, the EPRDF government established a federal system with regional and local administrations drawn along ethno-linguistic lines. However, this governing structure is contested by two dominant forces: ethno nationalist/centrifugal forces that strongly support the (ethnic) federal structure and call for its effective implementation including genuine self-rule and fair representation at federal level; and centripetal forces that criticize the federal system for undermining the country's unity. For the latter group, the federal system has intensified ethnic hostilities by eroding national unity, further augmenting lack of trust among ethnic groups and unleashing minority-majority tensions. The ethno-nationalist forces, however, attribute much of these challenges to the failure of the ruling party to effectively implement the federal system. According to this group, although the EPRDF adopted, on paper, a federal governance structure, in practice power is highly concentrated at the centre, with very little authority devolved to the regions. Rhetoric of respect and equality of all ethnic and national groups has been, for example, the emblematic motto of the party but the practice is quite different. There is sufficient evidence that the "ethnic card" has been used for divide and rule.

1.2 Journey of the Ethiopia Reformist Government

Since his election on April 2018, Abiy has transformed Ethiopia. He has moved to end political repression by releasing political prisoners, removing bans on opposition political parties and overseeing the prosecution of officials accused of human rights abuses. He has also restored diplomatic relations with Ethiopia's former long-time adversary, Eritrea. Under his premiership, the country witnessed reforms on several fronts. On the political front, deliberate efforts were made to restore trust in public authority, enhance social cohesion and tackle the growing ethnic tensions by promoting Ethiopian nationalism (Ethiopiawinet, meaning Ethiopianness) as a unifying factor. In a bid to broaden the political landscape, he reshuffled his cabinet, released political prisoners, amended some of the country's restrictive laws, and legalized prominent opposition groups formerly labelled as "terrorists", thereby convincing several rebel movements to renounce their armed struggle. New structures such as Ministry of Peace and Reconciliation Commission were introduced and institutions such as the National Electoral Board of Ethiopia (NEBE), Human Rights Commission and the security sector were reformed. The current government of the country believes that Ethiopia is now at a historic moment of great potential for political, economic and social transformation. Besides an ongoing reform in the country on different spheres of development, much will remain to bring up the needed reforms.

Challenges at the Age of Abiy's Rule

Since April 2018, ethnic and religious-based conflicts have alarmingly escalated in several parts of the country including Somali, Oromia, Amhara, Benishangul Gumuz, and SNNP regional states as well as Tigray and Amhara border areas, leading to the death and displacement of unprecedented number of people. Taking different forms and affecting establishments ranging from universities to religious institutions, the spiraling violence has had a devastating impact on Ethiopia's social fabric.

Despite the merger, the ruling party is highly fractured and divided as manifested by the bickering over state power (competition to control the central government), administrative border disputes, as well as controversy over the merger itself. Given the party's deep entrenchment in all tiers of state structures, its volatility fuels ongoing ethnic violence by emboldening radical elements and further dividing the already polarized elite/ethnic communities.

The deep division and mistrust between political forces including within the ruling party itself and the regional governments, underscores the complexity of the challenges facing the new leadership. The condition poses a formidable threat to the integrity of the state, hence necessitates a deeper reflection on the modes operandi including a re-negotiation between the two layers of the government. If not managed well, this trend threatens the country's capacity to sustain the initiated reforms and organize fair and free elections in 2020, which will eventually hinder its transition to democracy. Considering the apparent lack of elite consensus at the central and regional levels, the struggles between major ethnic forces and centripetal forces could pose a threat to the country's unity. As the election is approaching, how much these forces will be able to put their conflicting interests aside and execute their respective mandates in a non-partisan manner will be the key to conducting peaceful co-existence and transition to democracy.

Furthermore, political assassination was one of the huge challenges to the new prime minister. Assassination of Ambachew Mekonnen (PhD), President of Amhara regional state, and Azeze Wasse, the regional administration's public organization advisor and Migbaru Kebede, the Attorney General of Amhara regional state, who died of his injuries while receiving medical treatment. Migbaru become the latest victim in a wave of political assassinations that saw the shooting to death of General Seare Mekonnen, Chief of staff of the National defense force of Ethiopia. Also killed along with General Seare was Major General Gezai Abera, a retired general. Why they were killed and who were behind to their assassination was still unclear and not made public by the government for unknown reasons.

Exactly a year after political assassination on top government officials, another shocking assassination has been made on Hachalu Hundesa who is famous Oromo musician in the Capital Addis Ababa. Hachalu was killed on June 29, 2020 in Ethiopia's capital Addis Ababa in unclear circumstances. This shocking event has resulted in anti-government protests across Oromia, killing of civilians by government forces, an attack on some targeted groups by unknown organized groups in different parts of the region. Following the young Artist assassination, different people who were unrelated with the event has paid their life and properties. According to Ethiopian Orthodox Tewahedo Church released grim report on recent attacks on parishioners, 67 Christians were brutally killed; 38 severely injured and 29 sustained minor injuries. More than 7,000 parishioners were also displaced. Per government figures, of the 167 killed, 68% (114) are ethnic Oromos. Despite the differences in reporting the crises, civilians had paid unnecessary prices following assassination of Hachalu.

Immediately after the assassination of Oromo Artist Hachalu Hundesa's, the government had detained famous political leaders such as Jawar Mohammed, Bekele Gerba, Eskindir Nega, Lidetu Ayalew, and others. After this event, some claims that the government is wiping out opponents under the umbrella of rule of law. Some are even started to question how the Abiy's government is successful in managing the peaceful journey to democratic election imprisoning political opponents. Especially these kinds of comments come from radical nationalist organized with ethno-federalism.

1.3 Centripetal and Nationalists Groups

The country is bracing itself to organize elections in 2020, which is anticipated to be one of the most contested in its history. In the meantime, several forces, including the parties that have recently returned from exile, are prepared themselves and forging alliances with other like-minded parties. Although most of the parties are weak, disjointed and the alliances formed are still at their formative stages, essentially the upcoming election will largely be a competition between centripetal and ethno-national based centrifugal forces.

The centripetal forces consider themselves composed of individuals/groups of different ethnicities who place less emphasis on the issue of identity and call for a federal structure that looks beyond ethno-linguistic lines and advocate for a strong central government, they accuses of the centrifugal forces as they represent a single ethno-national group centering their argument around identity and contending for greater autonomy/self-rule and power devolution to the regions. While the centripetal forces includes Ethiopian People's Revolutionary Democratic Front (EPRDF) — now Prosperity Party (PP), and Ethiopia Citizens for Social Justice (ECSJ), whereas the Ethno-national-based Centrifugal Forces includes Oromo Federalist Parties, National Movement of Amhara (NaMA), Ogaden National Liberation Front (ONLF), Tigrayan People's Liberation Front (TPLF). These are some of the major parties expected to actively participate on the coming Ethiopia's election.

TPLF is a Marxist oriented movement established in 1974. As a political party that was instrumental in the formation of the other EPRDF coalition members, TPLF had largely dominated the front since its establishment, providing ideological and leadership direction. However, its influence began to weaken as a result of the post 2015 nation-wide resistance. Subsequently, the relations between the coalition parties deteriorated. The controversy reached its height following TPLF's open criticism of EPRDF's merger and its decline to join the newly formed Prosperity Party citing procedural and legal mishaps. The front officially broke away from the ruling party (PP) in January 2020, indicting its resolve to work along with other like-minded federalist parties to contest in the upcoming elections.

Given the relations between PP and TPLF are rocky, those between the federal and Tigray regional government also remain tense. Recently the relationship has been put to test when the federal government dismissed TPLF officials, including senior ministers, from the federal government. With such growing tension and animosity between the political elite, Tigray nationalism is also on the rise and if not handled carefully, any minor incident can trigger dispute and conflict between the centre and the regional government.

As a governing party, TPLF garners wide support in the Tigray region and was expected to collect substantial votes in the coming election. Unfortunately TPLF had decided to conduct the election under COVID-19 global pandemic crises and won the election with greater far result from its opponents. Despite repeated warning from the federal government on the illegitimacy of the election, Tigray went on forming its new government, resulting in the appointment of Debretsion as regional president. It came a few days after Ethiopia's parliament Okayed the country to hold the 6th general elections, which was postponed due to COVID-19. Tagesse Chafo, Speaker of the House of People's Representatives (HoPR) said that the general election will be held throughout the country, including Tigray. In response, Getachew Reda, TPLF executive member, told Dimtsi Woyane Television that this was not going to happen in Tigray. "As far as Tigray is concerned, the next election is going to be in five years from now." What is uncertain in this regard is the relation between the TPLF and federal government pre, during, and post election period.

The sudden emergence of corona virus global pandemic has forced them to postpone election period as per government report. The ruling party and NEBE have faced support and criticisms from different political party on postponing the election schedule. The ongoing 5th year, 4th emergency meeting of the Parliament decided Ethiopia can hold deferred general elections taking precautionary measures against COVID-19. The recommendation was presented at the meeting by the Women, Youth and Social Affairs Standing Committee.

1.4 Medemer Political Philosophy and the Ground Reality

Medemer represents synergy (from the Latin root "syn" (together) and "ergy" (work)). Medemer describes a synergistic process of coming together of individuals, groups, leaders and institutions to work more energetically, effectively and creatively for the common good and in the public interest.

Medemer philosophy aims to bring synthesis to Ethiopia's fractious politics. It aims to harmonize the politics of identity, sectarianism and communalism into a synthesis of nation-building, civility, tolerance, love, understanding and forgiveness. Medemer philosophy favors cooperation over competition because humans as social/political creatures (animals) maximize their rational self-interest through cooperation. Drawing on natural analogues, the author posits the precedence of cooperation over competition.

In the author's medemer synergy, the idea I believe is that "the whole is greater than the sum of its parts". In other words, for an organization or society to be successful, the functional elements cannot consist of merely individuals working independently and exclusively in their own self-interest. They must be part of a larger community that shares a common purpose, goals and objectives and apply social, political and economic synergy to create a public good.

The book of *Medemer* has different layers. In one layer, it is a philosophy as the author characterizes it. But in different layers, "medemer" could be understood as a vision, a theory, a road map, a paradigm shift, a mindset, a (meta) concept, an outlook, a call to action and an appeal to common sense. The author broadly argues "medemer philosophy" is a comprehensive socio-political and economic perspective necessitated by the events of the past several decades in Ethiopia. Ethiopia's political problems are rooted in ethnic identity, ideological polarity, lack of democratic political culture, etc. These problems can be solved when institutional stakeholders work at the grassroots level for a common goal.

Medemer is a critique of the approach to change particularly in the past one-half century. The author rejects the tendency Ethiopians have shown to always tear down everything of the past and urges that it is far more profitable to build upon what has already been done. Medemer politics argues for use of political energy not to fight the old and tear down the past but to build a brave new society of the future that thrives on consensus and cooperation for a common destiny.

Those who have fear or anxiety about "medemer" avoid efforts aimed at building national consensus on a common destiny or shared national goals. Nations, nationalities and peoples in Ethiopia share a common destiny emanating from historical, cultural and social ties. But those afflicted by "medemer-phobia" will spread fear and loathing to keep the population in a state of alarm and uncertainty hoping it will open an opportunity for them to grab power. Another obstacle is "walta regetenet" ("narrow-mindedness" or "dogmatism"). Those suffering from this affliction are sources of polarization. They see things in stark contrast of black and white. They do not appreciate reality is shaded and with gradation. There is nothing that is all bad and all good. Human beings have some elements of each. Medemer is a forward-looking philosophy and requires people to look at yesterday to learn lessons and not repeat mistakes.

Based on the above political philosophy of medemer, the new prime minister has pledged to review restrictive laws of the past, including the antiterrorism law, often used to silence opposing views. In addition, over 13,000 prisoners were freed as part of an amnesty campaign and the parliament legalized two opposition groups with secessionist aspirations, the Oromo Liberation Front (OLF) and the exiled movement "Ginbot 7". A revised civil society law was also introduced.

Another paradoxical issue under medemer political philosophy is Federal Attorney General allegation of political prisoners with terrorism and other charges against prominent politicians like Jawar Mohammed and 23 other Oromo politicians. The radical nationalist at different sides of political wing is saying that Ethiopia's government filed terrorism and other charges against prominent opposition leaders and activists in one of the most outrageous and fraudulent legal proceedings in the country. Federal prosecutors have also filed terrorism charges on Eskinder Nega, founder and leader of the opposition party Balderas for Genuine Democracy, and two others with him. It is said that the same government who denounced TPLF's use of "terrorist methods to stay in power", who told the public he is different and committed to democratic transition, the rule of law and justice is now using the anti-terrorism legislation and the political narrative that go with it, against the political opponents.

Anti Abiy's government groups are saying that the PM betrayed the opponents, betrayed his colleagues, and abandoned the transition, and turned into a typical dictator. The supporters of the "political prisoners" and detainees are repeatedly telling that it is highly likely that the narrative structure for the case was set by the ruling government himself. As it has been pointing out since top political leaders and several others were arrested, it is said that this decision is entirely political and it is motivated by the government's dictatorial desire to eliminate his formidable political opponents from Ethiopia's political scene.

On the other side, in a recent press statement, Attorney General (AG) Gedion Timothewos told local and international journalists that Jawar Mohammed and the 23 individuals who are facing terrorism and other criminal charges are "ultra-nationalist, militant, violent" individuals. This AG statement had been criticized as the description is a disturbing display of partiality and prejudice by the AG and constitutes an outrageous disregard for the defendant's fundamental right to presumption of innocence. Despite the medemer political philosophy of addition, it is unclear how this political philosophy will be successful in the condition where competition for power between major nationalists and centripetal groups are at its climax.

1.5 Future Prospects

Established on 16 October, 2018, the Ethiopian Ministry of Peace is one of the critical structures built by the new leadership to sustain the on-going reforms through undertaking peace-building measures. This involves the development and strengthening of peace and security structures/institutions to ensure the rule of law and lasting peace. The Ministry oversees key peace and security offices, including the National Intelligence & Security Service (NISS), Information Network Security Agency (INSA), Federal Police Commission and the Administration for Refugee and Returnee Affairs.

One of the principal mandates of the Ministry is ensuring the maintenance of public order; through among others identifying factors that trigger conflicts among communities. As part of its efforts to deliver on its mandate, the Ministry has so far undertaken several initiatives. This includes the conducting of a national Conflict Mapping study and introduction of a Conflict Early Warning and Rapid Response System (CEWRRS) which aims to detect and promptly respond to potential conflicts. If accorded the political backing and resources it requires, the Ministry — through the strategies and instruments being introduced — has the potential to efficiently respond to emerging conflicts that can threaten the peace and security of the country and its people — particularly around the much-anticipated election. It will also certainly bring the different political groups to negotiate on country's agenda.

The establishment of the Ministry of Peace and the National Peace and Reconciliation Commission by the government is a commendable step towards addressing entrenched grievances among the people and the prevailing deep divisions in the society. Nevertheless, the government must effectively use these structures to strengthen its national peace infrastructures and strive towards creating national cohesion and strengthening tolerance. But most importantly, given the increasingly polarized and already tense political landscape, the government should create a genuine platform that would pave the way for a negotiated political solution as a way out from the current stalemate and for peace and development in the long run. For this purpose, an inclusive national dialogue forum must be convened involving political leaders, traditional and religious leaders, youth representatives and other relevant stakeholders. The Reconciliation Commission must also expeditiously develop a clear activity plan and engage in implementation.

Part Two

Under this particular section, issues with regard to displaced population and persons with disabilities in the lens of medemer had been presented as follows.

2.1 Forced Displacement in Ethiopia

The major challenge facing the new administration has to do with an increasing number of internally displaced persons (IDPs). Since 2016 the number of displaced persons was reached its climax and this number has risen to 70.7 million at the end of 2018. The majority (41.3 million) was reported to be persons displaced in their own country. Refugees and asylum seekers constitute 29.4 million, where 25.9 million and 3.5 million were refugees and asylum seekers respectively. At Ethiopia's level, the press debriefing made on 2018 by the Federal Democratic Republic of Ethiopia Prime Minister to different medias has shown that within one year alone around 1.5 million people were displaced from their home excluding the 1.5 million displaced persons before he come to power. Ethiopia recorded more than 1.8 Million Internally Displaced in 2020 The report, which was completed in September and endorsed by Ethiopian authorities, contains data collected between June and July 2020 through the assessment of more than 1,200 sites and over 1,200 villages where IDPs had reportedly returned. The primary cause of displacement: conflict, which has resulted in 1,233,557 IDPs across this country. The second highest cause: drought, which displaced 351,062 IDPs, followed by seasonal floods (displacing 104,696 IDPs) and flash floods (50,093).

The number of persons displaced in their own country outnumbers the number of refugees. However, their situation is overlooked by international partners working on forced displacement. Reports are disclosing that children constitute 50% of the world refugees. The impact of displacement is somehow different for at risk groups such as children, women, and elderly people. This group should be the focus because of their vulnerability to life problems.

It had been said that Oromo communities displaced from Ethiopia's Somali region and

Gedio West Guji were the parts of the country impacted by huge and severe displacement regardless of the root cause(s). Although other factors such as environmental challenges also contributed to the country's displacement crisis, the significant portion was conflict-induced. To deal with the situation, the government, with the leadership of the newly established Ministry of Peace, has undertaken extensive work since April 2019 to return IDPs to their original homes. Humanitarian agencies have, however, accused the government of breaching international humanitarian principles by returning IDPs to their areas of origin with minimal or no assistance, including by force. This, in some instances, has led to secondary displacement of returnees as seen in the case of East and West Wollega zones. To address the challenges faced by returnees and displaced people who are still residing in shelters, the government has recently launched Durable Solution Initiative (DSI). The extent to which the DSI will succeed in resolving the issues of IDPs in a systematic manner will be key to ensuring peace and durable solution to Ethiopia's internal displacement challenges.

There are different legal instruments in Africa developed to protect internally displaced persons before the Kampala Convention was come to effect. Among them African Charter on Human and People's Rights (1981), Guiding Principles on Internal Displacement (1998), Protection and Assistance of Internally Displaced Persons which is one of ten protocols contained in the Great Lakes Pact on Security, Stability and Development (2006) were some of them.

At Ethiopia's level, a response to internal displacement largely focuses on provision of food and shelter. In fact, the provision of basic services (food and shelter) to internally displaced persons is very crucial as safety net; however, transition to development oriented assistance is equally important. Ethiopia does not have comprehensive policies on internal displacement. Disaster Risk Management (DRM) policy of 2013 with its associated Strategic Programme and Investment Framework is the current most relevant policies. DRM does not specifically address either the emergency or the development assistance needs of IDPs, but its objectives are to reduce risks associated with disasters and to protect those at risk in disaster circumstances. Besides the lack of comprehensive policies to address issues of internal displacement, the Government of Ethiopia has signed the Kampala Convention, but it has not yet ratified it, claiming instead that existing domestic legal and policy frameworks provide adequate guidance for addressing internal displacement.

Currently there are some positive changes to respond to the crises of internal displacement in the country. An IDP Advisory Group (comprising the UN Resident/Humanitarian Coordinator, the UN Office for the Coordination of the Humanitarian Affairs, IOM, the UN Refugee Agency, the International Committee of the Red Cross and the Danish Refugee Council), and a national steering committee (under the leadership of the Deputy Prime Minister) to support over a million individuals displaced following the border conflict between Somali and Oromia Regional States are among the new initiative of Ethiopia's on internal displacement. The Ethiopian government is also implementing, with support from the international community, the New Way of Working approach; emerging from the World Humanitarian Summit, this approach is defined as working over multiple years, based on the comparative advantage of a diverse range of actors, including those outside the UN system, towards collective outcomes.

The new national approach is Durable Solutions Strategy (DSWG) developed and endorsed by Ethiopia's Somali regional state in October 2017, which is the fist in its kind both at the region and nation level. The strategy adopted the definition of IDPs from the Guiding Principles on Internal Displacement and tried to contextualize it given the circumstances of pastoralists in the region. The strategy was connected with international principles and frameworks including the Guiding Principles, the Inter-Agency Standing Committee Framework on Durable Solutions for IDPs and the Kampala Convention, plus relevant national tools as well. The strategy was designed first at regional level but attracted the attentions of different regional states and policy makers at national level in Ethiopia.

Still there are some practical challenges to the strategy such as low level of efforts from stakeholders, and limited resources and insufficient capacity of regional implementers. The lack of systematic data collection on IDPs is an additional challenge to policy makers. This should be resolved by expanding of the existing information management system on internal displacement such as IOM's Displacement Tracking Matrix (DTM) for the collection of data for the purpose of guiding planning and coordination of short-term humanitarian response to the generation — by academia and/or multiple agencies in collaboration — of a body of evidence that can support progress towards solutions and future policy decisions. Displacement Tracking Matrix (DTM) is used by all cluster leads for their sectoral planning in Ethiopia from 2017. Before that there were no data on displacement because the government was sensitive of politicized data on internal displacement. The availability of systematic data in place plays a crucial role in changing the crises of internal displacement by gaining the attention of academicians, policy makers, and international partners.

In short, the work done at Somali and Gambella regional state that had experienced massive and recurrent internal displacement paved the ways for making comprehensive policies and strategies at national level to respond the humanitarian crises of internal displacement in Ethiopia.

Despite the initiation by local authorities and international communities to support the internally displaced persons, access to basic services like education of internally displaced children is unpredictable in an emergency situation due to lack of facilities.

On the humanitarian front, considerable support has been directed to supporting the government's IDP's return initiative that began in April 2019. International Organization for Migration (IOM) and other international organizations have also played a crucial role in the development and implementation of the Durable Solution Initiative (DSI) launched by the Ethiopian government.

Despite the devastating scale of internal displacement, which reached a world record high in

2018, and dedication of the year 2019 to the issues of refugees, returnees, and internally displaced persons, the AU has chosen to remain surprisingly silent about the situation in Ethiopia. This may be, to a certain extent, due to Ethiopia's strategic position as host of the African Union Commission and valuable partner in regional security (prominent contributor to AU and UN-led peacekeeping operations, a staunch ally in the fight against terrorism and migration, and host to close to 900,000 refugees). Although the country is yet to ratify the Kampala Convention, and as a sovereign state, the responsibility of protecting its internally displaced falls within its jurisdiction, the AU, as a continental organization to which Ethiopia is a member, should have made efforts to strategically support the protection of IDPs in the country.

Despite the huge internal displacement crises in the country, the real cause of the displacement is unknown. However, almost all of the displaced population had been displaced by the triggering of armed conflicts on civilians. At this moment the displacement crisis due to armed conflict is decreasing but it's still there in some parts of the country such us Benishangul Gumuz regional state.

Similar to the huge number of IDPs in the country, according to the UNHCR (United Nations High Commission for Refugees) report, Ethiopia is the second largest host of refugee population in Africa, sheltering 920,262 refugees in 2018, next to Uganda which hosts 1.1 million. Ethiopia's "open door policy" to refugees and the relative peace in the country as well as brutal conflicts in its neighboring countries are some of the reason for the current refugee influx in the country. Ethiopia opened 18 refugee camps in the last 7 years in which 10 of the camps were opened in western part of the country and destination for South Sudanese refugees.

The new development occurred granting refugees the right to work in Ethiopia. Ethiopia is party to the 1951 Convention relating to the status of refugees and its 1967 Protocol, although it has maintained reservations relating to refugees' right to work, until Ethiopia's house of people's representatives approved a new proclamation in January 17, 2019 granting refuges the right to work. This proclamation is believed to clear the road for the implementation of the "Ethiopian compact" as part of the Global Compact for refugees. The new refugee proclamation provides refugees the right to engage in wage-earning employment, in the areas of agriculture, industrial parks (special economic zone), small and micro-scale enterprises, handicrafts, and commerce. Since the proclamation is new and not yet implemented, it is hard to reflect on it at this level.

2.2 Persons with Disability

The education of children with disabilities made a paradigm shift from the individualized, medical-oriented special education to a social disability-based special need or inclusive education model. The social approach to disability makes an identification and analysis of the social, political and economic conditions that restrict the life opportunities of those suffering from impairment

(Butler & Bowlby, 1997). This newly emerging paradigm is premised on Universal Declaration of Human Rights (UN, 1948), the World Declaration on "Education for All" (UNESCO, 1990), the Declaration on the Rights of Disabled Persons (1975) to all services, the UN Convention on the Rights of the Child (1989) with special needs for social, educational integration, and such other recent derivatives as the Standard Rules on the Equalization of Opportunities for Persons with Disabilities (1993), the World Education Forum (2000), and the Salamanca Framework for Action (1994) which unequivocally endorsed inclusion as the best mode of educational delivery for children with disabilities. The principle of inclusive education was adopted at the Salamanca World Conference on Special Needs Education held in Spain in 1994, and was reaffirmed at the World Education Forum in 2002.

Ethiopia subscribes to many international conventions that require members to domesticate inclusive education agendas, including the "World Conference on Education for All" (1990) and "Salamanca Statement" (1994). Ethiopia has already signed the "UN Convention on the Rights of the Child" (1989), its African version, the "African Charter on the Rights and Welfare of the Child" (1999) and a number of other international declarations protecting and promoting the survival and development of children including their education. Ethiopia's commitment is demonstrated in her local frameworks such as: the Ethiopian Constitution (1994), the Ethiopian Education and Training Policy (MoE, 1994) and the five Education Sector Development Programs (ESDPs) (starting from the first one covering the period from 1997/1998 to 2001/2002). The fifth Education Sector Development Program (ESDP-Ⅴ) was developed in 2015 as a five-year plan (2015/2016-2019/2020) following the ESDP-Ⅳ, National Development Plans (GTP Ⅰ 2010/2011-2014/2015 & GTP Ⅱ 2015/2016-2019/2020), Master Plan for Special Needs Education/Inclusive Education 2016-2025, National Plan of Action of Persons with Disabilities 2012-2021, and the Higher Education Proclamation No. 650/2009 of Ethiopia.

Even though, one may come across a number of legal and strategic instruments to promote inclusion in Ethiopia, there were gaps in intention and action in Ethiopia's policies of Persons with Disabilities. While the legal instruments (intention) are fruitful to practice the essence of inclusion, the ground reality (action) doesn't reflect the intention written on the papers.

Part Three

Conclusion and Recommendation

Based on the issues discussed so far, it is time for Ethiopians to reflect on the failures of the past and the possibility of re-setting the clock for a new beginning. In recent times, it has been concerning to witness the curtailment of hard-won fundamental freedoms and the narrowing of political space. Today, it appears that we are almost back to a pre-2018 state of affairs, if not worse. The government's crackdown on opposition groups following the wrongful death of Hachalu has led to the prisons that were emptied in 2018 being filled with political prisoners once again. This is a frequent and well-trodden path characteristic of the Ethiopian state machinery, and it is a path to destruction that successive regimes have come out of as unsuccessful. However, there is still an opportunity to depart from this path, government officials must realize that moving Ethiopia backwards is not an option, nor is maintaining the status quo. The only option is to move forward as the very survival of this country relies upon realizing and effectively instituting the essence of true democracy and justice.

Achieving a consensus on the country's future requires the Ethiopian government and people to undertake a genuine national dialogue that will allow them to craft an acceptable constitutional design, including the re-defining of power relations between the centre and regions. Who wins the election and what trajectory it chooses to take will significantly determine the future of the country.

In hopes of re-setting the clock, I suggest for the immediate release of political prisoners, for the government to cease the attack on media and free speech and to stop weaponizing communication channels as a means of repression. Further, a genuine national political dialogue to discuss the way forward for this country is should be in place asap. This is a time that the government should task itself with remedying the deep-rooted legacies of state-violence and other repressive tendencies by charting a new path forward, not sliding back to its usual undemocratic disposition.

For those who are gathered together under the umbrella of radical nationalism, I strongly suggest views of previous US president Bill Clinton on nationalism. He said that an inclusive nationalism works better than exclusive nationalism in a world full of problems. As Ethiopians we are full of problems which must be solved by coming together for the common good. The medemer political philosophy also fosters cooperation which will help everyone involved as most of us share common goals if our interest is transforming the country.

As far as the issue of special population such as Persons with Disabilities and displaced population are concerned in medemer, the book lacks detail description about this issue. I strongly recommend reconsidering the issue as it is a sensitive problem of the country.

References

[1] ABEBAW Y A. 2013. Diversity in Ethiopia: a historical overview of political challenges. International Journal of Community Diversity. http://ondiversity.com/.

[2] ALI A. 2019. Medemer. Addis Ababa: Tsehaipublishers.

[3] BUTLER R, BOWLBY S. 1997. Bodies and spaces: an exploration of disabled people's experiences of public space, environment and planning development. Society and Space, 15 (4): 379-504.

[4] ENGEDAYEHU W. 1993. Ethiopia: democracy and the politics of ethnicity. Africa Today,

40(2): 29-52.

[5] GASHAW S. 1993. Nationalism and ethnic conflict in Ethiopia// YOUNG C. The rising tide of cultural pluralism: the nation-state at bay? Madison: University of Wisconsin Press.

[6] HAILE M. 1996. The new Ethiopian constitution: its impacts on unity, human rights and development. Suffolk Transnational Law Review, 20(1): 1-84.

[7] MENGISTEAB K. 2001. Ethiopia's ethnic-based federalism: 10 years after. African Issues, 29(1/2): 20-25.

[8] NAHUM F. 1997. Constitution for a nation of nations: the Ethiopian perspective. Asmara: The Red Press Inc.

[9] NIELSEN K. 1998. Liberal nationalism, liberal democracies and secession. University of Toronto Law Journal, 48(2): 253-295.

[10] MOKADDEM S. 2019. Abiy Ahmed's "Medemer" reforms: can it ensure sustainable growth for Ethiopia and what are the challenges facing the new government? https://www.policycenter.ma/publications/abiy-ahmed%E2%80%99s-E2%80%98medemer%E2%80%99-reforms-can-it-ensure-sustainable-growth-ethiopia-and-what-are.

[11] TSION B. 2020. Ethiopia conflict and insight: peace and security report. https://www.ipss-addis.org/publications.

[12] UN. 1975. Declaration on the rights of disabled persons. https://www.ohchr.org/EN/ProfessionalInterest/Pages/RightsOfDisabledPersons.aspx.

[13] UN. 1948. Universal declaration of human rights. https://www.ohchr.org/Documents/Publications/ABCannexesen.pdf.

[14] UN. 1989. UN convention on the rights of the child (1989). https://www.ohchr.org/en/professionalinterest/pages/crc.aspx.

[15] UNESCO. 1990. World declaration on education for all: meeting basic learning needs. https://bangkok.unesco.org/sites/default/files/assets/ECCE/JomtienDeclaration.pdf.

[16] UNITED NATION, MINISTRY OF EDUCATION AND SCIENCE OF SPAIN. 1994. Salamanca statement and framework for action on special needs education. https://www.right-to-education.org/sites/right-to-education.org/files/resource-attachments/Salamanca_Statement_1994.pdf.

[17] UNESCO. 2000. The open file on inclusive education support materials for managers and administrators. https://unesdoc.unesco.org/ark: /48223/pf0000125237.

[18] UNESCO. 2001. Including the excluded: meeting diversity in education — example from Uganda. Paris: UNESCO.

[19] UNESCO. 2003. Overcoming exclusion through inclusive approaches in education: a challenge and a vision. http://www.ijssh.org/vol6/654-H007.pdf.

[20] UNESCO. 2006. Strong foundations — early childhood care and education. http://www.unesco.org/new/en/archives/education/themes/leading-the-international-agenda/efareport/reports/2007-early-childhood/.

[21] UNESCO. 2007. Education and inclusive education: priority issues for inclusive quality education in Eastern and Western Sub-Saharan Africa. https://unesdoc.unesco.org/search/N-EXPLORE-c7fb3464-a658-44f9-8703-9ea240caaa83.
[22] UNESCO. 2010. Reaching the marginalized. Oxford: Oxford University Press.
[23] VAN DER BEKEN C. 2008. Ethiopia: constitutional protection of ethnic minorities at the regional level//BREMS E, VAN DER BEKEN C. Federalism and the protection of human rights in Ethiopia. Zurich: Lit Verlag GmbH & Co. KG Wien.

Medemer in the Context of Radicalism and State Making under the Derg and EPRDF

Fasil Merawi[①]

Abstract: By taking the introduction of a radical Marxist thesis during the period of the Ethiopian students' movement as a point of reference, this paper explores the epistemic terrain that is occupied by medemer which is introduced by the current Ethiopian Prime Minister Abiy Ahmed. In the existing debate, medemer is understood as an eclectic approach that synthesizes elements of Pan-Ethiopian identity, the indigenous Gada system of the Oromo, Pentecostal Christianity, populism, postmodern leadership and the Afrocentric philosophy of Ubuntu. In this paper the nature of medemer will be understood against the background of socialist ideology and the models of revolutionary democracy and the developmental state. The ideological operations of the Derg and the EPRDF are dictated by a radical Marxist-Leninist approach that is vividly manifested in the Ethiopian students' movement. Being founded on the Marxist thesis of class struggle, such an approach dictated Derg's attempt to introduce a proletarian revolution and the EPRDF's approaches of revolutionary democracy and the developmental state. Such a socio-ideological movement of radicalism used the colonial thesis to introduce a narrow characterization of Ethiopian history as a battleground between different ethnic groups and culminated under the EPRDF in a one-party state that promotes ethnic hatred and cultural dislocation. It resulted in ethnic polarization and the proliferation of ethnically organized political parties all vying to establish their dominance. There is a need to situate medemer in such a discourse on radical Marxism thereby exploring whether it manages to overcome the radical Marxist paradigm or not. After discussing the origins of the radical Marxist paradigm and how it manifests itself in the Derg's socialism and EPRDF's revolutionary democracy and the developmental state, the paper explores the conceptual space that is occupied by medemer in trying to introduce a new approach that overcomes a politics of polarization.

Keywords: Medemer; Radicalism; Marxism

① Assistant Professor, Department of Philosophy, Addis Ababa University.

Introduction

After coming to power, Prime Minister Abiy Ahmed introduced reforms which among other things include establishing strong relations with neighboring states and in the world of diplomacy, releasing political prisoners and widening the public space. The reforms that are introduced by Abiy's government are said to have both domestic and regional implications. With regards to domestic affairs, the reforms are said to contribute to the process of democratization by broadening the public sphere and the context within which political participation is being carried out. In terms of international relations, the reforms can stabilize the relations between Ethiopia and the neighboring states that are especially found in the horn of Africa. Still, ethnic polarization and the separatist movements of ethno-nationalistic groups are the major challenges to such reforms. The process of state formation is still contested and there is a need to come up with a narrative that can mediate the polarizing positions of the unionist and ethno-nationalistic camps. Matshanda tells us that the stability of the horn largely depends on the relations that are founded between Ethiopia and Eritrea and there is a need to strengthen the various efforts that are made on the ground. In this regard, Abiy's administration needs to "build trust and goodwill" (Namhla, 2020: 10). This contributes the broader peace building efforts.

The promise of societal progress and democratization that is promised by the government of Abiy Ahmed resists on the creation of a political playing field within which all political parties can equally participate in. Bratt (2020: 19) argues that realizing a multi-party political system, ensuring the independence of the judiciary and establishing a competent electoral commission are some of the things that the government needs to realize. Mokaddem (2019:1) claims that the freeing of political prisoners, stabilizing the horn and broadening the Ethiopian political space are some of the major reforms that are introduced by Abiy's government. Compared to previous times, "Ethiopia is now at a historic moment of great potential for political, economic and social transformation". Trying to cast a new image for Ethiopia, Abiy's government has embarked on bold progressive measures. The major challenge to his reform measures in the domestic front is polarized ethnic politics. This tends to destroy the centuries old values and the moral fabric which holds Ethiopian together. There is a need to introduce a new organizing principle for the Ethiopian federation that goes beyond ethnic identity. There is also a need to find an immediate solution to the rising costs of living and to stabilize the economy. Biru (2019: 65) further adds that establishing a moral compass within which the activities of the state are being guided and also insuring lasting peace and stability are some challenges that the Ethiopian state is currently facing.

At the heart of his reforms is his approach that he identifies as medemer. Although there is a lack of conceptual clarity in identifying what the normative and political presuppositions of medemer are, still in the existing debate it is introduced as an eclectic approach that borrows from several sources with an aim of introducing a new political culture that is founded on common goals and solidarity. There are arguments that Abiy's medemer brought major transformations in the political culture of Ethiopians and is also ideologically significant since it emphasized the themes of synergy and tolerance and in the process introduced an approach that overcomes the opposition between the Pan-Ethiopian identity on one hand and intimate affiliation to one's ethnic background on the other hand. Against the idea of fixed identities which are opposed by one another which is developed in the name of federalism, it is alleged that Abiy's approach focuses on relations of interdependence and a shared history.

Asegidew maintains that it is the inability to uphold basic individual rights and broaden the public sphere within the revolutionary democratic and developmental democracy models that gave birth to Abiy's medemer approach. As such, "TPLF/EPRDF's revolutionary democracy lacks willingness and attention for humanity as equal as the economic 'development' agenda" (Asegidew, 2019: 130). In medemer, an emphasis is given to shared history, problems that are encountered as a nation and the need to build the future together.

The discourse on ethnic identity in Ethiopia pictures the past as a source of assimilation and homogenization. The approach that is introduced by Abiy in return situates the historical past as the source of cultural pride and a common sense of identity. The common wars that Ethiopian fought are among other things situated as a foundation of a common sense of destiny and purpose for Ethiopians. Furthermore, there is a moral imperative within medemer that is communal and relational in its nature. Medemer does not exalt the role that is given by the isolated individual in societal progress. On the opposite, it pictures societal changes as a result of coordinated actions among the members of a community.

Part of the medemer approach that is introduced by the Prime Minister is establishing a relationship of solidarity between the Amhara and the Oromo which are the two larger ethnic groups of the country. Medemer here constitutes an Oromara element which is a strategic relationship that is envisioned between the Amhara and Oromo having two major goals in mind. The first one is mounting a strategic alliance that can be used to dismantle the hegemony of the TPLF within the ruling coalition. The second one is deconstructing the distorted historical past that used the categories of the oppressor and the oppressed to analyze the relations between the Amhara and the Oromo and in return to realize relations of fruitful cooperation. Such a partnership as Barkessa (2019:10) sees it was used to "stand together and challenge the corrupted and abusive governance system". But is this a temporary partnership or an operation that is needed to envision relations of equality in the nation?

The coming to power of Abiy signifies the emergence of a new alliance in the form of Oromara in the ruling coalition which also spells the end of TPLF's hegemony in the ruling party. Temin & Badwaza (2019:142) argued that Abiy came to power in a context where the ruling party, "had to decide whether to make leadership changes that would be sweeping enough to match the intensity of protestor demands, or risk fragmentation and eventual collapse". Instability in the regions and inter party struggle ensued in the aftermath of the reform measures that are introduced by Abiy's government.

One could discern several elements of medemer by looking at the book of the Prime Minister and also the discourse that is currently dictating political discussions in Ethiopia. Among other things, there is an element of a pan-Ethiopian identity in medemer as it is situated as an approach that revitalizes relations of solidarity and oneness that have resulted out of centuries old relations among Ethiopians. Medemer is also seen as an indigenous approach that pays attention to the Oromo Gada system and indigenous ethics. Besides this, one can also discern elements of Pentecostal Christianity in the theme of synergy that is being advocated by medemer. One also observes that medemer is more attentive to populism as it an approach that mobilizes the masses. As it is witnessed in the appointments that are made by the Prime Minister, medemer is more attuned to technocrats rather than the strict bureaucrats. It also has an element of Ubuntu ethics as it identifies the intimate relations that are found between the individual and the community.

The aim of this paper is not to identify the different sources of medemer. It has an aim of situating medemer in the context of the thesis of class struggle which directly informs the ideologies of the Derg and EPRDF. In light of this background, it makes sense to ask, what can kind of conceptual terrain is occupied by medemer and how does it differ from the ideological operations of the Derg and EPRDF. This also invites a discussion into some of the inherent ambiguities that are found in medemer as well as the potential threats that such an approach happens to harbor.

Marxism and the Origins of the Radical Paradigm in Ethiopian Politics

There is a radical paradigm in Ethiopian politics whose origins are traced back to the Ethiopian students' movement. Such an approach constitutes the usage of Marxist categories of class struggle and the emancipation of the working class as a way of providing solutions to the subjugation that exists within the Ethiopian context. Such a radical approach was introduced in the setting of the university and later on served as a foundation of the struggle for ethnic identity. In such a process, one witnesses a significant transformation in the application of the principles of Marxism. The classical Marxist thesis of class antagonism was replaced by the relationship that exists between the oppressor and the oppressed being approached through the prism of national identity.

In the attempt to make sense of the dominance of a Marxist inspired thinking in Ethiopian politics, one could ask, why was there such an interest in Marxism in the first place and how did it manage to provide the theoretical impetus for the Ethiopian revolution? Hughes (1992) tells us that not just in Ethiopia but generally the introduction of Marxism in Africa is characterized by both pragmatic and moral imperatives. Practically, it was seen as an ideology that appealed to the questions of the other and the oppressed. Morally, it was situated as a theory of emancipation which emphasizes solidarity among the oppressed and the exploited (Hughes, 1992). In such a background Ethiopian university students understood Marxism as the one practical philosophy that can free farmers from relations of oppression.

Others like Mennasemay (2008) contend that the introduction of Marxist and other political principles in the Ethiopian soli is characterized by a concept stretching that sought to impose foreign concepts on local realities. Recognizing this, there is a need to indigenize the political discourse and introduce a conception of political progress that is suited to our local realities. In recognition of this, "one cannot respond adequately to the questions that arise from the history and life-conditions of Ethiopians without a democracy — that integrates freedom, prosperity, and social justice" (Mennasemay: 2008: 4). The solution to the dominance of such alien concepts in Ethiopian politics is to initiate a process of cultural affirmation that allows us to engage in a reconstructive process that help us study local political concepts and modes of organization.

Mennasemay (2005) maintains that the application of Marxist categories in Ethiopia has led into a radical and polarized discourse that situated relations of the oppressor and the oppressed as the locus of the modern Ethiopian state. The limitation of such an understanding is that it fails to consider relations of interdependence that gave birth to the modern Ethiopian state. Mennasemay tells us, that "the problem in depicting Ethiopia as a colonial state is that the Marxist concept of colonialism is derived from the logic of capitalist reproduction, whereas traditional Ethiopia is not a capitalist society" (Mennasemay, 2005: 8). This showed why the application of the principles of Marxism to analyze Ethiopia's problems was a wrong attempt that did not take into consideration the specificities of the nation and the political economy of an agrarian economy.

Because it was grounded on a Eurocentric political philosophy that did not promote genuine political dialogue and engagement, the attempt to dismantle the feudal order with a Marxist revolution resulted in the institution of a military regime that eliminated all of the oppositions from the political landscape. Chege (1979) claims that Marxist ideas were championed by university students that mostly came from the class of the petite bourgeoisie and that in such a context, "the task of infusing ideological cohesion into the various petty-bourgeois and working-class forces fell to students in general" (Chege, 1979: 366). This gave birth to a polarized political culture that soon resulted in open confrontations and conflicts.

Clapham (1992) maintains that Marxism in Ethiopia served as a tool of centralized control for the government and an organizing principle which united the oppositions groups against exploitation. In comparison to most African states, Marxism enjoyed a higher status in Ethiopia. This is explained by the fact that just like the case in Russia it was assumed that Marxism is the perfect response to the centralizing tones of a feudal state that marginalized ethnic identities and imposed a dominant culture (Clapham, 1992: 106). There were several functions that Marxism served in Ethiopia especially for those who are in power and the elites. To start with, it served as a doctrine of revolution that helped mobilize the masses against the regime in the name of the overcoming of relations of class antagonism.

Besides this, Marxism also served as a way of modernizing the nation in line with an instrumental form of rationality. It also served as a way of answering the ethnic question by building a multi-ethnic state that resolved the questions of identity and difference (Clapham, 1992). It was used to subjugate and mobilize the masses in accordance with a material vision of the common good. Marxism was also used to forge ties with other nations in the world and to join the international struggle against imperialism and capitalism. The Derg and the opposition begin to abandon Marxism with the collapse of Soviet Union and the emergence of a new goal order that was dictated by the liberal policies of the Western world. The EPRDF which come to power after the Derg always remained faithful to its Marxist ideals although it made a tactical change and declared that it has accepted liberalism.

The attempt to introduce Marxism in Ethiopia took on the form of militant conflicts among Marxist groups and was not aimed at other groups once the revolution managed to get rid of the old feudal order. In the introduction of Marxism in Ethiopia, no attempts of indigenization were made and it was an imposition of a Eurocentric concept on Ethiopian indigenous realities that was carried out. Teshale (2008), remarks that there are two things that are so striking about the Ethiopian revolution compared to other Marxist revolutions in other parts of the world. First of all, it is that "the ruling class of the old regime collapsed without putting up a fight" (Teshale, 2008: 348). No considerable resistance was offered by the ruling class. Secondly, equally significant is that once the feudal order was dismantled, conflict ensued not between the Marxists and the guardians of the old order but between different factions which all espoused the principles of Marxism.

Abbink (2015) contends that the downfall of the feudal regime in Ethiopia could be seen as a revolution primarily because of two factors. First of all, it was not a mere unrest and upheaval but an attempt to dismantle the old structure and come up with new socio-political and economic modes of organization. Secondly, it was accompanied by a new Marxist ideology that replaced the old relations with a dialectical reading of history and analysis of relations of class antagonism. It was as such, "a fundamental social upheaval changing the political order and the basic structures of society" (Abbink, 2015: 335). Marxism dictated the spirit of the times and its practical application in nations like Ethiopia was characterized by violent conflicts. It had no space for genuine political dialogue and engagement.

The revolution that led into the coming to power of the Derg culminated in one of the most violent episodes in Ethiopian history that are characterized by extreme violence and bloodshed as there was an active conflict mostly in urban centers between different Marxist militant groups (Gashu, 2014: 334). Also, with the coming to power of the EPRDF what one witnesses is not the end of the Marxist paradigm in Ethiopian politics but its emergence in another form in the name of ethnic federalism. With the coming to power of the EPRDF in Ethiopia, a polarizing culture of violence and also alien political discourse continued to be employed. The EPRDF is also dictated by a Marxist orientation and the only difference between the Derg and the EPRDF is the manner in which the question of ethnic identity is being addressed. The Derg neglected such a question while the EPRDF made it the organizing principle of the federal structure.

Just like other nations, Marxist radical views came to be entertained in Ethiopia in universities which are secluded places that provide the context within which such ideas could be freely discussed. A relatively vibrant political space existed in the university compared to the society at large where political dissent and opposition was heavily crushed. Messay (2008) claims that for students, there were "special treatments compared to the complete silencing of the rest of the country" (Messay, 2008: 13). This served as a breeding ground for radical movements that soon begun to be articulated in terms of the nationality question.

Messay (2015) thinks that characterizations of the Ethiopia students movement like the ones that are developed by historians like Bahru Zewde tend to situate the origins of the process of radicalization in the moral development of those who participated in the revolution, in the process overlooking the elitist factors and the forces that exerted an impact on the thinking of the students from the outside. Besides this, such analyses are "unable to show concretely how the structural features of the imperial regime impacted on the radicalization of students" (Messay, 2015: 177). Messay's analysis of the origins of radicalism in the eyes of Bahru (2015) does not give an explanation of the attempts to change the system from within. He fails to see that, "it was the failure of these liberal recommendations for reform that made the radical option inevitable" (Bahru 2015: 188). Besides this, there is also a need to make sense of the contribution of international factors in the radicalization of students that take place in Ethiopia.

Marxism in the Derg and EPRDF

The Marxist ideals that were introduced in Ethiopia during the students' movement managed to have a lasting impact on Ethiopian political culture. They essentially constituted an attempt to impose a Eurocentric mode of rationality on Ethiopian indigenous realities. In a country with an agrarian economy and an intimate relationship between the individual and the community, an attempt was made to introduce a revolutionary philosophy that facilitates the emancipation form relations of exploitation that existed under the capitalistic system. Such an attempt culminated in a polarizing discourse and a radical political culture that did not tolerate any form of opposition to the absolute power of the government. The impacts of such a Marxist thinking are so influential that it continues to dictate contemporary Ethiopian politics. Its impact is mostly felt in the Derg and EPRDF regimes and their experimentation with the ideals of socialism, revolutionary democracy and developmental state.

Kelemen (1982: 246) situates the introduction of Marxism in Ethiopia as part of a revolution that was imposed from the above and did not originate from the actions of the masses. It was an ideology of the elites and the ruling classes that tried to control and normalize the life of the masses. In light of such an observation, Henze (1990: 4) adds that the Derg was mainly drawn into Marxism as it saw it as a way of consolidating its political power without encountering any resistance or opposition. There was no attempt that was mediate to mediate the principles of Marxism with the existing realities of the nation and to consider its value in light of indigenous political institutions and ideals.

Gashu (2014) maintains that the nature of contemporary Ethiopian politics is influenced by the importation of radical Marxist discourse during the time of the student movement of the 1960s. What started out as an attempt to bring an end to the feudal order, gradually resulted in a political discourse that is permeated with antagonism and polarizing political interests in contemporary Ethiopian politics that contains the ethno-nationalists on one hand and pan-Ethiopian identity advocates on the other hand. Such a Marxist radical approach to politics continued to dictate Ethiopian politics and is found behind the EPRDF. The introduction of Marxism in Ethiopia was not carried out through deliberative engagements that tried to appropriate the principles of Marxism to the Ethiopian reality. On the contrary, there was a shallow acceptance of the principles and the Eurocentric discourse was imposed on the minds of Ethiopians.

The introduction of Marxism did not just result in the overthrowing of the imperial regime. It continued to dictate Ethiopian politics and its influence is seen in the land policy and the right to secession that is practiced by the current government. There is a dangerous rhetoric in the application of the Marxist categories of the oppressor and the oppressed that was used to characterize ethnic relations in Ethiopia. Thus, "by applying the Stalinist notion of self-determination, the student groups simplistically attempted to classify the 'Amhara nation' or the *nefteya* as the oppressor and all the other ethnic groups as the oppressed" (Gashu, 2014: 95). Such a discourse continues to serve as a source of conflicts in Ethiopia.

The radicalization of Ethiopian politics is mostly attributed to the attempts to find an alternative to the non-progressive nature of the feudal order and the inability of students to bring forth a normative ideal that can bring gradual change and reform in their society. Radicalization gave way to ethnic mobilization as ethnic identity came to be regarded as a neglected issue in the Ethiopian revolution. When the EPRDF came to power it replaced the Derg's emphasis on social class with ethnic identity. It used a political reading of the modern Ethiopian state as a process of assimilation to situate ethnic federalism as a lasting solution to the questions of different Ethiopian ethnic groups for equal representation.

The EPRDF's supposed abandoning of the principles of Marxism and Leninism was part of a strategy of attracting Western donors and in reality; it like the Derg also used Marxism to create a polarized political culture that is against any form of opposition. Tsehai (2009) shows us that TPLF's acceptance of neo-liberalism was a tactical move that was meant to win the support of the Western nations and in reality the party was always dictated by a Marxist-Leninist ideology (Tsehai, 2009: 12). Particularly for Gashu (2014) the system of bureaucratic control and the absolute power that is exercised by the state during the rule of the EPRDF are inherited from Leninism. Even the revolutionary democracy model of the EPRDF is dictated by the "Marxist orientation of TPLF" (Gashu, 2014: 134). The TPLF took a pragmatic approach towards the interpretation of revolutionary democracy and used its fluctuating meaning in order to suppress political opposition.

The EPRDF pictures revolutionary democracy as a middle path in between the extremes of socialism and capitalism. In reality, it is a model that crushes political opposition in the name of realizing economic development. It perceives the political landscape as being made up of friends and enemies and sees the elite as standing against the interests of the masses.

The EPRDF tried to strengthen its rule in the name of developmental democracy after the 2005 elections. It established itself as a rule that is known for unlimited material progress. This is a model that surpasses the rights of citizens in the name of development. It is founded on the idea that "neo-liberal ideals do not work unless some degree of economic development is primarily achieved" (Gashu, 2014: 140). One of the features of the models of revolutionary democracy and the developmental state is that they are strategies that were meant to grab absolute power rather than clear political ideologies with moral and political imperatives.

Revolutionary democracy was presented by the EPRDF as the antithesis of neo-liberalism. Although it is used to crush all political opponents, there is no success so far in elucidating the nature of revolutionary democracy except in reference to other doctrines like Maoism and liberalism. Bach thinks that revolutionary democracy is founded on the attempt to find "a bridge between pre-capitalist and socialist societies" (Bach, 2011: 641). It is part of a strategy of ideologization in the part of Meles Zenawi to strengthen his place within the ruling party and also crush any opposition that comes from other parties. The TPLF's revolutionary democracy model initially originated as a war time ideology although it was subsequently used as a pragmatic approach in order to strengthen the power of the state. Lovise (2019: 3) argues that from the beginning the TPLF appropriated Marxism in its own terms employing the class of the oppressed nationalities rather than the exploited class as a major principle. Thus the idea of the working class was replaced by the suppressed and exploited ethnic group.

The idea of the ethnic identity which is marginalized in the previous regimes is the major principle that the EPRDF was founded on. Such a party sees itself as a party that has realized unlimited growth and has also ensured the equal representation of previously marginalized ethnic groups. Still Tobias & Jon (2011) identify as the basic feature of the EPRDF, the "unwillingness or inability to share power, its de facto rejection of political pluralism and its disregard for civic rights and political freedoms" (Tobias and Jon, 2011: 582). The developmental model which is adopted by the EPRDF still retained the idea of the oppressed ethnic identity and crushed all political voices in the name of attaining economic growth.

Although it has managed to create the image of the fastest growing economy to foreign nations, internally there was strong resistance and opposition to the policies of the EPRDF. Thus the Ethiopian developmental state has failed to find legitimacy especially in the domestic front. Because of this, Eyob observes that, "the transition from authoritarianism to democratic plurality remains incomplete and this continues to undermine attempts to consolidate and deepen democracy in Ethiopia" (Eyob, 2018: 65). The government of Prime Minister Abiy Ahmed came to power in such a context. Soon after assuming power, a set of radical reforms that focused on broadening the public sphere in the domestic front and renewing ties with the international community were carried out.

Abiy Ahmed's Medemer

Medemer is presented as an approach that is able to transcend the politics of antagonism and violence. It is also seen as an approach that can overcome the pitfalls of neo-liberalism and social democracy. As an approach that can appropriate elements of pan-Ethiopian identity, the Gada system of the Oromo, Pentecostal Christianity, elements of a populist rhetoric and Ubuntu relational and ecocentric ethics, medemer is conceptualized as a new approach that finds the middle ground between the unionist discourse on one hand and the ethno-nationalistic cause on the other hand. Whereas in the previous sections, I have discussed the origins of the Marxist discourse in Ethiopian politics and its presence in the Derg and EPRDF regimes, in this part of the paper I will discuss three major things. The first one is elucidating the essence of medemer. The second one is considering its nature against the background of Marxist discourse. The third one is identifying some of the inherent ambiguities that are found in medemer.

Jonathan & Meresa (2018: 205) proclaim that Abiy's medemer emphasizes the need to forgive one another and engage in common projects for the future. It is situated as an approach that stands against a politics of hate and violence. Some of the radical measures that Abiy took as part of his medemer agenda include strengthening diplomatic relations with neighboring states, broadening the public space and the releasing of political prisoners. Still as Worku & Ephrem (2020) show, some of the major challenges that his government is currently facing include the ethnically motivated conflict that is occurring in the different parts of the country, polarized political interests, power struggle within the ruling party, mob justice, rising costs of living and inflation and the absence of fair and impartial institutions.

In his book *Medemer* Abiy Ahmed (2019) argues that his medemer approach is founded on two major assumptions about the nature of human beings and what Ethiopians hope to accomplish as a nation. The first one is the centuries old values that Ethiopians managed to develop as a result of relations of interdependence. This serves as a force of social cohesion which holds Ethiopians together and provides the moral fabric through which a common sense of destiny is being instituted. The second assumption is that the laws of nature manifest themselves in relations of symmetry and harmony. This leads to the conclusion that human beings by nature have a desire to cooperate with one another. This is an altruistic ethics which ion the contrary to the ethics of capitalism assumes that human beings engage in acts self-sacrifice, and are not driven by their egoistic drives and inclinations.

Abiy tells us that ideological assumptions which are imported from the outside must be creatively appropriated to the local context. This still does not mean that Ethiopians do not have to borrow ideas that have a foreign origin. He also argues that human beings mostly have an altruistic attitude although their aspirations are dictated by existing circumstances (Ali, 2019: 2). Besides a description of the moral motivations of individuals that lead a communal life, medemer is situated as an approach that is critical towards both social democracy and neo-liberalism. It is assumed that both approaches although one advocates the active role of the government in the life of individuals and the other one focuses on the rights of non-interference, are founded on the appropriation of a wealth that is accumulated through the exploitation of non-westerners (Ibid: 21).

Abiy's medemer also attempts to identify the limitations of ideological programs that were introduced in Ethiopia like revolutionary democracy. Six major limitations of EPRDF's revolutionary democracy are identified in medemer. The first of such limitations is that revolutionary democracy has a contradictory view of the roles of elites in societal transformation. On one hand it sees all human beings as being driven by an egoistic drive while on the other hand it assumes that elites care only about the public good. Secondly, revolutionary democracy is a reductionist approach since it perceives the problems that are faced by a society only from an economic angle and a materialistic perspective. Thirdly, there is failure to see that revolutionary democracy is not an end in itself and must be seen as a way of transforming pre-capitalistic societies into capitalistic ones (Ibid: 28). We also need to remember that one of the failures of the Derg is that it employed the principles of Marxism as a way of transforming the state into the world of socialism when in fact what existed in Ethiopia was not a capitalistic state but a feudal one. Fourthly, revolutionary democracy is criticized for leading into the diminishing of the political space in its attempt to replace multi-party system with a one party dominated system. Fifthly, in being only interested in pre-capitalistic modes of production, revolutionary democracy does not give an account of other relations of production (Ibid: 31). Sixthly, revolutionary democracy exists in a context in which there are no strong and resilient social and political institutions in the country. Because there is no political culture that can promote genuine dialogue and criticism and a public sphere that can host a space in which all citizens could equally participate irrespective of their differences from one another, there was no success in instituting an inclusive political culture. Medemer is also critical towards the idea of the developmental state. It is argued that developmental democracy succeeded in bringing economic growth although it does not give an attention to the private sector and also resulted in the violation o0f basic individual liberties.

The essence of medemer is found in protecting our integrity and autonomy by using our material resources, knowledge, action and daily social life in unison (Ibid: 40). One of the core principles of medemer is standing for a common goal and purpose. Another principle is being motivated. This is initiating new things in our relations with others and the social reality that we happen to inhabit. National unity and giving equal respect are other major principles of medemer. Abiy also identifies the major obstacles that stand against the realization of his medemer vision for the nation. Such obstacles focus on the narrow landscape within which the political culture is founded, obsession with temporal benefits and failing to develop a holistic perspective that makes sense of the problems that are haunting the Ethiopian state.

The first of such obstacles is ethnic and societal polarization (Ali, 2019: 50). The second obstacle is failing to make sense of the totality of human experience and concentrating on only one aspect of time like the present moment and the past. Thirdly, simply treating problems from one angle and failing to understand their complexity is another major challenge (Ali, 2019: 58). Fourthly not respecting one's profession is another obstacle. Fifthly, being only interested on the trends of the day, not paying attention to significant ideas and simply submitting to the will of others are also identified as major challenges.

Now that we have elucidated the basic tenets and principles of medemer, let's try to consider the relationship of such an approach to the Marxist radical approach that has dictated Ethiopian politics starting from the time of the students' movement, and whether or not medemer manages to overcome such a polarizing discourse. To start with medemer does not operate within a thesis of class antagonism and class struggle, and does not employ ethnic identity as an organizing principle. It did not use the Marxist idea of class struggle to erect the question of identity as a struggle between the oppressor and the oppressed.

It uses two interrelated theses about the nature of human beings and what Ethiopians stand for as a nation. Like the socialist programs of the Derg, medemer is not dependent on the idea that it is the revolutionary praxis of the working class against forces of capitalism that entails the path towards emancipation. It does not also view the trajectory of human history within the Marxist frame of class struggle eventually giving way to a new reality where there is justice and equity. Medemer is not also dictated by a dialectical analysis of history which pictures human destiny as a result of the prevailing material relationships that are found within a given society. Still although it does not use the Marxist idea of class struggle as a foundation of the question of identity, it does not take a clear stance towards the question of identity. It makes an attempt to relate the question of identity to questions that human beings ask in their gradual development. But it does not explicitly state what kind of stance the state should embrace towards the question of identity.

We can also add that the conceptual space that is occupied by medemer is not oriented towards polarization. As an eclectic approach that draws on the insights of different political programs and schools of thought, medemer is an attempt to find a middle ground between social democracy and neo-liberalism. Being equally critical of such approaches, it assumes that it the quest of human beings to cooperate with one another and their altruistic behavior that is a foundation of a society. This is antithetical towards the capitalistic ethics of greed and consumerism.

Compared to the Marxist ideology that dictated the political programs of the Derg and EPRDF, medemer is not a radical approach that divides the political landscape towards friends and enemies that are involved in relations of antagonism. The strength of medemer is found in the fact that it is able to appropriate insights from different practices and intellectual traditions. But, this also turns out to be its major weakness since there is no clear underling ideological framework or political philosophy that underlies the practice of medemer. Unless it is strictly defined in relation to a particular picture of the world and a mode of social and political organization, then medemer risks becoming a loose concept that characterizes relations of cooperation within a given community.

Medemer also manages to strike a healthy balance between indigenous political wisdom and practices on one hand and alien concepts on the other hand. It is able to appropriate several ideals related to a concept of leadership that is down to earth and a rule that is mainly based on technocrats with a populist rhetoric and an altruistic moral philosophy. It is also attentive towards indigenous knowledge systems that emphasize a relational and holistic ethics and also ideals like the ubuntu moral approach that focus on a common fate and destiny.

The most important feature of medemer compared to socialist ideology, revolutionary democracy and the developmental state, is that it is not trapped under the analysis of material relations. It does not conceive the foundation of human existence as the material substratum of life. It also does not assume that change exists within a given society only and only when material relations are being revolutionized. It pays attention alternatively to the role of value systems and normative ideals in making societal change possible. Although this helps to avoid material reductionism, it also harbors the risk of utopian degeneration as it is possible that the ideals that are found in medemer could easily turn into concepts of social engineering that are being used to mobilize the masses.

The political philosophies of the Derg and the EPRDF are grounded on a Marxist thesis which assumes that there is no such a thing as human nature. On the contrary, it is assumed that human beings have the capacity to create themselves and the world that they are living in through creative labor and that in the world of capitalism they are being alienated and that the goal of revolutionary practice is to restore creative labor. Medemer on the contrary is grounded on an altruistic view of human nature which assumes that human beings have the inherent desire to cooperate with one another.

Despite all these departures that medemer has made in reference to the radical Marxist paradigm that is found in the Derg and the EPRDF, there are also certain ambiguities within medemer that need to be resolved. First of all, to be conceived as a political philosophy, medemer needs to have a much broader normative framework which deals with the essence of human values, the trajectory of human history and the engines that drive such historical framework. It also needs to be supplanted by a theory of social development that details the logic that dictates the development of societies around the world thereby situating where the Ethiopian process of state formation is situated in such a process.

Medemer also needs to identify a clear alternative that can resolve the debate on Ethiopian political modernity and the fate of the modern Ethiopian state. On one hand there are the ethno-nationalists who advance the view that the process of state formation in modern Ethiopia resulted in cultural assimilation and homogenization. On the other hand, we have those that allege that it was relations of interdependence and a common moral fabric that was created through centuries that led into the creation of the modern Ethiopian state. In such a context, medemer needs to be properly situated. A way of addressing questions like what is the essence of Ethiopia's process of modern state formation and what challenges does it present in the current moment needs to be presented.

Conclusion

The foundation of political discourse in contemporary Ethiopian politics could be traced back to the introduction of the principles of Marxism during the period the students movements. The idea of emancipating the people from a feudal political economy was entertained by making recourse to the ideas of class antagonism and the revolutionary practice of the working class. Such an attempt was founded on the failure to analyze the existing realities of the Ethiopian situation and the attempt to impose a foreign concept that is part of a Eurocentric system that is grounded on the modern European state, into the Ethiopian soil. It eventually resulted in a radical political culture that completely sidelined existing relations. Moreover, tin the political landscape it served as a foundation for the political programs of the Derg and the EPRDF.

The Derg used the principles of Marxism with an aim of attaining a proletarian revolution whereas the EPRDF interpreted the Marxist concept of class antagonism from the perspective of ethnic identity and the quest for recognition. Once it came to power it introduced revolutionary democracy that retinas the Marxist idea of history being driven through relations of antagonism and later on introduced the model of the developmental state which typically in a Marxist from understand the attainment of material progress and instrumental rationality as the ultimate form of progress.

Abiy Ahmed's medemer in this context represents an attempt to overcome the logic of Marxist rationality as it is heavily expressed in Ethiopian politics. By introducing a reading of Ethiopian history that focuses on relations of interdependence and a common destiny and a view of human nature that focuses on an altruistic ethics and motivation, medemer tried to introduce a political platform that overcomes the limitations of socialism, revolutionary democracy, the developmental state and also the positions of neo-liberalism and social democracy.

Medemer does not employ the Marxist analysis of history or the analysis of ideology and emancipation as its foundation. It is not also grounded on an analysis of material relations and because of this it can host the grounds for a political culture that can broaden the political landscape and the public sphere. It can also serve as a foundation of a mode of criticism that identifies the limitations of a polarizing discourse as it is particular developed by the different ethno-nationalistic political parties. With all these strengths, medemer needs to be founded on a clear normative framework and a political philosophy. The role of medemer in reference to the ethnic question and the process of state formation in modern Ethiopia need to be further understood.

References

[1] ALI A. 2019. Medemer. Addis Ababa: Tsehaipublishers.

[2] AALEN L. 2019. The revolutionary democracy of Ethiopia: a wartime ideology both shaping and shaped by peacetime policy needs. Government and Opposition, 55(4): 663–668.

[3] ABBINK J. 2015. The Ethiopian revolution after 40 years (1974-2014) plan B in progress? Journal of Developing Societies, 31 (3): 333-357.

[4] TSEHAI A. 2009. The Ethiopian developmental state: requirements and perquisites. Journal of Business & Economics Research, 7 (8): 11-18.

[5] ASEGIDEW M. 2019. A shift of political discourse: critical discourse analysis of Ethiopian Prime Minister Dr. Abiy Ahmed's inaugural speech. Advances in Sciences and Humanities, 5 (5): 128-137.

[6] BACH J. 2011. Abyotawi democracy: neither revolutionary nor democratic, a critical review of EPRDF's conception of revolutionary democracy in post-1991 Ethiopia. Journal of Eastern African Studies, 5 (4): 641-663.

[7] EYOB B. 2018. The carrot and stick of Ethiopian "Democratic Developmentalism": ideological, legal, and policy frameworks//TAPSCOTT C, HALVORSEN T, ROSARIO T C. The democratic developmental state: north-south perspectives.Stuttgart: Ibidem-Verlag.

[8] BARKESSA A. 2019. Discursive strategies of "Oromara": a critical discourse analysis of Abiy Ahmed's political rhetoric. Ethiopian Journal of the Social Sciences and Humanities, 15(2): 1-24.

[9] BIRU A. 2019. Failures of ethnic politics in Ethiopia: a Machiavellian way out. Social Sciences and Education Research Review, 6 (1): 48-71.

[10] BRATT H. 2020. Uneven playing field: understanding Abiy Ahmed manipulation of democracy in Ethiopia. http: //uu.diva-portal.org/smashlget/divaz:1388429/FULLTEXT01.pdf.

[11] CHEGE M. 1979. The revolution betrayed: Ethiopia, 1974-1979. The Journal of Modern African Studies, 17 (3): 359-380.

[12] CLAPHAM C. 1992. The socialist experience in Ethiopia and its demise. Journal of Communist Studies, 8 (2):105-125.

[13] WORKU D, EPHREM Ahadu. 2020. Post 2018 political reforms in Ethiopia: Its achievements and challenges. AGATHOS, 11 (1) :439-451.

[14] JONATHAN F, MERESSA T. 2018. Briefing "Game Over"? Abiy Ahmed, the Tigrayan People's Liberation Front and Ethiopia's political crisis. African Affairs, 118(470): 194-206.

[15] GASHU S. 2014. The last post-Cold War socialist federation: ethnicity, ideology and democracy in Ethiopia, Burlington : Ashgate Publishing Company.

[16] TOBIAS H, Jon A. 2011. Twenty years of revolutionary democratic Ethiopia, 1991 to 2011. Journal of Eastern African Studies, 5 (4):579-595.

[17] HENZE P B. 1990 The Ethiopian revolution: mythology and history. Northeast African Studies, 12(2/3):1-17.

[18] HUGHES A. 1992. The appeal of Marxism to Africans. Journal of Communist Studies, 8 (2): 4-20.

[19] MESSAY K. 2008. Radicalism and cultural dislocation in Ethiopia: 1960-1974. Rochester: University of Rochester Press.

[20] MESSAY K. 2015. The Ethiopian student movement: a rejoinder to Bahru Zewde's *The Quest for Socialist Utopia*. Northeast African Studies, 15 (1):175-186.

[21] KELEMEN P. 1982. A critique of the Ethiopian revolution. Horn of Africa, 5 (2): 18-31.

[22] NAMHLA T M. 2020. Ethiopian reforms and the resolution of uncertainty in the Horn of Africa state system. South African Journal of International Affairs, 25: 10.

[23] MENNASEMAY M. 2005. Ethiopian political theory, democracy, and surplus history. International Journal of Ethiopian Studies, 2 (1/2):1-32.

[24] MENNASEMAY M. 2008. A millennium democratic goal for ethiopia: some conceptual issues. Africa Today, 55 1(1): 3-32.

[25] MOKADDEM S. 2019. Abiy Ahmed's "Medemer" reforms: can it ensure sustainable growth for Ethiopia and what are the challenges facing the new government? Policy Center for the New South. https://www.policycenter.ma/publications/abiy-ahmed%E2%80%99s-E2%80%-98medemer%E2%80%99-reforms-can-it-ensure-sustainable-growth-ethiopia-and-what-are.

[26] TEMIN J, BADWAZA Y. 2019. Aspirations and realities in Africa: Ethiopia's quiet revolution. Journal of Democracy, 30 (3):139-153.

[27] TESHALE T. 2008. Modernity, Eurocentrism, and radical politics in Ethiopia, 1961-1991, African Identities, 6 (4):345-371.

[28] BAHRU Z. 2015. Response to Messay Kebede's rejoinder. Northeast African Studies, 15 (1):187-198.

浅析埃塞俄比亚"发展型国家"道路与新自由主义思潮①

云 蔚 翟风杰

(天津职业技术师范大学非盟研究中心,天津 300222)

摘要:本文通过对埃塞俄比亚(简称"埃塞")"发展型国家"道路与新自由主义思潮的梳理,研究了这两种思想在近30年来此消彼长的发展关系。从1991年开始,伴随着政权更迭,新自由主义政策成为埃塞的主流经济思想,但21世纪之后该国转而采取"发展型国家"的经济政策。2018年,新自由主义思潮卷土重来,成为埃塞流行的社会思潮。两种思想的碰撞持续至今。

关键词:埃塞俄比亚;发展型国家;新自由主义

埃塞俄比亚在近30年中进行了多次经济改革,其背后体现了埃塞政府对经济发展道路的探索以及国内外力量的博弈。在这一段历史中,"发展型国家"道路与新自由主义思潮此消彼长,对埃塞经济产生了重要的影响,理顺二者的含义及其关系,对理解埃塞经济发展有着较为重要的意义。

一、埃塞俄比亚"发展型国家"道路

(一)埃塞俄比亚"发展型国家"道路的内涵

"发展型国家"(Developmental State)② 的概念源自查默斯·约翰逊(Chalmers Johnson)在1982年出版的《通产省与日本奇迹——产业政策的成长(1925—1975)》(*MITI and the Japanese Miracle*:*The Growth of Industrial Policy*,1925-1975)一书③。随后在20世纪80年代末至90年代初,诞生了一系列研究东亚发展经验的文献,一并被认为是"发展型国家"的开创性研究。约翰逊解释说,"将'资本主义发展型国家'(Capitalist Developmental State)的思想引入日本近代工业政策的历史,主要目的之一就是要超越与美国和苏联经济的对比"④。"发展型国家"道路是东亚国家选择的一条不符合主流经济制度"自由市场"或"社会主义

① 本研究受教育部国别和区域研究专项资金(19GBQY011)资助,系该研究项目阶段性成果。

② "发展型国家"的英文"developmental state"中的"state"不仅指国家,还包括地区。

③ Chalmers Johnson, *MITI and the Japanese Miracle: The Growth of Industrial Policy,* 1925-1975, California:Stanford University Press,1982.

④ Jostein Hauge, Ha-Joon Chang, *The Concept of a"Developmental State" in Ethiopia*, in F Cheru, C Cramer, A Oqubay (eds.), *The Oxford Handbook of the Ethiopian Economy*, Oxford:Oxford University Press, 2019.

经济体制”的第三条道路，具有开创意义。从内涵上来说，“发展型国家”允许私人市场经济运行，但同时要求政府进行高度干预。后续学者也在个人理解的基础上结合“发展型国家”在实践中的演变延伸了该概念。莱夫特威克（Leftwich）将“发展型国家”定义为“运用内部政治和对外关系，集中足够的权力、权威、素质和能力，来塑造、追求和鼓励实现明确的发展目标，无论是通过建立和改善经济增长的条件，还是通过直接组织经济增长，或通过二者的不同组合来实现”。格布雷马里亚姆（Gebremariam）和巴宇（Bayu）认为，发展型国家需要具备“促进发展主义（developmentalism）理想与议程”的意识形态和强大的国家机构作为制度保障，需要政府作为重要的经济和发展参与者，且经济发展目标和合法性可以持续，不因政权变动而变动[①]。豪格（Hauge）和常（Chang）认为，“发展型国家”有如下特征：①源于日本以及亚洲其他国家和地区经济的发展经验；②将重度国家干预与私有制相结合；③优先发展经济，并通过工业化来实现；④通过经济发展绩效将该道路或模式合法化；⑤拥有一个专业的行政机构，它在日常的政治活动中与私营部门保持距离，但同时也是私营部门的合作伙伴，共同致力于工业转型[②]。综上所述，可以将意识形态取向（即促进发展主义的理想和议程）及其制度安排（即制定和实施其政策和方案的制度能力）作为“发展型国家”的特征[③]。

1991 年，埃塞政党联盟埃塞俄比亚人民革命民主阵线（简称“埃革阵”；The Ethiopian People's Revolutionary Democratic Front，EPRDF）推翻德格政权（1974—1991），建立过渡政府。在统治初期，为了实现尽快重建国民经济的短期目标和减少贫困的长期目标，过渡政府接受了国际金融机构及其他西方国家的资助，资助的条件是推行“结构调整计划”（Structural Adjustment Programmes，SAPs）等一系列新自由主义经济政策。但新自由主义政策未能帮助埃塞实现预期的经济目标[④]，埃塞前总理、埃革阵的精神领袖梅莱斯·泽纳维（Meles Zenawi）于 2001 年[⑤]正式宣布进行改革，采取“发展型国家”道路。

埃塞“发展型国家”思想的起源可追溯至埃革阵的核心政党提格雷人民解放阵线（简称“提人阵”；The Tigrayan People's Liberation Front，TPLF）。提人阵具有强烈的知识分子倾向和精英意识，曾在 20 世纪 80 年代后期建立一所商学院，翻译列宁的作品，研究阿尔巴尼亚社会主义革命和韩国的产业政策。韩国、日本、中国等东亚国家和地区的国家主导的工业化经验对提人阵的影响不可低估。克拉帕姆（Clapham）认为，埃塞显然借鉴了东亚发展模式，并以中国为最重要的灵感来源，但也试图从其他案例中学习，包括韩国、中国和日本[⑥]。

梅莱斯·泽纳维是埃塞“发展型国家”思想的创始人和领航者，也是埃塞走上“发展型国

---

① Fesseha Mulu Gebremariam, Abtewold Moges Bayu, *Ethiopia: a Democratic Developmental State*, ILIRIA International Review, 2017, 7(2): 9-26.

② Jostein Hauge, Ha-Joon Chang, *The Concept of a "Developmental State" in Ethiopia*, in F Cheru, C Cramer, A Oqubay (eds.), *The Oxford Handbook of the Ethiopian Economy*, Oxford: Oxford University Press, 2019.

③ T Gebremariam, *The "Democratic Developmental State" in Ethiopia: Origins, Challenges and Prospects*, in J. Sonja, Dagnachew Assefa, BushaTaa (Eds.), *Cultures of Democracy in Ethiopia: From Theory to Lived Experiences*, Addis Ababa, A Publication of the Friedrich-Ebert-Stiftung Ethiopia, 2017: 88-104.

④ 非洲大陆上的很多国家都经历了新自由主义方向的经济改革，但是均未取得理想的效果。

⑤ 也有文献认为 2002 年，埃塞开始宣布选择“发展型国家”道路，见：A Teshome, *Meles's Development Paradigm and Its Impacts on Economic Transformation in Ethiopia*, Global Advanced Research Journal of Management and Business Studies, 2012, 1(1): 384-396。大多文献对于埃塞开始明确采取“发展型国家”道路选择的具体时间表述较为模糊，但是普遍认为是从 21 世纪初开始的。

⑥ 同②。

家”道路的坚持执行者。梅莱斯·泽纳维认为,自独立以来,非洲国家的发展主要遵循两种范式:一是持续到20世纪80年代初的掠夺性国家的范式;二是从20世纪80年代开始一直流行的新自由主义范式。为了实现复兴,非洲必须要对这两种范式进行全面评估,以分析是否需要引入新范式。梅莱斯·泽纳维部分同意新自由主义者的观点,即非洲在独立后第一个十年采取的“掠夺性国家”发展方向是一个“死胡同”,但他同时认为完全将经济交由市场、无视政府作用将走向第二个死胡同①。因此,梅莱斯·泽纳维在评估埃塞所采取的新自由主义政策的影响之后,改变了发展模式,加大了政府对经济的参与,为市场主体创造了更加合适的商业环境②。

根据梅莱斯·泽纳维的理论,埃塞的“发展型国家”道路可以总结为市场力量与政府干预作用的平衡,在这个平衡中,政府的干预作用不仅体现在提供基础设施和服务方面,也在为发展生产能力和制造能力提供有利的环境方面起到主导作用。政府应该致力于创造价值,并将加快经济增长、扩大经济收入作为关系国家生存的大事③。

在“发展型国家”的基础上,埃塞进一步提出了“民主”的目标,要“成为一个民主统治、良政和社会公正、人民自愿参与的国家”④。梅莱斯·泽纳维认为虽然很少有先例,但是非洲国家在选择“发展型国家”道路的同时,也必须选择民主。从外部环境来看,民主成为受援的条件之一,时任美国助理国务卿科恩(Herman Cohen)清晰地表明了美国援助和埃塞民主改革的关系:“没有民主,就没有合作。”⑤从内部环境看,民主合法性对种族多样化的非洲国家十分重要,而且与30年前不同,在21世纪初,民主被视为基本人权的组成部分之一,这也是埃塞不能推迟民主的原因之一⑥。

梅莱斯认为埃塞的“民主”与西方的“民主”有着不同的内涵。梅莱斯·泽纳维谴责自由主义为“(财富)向上渗透的民主”(trickle-up democracy,指穷人的财富逐渐转移到富人手中),他认为在一个贫穷的发展中国家,政党和非政府组织很容易成为赞助机构,而不是政治文化和可持续发展的真正基础。他担心各方为抢夺国家权力进行斗争而形成“无选择的民主”(no-choice democracy)⑦。梅莱斯认为埃塞的“民主”可以为长期执政提供基础,从而实现国家所需的政策连续性和稳定性⑧。

结合“民主”的重要作用,埃塞的“民主发展型国家”可以被定义为在约束下通过运用权威、信用和合法性来设计和实施机构变革和经济增长。国家以长期的经济增长、结构转型、平等作为总体社会经济目标,同时使得发展的成果赢得民众的支持。因此,埃塞的“民主发展型国家”通过经济表现和民主程序赢得合法性并长期保持自己的权力,该模式主要包括三个重要部分:实行民主、政府(在经济中)的积极作用以及政治支持基础。

---

① Meles Zenawi, *Africa's Development: Dead Ends and New Beginnings*, 2006, http://www.meleszenawi.com/african-development-dead-ends-and-new-biginnings-by-meles-zenawi/.

② A Teshome, *Meles's Development Paradigm and Its Impacts on Economic Transformation in Ethiopia*, Global Advanced Research Journal of Management and Business Studies, 2012, 1(11):384-396.

③ Alex de Waal, *Review Article: The Theory and Practice of Meles Zenawi*, African Affairs, 2013, 112(446):148-155.

④ 埃塞俄比亚联邦民主共和国,增长和转型计划(GTP)2010/11—2014/15,2010。

⑤ 周瑾艳. 作为非洲道路的民主发展型国家——埃塞俄比亚的启示. 文化纵横,2019(3):29-39,142.

⑥ 同②。

⑦ 同③。

⑧ 同①。

（二）埃塞俄比亚“发展型国家”道路的实践成效

与埃革阵执政初期经济规划中大量的新自由主义政策不同，埃塞政府在“发展型国家”期间的目标着眼于通过强国家干预模式来实现：由国家弥补自由市场在基础设施建设和人力资源发展上的不足，指导并帮助私有部门的发展，优先发展农业并带动工业和服务业发展。这种发展模式从埃塞国情出发，体现了埃塞对自主发展道路的探索。转型目标写在国家《增长和转型计划》（*Growth and Transformation Plan*，GTP）中。在第一期《增长和转型计划》中，埃塞俄比亚经济方面的规划是：“建设一个现代高效的农业和工业起主导作用的经济；保持经济发展和保障社会公正；提高人均收入以达到中等收入国家的水平。”①

1. 经济增长

20 世纪 80 年代直至 20 世纪末，埃塞的经济增长极不稳定。从 21 世纪初开始，埃塞的国内生产总值（Gross Domestic Product, GDP）稳步增长。经计算，2001—2010 年，埃塞 GDP 年均增长率达 8.63%，2011—2019 年，年均增长率达 9.45%，远超 20 世纪 90 年代结构调整时期仅 2.75% 的年均增长率，增长也更趋于稳定。不仅如此，埃塞的经济与撒哈拉以南非洲国家同期相比也有着更快增长（见图 1），在该地区经济规模所占比重也从 1985 年的 1.33% 提升至 2019 年的 3.65%（见表 1）。

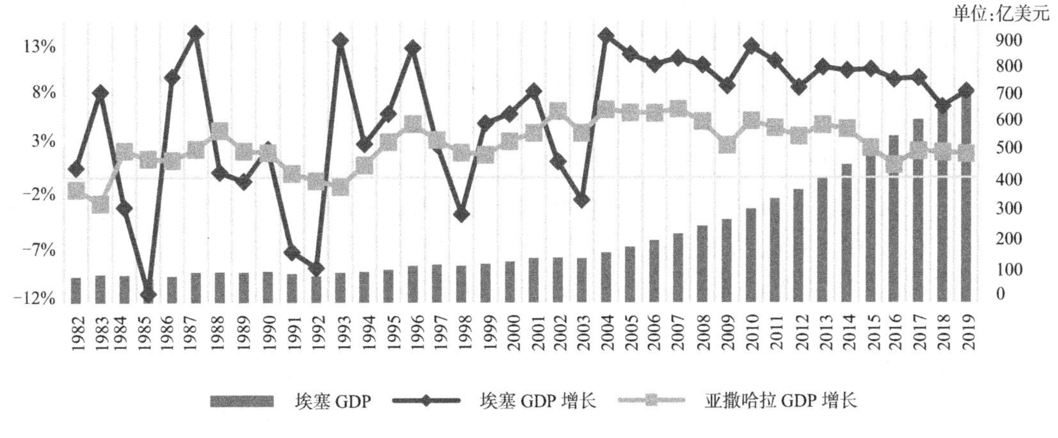

图 1　1982—2019 年埃塞 GDP 及埃塞与撒哈拉以南非洲国家 GDP 增长率 ②

表 1　埃塞 GDP 占撒哈拉以南非洲国家 GDP 总和的比重 ③

年份	1985	1990	1995	2000	2005	2010	2015	2019
比重	1.33%	1.50%	1.51%	1.60%	1.67%	2.17%	2.86%	3.65%

① 埃塞俄比亚联邦民主共和国，增长和转型计划（GTP）2010/11-2014/15，2010。

② 数据来源：世界发展指标数据库（World Development Indicators），更新时间为 2020 年 10 月 7 日。

③ 同②。

从产业结构来看,作为埃塞传统经济支柱的农业增加值在GDP中占比一直较高。近40年来,在1992年达到峰值63.83%,随后开始波动式地下降, 2014年开始下降至40%以下,2019年占比仅为33.88%。相对应的是工业和服务业占比的提升,工业占比由1992年的6.09%提高至2019年的24.77%,同一时间段,服务业占比由26.83%增长至36.87%(见图2)。相对于农业来说,工业和服务业提供了更为稳定和高速的增长率。

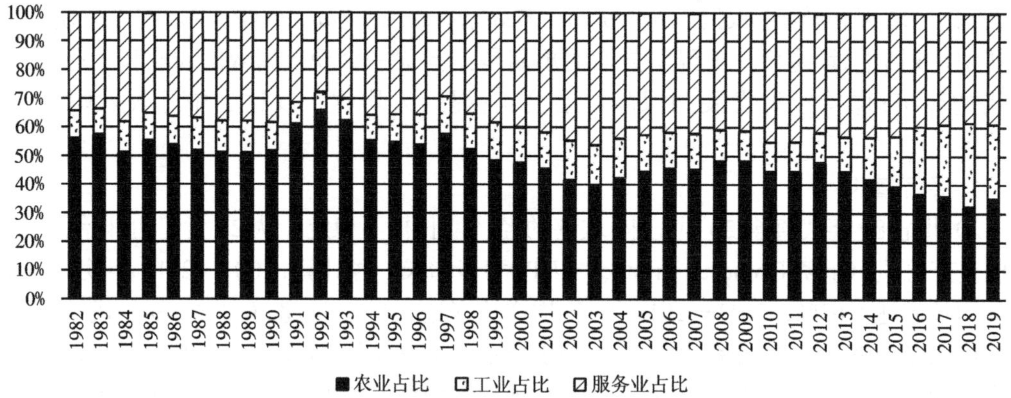

图2 1982—2019年埃塞三大产业GDP占比[①]

从减贫的效果来看,根据世界银行的贫困人口比率指标,按照2011年的国际价格衡量,埃塞全国范围内每天生活费低于1.90美元的人口所占比例由1995年的72.3%下降到2015年的32.6%。根据《人类发展报告2019》,埃塞的人类发展指数为0.47,从2000年开始逐年改善,在189个国家中排名第173名,比2013年提高了3个名次。

埃塞的基础设施建设较为薄弱,政府加大力度进行道路、铁路、电信、银行和电力等方面的建设。以运输为例, 2002年,埃塞公路网总长度仅为3.08万千米, 2019年,公路网达到13.81万千米,其中乡村公路长度达3.09万千米,占22.4%[②],大大提高了日常运输的效率。移动通信订阅人数从2000年的5万人增长至2017年的3960万人,在全国人口占比从7.18%提升至37.22%[③]。

2. 社会发展

埃塞政府在医疗、基础设施和教育等社会服务项目扩大支出。婴儿死亡率由2000年的8.7%下降至2019年的3.65%,降低了一半多。41%的人口可以使用基本的饮用水,比2000年提高了22个百分点[④]。埃塞政府践行了其对扩大教育的承诺[⑤],政府支出中教育占比由2000年的14.91%提升至2015年的27.10%。各级教育都得到了大规模扩展,特别是在小学和中学阶段。小学净入学率由2000年的40%提高至2015年的85.20%。政府通过加大对教育的投资提高人力资源的质量,一方面培养政府机构和公务员队伍的精英管理人才,另一方面培养现代化工业所需的技能型人才。

---

① 数据来源:世界发展指标数据库(World Development Indicators),更新时间为2020年10月7日。

② National Bank of Ethiopia, Annual Report 2018/2019 on Ethiopian Economy, 2019.

③ 同①。

④ 同①。

⑤ Alemu Asfaw Nigusieand Mohammed Seid Ali, "*Developmental State*" *as an Alternative Development Path in Ethiopia: Miracle or Mirage?* Bandung, 2019(6):50-76.

（三）埃塞俄比亚“发展型国家”道路遇到的挑战

第一，民主化进程受到质疑和挑战，民族问题仍是国家不稳定的重要因素之一。弗利茨（Fritz）和梅诺卡尔（Menocal）认为，埃塞处于民主的混合政权时期[①]，这种不完整的民主化进程可能产生破坏稳定的影响，包括加剧腐败、降低投资和增长潜力。国家能力仍然有限，民主压力带来的新要求可能使国家不堪重负，并且缺乏必要的机构和行政能力。埃塞2005年的大选危机就是这样一种民主化进程中的集中爆发[②]。2010年和2015年大选结果也遭到选民的质疑。1995年，埃塞通过《宪法》引入了联邦制结构，正式按照种族划分，促进该国民族和人民的自决权。种族联邦制和政策观念使奥罗莫人和阿姆哈拉人不成比例地处于边缘地位，导致种族冲突以及更普遍地针对国家政府的抗议活动。种族的极端政治化已将埃塞拖向广泛蔓延的社区冲突，甚至威胁到埃塞联邦的生存[③]。

第二，经济发展存在动力不足、发展不平衡等问题，与工业化、现代化目标还有较大差距。联邦政府与地方政府在经济能力、目标一致性、职责、效率、积极性等方面存在欠缺。公共部门与私人部门的关系有待理顺，过度依赖国有企业和外国公司作为市场参与者，导致私营经济发展乏力。政府没有充分发挥国有银行的政策性银行作用，贷款的发放也没有以工业化为导向。农业发展仍存在较强脆弱性，同时工业化道路发展缓慢，城市化水平较低，城乡之间发展不平衡，基础设施建设仍较为落后。埃塞仍然是世界上最贫穷的国家之一，人民的生活贫困现象仍较多存在。

第三，社会发展仍处于较落后的状态。卫生状况堪忧，医疗水平较差。劳动力素质普遍较低。教育政策更侧重于获得教育的机会，而不是教育的质量，缺乏必要的实验室、车间设备和信息通信技术设施等教学和培训场所和设备，学校教授的知识缺乏与行业需求进行融合或协同。

二、埃塞俄比亚新自由主义思潮

新自由主义建立在自由主义的基本思想基础之上，创立并形成了新的理论体系。在这个体系中，除了本文讨论的“自由主义经济学”方面的新自由主义之外，还有以意识形态为主要表现方式的新自由主义。“自由主义经济学”方面的新自由主义起源于20世纪30年代[④]，其在诞生后的90年间逐渐演变，内涵已超出了一种综合的理论体系范畴，所提倡的基础理论从个人层面的自由延伸至国家层面，表现为对国家干预经济政策的抵制，并被西方主要国家大力推行。

1991年，新自由主义思潮进入埃塞之后经历了30年的发展。从初期的用于发展中国家的统一“计划”和“套餐”逐渐演变为具有埃塞特色的思潮，其影响力经历了从波峰到低谷

① Fritz 和 Menocal 认为在发展中国家的民主进程中，政权过渡导致了混合政权而不是成熟的民主国家的出现。混合政权可以说是民主和威权主义的混合体——他们经历了正式的民主过渡，但还没有完全巩固其民主体制——并且在大多数情况下其发展记录还不是很强。混合政权被认为特别不稳定，仅举行选举并不能解决困扰许多发展中国家的更深层次的政治和社会问题。见 V Fritzand，A R Menocal，*(Re)building Developmental States: From Theory to Practice*，Working Paper，2006（274）.

② V Fritzand，A R Menocal，*(Re)building Developmental States: From Theory to Practice*，Working Paper，2006（274）.

③ Alemu Asfaw Nigusieand Mohammed Seid Ali，“*Developmental State*” *as an Alternative Development Path in Ethiopia: Miracle or Mirage?*Bandung，2019（6）：50-76.

④ 王珉. 当代西方思潮评介. 杭州：浙江大学出版社，2005：129-139；乔瑞. 当代主要社会思潮的动态研究与批判（下集）. 北京：中国社会科学出版社，2019：81-85.

再回潮的趋势。根据埃塞新自由主义思潮的发展特点，可大致分为三个阶段。

第一阶段：从 1991 年至 21 世纪初，这是新自由主义从在埃塞诞生到发展并对新政权的政治经济迅速产生影响的时期，新自由主义思潮作为一种外部力量，成为埃塞主流宏观政策，直接影响着埃塞国民经济的重建、市场开放程度、国有资产企业的经营、经济利益的分配等经济领域的各个方面，其标志事件是"结构调整计划"的实施。

第二阶段：从 21 世纪初至 2018 年，由于新自由主义改革方案在埃塞未取得预期效果，埃塞政府进行转型，采取了更加符合埃塞国情的"发展型国家"道路。在这个阶段，新自由主义作为一种重要的思潮，仍然通过国内外途径影响埃塞的政治经济，并引发了一系列的从意识形态到政治社会经济层面的辩论。

第三阶段：从 2018 年至今，以阿比·艾哈迈德·阿里总理上任为标志。新自由主义思潮卷土重来，对埃塞产生了重要和迅速的影响。阿比的政策中增加了诸多新自由主义的思想，主要体现在与厄立特里亚边境关系的处理、大刀阔斧的私有化改革、新政府内阁重组的年轻化和女性化等诸多方面。

三、埃塞俄比亚"发展型国家"道路与新自由主义思潮的论战

近 30 年来，埃塞俄比亚的政治经济处在不断的改革进程中，从最初的"新自由主义"政策到"发展型国家"道路，再到 2018 年之后的新政权，关于经济政策的争论从未停止。争论在不同时期有着不同的重点，很多争论延续至今。争论主要来自"革命民主派"和"自由民主派"，其中"革命民主派"主张埃塞政府需要对经济进行干预，推进"发展型国家"道路的实施，"自由民主派"主张政府作用最小化，推进"新自由主义"经济政策的实施。新自由主义思潮在埃塞出现之后，争论内容集中在对政府在经济中的作用等主题。在埃塞宣布实施"发展型国家"道路之后，又出现了大量"发展型国家"是否适合埃塞、埃塞是否称得上是"发展型国家"等主题的争论。归根结底，这些争论都是围绕在埃塞是应该采取"发展型国家"道路还是"新自由主义"政策的重要问题。争论背后体现了各方所代表的利益。阿比总理上台之后激进的改革措施也引发了人们对埃塞未来经济的担忧，同时体现了旧有政权与新政权之间的对抗。

（一）政府在经济中的作用

这个问题是"发展型国家"道路与"新自由主义"思潮两种政策的主要区别之一，也是论战双方的重大分歧之一。作为埃塞"发展型国家"代表人物的梅莱斯·泽纳维在《非洲发展：死胡同和新起点》一文中阐述了埃塞所采取的"发展型国家"模式，并对新自由主义所提倡的"守夜人状态"的政府进行了全面的批判。2012 年 5 月在亚的斯亚贝巴举办的非洲世界论坛上，他为埃塞的"发展型国家"道路进行了激烈的辩护，结合非洲在过去 30 年中基础设施投资严重不足的情况，他认为必须依靠政府主导的公共部门实施投资，埃塞也正是因为这样做才获得了亚洲式的增长[①]。

① William Davison, *From Meles's "Dead End" to Abiy's "New Horizon"*, 2019, https://www.ethiopia-insight.com/2019/06/10/from-meles-dead-end-to-abiys-new-horizon/.

自由民主派提倡有限政府，指责埃革阵频繁干预经济。革命民主派则称，埃革阵并非否定市场对经济的重要作用，但是对于埃塞这样的尚无健全市场经济基础的发展中国家，新自由主义能否帮助埃塞获得可持续的发展受到严重质疑。格贝耶胡（Gebeyehu）称新自由主义永远不会成为埃塞的选择，因为新自由主义体系中需求和供给主导的市场经济未能充分考虑埃塞的实际情况，"人们可以总结出像我们这样的第三世界经济体中政治经济学的基础，因为无论是在实际还是在理论层面都缺乏市场（机制）。而当市场（机制）存在时，它们又是不完善的，并且没有适当的机构支持。因此，政府应该在没有市场（机制）的情况下创造市场（机制），在市场（机制）存在时为其正常运作建立机构"[①]。哥达（Geda）认为，埃塞的经济增长在很大程度上取决于政治经济因素、气候风险、机构的能力和效率、公共政策的质量以及与战争和财产权相关的风险。产品和投入品市场不仅薄弱而且缺乏弹性，加上不稳定的政治环境，极大地限制了长期增长的潜力和短期增长的可持续性。因此他呼吁建立健全的机构，呼吁政府进行适当的干预直至市场体制完善[②]。

（二）"发展型国家"道路是否可行

21 世纪初，埃塞摒弃先前 10 年的新自由主义政策，采取了"发展型国家"道路的模式，梅莱斯·泽纳维将这种模式视为符合埃塞乃至非洲自身情况的发展模式。激烈的争论由此展开，考虑到埃塞的政治和社会经济情况，发展型国家范式是不是正确的选择？埃塞是否符合"发展型国家"的定义？埃塞是否处于"发展型国家"道路的正确轨道上并产生了所预期的效果？

关于"发展型国家"的模式是否适合埃塞，支持者（包括梅莱斯本人）都认为，这是埃塞在短期内实现经济增长的唯一出路。反对者则认为"发展型国家"模式自然地倾向于精英和非民主形式的政府，给了少数人以专制特权，牺牲了群众的自由。

转型之初，关于埃塞是否称得上是"发展型国家"，大多数讨论者对比"发展型国家"的定义和特点与埃塞情况的差异，支持者认为埃塞是非洲唯一的"发展型国家"，而反对者认为埃塞只是通过发展的名义掩盖其专制本质的国家，而不是"发展型国家"。勒福特（Lefort）在《埃塞俄比亚经济：发展型国家与自由市场》（*The Ethiopian Economy: the Developmental State VS. the Free Market*）一文中对埃革阵的动机提出质疑，他认为埃革阵在掌握政权初期表面上采取新自由主义政策，而实质在埃革阵领导层内部仍然深受马克思主义和列宁主义的影响，仅仅是为了"获得西方力量的支持"。而埃塞的"市场力量"由政党领导和操纵，也就是"政党主导的经济"[③]。

转型进行一段时间之后，部分争论的焦点转移至"发展型国家"产生的结果。支持者将连续的经济增长归功于政府的战略选择，反对者则认为增长仅是数字游戏，并没有真正改变人们的生活，他们坚持认为转型之后的通货膨胀、腐败和收入分配不公严重损害了增长的成果，并创造了极富的极少人和极穷的多数人这两个阶级。勒福特称"发展型国家"道路并未

---

① Yohannes Gebeyehu, *Neoliberalism Will Never Be a Political Economy Options for Ethiopia*, 2017, https://www.thereporterethiopia.com/content/neoliberalism-will-never-be-political-economy-options-ethiopia.

② Alemayehu Geda, *Macroeconomic Performance in Post-Derg Ethiopia*, Northeast African Studies, 2001, 8（1）: 159-204.

③ René Lefort, *The Ethiopian Economy: the Developmental State VS. the Free Market*, in Gérard Prunier, Éloi Ficquet (Eds.), *Understanding Contemporary Ethiopia*, London: C. Hurst & Co. (Publishers) Ltd, 2015.

为埃塞带来所谓的“经济奇迹”，并对埃塞经济连续增长的数据，包括政府公布的农业产量数据提出质疑①。

埃塞的“发展型国家”的道路在借鉴东亚经济体“发展型国家”模式基础上引入了“民主”的概念，由此也引发了人们对“民主”的辩论。其中一个重要主题就是发展和民主之间的关系，人们对于发展需要先于民主还是民主是发展的（前提）条件展开了激烈的争论。在大多数情况下，尤其是回顾东南亚的发展历史时，一些学者认为“发展型国家”和民主的概念不能在同一国家中同时实现，这种观点被称为“不可能的论点”（Impossibility Theses）。莱夫特威克明确指出，民主和发展型国家的目的不同，因此需要不同的制度环境，“稳定和巩固的民主对制度的要求与迅速而变革的增长对制度的要求在结构上是不同的。发展过程包括正式和非正式社会政治和社会经济体制中的必需的、根本性的、变革性和普遍性的变化，但这些变化与民主所需的制度大不相同。民主本质上是保守的权力体系，旨在稳定而不是改变。”②

斯特凡·安德雷森（Stefan Andreason）将新自由主义理解为一种意识形态，鼓励西方经济和政治价值观念的传播，例如民主化和多党制。也因此有人认为新自由主义政策可以在非洲传播民主化、多党制中发挥重要作用③。但是梅莱斯等政治家认为，埃塞选择将发展和民主同时推进，也是国内外形势所决定的④。

此外，关于埃塞是否做到了所宣称的“民主”，尼西（Nishi）认为埃革阵建立“事实上”的一党制并限制其他非政府组织的活动，以垄断发展资源⑤。尤其是在2005年埃塞大选之后，执政党的胜利备受争议。反对党、民间社会和媒体均被镇压，埃塞的民主进程和民主程度更是遭到了很大质疑。民主和发展之间的关系也再次受到挑战。

（三）结构调整计划是否可行

20世纪90年代至21世纪初，埃塞的新自由主义思潮很大程度体现在“结构调整计划”为代表的新自由主义政策上，也由此引发了该计划的成功与失败、失败原因等激烈争论。

首先，人们对“结构调整计划”的影响有着不尽一致的看法。国际金融机构认为“结构调整计划”取得了较好的效果，提升了埃塞的市场经济程度。但以梅莱斯·泽纳维为代表的埃革阵、部分非洲和埃塞学者认为“结构调整计划”未能达到所期望效果，未能提高埃塞产业竞争力。瓦塔纳贝（Watanabe）和哈纳塔尼（Hanatani）认为国际金融机构敦促非洲国家实施的经济改革对非洲新产业的产生和发展的促进作用非常有限。阿尔卡贝·奥克贝认为“结构调整计划”是个“痛苦”的调整过程，对非洲社会产生了负面影响（如失业），国家政府的作用也遭到了削弱⑥。

---

① René Lefort, *The Ethiopian Economy: the Developmental State VS. the Free Market*, in Gérard Prunier, Éloi Ficquet (Eds.), *Understanding Contemporary Ethiopia*, London: C. Hurst & Co. (Publishers) Ltd, 2015.

② Fesseha Mulu Gebremariam, Abtewold Moges Bayu, *Ethiopia: a Democratic Developmental State*?, ILIRIA International Review, 2017, 7(2): 9-26.

③ Kebede Lemu Bekelcha, Aregash Eticha Sefera, *Advantages and Disadvantages of Neoliberalism/Neoliberal Economic Policy in General and the Case of Ethiopia in Particular*", Journal of eSciences, 2019(2).

④ 同②。

⑤ Makoto Nishi.*Problems*, *Possibilities of Democratic Developmentalism in Ethiopia*, Conference Paper, 56th Annual Meeting of the African Studies Association, Kyoto University, 2013.

⑥ 阿尔卡贝·奥克贝. 非洲制造——埃塞俄比亚的产业政策. 潘良、蔡莺，译，北京：社会科学文献出版社，2016：52。

其次，在认定"结构调整计划"失败的观点中，有些人将其归因于"结构调整计划"本身，即新自由主义政策的失败。也有些人将其归因于埃塞在执行上出了问题。根据格塔洪·塔费塞（Getahun Tafesse）的说法，"结构调整计划"在普遍范围内失败的一些原因包括：该计划由"华盛顿共识"推动，具有"自上而下"的制约性。埃塞缺乏适合"结构调整计划"发挥的"经济基础"，新自由主义可以更好地解释当前高度发达的经济体的运作方式，而不能很好地促进贫穷经济体振兴。同时，该计划未能理解和考虑"体制"因素。非洲实施新自由主义经济政策的几十年如今经常被称为"迷失的几十年"，贫困的顽固存在导致国际捐助者重新思考、修改和调整关于减免债务减贫战略的援助计划。这也是自 20 世纪 90 年代中期以来，国际金融机构承诺制定新政策替代新自由主义发展范式的原因①。

（四）阿比政府的新政将带领埃塞去往何处

2018 年后阿比总理的政治经济改革同样引发了大量讨论。观察家们很快觉察出阿比总理的动向，阿比政府在上任后 7 个月中进行的改革表明，执政联盟实际上已基本放弃了前任政府的革命民主思想和"发展型国家"道路②。对于新政府采取的经济自由化政策，亚伯拉罕（Abraham）认为，阿比总理正在带领埃塞"陷入社会、经济和政治悲剧"，他举例称，"不敢想象沃尔玛在亚的斯亚贝巴、默克莱、巴哈达尔和其他城市开设超市时，埃塞俄比亚的中小微企业将会发生什么"③。而原提人阵主席德布雷齐森·格布雷迈克尔 (Debretsion Gebremichael)④ 则明确表示脱离政府干预的经济存在"严重危险"，他称"如果我们按照新自由主义者的建议行事，这将脱轨"。他认为，从埃塞之前经济增长记录来看，国家在经济中仍然发挥着积极作用⑤。除此外之，私有化、对外开放等方面也成为论战的重点。杰（Jay）认为外资的进入引发了外资对埃塞国有资产以及自然资源和劳动力的"争夺战"⑥，这可能导致国有资产的流失，而且外资与私人部门迅速发展可能将在创造就业的同时产生严重的不平等，加剧富人对穷人的剥削⑦。尽管阿比政府频繁采取新自由主义的政策，但是为应对国内日益激化的民族矛盾和经济问题、逆全球化的外部环境等复杂因素，阿比总理提出了"Medemer"（阿姆哈拉语，意为"协同"）的理念，可以理解为这是埃塞对自主发展道路开始的新探索。

四、结论

本文简要回顾了近 30 年来主导埃塞政治经济的"发展型国家"和"新自由主义"思潮，以及围绕埃塞经济发展道路产生的论战。"发展型国家"体现了埃塞对经济发展的自主探

---

① A Teshome, *Meles' s Development Paradigm and Its Impacts on Economic Transformation in Ethiopia*, Global Advanced Research Journal of Management and Business Studies, 2012, 1(11): 384-396.

② Tim Worstall, *Congratulations to Ethiopia-Getting Richer by Going Neoliberal*, 2018, https://www.continentaltelegraph.com/2018/10/congratulations-to-ethiopia-getting-richer-by-going-neoliberal/.

③ A Mogos braham, *Characterizing Neoliberalism: A Bird' s Eye View on Ethiopia' s Predicaments*, 2019.

④ 在梅莱斯·泽纳维时期担任国家信息和通信技术部部长。

⑤ Lionel Barber, David Pilling. *My Model Is Capitalism: Ethiopia' s Prime Minister Plans Telecoms Privatisation*, 2019, https://www.ft.com/content/433dfa88-36d0-11e9-bb0c-42459962a812.

⑥ Stephanie Jay. *The New Scramble for Ethiopia*, 2019, https://www.jacobinmag.com/2019/06/ethiopia-abiy-ahmed-meles-zenawi.

⑦ Stephanie Jay, Ethiopia' s Capitalist Turn, 2019, https://africasacountry.com/2019/03/ethiopias-capitalist-turn.

索,“新自由主义”则是西方为发展中国家提供的“药方”。从埃塞发展实际来看,“发展型国家”更加适合埃塞的现阶段发展,但是也面临着严峻挑战,“新自由主义”缺乏对埃塞具体国情的充分考量,难以提供埃塞工业化和现代化发展的根本动力。对于发展中国家,如何在经济发展的过程中,保持政策的独立并提高自主发展能力,需要进一步深入思考。

Rethinking Democratic Developmental State in Ethiopia

Biruk Shewadeg[1]

Abstract: Ethiopia adopted a democratic developmental state following the success stories of the East Asian Tigers. Indeed, many of the exemplars of the developmental state claimed to ignore the democratic aspect of a developmental state. The Ethiopian government, before the current reform, claims to fill the gap and attempts to implement developmental state while incorporating democracy as well. An achievement of a fast and sustained economic growth for the past decade and half may not be contested. However, this paper with the help of analyzing intensive literature and deployment of discursive reasoning approach became cognizant of the tacit contradictions in an attempt of fully realizing the given political economy argues for rethinking of such a model. Heterogeneity of the constituents, and ethnic federalism that is responsible for a bureaucracy which appears to be ineffective and inefficient that can carry the huge government initiatives; the loss of a nation-wide public, and a limited elite commitment among others, pose a formidable challenge for the absolute success of democratic developmental state in the country. As a way of addressing the points thereof, the paper is categorized in to two sections of first an attempt is made to conceptualize the ideals of developmental and democratic developmental states and secondly the contradictions between the rhetoric of advancing democratic developmental state and the objective realities in the Ethiopian case is discussed.

Keywords: Democratic Developmental State; Ethnic Federalism

Introduction

The analysis of "rethinking democratic developmental state", by and large dwells on the time prior to the current reform. The country undergoes a political reform since April 2018. Following the resignation of his predecessor Hailemariam Desalegn, the new Prime Minister Abiy Ahmed shunned the state of emergency, realized the release of a number of political prisoners, allowed exiled politicians and activists to return home and freed many social media platforms and

① Lecturer of Philosophy at Addis Ababa Science and Technology University & a PhD candidate at the Centre for African and Asian Studies, Addis Ababa University.

TV channels that were formerly blocked. He also ended the state of enmity with the neighboring Eritrea by agreeing to unconditionally accept the Algiers Peace Agreement whereby normalizes relation with the long-time foe which in return awarded him the Nobel Peace prize. His leadership, however is not free from challenges. Massive displacement of people, the proliferation of vigilantes, and failure of securing the rule of law, among others reflect the predicaments of his regime. Despite the a forementioned points, his administration does not display an essential departure with regard to democratic developmental state. Neither, he introduced a new political economy in exchange for the already existed democratic developmental state. In one of his books titled "እርካብናመንበር" written in Amharic anonymously, Abiy Ahmed outlines the fundamentals of developmental state in the East Asian Tigers and its relevance for third world countries as Ethiopia. Thus, even though, the analysis of this piece exclusively relies on the time before the current reform, not only is a retrospective engagement, it rather obtains a due implication to the present day Ethiopia as well.

Ethiopia, notwithstanding its rank of 173rd out of 186 countries, have achieved a fast economic growth in the past decade and half under a normative statistical measures, averaging 10.8% per year in 2003/2004-2014/2015 where 5.4% was the regional average (UNDP, 2014; World Bank, 2017b). In the years between 2000 and 2016, the country yearly scores 9.8% average GDP growth, GNI per capita raised from 120 in 2000 to 660 in 2016, and life expectancy increased from 51.9 in 2000 to 64.6 in 2015. This growth significantly reduced the poverty leveldown from 45.5% in 1995 to 29.6% in 2010. According to the international poverty line measurement of less than $1.90 per day 55.3% of Ethiopians lived in absolute poverty in 2000, by 2011, this figure was considerably reduced to 33.5% (World Bank, 2017a; World Bank, 2017b). Generally, Ethiopia's economic performance in the past decade and half has been impressive.

It achieved a double digit economic growth, huge investment in socioeconomic infrastructure; high pro poor investment in social service; and a conforming enhancement in a number of social indicators (UNDP, 2014; cited in Belay, 2017).

Essentially, the Ethiopian government has been doing to emulate all aspect of the East Asian Tigers model. In various party documents and government policies, the regime saw itself as having a strong government commitment for development; the government capability in avoiding state capture and maintaining autonomy from the political and economic influence of the private sector; the progressive conception of developmental hegemony in the country; and democracy and the federal structure as substantial underpinnings of the country's renaissance (EPRDF, 2010).

This being the case, however, inner contradictions have always existed between the country's rhetoric for an establishment of a democratic developmental state and the objective realities at hand.

Understanding Developmental and Democratic Developmental States

Developmental State

The literature of developmental economics and international political economy is not entirely new to the idea of a developmental state. It has been widely referred to the 1970s onwards state-led economic planning practices in the East Asian countries. The concept of the developmental state, in its contemporary usage, came from Chalmers Johnson (1982) who used it to define the remarkable growth of the Japanese economy and its rapid industrialization in the aftermath of the Second World War. Central to Japan's "economic miracle", Chalmers argue was, a "planned rational state" — a developmental state that was capable of inspiring and proactively support and promote economic development.

Castells (1992) maintains the ability to realize sustain development — steady and high rates of economic growth and structural change in the productive system, both internally and its relationship with the international economy as a principle can define a developmental state.

It is a kind of state, which is capable and enthusiastic to create and sustain a policy climate that promotes development by realizing productive investment, export, growth, and human welfare (Castells 1992: 56).

It is a state with a sufficient organization and power to achieve its goal of development that seizes the ability to prove consistent economic guidance and the power to support sustained economic policies by resisting external pressures triggered by "multinational corporations and internal resistance that may arise from groups bent on transient political gains or short term benefits" (Edigheji, 2010: 10). Moreover, the developmental state is not engulfed by particularistic interest groups.

Bureaucratic coherence, which is a key instrument behind developmental state model, is achieved by, among others, meritocratic recruitment, which in turn leads to the establishment of coherent networks within the state. This heightens the ability of the state to identify and implement independent goals. Meritocratic recruitment, in view of Edigeji (2005: 12) is "complemented by predictable career paths and long term rewards for bureaucrats both of which help to generate a sense of corporate coherence".

A developmental state needs to possess the capacity to control domestic wrangling and build consensus among the larger mass on national developmental agenda by drawing attention to long-term benefits to all. To this effect, a developmental state ought to be a persuasive state with the ability to mobilize the people and resources around its developmental plan. As Evans (1995) avers, developmental state is founded on an institutional design which is meant to advance transformative role of the state. Rather than constraining the state, developmental state obtains the capacity to articulate and device its developmental objectives in "an authoritative and binding fashion", for the betterment of economic performance (Schmiz, as quoted in: Edigheji, 2005, 6).

The developmental state is at times called an "*emphatic state*" — a "hard state" that achieves a remarkable autonomy and appears distinctly interventionist in the key economic sector by monitoring and controlling, in addition to regulating, guiding and shaping it. The autonomy of a developmental state implies the presence of high degrees of coherent state agencies that are able to promote and implement coherent developmental goals (Edigheji, 2005). It is known by its ability to balance strategic linkages with, and relative autonomy from, different societal forces. Such autonomy allows the state to preside over the trajectory of the economy, which is often situated with the direction of the developmental process.

Generally, a developmental state is characterized by character traits such as; economic nationalism, focus on foreign technology transfer; corporatism — state, labor, and industry nexus; skepticism about the joint neoliberal — "Washington Consensus" fundamentals; prioritization of economic growth over political reform; legitimacy and performance. Its basic features include, strong, competent, depoliticized bureaucracy; strong, visionary, capable and committed leadership; effective national developmental planning; trust and confidence building institutions and norms such as the rule of law, justice, political stability and peace (UNECA, 2011; UNDP, Ethiopia 2012).

Developmental state manifests itself in many forms. Typical examples include East Asian countries i.e. the Republic of Korea, Singapore, Japan, and Vietnam (Routley, 2012: 4). Less obvious examples include the "Nordic countries of Sweden and Norway and Japan" (UNDP Ethiopia, 2012: 9). Drawing a lesson from those countries, to lift African continent from deep poverty and widespread unemployment, the United Nation Economic Commission for Africa (UNECA, 2011) has challenged the states in Africa to adopt the developmental state model and fundamentally transform their economies from an agrarian to a more industrialized economy. Furthermore, on its quest for the realization of developmental state the UNECA (2011) argues, African countries will have to build transformative institutions, primarily operated under competent and professional bureaucrats. All developmental projects have to be managed by "competent and professional bureaucrats", recruited solely on meritocracy, and autonomous from the influences of rent-seeking groups (UNECA, 2011: 8). The commission recommends that as autonomous professionals, the state bureaucrats should preside over the power to design, pursue, and implement policies to enable their respective countries to move away from their subsistence economies to industrial societies.

Such a conception of the developmental state has been however eventually criticized for its failure to pay any heed to the democratic aspect. This is primarily because the repressive nature of the state was presented as an important factor which enhanced its development capacity in most of East Asian Tigers. State authoritarianism was the most distinguishing characteristics of the exemplars of the developmental state model.

This has a resultant effect of developing a perception that the model of developmental state is intrinsically inconsistent with the mode of a pluralistic form of democracy, in which a multitude of interest groups enjoy broadly equal and unrestricted access to the state. None of the Newly Industrialized Countries, aka the East Asian Tigers, Brohman(1996: 174) argues, "have made much progress in creating democratic structures that would facilitate meaningful political participation by the majority". In recognition of the limitations of the dominant conception of the developmental state, Robinson & White (1998) came up with the notion of the democratic developmental state.

Democratic Developmental State

Developmental state, at the first glance seems difficult to sustain in a fully democratic systems in which people enjoy extensive political rights. This is primarily because the source of legitimacy of authority, Johnson (1999) maintains, is not one of the Weber's Holy-Trinity of tradition, rational-legal, or charismatic sources. Rather it is "Revolutionary authority: the authority of a people committed to the transformation of the social, political, or economic order. Legitimization occurs from the state achievements, not the way it came to power" (Johnson, 1999: 53).

The concept of democratic developmental state, however, designates that a given state to be a developmentalist and democratic at the same time for the two can arguably reinforce each other. In Matlosa's view, a sustainable economic nationalism, which is prerequisite for the existence of a developmental state, democratic governance is an imperative and contends that the notion of democratic developmental state "makes liberation of the people, state, society, and economy from domestic tyranny and foreign domination fundamental to democratization, and development" (Matlosa, 2005: 4). In this sense, democratic developmental state is a one that forges broad based alliances with society and guarantees popular participation in the governance and transformation process. Irrespective of the form of government that is instituted — federalist or unitary, a parliamentary or presidential systems, democratic developmental state is guided by the goals of coherence governance, accountability, inclusiveness, stability, ability to generate consensus and popular participation. What is essential in a democratic developmental state is a political modus operandi accommodating diverse political interests and voices.

Central to a democratic developmental state is a notion that a developmental state and democracy are not antithetical to each other. It rather asserts the two as complimentary and looks for a possibility where the two may reinforce each other. For, there is a limit to legitimacy that emanates solely from economic performance, a developmental state without democracy, is not only impossible but also unsustainable in the longer term.

Democratic developmental state is predicated on an inclusive approach to public policy making. White (1998) coined the concept of "inclusive embeddedness" — a notion marking "the social basis and range of accountability goes beyond a narrow bond of elites to embrace broader sections of society" (White, 1998: 98). The nature of the political system is also a source of autonomy for the democratic developmental state. "Institutional coherence", as White calls, implies "the distribution and use of political power, in the relation between different sections of the bureaucratic apparatus, and in the nature of the party system in political society". This emphasis presupposes that political society creates "channel of political participation, particularly in the structure of the party system" (White, 1998: 31).

The UNECA in its part argues that the East Asian developmental paths were predominantly designed on the premise that Western democratic values were foreign luxury, and thus unsuited for the promotion of development in Asia. The African states however are required to follow the basics of developmental state, yet they are expected to meet set of standards based on Western democratic values designed by UNECA (Mohamad, 1994).

Ethiopia and Its Quest for Advancing Democratic Developmental State

The late Meles Zenawi, in his speech on the 5th conference on Federalism, Addis Ababa, said "Democratic federalism is one of the two pillars of our national renaissance. Together with the establishment and consolidation of an effective developmental state in our country, it has enable us begun the long road back to the frontiers of our civilization" (UNDP 2012, 1).

Over the years, the Ethiopian government in general and the late Meles Zenawi in particular, boldly criticize the Western development model and searches for alternatives with showing a disregard for the neoliberal economic doctrines which faced its "*dead-end*" in realizing development in the country. Zenawi challenged the neoliberal policy recommendations anchored in aid conditionality and openly stated that unless Africa marks a paradigm shift away from the predatory state driven by neoliberal policy to a more progressive one that is the democratic developmental state, the goals of development and good governance will remain unattainable (Zenawi, 2006).

The Ethiopian government, after the disputed 2005 election, has explicitly declared itself as a democratic developmental state. However, substantial challenges existed as regards to how the country empirically operates and its rhetoric for implementing a democratic developmental state. This being the case, however, deep and adequate scientific analysis have made neither by the Ethiopian government itself nor by the researchers to evaluate whether an ethnically divided country where the political modus operandi intricately intermingled ethnic identity and politics, can afford such a model. There are some in fact, from the outset question whether Ethiopia has been really a developmental state pointing to the tenacity of deep-rooted poverty in the country (Tesfaye, 2010; Atlaw, 2013). Others on the other hand, by accepting the policy of the country as developmental, remained skeptical whether the developmental state of Ethiopia is determined to democratic principles and practices mentioning the abuse of power by the government officials and ignorance of basic democratic rights such as freedom of press by the ruling party (Kebede, 2011; Clapham, 2006). In the same vein, others point to the party's vision of staying on power for the decades long in the future, to support their argument for its undemocratic characteristics.

Putting aside the contending debates, the government, ipso facto, firmly stated the adoption of democratic developmental state. Moreover, the Ethiopian government's overwhelming emphasis on economic growth has manifested itself in official documents and in practices as well. The government's highly ambitious five year plan of the Plan for Accelerated and Sustained Development to End Poverty (PASDEP) in 2005 is a case in point.

The even more ambitious Growth and Transformation Plans (GTP Ⅰ and Ⅱ, 2010 and 2015, respectively) which aims to double the country's GDP by 2015 and achieve "middle income status" by 2025 (MoFED, 2006 & 2010), are development policies, programs, and strategies designed for achieving a fast and sustained economic growth. The government also holds the rhetoric that it's democratic as well mentioning the constitution and mostly comparing itself with the past regimes.

Whenever we approach the democratic developmental state against the background of heterogeneity and federal state structure, there are plenty of factors that can cause pessimism on its feasibility. Primarily, as a matter of fact, almost all the exemplars of developmental state including "Japan, Republic Korea, Singapore, Malaysia, and Thailand" are relatively homogeneous society and adopted a unitary state structure (Abera, 2015: 294). Ethiopia, by contrast is an ethnic-based federal state and well-diversified in terms of ethnic composition. Though, the typical examples of developmental state are homogenous and adopted a unitary state model, ethnic heterogeneity and federal state structure per se may not be a problem either. For, countries like South Africa and India, democratic developmental states in the broader spectrum, are able to build a relatively stable political economy. The challenge however is when ethnicity become an element of political mobilization and the federating units are those that are organized under an ethno-linguistic divide, ethnic heterogeneity appears a curse and have a capacity to endanger nation-wide policies and practices which is a key factor in developmental states. Developmental state vigorously needs mobilizing the people and creating a national consensus for development (Johnson, 1982; Edigheji, 2010; Equbay, 2015). Furthermore, nationalism used as a driving force for mobilization, possibly creates a sentiment of social cohesion and an awareness of that the populace in a given state are all in the same boat(Pempel, 1999; Woo-Cumings, 1999). Thus perceived, the bond of nationhood and homogeneity can bring a better social cohesion and makes the task easier as it was helped in Republic Korea, and Japan (Pempel, 1999: 168). However, ethnic, religious and/or any other form diversity and employing this diversity further for political mobilization facilitates fragmentation may pose a serious challenge to mobilize the people in one grand development objective.

Ethiopia, despite its ethnic-based federal state structure and heterogeneity of its constituencies, opt for a developmental state model. The government maintains that the main reason behind the adoption of ethnic federalism is to respond to the historic "nationalities question" by devolving power through decentralization and empower the decentralized unit to make decision on their respective domains. By contrast, developmental state needs a strong central power that can make decisions at the center and perhaps at the expense of lower tier units. This then calls for a rethink in the compatibility of the model thereof in such ethnically divided and perhaps federal state of Ethiopia.

Apart from social heterogeneity, self-determination is the most renowned pillar of ethnic federalism in Ethiopia. The polarization on mere ethnic identity for self-identification, if not successfully managed, probably causes a tendency towards disintegration. More importantly, elites in such a system are more dedicated to the betterment of their ethnic groups than any other group or national well-being. Developmental state, by contrast, opts for an unshakable elite commitment at national level who can strive for the common good of all, than those who only display an attachment to a particular interest. Ethnic federalism, thus, appears to be a most combative policy when viewed against the demands of a developmental state. As considered by its supporters as the only viable solution for holding multi-ethnic Ethiopia together and retaining its territorial integrity, it's denounced by others as a dangerous concept that may have a capacity to dismember the country, eventually.

Some pan-Ethiopianists consider the policy as a deliberate play in undermining the national identity — a conscious step backward from nation building process. Similarly, others understood the federal system as a malevolent TPLF (Tigrayan People Liberation Front) tactic to plant divisions among ethnic groups so as to facilitate rule by the Tigrayan minority (Ottaway, 1995). Paulos Chanie (2007) for instance, observes the federal system as one that divides rather than unites people by way of promoting mutual suspicion and instituted ethnical dynamics that could easily spiral out of control. The constitutional clause that offers nationalities the right to secede is toasted as a proof of the regimes' anti-Ethiopian stance. Eritrea's independence, which turned Ethiopia into a land-locked country, is viewed by some, as an evidence of a desire to dismember. Proponents of ethnic federalism, on the other hand acclaim the recognition of group rights, seeing ethnic based administrative entities as the only meaningful approach for diffusing ethnic identities.

Moreover, Ethiopia's ethnic federalism, they believe, redressed historic injustices that minorities suffered centuries of domination by a central state which imposed Amharic language and culture up on them.

In spite of the above contentions, it seems justifiable to argue that ethnic federalism affected elite commitment which is considered to be an important element for the triumph of democratic developmental state in a given country. Merera Gudina (2003) sees the composition of ruling elites in Ethiopia as tyrants and despots owing to the politics of exclusion the government persistently employs. Such practices of exclusion instead of integration or coalition represents the lack of development oriented elites and the dominance of rent-seeking and predatory elites. Since, the major criteria of the ruling party to incorporate elites is on the basis of ethnicity and political loyalty, there is hardly enough space for multi-dimensional competent elites.

As Ghani, Lockhart, and Carnahan (2005) argues, one of the underlying requirements of the developmental state is the creation of nation-wide public. It has been argued by many scholars that the success of the East Asian miracle was driven by nationalism, and not regionalism or ethnicity, whatsoever. Practically, the main force behind the development ideology has been nationalism which seeks to subordinate the energy of the people behind a single national goal. The assumption is that all citizens should be able to see themselves as Ethiopians rather than their ethnic and/or any other group identification. And, ethnic federalism contributed a lot to the absence of national consensus in the country. In a state where civic identity and nationalism remains a subordinate of ethno linguistic identity and nationalism, the possibility of creating a nation-wide public which could easily mobilize for a single development agenda is highly challenged and also hinders national consensus. This absence of elite's commitment towards the designing and effective implementation of holistic development policies and strategies put its own limit on succeeding the goals of a developmental state and made the ideology of developmental state to face a formidable challenge. As De Waal (2012) warns, that in a country as wide and diverse as Ethiopia, implementing such a grand policy as democratic developmental state without creating a common mind set first runs the risk of degenerating the principles, no matter how erudite the theoretical foundations are, "into a set of dogma parroted by party cadres," with hardly any indulgence of the actual meaning and implication of the policies and strategies (De Waal 2012, 154).

Bureaucracy is the other major predicament that needs evaluation in Ethiopia's attempt to build a developmental state. It is believed that the capacity of public institutions, particularly the bureaucracy is an important element to economic performance in a developmental state. The bureaucracy is said to constitute "the soft underbelly of the state" which advices the political executive and frames and gears public policies professionalism. Technical skills and disciplines are core issues in administrative, competence, and capability of the bureaucracy (UNECA, 2005). What is required of the bureaucrats, Messay Kebede (2011: 5) argues "is less political allegiance than efficiency in exchange for handsome remunerations". The Ethiopian system of bureaucracy, viewed from the vantage point of a bureaucracy that a developmental state which requires a system that is based on merit, has been incapable of realizing grand development plans. The bureaucracy is managed by civil servants who are mainly recruited on the basis of political affiliation and ethnic based quota system, and not on the basis of meritocracy. This is the reason why it failed to serve competently.

Moreover, the bureaucratic institutions that the functionaries maneuver are not autonomous. For, the prevalence of a strong influence by the ruling elite. It's not uncommon to see the allocation of higher positions in many governmental departments including ministries per ethnic based quota system. The bureaucracy, instead of allowing autonomy, is using "an extended organ of the political machinery, thereby dejecting impartiality and professionalism, and distributing favourable treatment on the basis of political patronage and, ethnic affiliation" (Kebede, 2001: 7). This negatively affects autonomy of the bureaucracy and structurally weakens its functions. Such reality is in a sharp contradiction with the bureaucracy demanded by a developmental state.

Even when the bureaucracy, in some cases, obtain the functionaries which are recruited on meritocracy, owing to the perception held by the public, willingly or unwillingly the bureaucrats are expected to work in "conformance with their ethnic affiliation rather than in pursuit of the goals of their organization" (Abera, 2015: 296). This then results in the absence of transparency, and the promotion of the desire to bear out the wishes of the political agenda that introduces the enticement for corruption that has become pervasive in the functioning of bureaucracy in the country.

It is undeniable that some of the government initiated development goals and plans were very rational and had it been the case that are systematically executed, they could efficaciously achieve their intended goals. But, many prolific projects were unjustifiably delayed because the bureaucracy lacked the professionalism and commitment needed to mobilize the limited resources of the country. In such a situation whereby the bureaucracy is handicapped by the wrongly interpreted division of the country based on ethnic line, the implementation of the developmental state remained a mere rhetoric. Furthermore, owing to the lack of competent, merit-based bureaucracy, the country faced implementation failure and exposed to the danger of rent-seeking as the highest officials publicly confessed.

The other quandary of ethnic federalism viz building a democratic developmental state is the generation and transformation of intra-regional autonomy conflicts and intra-regional conflicts. The eruption of ethnic clashes still remained intact in the country as well. The most noticeable change regarding ethnic conflicts in the post 1991 setting has been the emergence of localized violent conflicts involving many of the ethnically constituted regions which drastically hurt to create viable society. At the same time, there are centrifugal forces pertaining to secessionist movements engaged in low-level guerilla warfare portraying the central government as an ethnic group domination of one group over the other. Thus, an attempt at building democratic developmental state without primarily stabilizing ethnic clashes over resources and power distribution would remain difficult. The cumulative effects of all these rivals would undermine solidarity, fraternity, and unity among neighbor ethnic groups, and if not managed timely, it may lead to hated civil wars which adversely affect the country's development.

Finally, regarding the democratic nature of the developmental state, some view the Ethiopian developmental state is democratic enough in addressing the democratic causes of the society and strong enough to enforce the developmental policies to attain the highest possible growth in a stable environment (Tiruneh, 2015). Others characterize the regime as a one that uses "democratic jargon in undemocratic part-state structure" (Bach, 2011: 647). In fact, it is not uncommon hearing Ethiopian democracy is in its nascent and fledgling stage and democracy is a process. Over quarter of a century, such an excuse can hardly work. The Ethiopian democracy is not only "an incomplete democracy; it is also characterized by an authoritarian state swathed in democratic window-dressing in which multiparty elections are only manipulated as a means to sustain power" (Aalen & Tronvoll, 2009: 203). Moreover, the tacit "development first" thinking of the government towed the democratization process. Particularly, later the 2005 infamous election there is a visible step back of democracy in Ethiopia, the genuine system is also gone and the dominant one party system prevailed. Political pluralism and accommodation of politically dissident voices are hardly tolerated in the country. The colossal violation of human rights on the development guise remained the norm of the government. Arrest and intimidation are the expected outcomes whenever challenges occur regarding government development policies. There were also repeated reports of forced displacement from development projects across the country (Human Rights Watch, 2016 & 2017).

Conclusion

The democratic developmental state that is adopted under ethnic federal state of Ethiopia faced potential contradictions and serious challenges. Heterogeneity of the populace, not by itself a problem, owing to its legal and practical measures to sustain political mobilization, however hampered civic nationalism which is crucial in fulfilling the demands of a developmental state. In ethnically diverse and deeply divided society it is hard to create a national consensus which is a requirement for effective developmental state. Furthermore, ethnic federalism accelerates ethno nationalism and exacerbates ethnic conflict with the creation of new minorities at regional level which erodes national consensus, the core element for the success of developmental state.

Though, the vanguard EPRDF has been characterized by democratic centralism, the ethnic federal arrangement de jure delivers autonomy and decentralization in many aspects of judicial, legislative, and executive, and fiscal powers while the developmental state obliges development planning and resources mobilization to be centrally dwelled. Theoretically, central planning, central mobilization of national resources and uniform implementation of the national development plan in an ethnic federal states is a difficult task. Any development strive and partnership in ethnic federal states is ethnic oriented than national oriented.

The highly celebrated politics of self-determination drastically hindered the elite commitment, and ethnically affiliated bureaucracy has been cultivated instead of meritocracy that negatively affects developmental state. While, the bureaucracy in developmental state needs to be competent, meritocratic, depoliticized, and effective, the ethnic federal Ethiopian bureaucracy is politicized and ethnic oriented. Rather than meritocracy, it largely favors mediocrity.

Lastly, a democratic developmental state that the Ethiopian government claims to implement necessitates legitimacy to not only be gained along performance alone. Democratic credentials are also an equally important sources of legitimacy. But, the poor records marked under human right issues; multi-party democracy, and forced displacement of people in the name of development assures that the democratic developmental state rhetoric in the country is obsolete and eventually urge for rethinking of the model.

References

[1] AALEN L, TRONVOLL K. 2009. The end of democracy? curtailing political and civil rights in Ethiopia. Review of African Political Economy,36(120):193-207.

[2] BACH J. 2012. Abyotawi democracy: neither revolutionary nor democratic, critical review of EPRDF' s conception of revolutionary democracy in post 1991 Ethiopia. Journal of Eastern African Studies, 5 (4): 661-663.

[3] BELAY M. 2017.The feasibility of democratic developmental state in ethnic based federal polity: the Ethiopian experiment. Bradford: University of Bradford.

[4] BERESA A. 2015. Ethnic federalism and democratic developmental state in Ethiopia: some points of contradiction. Inter J Polit Sci Develop, 3(7): 291-300.

[5] BROHMAN J. 2015. Postwar development in the Asian NICs: does the neoliberal model fit reality?Economic Geography, 72 (2): 107-130.

[6] CASTELLS M. 1992. Four Asian tigers with a dragon head: a comparative analysis of state, economy and society in the Asian Pacific Rim//APPLEBAUM R, HENDERSON J. State and development in the Asian Pacific Rim. Newbury Park: Sage Publications.

[7] CHANIE P. 2007. Clientelism and Ethiopia' s post-1991 decentralization. Journal of Modern African Studies, 45(3): 355-384. https://www.jstor.org/stable/4501295.

[8] DE WAAL A. 2012. The theory and practice of Meles Zenawi. African Affairs, 112 (446): 148-155.

[9] DEMEKE A. 2012. Promising democratic developmental state in Africa: evidences from Ethiopia. International Journal of Educational Research and Development, 2(7): 168-177.

[10] EDIGEJI O. 2010. Constructing a democratic developmental state in South Africa. Cape Town: Human Sciences Research Council.

[11] EDIGHEJI O. 2005. A Democratic Developmental State in Africa: A Conceptual Paper. Johannesburg: Centre for Policy Studies.

[12] EPRDF. 2010. የተሃድሶውመስመርናየኢትዮጵያህዳሴ. Addis Ababa: Mega Printing Enterprise.

[13] EQUBAY A. 2015. Made in Africa: industrial policy in Ethiopia. Oxford: Oxford University Press.

[14] EVANS P. 1995. Embedded autonomy: states and industrial transformation. Princeton, NJ: Princeton University Press.

[15] GHANI A, LOCKHART C, CARNAHAN M. 2005. Closing the sovereignty gap: how to turn failed states into capable ones. London: Overseas Development Institute.

[16] GUDINA M. 2003. Ethiopia: competing ethnic nationalism and the quest for democra cy, 1960-2000. Netherlands: Shaker Publishing.

[17] HABISSO T. 2016. The challenges of implanting and building multiparty democracy in human rights watch. https://www.hrw.org/world-report/2016/country-chapters/ethiopia.

[18] HUMAN RIGHTS WATCH. 2017. Ethiopia: Human Rights Watch. https://www.hrw.org/world-report/2017/country-chapters/ethiopia.

[19] JOHNSON C. 1999. The developmental state: Odyssey of a concept//WOO-CUMING M. The developmental state. Ithaca: Cornell University Press: 32-60.

[20] JOHNSON C. 1982. MITI and the Japanese miracle: the growth of industrial policy 1952-1975. Stanford, CA: Stanford University Press.

[21] KEBEDE M. 2011. The fallacy of TPLF' s developmental state. Ethiopian Review, Ethiopian News Journal. https://www.ethiopianreview.com/index/33340.

[22] MATLOSA K. 2005. The state, democracy and development in southern Africa. The Journal of New Paradigm Research, 63:443-463.

[23] MINISTRY OF FINANCE AND ECONOMIC DEVELOPMENT (MoFED) of GOVERNMENT OF ETHIOPIA. 2006. Ethiopia: building on progress, a plan for accelerated and sustained development to end poverty (PASDEP) 2005/2006-2009/2010, 1: Main Text, Addis Ababa.

[24] MINISTRY OF FINANCE AND ECONOMIC DEVELOPMENT (MoFED) OF GOVERMENT OF ITHIOPIA. 2010. Growth and transformation plan (2010/2011-2014/2015).http://www.ethiopians.com/Ethiopia-GTP-2015.pdf.

[25] MOHAMAD M. 1997. Speech by Dr. Mohamad at rethinking human rights//LEE H P. Constitutional values in a turbulent Asia. Monush University Law Review, 23(2): 375-396.

[26] OTTAWAY M. 1995. The Ethiopian transition: democratization or new authoritarianism? Northeast African Studies, 2 (3): 67-84. http://www.jstor.org/stable/41931114.

[27] PEMPEL T J. 1999. The developmental regime in a changing world economy//WOO-CUMINGS M. The developmental state. Ithaca: Cornell University Press: 137-181.

[28] ROBINSON M, WHITE G. 1999. The democratic developmental state: political and institutional design. Oxford University Press: Oxford.

[29] ROUTLEY L. 2012. Developmental States: A Review of the Literature. Manchester: Effective States and Inclusive Development Research Centre (ESID), University of Manchester.

[30] TIRUNEH S. 2015. Ethnic federalism and democratic developmental state in Ethiopia challenges and prospects. M. A. Internationl Development Studies: Hankak University.

[31] UNDP ETHIOPIA. 2012. Democratization in a developmental state: the case of Ethiopia issues, challenges, and prospects. http://dcollection.hufs.al.kn/isplsearchF/DcRetailView.jsp?itemId=00000011688.

[32] UNDP ETHIOPIA. 2014. National Human Development Report 2014: Ethiopia. Addis Ababa: UNDP. http://hdr.undp.org/sites/default/files/nhdr2015-Ethiopia-en.pdf.

[33] UNECA, AU. 2011. Governing development in Africa — the role of the state in economic transformation. Addis Ababa: Economic Report on Africa.

[34] UNECA. 2005. African Governance Report. Addis Ababa: UNECA.

[35] GORDON, W. 1998. Constructing a democratic developmental state// ROBINSON M, GOR-

DON W. The democratic developmental state: political and institutional design. Oxford: Oxford University Press.
[36] WOO-CUMINGS M. 1999. Introduction: Chalmers Johnson and the politics of nationalism and development// WOO-CUMINGS M. The developmental state. Ithaca: Cornell University Press.
[37] WOO-CUMINGS M. 1996. The ties that bind? autonomy, embeddedness, and industrial development. Political Power & Social Theory, 10: 307-319.
[38] WORLD BANK. 2017. Ethiopia overview.http://www.worldbank.org/en/country/ethiopia/overview.
[39] WORLD BANK. 2017. World development indicators | Ethiopia. http://databank.worldbank.org/data/reports.aspx?source=2&country=ETH.
[40] ZENAWI M. 2006. Africa's development. dead ends and new beginnings. http://cgt.Columbia.Edu/files/conferences/Zenawi-DeadEnds-and-NewBeginning

The Paradox of the "Developmental State" Experiment in Ethiopia: a Critical Examination

Mohammed Seid Ali & Alemu Asfaw Nigusie[①]

Abstract: Nowadays many of the developing countries particularly in Africa are attempting to emulate the Asian "miraculous" economic growth and Ethiopia is one of these countries. A critical examination of the adoption of such "developmental state" project in Ethiopia has revealed mixed results, however. On the one hand, Ethiopia is said to have registered a remarkable double-digit economic growth for over a decade. On the other hand, the same success story appears to be marred by major weaknesses like excessive state intervention in the economy, prevalence of low level of education standard and poor quality of the labor force as well as lack of an effective, meritocratic, and independent bureaucracy. Accordingly, Ethiopia's developmental state and its concomitant economic growth shows element of paradox and irregularity. In this paper, therefore, we argue that this paradox pertains to the inherent limitation (anomalies) in the foundation of the developmental state project in Ethiopia that lacked an institutionalized ideology and a strong state, which are the cornerstones to successful developmental state project.

Keywords: Developmental State; East Asia; Ethiopia; Anomaly

Introduction

Following the end of WWII, the so-called East Asian Tigers embarked on a development path that eventually led them to economic growth and prosperity. The successful development path these countries took, hailed as a "miracle", was not essentially an orthodox liberalism project, rather it was based on "heterodox" economic policies (Fantu & Obi, 2010). As such, it is difficult to explain the economic success of the East Asians through the vantage point of one theory since a combination of internal and external factors were behind this success (Krugman, 1994; Wade, 1992).

① Mohammed Seid Ali, Assistant Professor and PhD Candidate;Alemu Asfaw Nigusie, Lecturer and PhD Candidate,*Department of Political Science and International Studies, Bahir Dar University, Ethiopia.*

It is against this successful development background that we tend to see now a days many of the developing countries particularly in Africa desperately attempting to emulate this Asian "alternative road to development" and bring economic growth of their won and Ethiopia happens to be one of these African countries. In fact, as Clapham (2017: 11) stated, "Ethiopia clearly ranks as one of the clearest examples in Africa of the application beyond East Asia of the idea of the developmental state". Now it has been more than a decade since the Ethiopian developmental state has been declared. But, the question is, what is the rationale behind the adoption of the developmental state philosophy? Does Ethiopia has the necessary ingredients to run a developmental state? And above all, why Ethiopia's experiment of developmental state project is paradoxical? Such questions apparently appeared not to be addressed by the available literature on the subject. For instance, Clapham (2017) and Ayenachew (2015) focused on the implementation aspect of the developmental state of Ethiopia and the challenges it faced. Tewelde (2017), who took the presence of the developmental state in Ethiopia for granted, analyzed the democratic aspect of Ethiopia's developmental state. Jebena (2015) highlighted the contradiction between Ethiopia's political system (ethnic federalism) and development doctrine (democratic developmental state). Sehen & Tsegaye (2012) tried to identify the challenges the Ethiopian democratic developmental state is facing and appeared to be optimistic about the combination of democracy and developmental state in Ethiopia. Evidently, thus, all of them (Jebena, 2015) failed to interrogate whether there is a fertile environment for the proper application of the concept in the first place in Ethiopia, the very sources of the challenges and paradoxes the Ethiopian developmental state is facing.

Therefore, the main objective of this paper is to examine the justification for the adoption, implementation and above all the anomalies that challenged the germination of developmental state or the paradoxes of the project in Ethiopia. Methodologically, this paper adopted a qualitative document analysis (QDA) method of analysis that entails interpretation of texts or documents and looks for context and meaning in the process (Wesley, 2010). In this paper, therefore, an interpretation of the primary and secondary documents was conducted to understand and explain why Ethiopia adopted a developmental state project, and at the same time why the experiment of the same project has become paradoxical. To this end, this paper employed the developmental state concept as its point of reference to scrutinize the fabrics of Ethiopia's developmental state. Primary and secondary sources were utilized. Particularly, the 2017 official press statements of EPRDF (Ethiopian People's Revolutionary Democratic Front) and TPLF (Tigray People's Liberation Front) were found to be insightful as they provide us with much needed fresh and insider ideas about the politics and economy in Ethiopia at the moment.

This essay is divided into three major sections. The first section highlights the main features of the East Asian development success and the developmental state concept. The second section deals with Ethiopia's adoption of the developmental state path. Particularly, this section will look into the justifications, the national context, and the emerging issues in the utilization of this philosophy in Ethiopia. Eventually, the paper presents the concluding remark in section three.

Theoretical Aspects and Practical Lessons — the Developmental State in East Asia

There is no disagreement among scholars about the remarkable economic development registered by the East Asian countries (Herms, 1997; Krugman, 1994). And this has been made clear by Herms' (1997: 1) unequivocal statement: "Without a doubt East Asia's economic expansion during the past twenty years is one of the most remarkable economic changes since the Second World War". This remarkable growth was reflected by the consistent higher GDP growth, which was more than 5%, of these countries for close to three decades from 1965 to 1990. Comparatively speaking, this GDP growth was higher than the combined GDP growth of Latin America, Sub-Saharan Africa, and OECD in the same period. Six of the seven fastest growing economics in the period from 1960 to 1985 were East Asians, too (Herms, 1997).

At the heart of the economics success lies state interventions, the fact that has been even recognized by the World Bank's 1993 report on the region. But, what were the dimensions these state interventions? Let me briefly discuss the practical aspects. Herms (1997), following the arguments of the new interventionists, mentioned five aspects that are taken as the basis for the successful economic growth in the region. First, the industrial policy of the government was such that it selectively promoted those industries that were assumed to be of critical to the long-term development of the nation at large. Second, the government used various instruments to stimulate the economy like providing subsidies to selective investments that were thought to be of great importance to the future of the country. But, the relationship between the state and the firms was, according to Amsden (1989), characterized by reciprocity, where the state offered firms a subsidy and the firms were expected to do well in the export market. In essence, subsidies were earned, not given. Third, the government promoted and supported export-oriented economy. Even, the government deliberately created comparative advantage for its industries that were not able to compete against the Western goods hitherto. Fourth, there was strong collaboration between the state and the private sector that reduced the coordination problem in the economy. Lastly, the initial conditions were vital to the success of the East Asians. These initial conditions include relatively high standard education of the labor force, investment in physical infrastructure as well as stable political system before the state embarked on the developmental state project. Besides, such factors as the presence of, in economies like Republic of Korea, an equal income distribution through the land reforms of the 1950s, a culturally homogenous society, and finally absence of significant natural resources and its concomitant paucity of elite competition are listed as preconditions (Herms, 1997: 9-20).

On top of these internal factors, the external environment was also said to be conducive to the economic growth of these countries. The East Asians were able to benefit from the war economy of the Cold War as well as the absence of binding laws in the international trade like intellectual property rights. In the absence of restrictive intellectual rights, these countries were able to copy or steal technologies and ideas without any significant repercussion (Wade, 2003). This and the above mentioned factors contributed to the economic development of Republic of Korea, the one role model of Ethiopia.

Given these heterodox policies and realities, the East Asian economic experience is best described by *dirigisme* economy whereby the government was able to "govern the markets" to its advantage by controlling the pace and direction of the economic development. This *dirigiste* experience was also was achieved in short through what is called "developmental state" approach (Mkandawire, 2001). But, the question is, what are the defining features of a developmental state that makes it different from other types of states? It is to discussion of this concept I now turn so that the examination of Ethiopia could make sense.

According to Mkandawire (2001), the notion of "developmental state" entails the nexus between ideology and structure. Ideologically, it means the state makes it clear that it is "developmentalist" and that its holy mission is to bring about economic growth that is reflected in terms of capital accumulation, industrialization, and, more generally, structural transformation. But in order that this happens, developmental state needs a developmental leadership and elite who works hard to make the "developmental project" the "hegemonic ideology" by superseding other ideologies in the country and mobilize citizens and key actors so that they could embrace it willingly and make it happen on the ground. The main force that is assumed to be behind such developmental state's inclusive ideology is nationalism, a force that galvanizes the society at large in defense of its country and makes justifications to policy choices by the ruling elite easier. Simply put, nationalism serves as the "opium of the masses"; and finally, it integrates the ruling class. Thus, nationalism that is anchored on clear ideological orientation becomes critical to the success of the developmentalist project.

On the structural side, the state should have adequate capacity to marshal its mission and implement its economic policies effectively. State capacity entails institutional, financial, administrative, technical, and political capacities. Likewise, Johnson (1982, cited in Ayenachew, 2014) emphasized the centrality of pilot agency (institutional capacity) in the developmental process. As to him, pilot agency that has the power to plan, supervise, and direct the whole developmental process in the right direction is imperative. Examples of such agencies in East Asia include the Ministry of International Trade and Industry (MITI) of Japan, Economic Planning Board of Republic of Korea, and the Economic Development Board of Singapore. These institutions basically play the role of a conductor, in the music world sense, where they coordinate, collaborate, and share information between the government and the private sector.

As to Mkandawire (2001), the state-structure dimension of a developmental state emphasizes the state to have autonomy to formulate and execute its policies without negatively affected by social forces or by avoiding state capture by some interest groups. The notion of "autonomy" in turn implies the necessity of a strong state that exhibits the four capacities mentioned above. It is this core integration of the two components (ideology and state structure) that sets the developmental state different from other types of states. Of course, Weiss (2010, cited in Ayenachew, 2014) has identified these two components as the "software" (ideology) and "hardware" (structural capacity) of developmental states.

Levi-Faur's (2012) concise definition of the developmental state captures the essence of what Mkandawire argued. Levi-Faur's (2012: 10, cited in Ayenachew, 2014: 4) defined the developmental state as "a state with a dutiful and credible commitment to development". This definition underpins two pillars that a developmental state should have: duty and credibility. The state has the duty or obligation to deliver development to its citizens and has to actually deliver its promises as expected so that it could be trusted and supported. So, in essence, if the developmental state full fills these two requirements, then it meets the social expectations (duty) and acquires legitimacy (credibility). Yet, this to happen, the state must be complemented by meritocratic and autonomous bureaucracy. Given such definition of a developmental state, it means that such kind of state derives its legitimacy from its ability to register economic development (Mkandawire, 2001).

Yet, as Mkandawire (2001) has argued, some people do not think or expect that such kind of developmental state that worked in East Asia would flourish in Africa because for these group of people the African states are understood to be inherently weak and thus they are not in a position to correct the illnesses of neoliberalism (market failures) through state intervention which the East Asians were able to do it: "The most important case against developmental states in Africa is not faith in flawless markets, but rather that whatever the degree and extent of 'market failure' African states cannot correct them in ways that do not make things worse." (Mkandawire, 2001: 294) And Ethiopia's adoption of East Asian developmental state project can be understood as a defiance to this general neoliberal negative diagnosis and prescription. It is to the examination of this project in Ethiopia that now I turn to.

Ethiopia's Developmental State: Justification, Balance Sheet Card, and Anomalies

It has been more than a decade since the government of Ethiopia proclaimed its allegiance to the developmental state ideology and its commitment to realize it. To this end, the Ethiopian government tried to emulate the success stories of the East Asians (particularly Republic of Korea) at the time when questions were being raised against the efficacy of the neoliberal development model to the Africa following the failure of the Structural Adjustment Programs (SAPs). Thus, the East Asian development model was taken as alternative model to bring economic prosperity and development and this has been embedded in the country's five year plans called Growth and Transformation Plan (GTP) I (in 2010) and Growth and Transformation Plan (GTP) II (in 2015). These GTPs could be understood as the living embodiments of the developmental state ideology that Ethiopia was able to articulate, with all its limitations, for the first time by itself. In fact, GTP I has clearly stated the establishment of "suitable conditions for sustainable nation building through the creation of a stable democratic and developmental state" as its main objectives (FDRE, Growth and Transformation Plan (GTP I), 2010: 22).It also shows the relative policy space Ethiopia has vis-à-vis the external pressure. Indeed, over the period of 2000-2013, Ethiopia has registered remarkable economic growth, with a consistent GDP growth of two digits. This can be clearly seen in the expansion of the physical infrastructure, education, reduction of poverty, and the improvements in the health sector (Fantu, 2015).

When exactly was the developmental state introduced in Ethiopia is not clear. Nonetheless, here it is argued that the ideology of developmental state might have been articulated in the early 2000s, but the 2005 election crisis made its introduction urgent due to two fundamental points. On the one hand, EPRDF's (Ethiopian People's Revolutionary Democratic Front) initial concern was to establish its political base in the new political environment of ethnic federalism (1991-1998) (Clapham, 2017); then Ethiopia fought a bloody war against Eritrea (1998-2000); lastly, there was political schism within TPLF (the single most important member of the ruling EPRDF coalition party) as the party was going through reconfigurations. Thus, in effect, these conditions made it difficult for the government to have the time and space to critically think and formulate national policies that are embedded in an over-arching ideology.

On the other hand, the 2005 national election crisis vividly exposed the real nature of the Ethiopia state even towards peaceful opposition groups. As Clapham (2017: 4) stated, "it has become abundantly clear since 2005 that no significant challenge to the regime would be permitted" and tolerated. The next two national elections (2010 & 2015) were also won by EPRDF, particularly EPRDF won all seats in the 2015 election. And the title of Arriola& Lyons' (2016) article sums it up: *Ethiopia: the 100% Election*. As such, Ethiopia has effectively become a "... a single-party state in all but name" (Clapham, 2017: 4). Hence, the state appeared to lose trust and support among its citizens. So, in a sense, the developmental state project was launched as a response to the declining popular support and the legitimacy to rule as well as the need for something to galvanize the Ethiopian society around it and this was supposed to be accomplished by bringing fast economic growth through the adoption of the developmental state ideology.

Yet, two contending views have emerged regarding the felicity of the developmental state project to the Ethiopian context. The incumbent government has made clear that the developmentalist state is the only way forward to address Ethiopia's chronic economic, social, and political illnesses. EPRDF stated that poverty and lack of good governance and democracy will cause political disorder in Ethiopia, even to its disintegration. So, poverty has been singled out as the existential threat to Ethiopia and the developmental state as its panacea (EPRDF, 2010). While others opposed the developmentalist project on the ground that such a project would condone dictatorship that the country cannot afford anymore given its past political problems (Ayenachew, 2014).

Now it has been quite some time since the developmental state has been put in to practice, but the balance sheet does not look great. Firstly, if one looks at state intervention and the public-private interface, the Ethiopian state appears to have excessively intervened in the economy so much so that its actions became market unfriendly and a distortion to the balance it should maintain to effect healthy economic change. The state has directly involved in the economy through the continued ownership of the hitherto public services like telecommunication, electricity, and the Ethiopian Airlines; investment in sugar and fertilizer production; construction of huge projects like road, rail way transport between Ethiopia and Djibouti, and of course the Grand Ethiopian Renaissance Dam (GERD); establishment of the Metals and Engineering Corporation (Metek) company, Ethiopia's chaebol (Clapham, 2017).

Apart from the state, the two major players in the Ethiopian economy are the MIDROC group and the so-called endowment companies that are categorized under the "private sector" umbrella. Endowment companies have emerged in the four regional states and are associated with each of the four constituting parties of EPRDF, namely, the Endowment Fund for the Rehabilitation of Tigray (EFFORT) in Tigray; *Tiret* in Amhara; *Dinsho* in Oromia; and *Wendo* in the Southern Nations, Nationalities and Peoples' (SNNP). These conglomerate companies, by virtue of being close to these ruling parties, appeared to have an advantage in the market (Vaughan, Mesfin, 2011). On the contrary, the MIDROC group is owned by the half-Ethiopian Saudi entrepreneur Mohammed Al Amoudi who is also said to be affiliated with the government. Al Amoudi has investments in many sectors, namely hotel and tourism (Sheraton Addis), bank (Dashen), cement (Derba), real estate, commercial agriculture, as well as the country's largest gold mine, at Lega Dembi. Except for these examples of private sectors, there is no meaningful collaboration between the government and the private sector (Clapham, 2017).

The state-owned companies and the endowment enterprises appeared not only to greatly benefit from their close association to the government, but also they did not perform in a way they should act in a developmental state as they merely enjoy the state "rents" without any responsibility, supervision and punishment when they fail (Vaughan, Mesfin, 2011). In such a way, one of the central lessons taken from the East Asians looks to be lacking in Ethiopia. In short, Clapham's observation of the interface between the state and the private sector sums up the whole idea: despite the regime's formal recognition of the need for the private sector to assume a dynamic role in expanding the economy, its underlying attitudes remain instinctively statist, and correspondingly suspicious of private businesses, which are subject to an uncertain regulatory environment and readily targeted as "rent-seekers" (Claphm, 2017: 10).

Second, the land policy appears not to support the developmental project the state wishes to see on account of the state ownership of the land and the processes of allocation of land to investors that make it difficult to increase productivity. The land policies are related to rural and urban lands. The 1997 federal proclamation gave the federating units the responsibility to devise appropriate land policy according to their context, eventually leading to inter-regional diversity of land policy. In an attempt to solve this unevenness, resolve the tenure insecurity, and encourage investment and productivity, the federal government passed a decision in 2003 to implement the land certification process in Ethiopia's main regions like Tigray, Amhara, Oromia, and SNNP. The benefits of this land reform certification process are immense for small farm holders. For instance, it recognizes their legal ownership to the customary rights, enhances women's property rights and allows them to use this certificate as a collateral to borrow money from financial institutions. Despite such benefits, the new rural land reform has been marred by implementation predicaments and inter-regional variations (Deininger, et al, 2008). Also, the state has ushered in the commodification of urban land through its lease policy (FDRE, 2011), which in effect has benefited the rich people at the expense of the poor ones. The state is collecting huge amounts of money from the lease policy.

Third, it is recently (2013) that we see the establishment of Ethiopia's pilot agency, the National Planning Commission, which is in charge of preparing five-year plans of national development and conduct periodic evaluation of the implementation of the plans (FDRE, 2013). Before this commission, it was the Ministry of Finance and Economic Development (MoFED) that was carrying out the coordination of the economic activities in the country and that prepared the GTP documents. But, MoFED was unable to enforce directives to its co-ministries (horizontally) and to the regional states (vertically). In short, it lacked the institutional autonomy to enforce, supervise, steer, and shape the direction and pace of the economic change as planned at all levels wherever and whenever it is required (Ayenachew, 2014). Likewise, the actual synergy between the Ministry of Industry and Trade and the newly established Industrial Parks Development Corporation (IPDC) which has been given the task to oversee the development of large, medium and light industrial parks and the ministries of industry and agriculture is open to question (FDRE, Council of Ministers Regulation 326/2014).

Fourth, prevalence of low level of education standard and poor quality of the labor force. The government of Ethiopia has shown its commitment towards the expansion of education to realize the stated objectives of the growth and transformation plan and achieve the 2025 middle-income vision. Indeed, this policy has resulted in an amazing expansion of education at all levels, particularly the expansion of universities is clear. The government has also adopted the 70 : 30 formula whereby 70% of preparatory students will be directed to natural sciences and the remaining 30% to social sciences. And in the same manner the focus has been on the expansion of science and technology fields of study, including Engineering and Technology, Natural and Computational Sciences Medicine and health science, agriculture and life sciences as opposed to such social sciences fields of study as Business and Economics, Social Sciences and Humanities. Yet, the country's education policy has emphasized more on the access to education aspect, rather than the quality of education. For instance, students are not learning practically as they do not have the appropriate tools and equipped laboratories to practice; financial support for research is very low; low quality of students is introduced to higher education; insufficient supplies of text and reference books, laboratory and workshop equipment and access to ICT facilities; insufficient staff, with no appropriate skills. Also, the problem is there is lack of integration or synergy of what is taught at school and what the industry demands. This has resulted in the unemployment of thousands of students. It is not uncommon now a days to see thousands of unemployed graduates as a result of this education policy. This implies that the state is not playing its role as a regulator of the supply and demand of graduates(FDRE, MoE, 2010, 2015;Salmi, Sursock, Olefir, 2017).

Fifth, an effective, meritocratic, and independent bureaucracy that a developmental state requires appears to be absent in Ethiopia because civil servants are not really selected based on their merits, but their ethnic-affiliation, loyalty to the ruling party, and even nepotism. This has finally resulted in the dearth of disciplined bureaucrat and parasite bureaucracy that is characterized by rampant rent seeking behavior, corruption, and inefficiency (Ayenachew, 2014; Medhane, 2017). Apparently, such socially wasteful patronage and rent-seeking behaviors were supposed to be stumped out by the developmental state. But, in Ethiopia, the opposite is happening.

Sixth, the executive branch, specifically the Prime Minister's office, has become powerful by suppressing the power of the legislative branch without any ramifications. And the judiciary branch has been the subservient of the executive branch. The government has exceeded the usually tolerated "developmental authoritarianism" limits and threatened the inclusiveness, accountability, transparency, and responsiveness required from it to bring economic growth (Ayenachew, 2014; Clapham, 2017). This scenario has hampered the exercise of free market economy and competition among firms and as a result it has resulted in the granting of concessions and access to the market based on narrow and temporary political calculations, rather than rational national economic imperatives.

Finally, developmental state means the state has the policy space where it can formulate and execute by itself as it sees it fit. Yes, it is true Ethiopia has developed GTPs by itself, but it is difficult for Ethiopia to do whatever it wishes given the existence of pervasive external pressure that are usually conflicting to each other. Also, instead of mobilizing domestic sources and build on domestically mobilized saving mechanisms, Ethiopia has continued to depend on foreign direct investment (FDI), different forms of foreign aid as well as remittance from its diaspora to achieve its developmental projects (Clapham, 2017). So, how can Ethiopia claim to be a developmental state and work towards achieving it given these situations?

The net effect of all these weaknesses has been a shallow acceptance of the developmental state and popular protest mainly in the Amhara and Oromia regions) against the state which has been going on since 2015 ((EPRDF official statement, 2017). It is true that in East Asia people obeyed the constrained political space because the state was punishing those individuals that were involved in irresponsible acts (like corruption) and because people were able to see, taste, and benefit from the developmental projects their respective governments were conducting; so, as Krugman (1994) stated, they were happy to sacrifice temporary satisfactions for future benefit. But, unlike this East Asian model, the Ethiopian state is not really providing economic and political provisions on equal basis so that the people could obey and tolerate. Accordingly, the people (mainly the youth) are demanding what the state has not been able to deliver, but promised to deliver (Al Jazeera, 2016; Human Rights Watch, 2017). Even the government itself has recognized these demands and has vowed to repair them to avoid the degeneration into dangers situations (EPRDF official statement, 2017; TPLF official statement, 2017).

Given such characteristics of the implementation of the developmental state in Ethiopia, one will not hesitate to ask such questions as does Ethiopia has the necessary ingredients to start and sustain the developmental state project? Does Ethiopia has what it takes to be a developmental state after all? How does Ethiopia's political and economic system relate with the developmental state project? These questions lead us to the discussion of the inherent limitations (anomalies) in the foundation of the developmental state project in Ethiopia that affected its realization.

The initial ingredients or the foundations that help a developmental state successful (like the East Asians) appears to be lacking in Ethiopia. This has been reflected in the absence of national consensus and nationalism in Ethiopia and this emanates from both the presence of competing narratives of the Ethiopian statehood that were not yet addressed (Merera, 2006; Medhane, 2017) and that of the ethnic federalism political system the country follows (Jebena, 2015). According to this political system, people first and for most have ethnic or sub-national citizenship, then they have the Ethiopian national citizenship; elites are allowed to form political parties along narrow-based ethnic lines; diversity than unity is pronounced and institutionalized; public memory is being built on past and present issues of marginalization and exclusion; the system encourages ethnic entrepreneurs who use ethnicity as an instrument to access power and resource; ethnicity has been politicized and politics has been ethicized (Medhane, 2017; Jebena, 2015). So, how can one implement the developmental state project and expect it to be successful in such hostile political environment?

The other anomaly is linked with the education system and the level of education of the working force required to serve the developmental state. When it comes to the development of manpower, in Ethiopia, unlike what was the case in the developmental states of East Asia, there is a paucity of skilled manpower at the beginning of its developmental state path and the problem looms even large when one examines Ethiopia's poor record towards achieving quality education after the introduction of developmental state ideology in the country. In fact, the problem is not so much about to what extent Ethiopia had skilled manpower before launching its developmentalist ideology, but rather the question is to what extent Ethiopia is addressing its shortage of qualified labor force through appropriate education that has standard and endows quality so that it could provide the necessary skilled labor force trained theoretically and practically for its industries. The answer to this question is clear: so far this has not been the case as the government of Ethiopia appears to focus on quantity, not quality of education (FDRE, MoE, 2010, 2015).

Moreover, Ethiopia's developmental state ideology looks to be problematic. A developmental state should make its mission to be 'developmentalist' at any cost and is endowed with visionary and devoted elites that make this ideology a "hegemonic ideology". But, in Ethiopia, not only the rank and file, but also the higher leadership (the executive committee in particular) of the ruling party (EPRDF) lacks the ability and commitment to deliver this promise because "Many in the party simply bought to the idea out of self-interest and there is no strong ownership of the agenda in both political and academic terms" (Medhane, 2017; EPRDF official statement, 2017). Such scenario inhibits the emergence of an effective, meritocratic, and independent bureaucracy that a developmental state requires. Another problematic issue related with this problem is the short-sightedness of government's endorsement of the ideology of developmental state. The Ethiopian state did not whole-heartedly supported the ideology, rather it was supposed to serve as a source of legitimacy, "performance legitimacy" as Clapham (2017: 4) called it, that it could not achieve through the democratic process. Developmental state is seen as an escaping plan or replacement to the intrinsic way of achieving legitimacy that comes democratically through the will of the people.

Besides, the developmental state ideology has been the brainchild of the late PM Meles Zenawi (ENA, 2017) and hence, the ideology has become personalized, not institutionalized and deliberated among the population for consensus. As it emerged, it was Meles that is assumed to have been the engine and the master mind behind the attacks against the neoliberal principles and the articulation and adoption of the alternative East Asian development model in Ethiopia. The papers he wrote (Meles, 2006, 2012) and the testimonies of external scholars actually further consolidates this argument. For instance, Clapham's (2017: 3) admiration of Meles that Meles Zenawi "proved exceptionally capable of articulating an ideology of development that drew heavily on the East Asian model, while adapting it to Ethiopian circumstances" confirms this. And when he died, the ideology of developmental state appears to see no new champion, rather the main job of the post-Meles leaders has become about the "legacy of Meles" and about how to extend these legacies.

The Ethiopian state's ambition to be both developmental and democratic at the same time, democratic developmental state, is also another critical issue. These two concepts did not go hand in hand theoretically and practically in the East Asian case (the exception being Japan) at least at the beginning or until the developmental state reached some level of development which makes it imperative for the state to open up for values of liberal democracy (like respect for civil and political right, individual freedom, the right to press, accountability, and transparency). So, this means that the developmental state has to be undemocratic for some time until it brings successful development. Yet, there are some authors who argue that the two concepts are not really antithetical to each other and that it is possible to achieve them simultaneously provided that the developmental state must be complimented by democratic processes like accommodating various political interests and voices (Matlosa, 2005; Edigheji, 2005 cited in Sehenand Tsegaye, 2012). For instance, as to Anderson (2010, cited in Sehenand Tsegaye, 2012: 14) "a developmental state without democracy is not only impossible (because such a state lacks the much needed consensus among the populace and coherence in the state), but also unsustainable in the longer term (for there is a limit to legitimacy that emanates from economic performance)".

Likewise, the government of Ethiopia's justification to build a democratic and developmental state at the same time arose out of its conviction to address the hitherto unsolved national question or marginalization and oppression of ethnic groups (internally) and the rise of religious fundamentalism and terrorism in the Horn of Africa (internationally) (EPRDF, 2010). Indeed, the idea of constructing a democratic developmental state of Ethiopia has been clearly stipulated in the vision of GTP I, which states that Ethiopia's vision is "to become a country where democratic rule, good governance and social justice reign, upon the involvement and free will of its peoples, and once extricating itself from poverty to reach the level of middle-income economy as of 2020-2023" (FDRE, Growth and Transformation Plan (GTP I), 2010: 21). As such, the idea of being democratic may sound good and even tempting to use for Ethiopia given its past and present threats both at home and abroad, but the truth is democracy does not mean simply allocating each ethnic group, through the agency of national liberation front, its own region to govern or other sub-national groups to form special zones or woredas and conducting an election every five year, rather it means to be representative, participatory, inclusive, transparent, accountable, competitive, fair and free and finally rule of law, which apparently is non-existent in Ethiopia (Tewelde, 2017). Thus, the dream of seeking a democratic developmental state of Ethiopia remains to be rather a rhetoric, than a reality at least for now. However, if Ethiopia wants to still to construct a democratic developmental state, then it has to address some of the formidable challenges like overcoming the legacy of authoritarianism, ethnocracy, and neo-liberalism; managing the challenge of multiple transitions that demand: restructuring the state, opening the political space, and liberalizing the economy; living under a constitutional democracy with the onerous burden of protecting and enforcing human rights by harmonizing the relation between collective and individual, civil/political and economic/socio-cultural, rights (Sehenand Tsegaye, 2012: 16).

Furthermore, the nature of the governing party appears to be another thorny issue in the establishment of the hegemonic ideology of the developmental state and its implementation in Ethiopia. The ruling party of Ethiopia, EPRDF, is not one single party, rather it is a coalition of four major parties that represent different regions, namely, Tigray People's Liberation Front (TPLF) for Tigray people, Amhara National Democratic Movement (ANDM) for Amhara people, Oromo People's Democratic Organization (OPDO) for Oromo people, and Southern Ethiopian Peoples' Democratic Front (SEPDF) for the southern people. Apparently, as it is revealed now, these constitutive parties of EPRDF seems to have unequal power and domination in the united front and ipso facto a symmetric power dynamics has developed in the government. Such unequal power allocation has exposed the state to be captured by groups that have narrow economic interest, not national ideological base. Actually, this has been unequivocally confirmed by the incumbent EPRDF-led government in its official statement where it stated about the prevalence of non-principled relationship between individuals and groups, the slackening of intra-EPRDF democracy, and the attempts that are directed against weakening the equality of party system (EPRDF official statement, 2017: 1-2). It is, therefore, possible that such kind of asymmetric relationship has caused mistrust, competition and in-fighting among themselves and hence eroded the healthy germination of the developmental state in Ethiopia.

On top of these internal issues, Ethiopia does not have the luxury of maneuver that the East Asian had in the Cold War vis-à-vis the influence of Western powers. Ethiopia's adoption of the developmental state project in the era of neo-liberal world order appears to be much more difficult to implement. As it has been argued by the government, the Structural Adjustment Programmes(SAPs) the country has to go through or any other form of the "Bretton Woods" influence extremely restricts Ethiopia's policy space and ability to execute the developmental state idea (EPRDF, 2010).

Concluding Remarks

Despite its adoption of the East Asian development model, it has been vividly demonstrated that Ethiopia lacks the two major foundations for a successful developmental state paradigm, namely an institutionalized ideology and strong state that has the institutional and political capacity to realize it. Ethiopia's developmental state project is suffering from multiple limitations that emerged out of the absence of initial ingredients. The Ethiopian leaders appeared not to be genuinely committed to the project, instead they are just paying lip-service to the ideology so that it could serve them political expediency. Therefore, the decision to adopt the East Asian developmental path was mainly seen as a replacement for the absence of "intrinsic legitimacy". The overriding implication of such analysis is that the Ethiopian state is not yet a developmental state in the East Asian sense and it has to become one. And this appears to be supported by the recent works of Clapham (2017) and Vaughan and Mesfin (2011) who tried to understand the Ethiopian state, following the contribution of Kelsall (2009, 2010, 2013), rather through the "developmental partimonialism" framework which is explained in terms of the mixture of clientelism (patron-client relationship) and the emergence of technocratic class. To what extent this concept explains the Ethiopian state is beyond the scope of this paper and needs further investigation.

References

[1] JAZEERA A. 2016. Ethiopia declares state of emergency over protests. http://www.aljazeera.com/news/2016/10/ethiopia-declares-state-emergency-protests-161009110506730.html.

[2] AMSDEN A H. 1994. Why isn't the whole world experimenting with East Asia development model? Review of the East Asian miracle. World Development, 22(4): 627-633.

[3] ARRIOLA L R, LYONS T. 2016. Ethiopia: the 100% election. Journal of Democracy, 27(1): 76-88.

[4] AYENACHEW A W. 2014. The Ethiopian developmental state and its challenges. SSRN

Electronic Journal. https://doi.org/10.2139/SSRN.2512907.

[5] CLAPHAM C. 2018. The Ethiopian developmental state. Third World Quarterly, 39(6): 151-165.

[6] DEININGER K, DANIEL A A, HOLDEN S, et al. 2008. Rural Land Certification in Ethiopia: Process, Initial Impact, and Implications for Other African Countries. World Development, 36(10), 1786–1812.

[7] EPRDF. EPRDF official statement. 2017. http://www.tigraionline.com/articles/eprdf-meeting-concludes.html.

[8] ETHIOPIAN PEOPLE'S REVOLUTIONARY DEMOCRATIC FRONT (EPRDF). 2010. Yetehadisow mesmer ena ye itiyopiahidase. Addis Abeba: Mega Printing PLC.

[9] ETHIOPIAN NEWS AGENCY (ENA). 2017. Meles engineered democratic developmental state in Ethiopia: Scholars. http://www.ena.gov.et/en/index.php/politics/.item/3615-meles-engineered-democratic-developmental-state-in-ethiopia-scholars.

[10] FANTU C. 2015. Structural transformation and inclusive development in Ethiopia: results from GTP I implementation. http://www.un.org/esa/socdev/egms/docs/2015/Cheru.pdf.

[11] FANTU C, OBI C. 2010. Introduction — Africa in the twenty-first century: strategic and development challenges//Fantu C, Cyril O. The rise of China and India in Africa: challenges, opportunities, and critical interventions. London: Zed Books.

[12] FDRE-MINISTRY OF EDUCATION. 2010. Education Sector Development Program IV (ESDPIV) 2010/2011-2014/2015 Program Action Plan. https://planipolis.iiep.unesco.org/sites/default/files/ressources/ethiopia_esdp_iv.pdf.

[13] FDRE. 2010. Growth and Transformation Plan (GTP I) Volume I: https://www.preventionweb.net/files/28796_gtpenglishministryoffinanceandecono.pdf

[14] FDRE: URBAN LAND REFORM. 2011. Urban Lands Lease Holding Proclamation No. 721/2011. http://admin.theiguides.org/Media/Documents/Urban-land-lease-proclamaion-no-721-20111.pdf.

[15] FDRE-COUNCIL OF MINISTERS REGULATION. 2013. National Planning Council and the National Planning Commission Establishment Council of Ministers Regulation No. 281/2013. https://land.igad.int/index.php/documents-1/countries/ethiopia/legislation-and-policies-1/legislation-1/laws-on-land-1/249-national-planning-council-and-the-national-planning-commission-establishment-council-of-ministers-regulation-no-281-2013/file.

[16] FDRE-COUNCIL OF MINISTERS. 2014. Industrial Parks Development Corporation Establishment Council of Ministers Regulation No. 326/2014. https://chilot.me/wp-content/uploads/2017/04/regulation-no-326-2014-industrial-parks-development-corporation-establishment.pdf.

[17] FDRE-MINISTRY OF EDUCATION. 2015. Education Sector Development Programme V (ESDPV) 2015/2016-2019/2020 Program Action plan. https://www.unicef.org/ethiopia/media/1396/file/Education%20Sector%20Development%20Programme%20V%20(ESDP%2V).

pdf.
[18] JEBENA B A. 2015. Ethnic federalism and democratic developmental state in Ethiopia: some points of contradiction. International Journal of Political Science and Development, 3(7): 291-300.
[19] HUMAN RIGHTS WATCH (2017). "Fuel on the fire": Security force response to the 2016 Irreecha Cultural Festival. https://www.hrw.org/sites/default/files/report_pdf/ethiopia0917_web.pdf.
[20] KRUGMAN P. 1994. The myth of Asia's miracle. Foreign Affairs, 73(6): 62-78.
[21] HERMS N. 1997. New explanations of the economic success of East Asia: lessons for developing Eastern European countries. CDS Research Report, 3: 1-30.
[22] MEDHANE T. 2017. The developmental state in Ethiopia: congenital anomalies or inertia? The Current Analyst, 13. https://medium.com/the-current-analyst/the-developmental-state-in-ethiopia-congenital-anomalies-or-inertia-56bc3cdd927d.
[23] MELES Z. 2012. State and markets: neoliberal limitations and the case for a developmental state//NOMAN A, BOTCHWEY K, STEIN H, et al Good growth andgovernance in Africa: rethinking development strategies. New York: Oxford University Press.
[24] MELES Z. 2006. Africa's development: dead ends and new beginnings. http://www.meleszenawi.com/wp-content/uploads/2012/11/African_Development-Dead_Ends_and_New_Beginnings_by_Meles_Zenawi.pdf.
[25] MERERA G 2006. Contradictory interpretations of Ethiopian history: the need for a new consensus//TURTON D. Ethnic federalism: the Ethiopian experience in comparative perspective. Oxford: James Currey.
[26] MKANDAWIRE T. 2001. Thinking about developmental states in Africa. Cambridge Journal of Economics, 25(3): 289-313.
[27] SALMI J, SURSOCK A, OLEFIR A. 2017. Improving the performance of Ethiopia universities in science and technology: a policy note. http://documents.worldbank.org/curated/en/687231505250026457/pdf/119694-REVISED-PUBLIC-Ethiopia-ST-HE-Policy-Note-Ethiopia-Higher-Education-Science-and-Techn.pdf.
[28] SEHEN B, TSEGAYE R. 2012. Democratization in a developmental state: the case of Ethiopia issues, challenges, and prospects. UNDP Ethiopia, Development Brief, No.1.
[29] TEWELDE G. 2017. The "democratic developmental state" in Ethiopia: origins, challenges and prospects//Sonja J, Assefa B, Taa B. Cultures of democracy in Ethiopia: from theory to lived experiences. Addis Abeba: A Publication of the Friedrich-Ebert-Stiftung Ethiopia.
[30] TPLF. TPLF official statement. 2017. http://aigaforum.com/news2017/TPLF-official-statement-113017.pdf.
[31] VAUGHAN S, MESFIN G. 2011. Rethinking business and politics in Ethiopia: the role of EFFORT, the endowment fund for the rehabilitation of tigray. The Africa Power and Politics Programme (APPP) Research Report, No.2.

[32] WADE R. 1992. East Asian economic success: conflicting perspectives, partial insights, shaky evidence. World Politics, 44(2), 270-320.

[33] WADE R. 2003. What strategies are viable for developing countries today? The WTO and the shrinking of development space. Review of International Political Economy, 10(4): 621-624.

[34] WESLEY J J. 2010. Qualitative document analysis in political science. http://www.poltext.org/sites/poltext.orglfiels/pzwesley._09102010_131253.pdf.

埃塞俄比亚近年来引进外资与对外经济设计初探

张　歌

摘要：埃塞俄比亚（简称“埃塞”）是非洲人口第二大国，具有广阔的市场潜力，同时也是当前非洲经济发展比较快、比较成功的经济体之一。该国地处东非非洲之角，战略地位十分重要。近年来，埃塞俄比亚经济发展迅速，埃塞政府根据形势调整了国内的经济政策，将吸引海外投资设定为国家经济发展计划的重要因素，鼓励各种形式的国家层面、私人层面的外资进入国内。这其中，中国在各个方面都有抢眼的表现，在国与国、企业与企业等层面的合作上，双边关系形势喜人。本文通过对相关数据的分析，对当前埃塞经济发展中的对外资的态度及外资进入的渠道和主要领域作了简要分析，并对未来有较大发展空间的领域进行了论述。

关键词：埃塞俄比亚；中国；外资

埃塞俄比亚长期以来一直是东非大国，其历史文化影响不仅在东非、尼罗河流域十分深远，甚至跨过红海，在近东的文明演进中也发挥了重大的作用。进入现当代，埃塞俄比亚的发展充满坎坷，但该国人民一直自立自强，走出了一条具有自身特色的发展之路。在短短的百余年间，埃塞俄比亚不仅经历了民族国家的构建、国土的统一与抵抗外敌入侵等一系列重大历史事件，更是经过了长期的经验摸索走出了一条适合自身的国家发展之路。如今的埃塞俄比亚已经是非洲人口第二多的国家，从 21 世纪初至今将近 20 年来，埃塞国内政局逐渐稳定，经济发展已成为国家的绝对中心议题，在 2016 年之前的 10 多年里，国内生产总值（Gross Domestic Product，GDP）以每年 8% 到 11% 的速度增长，不仅在非洲国家中表现优异，而且是国际货币基金组织 188 个成员国中增长最快的国家之一。[①] 埃塞国内的新局面为国际经济体系之间的交往加入了一抹亮色，不仅其本国受益，也为更多国家开展海外投资、谋求共同发展提供了一种可能。

一、埃塞俄比亚国内当下经济状况的分析

埃塞俄比亚国内人口增长很快，进入 21 世纪，其国内人口已经达到了 8 400 万，随着政

① 美国中央情报局：https://www.cia.gov/library/publications/the-world-factbook/geos/et.html. 本章以下数据如无特别说明均出自美国中央情报局公开的相关统计数据。

局的平稳，埃塞俄比亚的人口年均增长率已达到 2.7%~3%，46.3% 的人口处于 14 岁以下[①]。虽然人口的迅猛增长给自然环境与资源以及国家基础建设方面带来了很大的压力，但是一支年轻而具有规模的人口大军也意味着该国具有潜在的巨大而活跃的市场。目前埃塞俄比亚国内政局稳定，其人口基数不仅在东非，甚至在非洲也处于前列，这意味着一旦其国内经济起步，对周边乃至整个非洲都将具有辐射作用。事实证明，埃塞俄比亚在对国内人口总量的规划中将其同国内市场、经济等要素进行了很好地结合，近年来埃塞国内经济增长的速度极快，国内生产总值攀升幅度很大。据美国中央情报局公开的相关统计数据显示，其国内生产总值在 2015 年达到了 1 676 亿美元，2017 年这一数值已增长到了 2 000 亿美元。在对埃塞国内的通货膨胀情况作出修正之后，可以看出其 GDP 实际增长率不可小觑。

2015 年、2017 年埃塞 GDP 修订后增长均达到 10% 以上，分别是 10.4%（2015 年）和 10.7%（2017 年），2016 年由于埃塞俄比亚国内各地方普遍进行了产业结构调整，影响了 GDP 数值，但当年的增长仍达到了 8%，远高于同时期非洲大多数国家的经济增长水平。

与此相对应，埃塞俄比亚国内人均收入水平也增长较快，由于这一数值和国民购买力水平密切相关，所以是国与国之间贸易往来、资本投资的重要参考。根据本地物价水平对相关数值进行修订后，可以看出 2015 年埃塞国内的人均收入购买力水平已达到 1 900 美元，2016 年达到 2 000 美元，2017 年达到 2 200 美元。相比较周边国家而言，埃塞俄比亚国内国民储蓄额占 GDP 的比重处于一个较高的水平。从数据上来看，从 2015 年至今，国民储蓄额一直都占到了 GDP 总量的三分之一，这显示出随经济高速增长而来的国民收入水平、生活水平的提高，但国民对于消费仍保持着一定的审慎态度，这也从侧面证明埃塞国内的市场仍具有较大潜力，经济仍具有上升空间。

在对 GDP 最终走向的划分里，以 2017 年为例，生产总值数据中埃塞国内家庭消费占到了总额的 69.6%，固定资产投资占总额的 43.5%，两项数据显示埃塞国内经济发展给埃塞国内所带来的良性效益。但与这两项指标相对应，商品和出口服务的投资只占 GDP 的 8.1%，这虽然比一些邻国要高，但在世界范围内仍属于低水平，特别是和埃塞国内近年来的经济发展形势相比，这些领域的投资状况无疑成了今后经济发展的绊脚石。而商品与进口服务占 GDP 的比重则更加严峻，数值显示为 -31.2%，这一低落的数据显示埃塞国内没有为进口商品提供完善配套服务设施的能力。虽然首都亚的斯亚贝巴附近通过加大基础设施建设力度、开设产业园区等措施试图加强这方面的保障，但是在首都以外地区，特别是西南和东北部山区其状况仍不乐观，这也是数据落差如此之大的原因，而且短期内很难得到改善。

造成这种形势的原因是多方面的。首先，埃塞地处东非内陆，没有出海口，传统的贸易外港在今厄立特里亚地区，但随着厄立特里亚独立，以及两国在 21 世纪初期围绕边境问题所形成的紧张态势，埃塞通向红海的传统出海口路线极度衰落，虽然近年来两国关系明显改善，但距离恢复之前的外贸路线的水平还有一段距离，且厄立特里亚目前港口基础设施、仓储条件也不尽如人意，在可以预见到的时期内，看不到明显改变的趋势。其次，虽然埃塞俄比亚本国国内政治环境稳定，但其周边存在着不安定因素，南苏丹独立不久，同苏丹之间还有着一系列领土与油田分配等方面的争端，埃南两国边境时常面临难民涌入与局部冲突等

---

① Jon Abbink, *A Decade of Ethiopia: Politics, Economy and Society,* 2004-2016, Koninklijke Brill NV, Leiden: The Netherlands, 2017, p.122.

紧张局势，而其东部邻国索马里的局势也仍不明朗，到目前为止索马里仍然处于分裂割据的状态，埃塞俄比亚同其国内一些割据的地方政权之间关系微妙，虽然索马里北部的港口也被埃方用作扩展对外贸易的桥头堡，但当地局势影响到了这一贸易路线的稳定。再次，由于埃塞俄比亚国内广大地区地处山区、高原，当地的制造业基础薄弱，特别是在广大农村地区，当地人口的生活自给自足的倾向仍然较强，传统的小农经济对外部商品需求较小，在基层社会缺乏对相关的外来工业产品的销售网络和服务设施。这些因素综合使埃塞国内的外贸配套服务体系十分落后，这对其对外经济交往的形式具有很重要的影响。从目前外资进入其国内的产业特色来看，以出口为导向的产品加工业大多聚集在首都亚的斯亚贝巴周边地区，内地很少，但以西方国家为代表的这些外资在首都附近已经形成了固定的格局，未来进入的外资再进入这一领域的前景并不看好。反之，只有在埃塞国内迫切需要的基础设施建设、国内农牧产品加工销售领域的投资意向有比较明显的发展前景。因此，未来的投资思路不在于出口导向型的加工产业，而在于旨在能打开埃塞国内市场、开拓其国内各地销路的方向上。

对埃塞俄比亚国内三大产业结构的数据分析从另一个角度也可以证明上面的推论。在其国内本地生产总值的数据比例中，根据近年来统计可以看出，农业占 34.8%、制造业占 21.6%、服务业占 43.6%。其中服务业比重大主要是同旅游业、民航运输业等部门相关的发展所致。由于埃塞俄比亚历史文化悠久，有众多的历史文化遗产，另外还有绮丽的自然风光，因而一旦政治局面安定，国内的旅游资源的发展速度是十分可观的；而埃塞俄比亚航空无疑已经成为该国交通运输业的一张名片，享有国际声誉。但除此之外，商品流通、国内金融信贷以及其他方面的物流、仓储服务业等部门欠佳的发展水平并不能在这项数据的指数中得到体现，因而只从本地生产总值的统计结果看，结论仍不能完全说清楚问题。如果从不同产业占国民经济总量的比重这一角度则可以看出，埃塞俄比亚国内农业占经济总量的 72.7%、制造业占 7.4%、服务业占 19.9%[①]。这一统计结果可以相对更真切地反映出埃塞国内三大产业目前的发展水平和状况，从中可以看出其经济结构主要呈现出以农业为主、制造业薄弱、服务业欠发达的状况。其中服务业的数据不仅参考了旅游文化产业和航运客运等方面的数据，更计算了包括进出口服务业、金融服务业等在内的同制造业紧密结合的工业服务业的发展水平。由于制造业在整个国民经济中比重过于弱小，连带相关服务业部门也裹足不前，这种状况说明至少在当前一定时期内，单纯投资以出口导向性为主的加工业而不顾及埃塞国内本身生产销售链的建设思路需要付出的成本较高。

埃塞俄比亚国内家庭消费在经济增速、国民收入增长的同时，埃塞国内尼基指数保持在 33.6 左右，在非洲国家中处于较低水平[②]，人类发展指数为 0.463，在世界属于中间水平，但仍处上升势头[③]。但同时要看到，埃塞国内的社会状况同所有发展中国家普遍存在的问题一样，存在着社会两极分化、贫富差距拉大等问题。在劳动力的相关统计数据方面，2014 年埃塞俄比亚国内贫困线以下人口占总人口数的 29.6%，其中最贫困人口大致占总人口数的 4.1%~10%，由于大量贫困地区地处偏僻，统计结果存在一定误差。与贫困率相比，埃塞国内

---

① 其中前两项数据是 2017 年的统计数据，服务业则为 2013 年的统计数据。

② Selima Jāhāna, Human Development Report 2015:Work for Human Development,United Nations Development Programme, 2018:232.

③ United Nations(ed).2018 *Human Development Report, United Nations Development Programme,* Retrieved 14, 2018.

的失业人口占总人口比重常年在 17%~18%，即使在外资进入、国内产业结构调整所带来经济增长之后，仍有占人口五分之一的人群无法找到工作，在大城市中生活成本较高，水电短缺，同时还有受到普遍指责的腐败现象等。这些从侧面反映出此前的引入外资领域与国家发展策略之间存在一定偏差。虽然富裕人口与中间阶层收入增长较快，尼基指数呈低水平，但通过比较所显示出的实际社会形势仍需要谨慎处理。

此外，对于经济形势的评估还需要考虑埃塞俄比亚的国家债务问题。应该注意到埃塞俄比亚国内债务有历史遗留问题，特别是在 20 世纪 90 年代后期，埃塞社会经济处于转型时期，举借了大量外债，这其中一部分一直延续到现在仍未完全偿清，但近年来的债务增长确实有过快的势头。据《埃塞俄比亚新商业》杂志 2019 年 7 月 1 号报道："埃塞财政部负责人表示，埃塞俄比亚国内外债务分别累计达到了 253 亿美元和 270 亿美元，国家债务负担总额达到了 523 亿美元。"① 国家负债情况虽然整体可控，但在非洲国家中，这项数值并不算低，对此埃塞俄比亚政府表示："从 2018 年 7 月到 2019 年 5 月，本国政府已偿还债务 94 亿美元，但债务总额仍较高，政府给出的解决办法包括尽可能减少商业贷款，积极推动债务重组，并从供给侧方面推动采矿、旅游业、制造业等产业的快速发展。"②

通过以上分析可以看出，虽然有需要多方面谨慎考虑的必要，但通过分析几项关键数据显示埃塞俄比亚经济总体呈现较好的形势，如能打开其国内市场，联络销售网络，让投资项目能够在其国内形成一套生产销售的网络，则能在降低成本的情况下使投资得到回报。当然，这仍然需要投资方在初期对当地的环境进行一些基本投入，但不同于西方单纯地利用当地廉价劳动力代工加工，直接走和当地经济关系不大的产品出口相比，这种思路下的投资本身和埃塞国内的经济建设需求联系在一起，随着投资项目的运转可以使其国内的经济体系和投资方结合在一起，是一种合作共赢的体系，因而在埃塞国内形成产销共同体则不啻为对埃塞投资的一条思路。然而这一系列产业部门的升级启动一级产业运作等方面都需要大量资金。如何增加外汇收入、吸引外资和相关技术进入埃塞国内，从而建立起一套可良性发展的经济体系，进而解决债务问题，维持本国经济高速增长的势头，埃塞政府需要找到切实可靠的解决办法。从现有埃塞俄比亚国内的经济结构看，其农产品的生产与出口以及国家大规模基础设施和工程建设等部门的效能的提高仍是推动其国内经济发展的最重要因素。在这方面所进行的产业结构调整，同外部世界经贸网络建立联系，在共赢的基础上寻求外部投资的支持是解决如上问题比较即时有效的方法。

二、埃塞俄比亚外资引入的情况以及中埃间的多层面合作的分析

中国在埃塞俄比亚社会经济方面的参与正在不断加强，《中国全球投资追踪》(*China Global Investment Tracker*) 对中国在埃塞俄比亚的经济活动和投资情况进行了专门的分析评论，中国在埃塞俄比亚的投资和合同从 2004 到 2016 年呈稳步增长的发展趋势，数据显示资金总额已达 176.2 亿美元③。中国在埃塞俄比亚的经济活动和投资方式塑造了一种新的国与国之间社会、经济等方面的交往方式，这可能会引起旧有国际政治经济格局的变动，也会

① 中国驻埃塞俄比亚使馆经济商务参赞处：http://et.mofcom.gov.cn/article/jmxw/201907/20190702879024.shtml.

② 同上。

③ Edson Ziso, *A Post State-Centric Analysis of China-Africa Relations*, This Palgrave Macmillan, 2018：5.

在埃塞俄比亚国内原有的社会政治力量、经济贸易网络的格局中引发一连串的反应，但相信这种变化会随着中埃两国之间的交往加深而向着好的方向发展。有观念认为中埃之间的交往实际上已超出埃塞俄比亚一国的范围，从而在整个东非区域的整体市场构建、区域性贸易网络的形成中发挥重要的影响。

从现有发展格局来看，中国对非洲经济的参与是多方面的，其中包括了援助、贸易往来、债务减免、发展筹资以及各种形式的投资。这其中东非地区以其相对稳定的政治局面和较非洲平均水平为优的基础设施成为中国在非洲上述经济活动的重点地区。根据联合国非洲经济委员会 (UNECA) 的数据，东非继续快速增长，人均收入在 10 年内翻了一番。2016 年，该地区人均收入达到 740 美元；UNECA 官方报告补充说，这一数字是 10 年前的两倍[①]。这其中埃塞俄比亚经济增长最为迅猛，当前埃塞俄比亚已经超过肯尼亚成为东非第一大经济体，埃塞俄比亚在基础设施建设上的投资远大于周边国家。该报告指出，埃塞俄比亚实施了一项雄心勃勃的出口导向型工业园区计划，宗旨是打造成埃塞俄比亚国内的一个制造业重镇，从而在国内建立起一条完整的产业链，不仅可以使投资方得到回报，而且本地也能得到相关技术和企业管理经验，从而带动本国制造业体系的完善与发展。在具体措施上，埃塞政府特别提到希望能广泛引入外资，不仅加工制成品出口，而且希望这一计划将对改善当地的私人经商环境有很大的助益。

该报告还指出："如果实施政策支持私营部门的活动，经济增长将会更强劲、更有弹性。"[②] 这一结论也得到了近年来埃塞俄比亚国内官方消息的证实，据埃塞俄比亚芳那广播公司 7 月 1 日报道："埃塞总理阿比当日向埃塞人民代表院作 2018/2019 财年政府工作报告时表示，预计埃塞 2018/2019 财年经济增长 9.2%，较 2017/2018 财年 7.7% 的增速以及 2016/2017 财年 8.6% 的增速有所增长。阿比在其报告中表示，在政府收入方面，过去 11 个月政府收入为 1 785 亿比尔（约 63.75 亿美元），较上财年同期增长 10%。预计到 2019 年 7 月 7 日，本财年结束之日，总收入将达到 1 890 亿比尔（约 67.5 亿美元）。在创造就业方面，去年政府新增 140 万个工作岗位。按照每年新增 200 万失业人口的趋势统计，目前仍有 1 100 万人失业。在吸引外国直接投资方面，贷款和侨汇较上财年增长 20%，银行存款总额增长 22%，银行发放贷款量增长 35%。在国企私有化改革方面，政府首先着力于电信业和制糖业，将其作为示范领域接受私有化投标，此后将在电力、铁路、物流、工业发展和航空航天业等领域展开私有化进程。阿比同时表示，埃塞目前通胀率较高，2019 年 5 月数据为 16.2%。此外，针对目前国内投资环境所面临的一些问题以及外国投资者的一些疑虑，过去一年政府在确保法治执行、恢复流离失所民众住所、扩展政治发展空间等方面做出努力。其中，2018 到 2019 财年共有 996 人因涉嫌恐怖主义、洗钱、煽动暴力、经济破坏和贩卖人口等活动被捕，并有 210 多万流离失所民众在政府帮助下返回故乡。此外，政府大赦超过 45 000 人，释放 10 多万名囚犯，准许超过 10 个流亡政党回国。政府还取消了对 260 家媒体和网站的屏蔽措施。阿比还表示，埃塞国家选举委员会、人权委员会、国家情报安全局和信息网络安全局等政府部门还落实了相关改革举措。"[③]

---

① 埃塞俄比亚沃尔塔信息中心: http://www.waltainfo.com/index.php/news/detail/39308.

② 同上。

③ 中国驻埃塞俄比亚使馆经商处：http://et.mofcom.gov.cn/article/jmxw/201907/20190702879025.shtml.

这则消息的前半部分反映了埃塞俄比亚政府目前希望能引入外资帮助改善国内经济的相关领域和每个领域中的具体部门，其中电信产业和电力等相关要害部门从 20 世纪 90 年代后期埃塞国内开始社会经济转型后一直都是由国家控制的专营领域，之前并不允许私有资本的进入，对于外部资本在这些领域也严格进行管控，这次伴随私有化改革对外部资本的开放程度在埃塞历史上是空前的。后半部分则显示了埃塞俄比亚国内改善投资环境、维持社会稳定的决心与具体措施，而且可以看出除了反恐和打击各种犯罪之外，埃塞政府将营造政治上的宽松环境、实行民主化改革作为工作的重点，这也是为了营造开放私有化、实现自由市场经济所摆出的重要政治姿态。

作为对这种发展局势的一种肯定与回应，中国国家开发银行设立了 10 亿元人民币作为中非发展基金，用于基础设施、工业等领域和农业项目。中国现在积极参与埃塞俄比亚的经济模式增长和积累。例如，中国几乎参与了埃塞俄比亚国内的所有发电项目，在运输和道路交通部门，参与的比重也很大[①]。

当前，中国已经超过了英国，成为非洲最大的经济体贸易伙伴，早在 2009 年中国在非洲的经贸与投资总和就超过美国在非洲的投资，双方的差距十分明显。截至 2012 年，中国的企业对非直接投资 147 亿美元，同比自 2009 年以来同比增长已经超过 60%。如果加上中方通过其他国际市场的渠道投放的资金，中国在非洲的直接投资总数已经超过 400 亿美元，中国对非洲的贷款已超过世界银行 (World Bank)[②]。其中，埃塞俄比亚是中国在非投资的一个主要集中地，这一态势的形成是两国基于经济、政治、外交、地缘等多方面考量之后所采取的审慎的措施。中国和埃塞俄比亚已经发展起来全方位、多层面的合作关系，具体特征为人与人、企业对企业，特别是政府对政府和政党对政党的长期战略合作的关系，这在中国与非洲国家间的交往中是不多见的。

中国在埃塞俄比亚的投资有独特的领域与策略，在非洲其他国家的中国投资领域中可以看出大多集中于矿产开发、能源利用等方面，而在埃塞俄比亚，并没有一个明显在国际市场份额中占有优势的矿产或能源种类，这说明资源开发并不是中埃经贸交往中唯一的动力，中国所看重的是埃塞俄比亚国内长期稳定的政治环境，在这一大背景下迅速增长的经济总量，以及随着收入不断增长其国内巨大的人口所带来的潜在市场。如前所述，埃塞俄比亚近年来国内国民可支配收入按照实际购买力计算已超过 2 000 美元，这表明其国内的经济发展水平已初步达到了中等发展中国家的水平，埃塞俄比亚对于世界来说是一个正在形成中的具有巨大潜力的市场，这不仅在产品销售领域，在投资领域也是这样。对于这样一个在东非乃至在整个非洲来说重要的战略合作伙伴，中国更加注重长线投资与经济网络联系所带来的远景效应，具体到目前的投资策略，可以看出目前在产业技术及产能转让、工农业原材料供给链、初级工农业产品加工及其与中国产业链对接等方面中方投入了更多精力。而埃塞也看到了这方面的合作对自身的经济发展、产业结构的调整与完善具有极大的好处，因而这是一种互补双赢的合作关系。也正是这一愿景，中国在埃塞俄比亚的很多项目都具有合作示范的深意。

从 2005 到 2016 年，中国在埃塞俄比亚的投资总额与合同总金额数合计达到了 176.2

---

① Edson Ziso, *A Post State-Centric Analysis of China-Africa Relations*, This Palgrave Macmillan, 2018 : 8.

② 同上。

亿美元,这其中有很多是私人企业的投资,但是更多的中国国有大型企业也已经参与到这一合作中。中兴通讯为埃塞俄比亚国内提供先进的电信设备与运营解决方案;中国水电、华为技术有限公司等也在各自的专业领域同埃塞俄比国内相关领域展开了广泛的合作。中国万宝工程、中国路桥工程总公司、中国铁道工程总公司、中国航空基础进出口总公司、中地海外集团等利用自己在工程技术方面的优势参与埃塞俄比亚国内大规模基础建设的工程项目,在这方面中国企业取得了世界瞩目的成果。2009 年,埃塞俄比亚所有新建筑和 66.6% 的道路修复、升级和维修都是中国公司做的。当然,中国国有企业在埃塞俄比亚业务快速发展的同时也有一些结构性问题,比如,中国公司主导埃塞俄比亚的实际建设和重建工作等,特别是在基础设施方面,主要项目的资金来源仍为世界银行、欧洲委员会、非洲开发银行、石油输出国组织、国际货币基金组织和阿拉伯经济发展银行①,这导致在项目规划和成本计算等方面中方参与度不够,会在项目实行中受到一些限制。在这方面中国和埃塞俄比亚以及投资各方还有较大的商议空间。由中国路桥总公司承建的位于亚的斯亚贝巴的格特拉交汇路口立交桥工程(Gotera Intersection Flyoverbridge)在这方面作出了一种改革的尝试,该项目投资是中方直接承诺的 1 270 万美元,资金到位迅捷,工程进度很快②。这可以被视为目前中国在埃塞俄比亚项目投资中改变相对被动局面的一种尝试,在这项工程之后,中国国家进出口银行向埃塞俄比亚提供了 5 亿美元的贷款,用于包括公路和桥梁建设在内的 11 个开发项目,从而使原来中埃双方在经济合作中面临的结构性问题得到了很大程度的改善③。在此基础上,中埃双方又以合资企业的形式来加深合作:中国路桥工程总公司同埃塞合资成立了路桥建设公司(Road and Bridge Construction Company, RBC);中国北方工业总公司与拉利贝拉建筑公司合作组建的诺林—拉利贝拉工程建设公司股份有限公司 (The Norinco–Lalibela Engineering and Construction Share Company , Nori-La) 于 2004 年成立,目前正在亚的斯亚贝巴和奥罗米亚地区承建 8 座公路工程,投资 4 100 万美元,雇佣 500 名工人。自 2002 年起,发电量在 300 兆瓦的特克泽水电站开始兴建,该项目耗资 2.24 亿美元,不仅是中埃双方单项合作的最大项目,而且被认为是最大的中非合资企业联合项目,合资中中方参与企业有中国国家水利水电建设有限公司、葛洲坝集团,埃方参与企业为埃塞俄比亚电力公司。中国进出口银行提供 5 000 万美元 (年息为 1.75%) 作为工程队部分贷款④。由此可见,中方国有大型企业在走出对西方投资方的依赖、独立自主同埃塞俄比亚展开合作方面已经颇有成效。相关合作项目大多仍在进行中,已建成的基础设施在投入运营后的后继评估仍有待进一步统计公布,相信中埃双方会在后继运营中展开更深入的合作。

此外,中埃以及吉布提三方合作的埃塞—吉布提铁路建设因为关乎埃塞俄比亚的出海口规划与进出口贸易而尤其引起世人的瞩目。自厄立特里亚独立以来,埃塞俄比亚已经失去了所有的海岸线,这给两国之后各自的经济规划以及埃塞自身的利益诉求带来很多矛盾。世纪之交,两国曾围绕边境划界、民族问题爆发过几次冲突,但归根结底,这些冲突的背后都是经济诉求所导致的矛盾。应该看到,尽管两国最后达成了停火和解,但成为内陆国的形势

---

① Edson Ziso, *A Post State-Centric Analysis of China-Africa Relations*, This Palgrave Macmillan, 2018:121.

② Monika Thakur, “Building on Progress? Chinese Engagement in Ethiopia”, Occasional Paper, No 38, China in Africa Project, South African Institute for International Affairs, 2009, 6.

③ 同上。

④ 同上。

对于埃塞俄比亚的经济、进出口贸易的冲击很大,多年来其一直尝试寻找改变这种不利局面的突破口,其中包括同厄立特里亚关系正常化,利用该国港口,但为了避免贸易线路的单一,埃塞也一直在寻找另外可能的替代性外港。吉布提的地理位置正好占据了与埃塞相邻的另一段红海海岸线,而且从战略位置上说,吉布提扼住了红海进出的要道,显然是埃塞寻求替代出海口的绝佳选择。然而在东非以及红海沿岸诸国的微妙国际博弈中,这一方案受到诸多牵制,且交通设施的财力投入也远非埃吉两国所能独自承担。在这种局面下,中国的介入为解决这一难题提供了难得的机遇与方向。2014 年,这一项目取得了突破性的进展,中方在该项目中投入了大笔资金,同时作为该项目的扩展,亚的斯亚贝巴的轻轨铁路建设在中方的资金和技术协助下也有了较大的进展。87% 的轻轨建设与 80% 的埃塞—吉布提铁路建设在 2014 年进展顺利,而且已经完成,这为后来在 2016 年全线贯通、2018 年投入商业运营奠定了坚实的基础,为埃塞俄比亚打开了一条进出口贸易的交通要道。埃塞俄比亚这些工程成为中国与埃塞俄比亚之间合作的又一个突出事例[①]。在这一基础建设的保障下,2016 年 7 月 21 日,中、埃、吉三国政府宣布建设一个总计投入达 40 亿美元的天然气开发项目,其远景规划是在奥加登地区为进一步天然气开发做着准备[②]。这不仅极大地改善了埃塞俄比亚的经济与贸易的发展规划,为其寻找出海口打开了新的局面,而且对整个东非以及红海两岸地区的国际局势也形成了影响,在这一项目中,中国的立场与实力也更多角度地展现在世人面前。随着铁路的顺利开通运行,可以想见,这种合作模式及其良好的前景必将为中国与该区域的合作起到更大、更长远的作用。

三、埃塞俄比亚近年来新兴的鼓励外资领域的分析

在过去的几年中,埃塞俄比亚在亚的斯亚贝巴等地进行了大规模的技术开发区以及配套基础设施的建设,这给中国进一步的投资提供了良好的环境,而且在面对中国企业时,埃塞国内在同中方大型央企、国企广泛合作的同时,始终重视私营企业在其国内的投资和利益,试图全方位和中国的经济网络密切联系。2010 年,在埃塞俄比亚共有 348 家中国私有及国有企业拥有经营许可证,从事相关经济商贸活动,到 2013 年 12 月底,共有 701 家中国企业在埃塞俄比亚国内拥有经营许可证,并从事项目经营[③]。在这一巨大的涨幅中,除去已经提到的几家中国大型国有企业之外,大多数是中国私营企业,这也证明埃塞俄比亚政府对于不同类型企业的投资保障是切实有效的。

埃塞俄比亚 2010—2015 年五年《增长与转型规划》(GTP)由埃塞俄比亚议会于 2010 年 11 月批准,可以认为这是埃塞国内长期稳定政策的一个基石。2019 年已是埃塞俄比亚新政策推行,对外国投资的需求和开放的第九个年头,其政府承诺将在畜牧业、农产品加工业、制造业、建筑业、房地产业、旅游业等方面欢迎外部资本的进入。

在所有这些门类中除去上文所述和中国国有企业合作的方面之外,以畜产品、农产品加

① Jon Abbink, *A Decade of Ethiopia: Politics, Economy and Society,* 2004-2016, Koninklijke Brill NV, Leiden: The Netherlands, 2017:204.

② 同上。

③ Edson Ziso, *A Post State-Centric Analysis of China-Africa Relations*, This Palgrave Macmillan, 2018:118.

工出口为主轴的农业方面还具有未开发的巨大的投资机会[1]。以畜产品的生产能力为例，埃塞俄比亚国内牲畜常年存量大概有3 500万头牛、3 900万只绵羊和山羊、860万匹马和100万只骆驼，其牲畜总数值据非洲第一、世界第九。在此基础之上，其国内可年产兽皮270万张、绵羊皮810万张、山羊皮750万张[2]。在这一领域有一个中埃合作得很好的例子：中非海外皮革公司（China-Africa Overseas Leather Products S.C.）在中国新乡工藤达明与明良皮革有限公司（Xinxiang Kudroda and Mingliang Leather Co. Ltd.）和中非发展基金（CAD Fund）的出资合作下在埃塞俄比亚投资2 700万美元建立了一家工厂[3]，这是中国皮鞋制造业目前在埃塞俄比亚广泛进行投资尝试的一个缩影。埃塞政府认为这种外资的引入对于引起行业内部的良性竞争与产业重组具有促进作用，因而采取了鼓励的措施，这也和之前所说的埃塞政府平等对待私营企业外资在国内的表态相一致。对于中国皮革行业来说，这种投资尝试也符合目前国内有关"走出去"大战略的部署，使中国企业投身于国际竞争中，从而做大做强。正如格布列（Gebre-Egziabher）所说："认为竞争并不总是会取代竞争对手，但正如古典经济学告诉我们的，竞争可以增强那些处于竞争环境中的公司的生产率。"[4]

而在农产品的生产及贸易方面，据埃塞俄比亚政府2019年7月28日消息："在刚刚结束的埃塞俄比亚财政年度中，埃塞俄比亚从咖啡和油籽出口中获得的收入超过12亿美元。据隶属于国家的Fana广播公司(FBC)上周六报道，这些收入来自咖啡、绿豆、白芸豆、芝麻和大豆的出口。大量的出口收入来自咖啡的出口。埃塞俄比亚是世界第七大咖啡生产国，也是非洲最大的咖啡生产国、非洲最大的阿拉比卡咖啡生产国之一，咖啡生产被称为该国农业主导经济的支柱。"[5]其每年生产的咖啡除国内消费外，仍有一半供出口，埃塞俄比亚咖啡的主要市场是欧盟（约占出口的一半）、东亚（约四分之一）和北美[6]。从这一出口市场的配比份额中可以看出东亚地区占有比重不低，而中国近年来随着消费生活观念的变化，咖啡的消费量一直呈稳步增长趋势，双方在这一方面的经贸往来仍有较大的合作空间。不过，尽管出口量很大，但目前埃塞俄比亚国内的咖啡种植与生产仍然处于比较粗放的方式，传统的生产方式从古至今没有太大的改变，几乎所有的工作，如耕作和干燥，仍然是手工完成的。咖啡种植总面积估计约为4 000平方千米，由于咖啡农场的分散性质，具体面积和地区种植情况尚不清楚。但为了鼓励国内咖啡产业链的进一步发展，埃塞政府出台了一系列扶持政策，在这一良好形势下，"埃塞俄比亚最近还公布了一项新的倡议，要在今后5年内将目前每年近60万吨的咖啡产量提高到180万吨，而据埃塞俄比亚咖啡和茶叶管理局(ECTA)称，中国市场有望成为该国咖啡出口的主要目的地。"[7]2019年4月，中埃两国签署了《中国咖啡出口谅解备忘录》，深化双边贸易合作。据埃方消息称："随着中国年轻人对咖啡的需求不断

---

① Edson Ziso, *A Post State-Centric Analysis of China-Africa Relations*, This Palgrave Macmillan, 2018：117.

② Andualem Sisay Gessesse, "Better Local Price Challenges Ethiopia's Shoesexport", http://www.newbusinessethiopia.com/index.php/manufacturing/item/78-better-local-price-challenges-ethiopia-s-shoes-export.

③ Desalegn Sisay, "Ethiopia Gets a US$27 m Chinese Leather Factory",[2010-11-25], http://www.afrik-news.com/article18486.html.

④ Tegegne Gebre-Egziabher, "The Developmental Impact of Asian Driverson Ethiopia with Emphasis on Small-scale Footwear Producers", The World Economy, 2009：1.

⑤ 埃塞俄比亚沃尔塔信息中心：http://www.waltainfo.com/index.php/news/detail/49359.

⑥ Pascal Belda, Ethiopia, MTH Multimedia S.L., 2006：77.

⑦ 埃塞俄比亚沃尔塔信息中心：http://www.waltainfo.com/index.php/news/detail/49359.

增长，打入新兴咖啡市场也越来越被视为埃塞俄比亚咖啡生产商和出口商的一项主要任务。”

近年来，中国市场对埃塞俄比亚芝麻生产的兴趣日益浓厚。芝麻被认为是埃塞俄比亚仅次于咖啡的主要出口商品之一。埃塞俄比亚豆类、油籽和香料加工出口协会主席海尔·贝赫对新华社说，“目前，埃塞俄比亚向中国出口的芝麻占这个东非国家向全球市场出口芝麻总量的近70%。中国已经是这个东非国家的主要出口目的地。据埃塞俄比亚贸易部统计，在埃塞俄比亚2017—2018财年，埃塞俄比亚向中国出口了2.45亿美元的商品。”[①] 芝麻的出口针对中国市场的意向性较强，资料显示中国是芝麻使用量最大的国家，因而需要投资方与相关政府职能部门对市场导向的宣传和引导工作，同时需要对现有的生产方式、收购渠道以及出口代理等诸多产业环节优化重组，而这仍然离不开从中央到地方各级政府的支持，因而同咖啡贸易相比，芝麻产业对埃塞俄比亚国内的政治形势依附性更强。2015年中国开发银行为参与埃塞俄比亚芝麻产业的农业企业贷款2 500万美元，企业可以通过生产和销售芝麻的利润来偿付相关金融和其他服务的费用，贷款有效促进了中埃双方在芝麻产业上的合作，也加深了中国企业在埃塞国内芝麻生产收购出口产业链上的参与程度。

相对于国有企业所进行的大型投资而言，在埃塞俄比亚国内的农产品相关产业上的投资相对投入要求较小，而且在如上所述的一些特定农产品的产业链比较清晰，出口市场预期也比较明确，而在这些方面深入当地原材料的生产市场可以更深度地和当地社会的经济体系乃至政治文化展开合作，因而笔者认为这方面的投资合作不仅对于埃塞的经济发展具有重要意义，而且对于中国的政治经济利益来说也是具有战略意义的。因而在这和前文所述的埃塞国内农业的基本情况及其发展趋势是符合的。

结论

当前埃塞俄比亚的发展趋势是在整个非洲社会政治经济转型大背景下的一个优秀的范例，结合其国内目前的发展形势可以看出埃塞在引入外资上的态度是积极的，这不仅表现在相关鼓励性政策的制定上，而且表现在对于外国国有企业与私人企业的同等重视上。

埃塞俄比亚目前已是中国在非洲最重要的战略合作伙伴之一，仅在经济领域双方共同运作的项目的深度和广度都是空前的，而且在很多方面都起到了示范作用。西方企业将埃塞俄比亚视为原材料提供地，配合当地廉价劳动力搞单纯的出口导向型的产品加工业。中国则制定了更加长远的战略目标，以合资、合作的理念进入埃塞国内的经济体系中，同其整个国民经济发生更密切的联系。笔者认为在埃塞俄比亚当前国内政治经济形势下，外资的投资方向可以从参与埃塞国内经济建设、参与调整产业布局入手，从而在整个产业链条上同埃塞俄比亚国内的企业或相关经济部门展开合作，从而为企业在当地打开市场、建立商业网络创造可能。这种方式不仅将使中埃双方都能获益，避免同既有国际经济格局下由西方主导的全球贸易体系进行不必要的竞争，而且能真正在埃塞国内潜在的巨大市场上站稳脚跟。从目前中国国有大型企业在基础设施建设、技术转让、产能转移等方面在埃塞俄比亚所开展的业务情况可以看出这一方向大致是符合实际情况的，而且为中埃的合作奠定了一个良好

① 埃塞俄比亚沃尔塔信息中心：http://www.waltainfo.com/index.php/news/detail/49359.

的基调。中国的私营企业进入埃塞国内不晚,目前也可以在这一思路下考虑投资的方式和方向,本文仅就埃塞国内农产品产业链中几个市场化程度较高的门类进行了分析,可以看出中国私营企业在当地还是展开了一定程度的合作的,而且投资前景比较乐观,但还可以有更大的发展空间。

中埃的经济交往是当下国际交往中一个具有特色又十分生动鲜活的例子,未来的发展值得我们进行更深入的思考和研究。

The Question of Linguistic Identity and the Modern Ethiopian State: Can the State Justifiably Follow a Hands-off Approach towards Linguistic Issues?

Getahun Dana①

Abstract: Ethiopia has over the years faced several social, economic and political challenges. There are many divisive issues that pose challenge to the continued existence of the state. Linguistic issues have been one of the most divisive issues that the country faced over the past fifty years. There are two irreconcilable claims entertained by scholars with regard to the question of whether the country's political structure should run along linguistic lines. On the one hand, there are those who argue that since language is such a divisive issue, the governing structure of the public sphere should not be informed by linguistic issues. The government, in other words, should treat language as a private matter on a par with religion. On the other hand, there are those writers who reject this claim on the ground that the state cannot help supporting one or more languages to become widely spoken language/languages if it is to function well. So, they argue that the state should provide the same support for the other languages that are not going to be selected to function as national language/languages. The idea is that since the well-functioning of the state depends, partly on, the choice that it makes to make one or more languages of the land the national ones, it cannot justifiably withhold support from other languages that are not going to be candidates for the choice for one reason or another. In short, they insist that the state's structure can justifiably run along ethnic lines and linguistic issue can inform the functioning of the state. I argue in this paper that this later view can be rationally defended.

Keywords: Language; Identity; Multi-ethnic State; National Language

1 Introduction

In multi-ethnic societies where people are divided, among others, along ethnic lines the

① Lecturer and PhD Student at the Department of Philosophy, Addis Ababa University.

question of how the state should treat ethnicity has been one of the most controversial issues. African politicians also took the question of how the societies at large treat ethnicity as perplexing and critical[①]. Many African writers have argued that since ethnicity is just one of the several identities that matter to people, it should not be taken as one's primary identity[②]. But, it is also to be noted that disregard to matters of ethnicity will also get us nowhere. This is because although various measures have been taken by African governments to reduce ethnic tensions, it shows no sign of abating[③].

As a multi-ethnic state, the question of how should the state treat ethnicity is of crucial importance to Ethiopia as well. Many writers agree that the adoption of the 1995 constitution by the Ethiopian state marks a major break with the past in taking ethnicity as the most important factor in dealing with its citizens. Article 39 of the constitution provides the right to self-government to "nations, nationalities and peoples" of the state. By taking ethnicity as its most important governing principle, the internal boundary of the state was drawn along ethnic lines. As a result, nine regions and two special administrative zones were created. The central question that I will be dealing with in this study is whether the Ethiopian government was morally wrong in taking ethnicity as the most important organizing factor of the state?

Since the problem in question is the challenge that all multi-ethnic societies throughout the world are facing, it is of crucial importance to explore how the dominant political tradition dealt with this problem. The traditional liberals' approach towards ethnicity is to regard it as a private matter on a par with religion[④]. This means the state should neither support nor discriminate against any ethnic group. It should simply respond with indifference or "benign neglect"[⑤].

The assumption is that if the universal civil and political rights of individuals are respected, other rights such as the rights of vulnerable communities will necessarily be respected without supplementing it with special group rights for minorities[⑥]. But this view has received a wide range of criticisms from liberal nationalists such as Will Kymlicka who argued for supplementing those universal rights with special rights for vulnerable groups[⑦]. In this study, I shall attempt to defend Kymlicka's view by providing evidence from the Ethiopian federal experience.

The multi-national state that I will be referring to in this study is one that arose through the incorporation of previously self-governing groups into the larger state. In this sense, I will take Ethiopia as a multi-national state. The question is, given such diversity, can the state be neutral towards the ethnic and cultural differences of its citizens? I shall argue, following Kymlicka and

① Alemante G. Sellassie, "Ethnic Identity and Constitutional Design for Africa", Standford Journal of International Law, 1992, 29(1):5.

② Yonatan T. Fessha, "The Original Sin of Ethiopian Federalism", Ethnopolitics, 2017, 16(3):236.

③ Jon Abbink, "Ethnic-based federalism and Ethnicity in Ethiopia: Reassessing the Experiment after 20 Years", Journal of Eastern African Studies, 2011, 5(4):608-9.

④ Will Kymlicka, Multicultural Citizenship: A Liberal Theory of Minority Rights.New York: Clarendon Press, 1995:107.

⑤ Ibid, 2-3.

⑥ Ibid, 2.

⑦ Ibid, 5.

supporting it with the Ethiopian federal experience for nearly three decades, that there cannot be "strict separation of state and ethnicity"[①] and the state can legitimately take the ethnic identity of citizens as informing the governing structure of the state.

But, it is one thing to say that the state should not disregard ethnicity and it is quite another to say that the state should take ethnicity as the most important factor in dealing with its citizens as is the case with the current Ethiopian state. The problem is that we are a kind of being to whom different things matter. One may take his ethnic identity as the most important factor for his identity whereas some other person may take his religious identity as primary for him. Because of this reason, some writers argue that the state should not act paternalistically on its citizens' behalf and make just one of the many identities that an individual associate himself with as primary[②]. Without denying this point, I shall insist throughout the paper that the Ethiopian state can take ethnicity as the most important organizing principle of the state. The question then is, can this warrant drawing the internal boundary of the state along ethnic lines? I shall also argue that there are compelling reasons to do so.

Organization of the Study

The study has four parts. In the first part, I will introduce the main issue to be discussed. In the second part, I shall discuss the traditional liberal's approach towards ethnicity and reject it. In the third part, I shall discuss the Ethiopian federal experience. Here, I shall show how this experience disproves the myth of ethnocultural neutrality. In the fourth part, I shall conclude with some points to be taken for further research.

Methodology of the Study

The study is mainly based on the readings of secondary literature such as books, book chapters, journal articles and proceeding. But in few occasions I will also try to substantiate my claims with my personal observations.

2 The Liberals Approach towards Ethnicity

The dominant liberal tradition's approach towards ethnicity treats the individual human being as the ultimate unit of moral concern[③]. This means that the individual's ethnic and cultural identities, among others, are irrelevant for the functioning of the government and thus should be left for the individuals to exercise them in their private sphere. Ethnicity, liberals insist, should be treated as a private matter on a par with religion[④].

For them, citizens are fundamentally free to promote their cultural attachments and the

① Will Kymlicka, Multicultural Citizenship: A Liberal Theory of Minority Rights.New York: Clarendon Press, 1995:7.

② Yonatan T. Fessha, "The Original Sin of Ethiopian Federalism", Ethnopolitics,2017,16(3):236.

③ Chandran Kukathas, "Are There Any Cultural Rights?", Political Theory,1992,20(1):107.

④ Will Kymlicka, Contemporary Political Philosophy.New York: Oxford University Press, 2002:343.

responsibility of the state towards citizens' cultural attachments is that it "does not oppose the freedom of people to express their particular cultural attachments, but nor does it nurture such expression"①. Here, the state's obligation towards citizens' culture is merely a negative one in the sense that is should not discriminate against any group. Here, citizens "are free to maintain whatever part of their ethnic heritage or identity they wish, consistent with the idea of others"②. This again means that they cannot have a reasonable expectation from the "public agencies to attach legal identities or disabilities to cultural membership or ethnic identity"③. This "strict separation of state and ethnicity"④, as Kymlicka calls it, "precludes any legal or governmental recognition of ethnic groups, or any use of ethnic criteria in the distribution of rights, resources, and duties."⑤

The idea is that as far the citizens' universal civil and political rights such as the right to association and assembly are protected, members of a given ethnic group can ensure their continued existence as distinct society without any need for supplementing these rights with special group rights for vulnerable groups⑥. This means vulnerable groups can "visibly and proudly"⑦ affirm their identities both in public and private spheres without fear of discrimination if these rights are respected. Claud also writes, the general tendency of the postwar movements for the promotion of human rights has been to subsume the problem of national minorities under the broader problem of ensuring basic individual rights to all human beings, without reference to membership in ethnic groups. The leading assumption has been that members of national minorities do not need, are not entitled to, or cannot be granted rights of a special character. The doctrine of human rights has been put forward as a substitute for the concept of minority rights, with the strong implication that minorities whose members enjoy individual equality of treatment cannot legitimately demand facilities for the maintenance of their ethnic particularism⑧.

But can the state be neutral towards ethnicity? I shall argue in the following section that formal equality of treatment does not guarantee the continued existence of vulnerable groups. I shall first show how an "ethnically neutral state" is a metaphysical absurdity, at its best.

2.1 The Myth of the Linguistically and Culturally Neutral State

As Kymlicka argues, the idea of a culturally neutral state is a myth because the state cannot help lending support for the culture from which it arose. It does so when, for example, it chooses the national symbol and national holidays⑨. It cannot also help lending support to the dominant

① Will Kymlicka, Multicultural Citizenship: A Liberal Theory of Minority Rights.New York: Clarendon Press, 1995:3.

② Ibid, 3-4.

③ Ibid, 4.

④ Ibid, 4.

⑤ Ibid, 4.

⑥ Ibid, 2.

⑦ Will Kymlicka, Multicultural Odysseys. New York: Oxford University Press, 2007:72.

⑧ Inis Claud, National Minorities: An International Problem. Cambridge, Mass: Harvard University Press, 1955:211.

⑨ Will Kymlicka, Contemporary Political Philosophy. New York: Oxford University Press, 2002:111.

language when it decides to make it the national one that every citizen speaks irrespective of their ethnic differences and also the language of schooling. One of the conditions required to ensure the continuation of a language to the next generation is the making of that language the language of schooling and the language of communication in its various institutions①. The well-functioning of any modern state, as will be discussed later on, partly depends on the state's making such choices. So, when it does this, it inevitably lends support for the language in question to continue as a living and developing one. The problem here is that the state's inevitable bias in favor of the dominant language and culture puts a subtle assimilative pressure on ethnic minorities. One area that proves this is the *de facto* language requirement for employment.

As Kymlicka rightly notes, the modern states with their vibrant economies require, among other things, mastery of the language of the dominant group②. Here, I will be focusing on the *de facto* language of requirements of mainstream societies in Ethiopia. By mainstream society, I am referring to mega cities where different ethnic groups live together such as Addis Ababa. I shall argue that, the Ethiopian state has provided Amharic the most important form of support that it needs to continue as a living and developing language when it made it the country's working language. This inevitable bias in favor of the dominant language tends to threaten the development of other languages for the reasons that will be mentioned later on. The question thus is, what should the state do to ameliorate the effects of its inevitable bias in favor of the dominant language?

The *de facto* language requirement of the mainstream society puts a subtle assimilative pressure on ethnic minorities who have migrated to citizens for livelihood purpose. This is because if members of ethnic minorities do not have mastery of the majority language, they will have limited economic opportunity, and they cannot easily access the culture of the mainstream society③. Since national minorities do not in most cases have mastery of the national language, and since the de facto language requirement for employment in government institutions is having a mastery of the language in question, minorities will be forced into learning the language so as to enlarge their chance of employment often at the cost of their local language. That is, even though they are not discriminated against on ground of their ethnic identity, the *de facto* language requirement puts a subtle assimilative pressure on them.

Here, I am not arguing against the learning of the majority language and culture by ethnic minorities as such. In fact, they should in some sense. Otherwise, they will be politically marginalized④. This is also because the *de facto* language requirement for active political participation is also the mastery of the language of the culturally dominant group⑤. Research findings show that ethnic minorities who are found in a geographically remote area tend to preserve their cultures

① Will Kymlicka, Contemporary Political Philosophy.New York: Oxford University Press, 2002:343.

② Ibid, 76-77.

③ Will Kymlicka, Allen Patten, "Language Rights and Political Theory", Annual Review of Applied Linguistics,2003,23(3): 13.

④ Ibid, 13.

⑤ Will Kymlicka, Contemporary Political Philosophy.New York: Oxford University Press, 2002: 346.

and identity without any problem①. But, as long as they are part and parcel of the larger state, the preservation of their cultural identity comes only at the cost of political and social marginalization.

The other moral problem here is, when the state makes a language the national one, it by the very same act puts the speakers of the language in privileged position as far as, among others, their chance of employment is concerned. Since the government bureaucracy and institutions require, among other things, fluency in the working language, those who speak the language with fluency are the ones who are going to meet the *de facto* language requirement. But, members of ethnic minorities who do not speak the language in question in the same level of fluency with members of the majority ethnic group, are not likely to compete equally, other things being equal, with the speakers of the language. Abraham Demoze writes:

"As soon as you designate one language the official/national language, you thereby give a major competitive advantage...to the native speaker of that language. You also, at the same time and by the very same act, disenfranchise the speakers of all other language in the nation. You eliminate or heavily constrain their access to education, to employment, to information in general and to power and prestige in many forms." ②

Arguably, the members of the Amhara , one of the two largest ethnic groups, are one of the most mobile groups in Ethiopia in the sense that they have moved to other regions in greater number than any other ethnic groups③. Part of the reason for this is their mastery of the *de facto* language requirement in many parts of the country. Just by virtue of being Amharic speakers they have a comparative advantage over non-Amharic speakers in securing job.

Here, I am not categorically denying the fact that some members of the dominant linguistic communities are also facing the threat of assimilation from other linguistic groups. As some parents recently testified, the children of the Amhara ethnic groups who were born and raised up in the Oromia region are required to learn in Afaan Oromo, at the cost of their parents' language. They may speak their parents' language, but only as their second language. In this limited sense, one can say that the continued development of Amharic as a living and developing language has already faced a challenge by the ethnic-based structure of the state. Thus, one may conclude that , things remaining constant, such parents cannot realistically hope to ensure the continued existence of their languages into the future in regions where they form ethnic minority.

What makes a language a living and developing one is its transmittability from one generation to the other and that again depends on the size of the speakers. If the language of ethnic minority is not transmitted into the future, its chance to go extinct its greater than the language of ethnic majority. Those who come to the city often prefer to speak Amharic at the cost of their local

---

① Will Kymlicka, Contemporary Political Philosophy.New York: Oxford University Press, 2002:343.

② Abrham Demoze, "Language Identity and Peace in Ethiopia and the Horn", Proceedings of the 4th International Conference on the Horn of Africa. New York: Center for the Study of the Horn of Africa.

③ This assertion is based on my personal observation in different parts of the country.

languages, and teach their children Amharic so that they can easily meet the requirements of the mainstream society. Since many children of ethnic minorities are coming to the mainstream society so as to make their living there and since they often tend not to go back to their "historic homeland" so as to resettle there, there is little or no chance of transmitting their language to their children. And we should not forget the fact that the issue of assimilation is multi-generational and thus it may not happen within a single generation of migrants.

Members of ethnic majorities do not face such challenge. They often take the development of their language for granted, and fail to see that ethnic minorities are facing a subtle assimilative pressure emanating from the requirements of the mainstream society.

2.2 The Need for One or More National Languages

One of the main reasons why there cannot be a culturally and linguistically neutral state emanates from the fact that a multi-ethnic state needs one or more national languages. Unless the state makes one or more languages the languages of public serves that every citizen speaks irrespective of their ethnic differences, obviously government employees among others will not "be able to communicate effectively with one another"①. Worse still, "[I]f citizens cannot understand each other, or if they communicate only with their co-linguists, then democratic politics will be compromised."②

The Ethiopian federal experience for nearly three decades proves this fact. After power decentralization started to take root in Ethiopia, different ethnic groups have started to use their self-government right to a limited extent. This meant that they started to exercise an important control on crucial issues that affect their lives. One such issue is language. So, several ethnic minorities have made their language the language of schooling. But the problem is that in the last nearly three decades due emphasis have not been given for teaching the language of wider communication. Because of this, we have reached to the point where no communication is possible across ethnic groups③. Thus, many scholars insist that if we have to continue as a multi-ethnic state, we have to have one or more language of wider communication to curb the communication breakdown that we are facing. The problem here is if we have to build one common nation together, as Adeno suggests, we need to engage in shared deliberations which is impossible "without the dominant group coercively imposing a single language on all citizens"④. But inevitably, this threatens linguistic diversity in a multiethnic country such as Ethiopia. This again requires some positive measures by the state to mitigate the effect that this decision has on vulnerable communi-

① Will Kymlicka, Allen Patten, "Language Rights and Political Theory", Annual Review of Applied Linguistics,2003,23(3): 10.

② Ibid, 13.

③ In the University where I am teaching, I have observed in numerous occasions communication breakdown among different ethnic groups because of the fact that members of each group speaks only his or her language.

④ Addis Adeno, "Human Diversity and the Limits of Toleration", in Ethnicity and Group Rights, ed. Ian Shapiro, Will Kymlicka. New York: New York UP, 1997:117-120.

ties. But, the sharing of common institutions and boundary alone cannot explain our membership in a given bounded political community. If we are not able to communicate with each other due to the absence of one or more widely spoken languages, it is very difficult to take the people in question as composing a nation.

As Miller notes "the people who compose a nation must believe that there is something distinctive about themselves that marks them off from other nations, over and above the fact of sharing common institutions"①. Without disagreeing with Miller on this particular point, I would add that the people who compose a multi-ethnic state should have "something distinctive about themselves"② that goes above and beyond sharing a common boundary and common institutions. The demand for this "distinctive something" is, it seems to me that, greater in Africa than elsewhere in the world because of the fact that the boundaries of Africans states were arbitrarily drawn by the former colonial masters. Today we take, by and large, these boundaries for granted. But, unfortunately we fail to see the need for one or more languages that every citizen irrespective of their ethnic differences speaks and takes it as "theirs" in some sense. Now, the question is, what should the state do to ensure the continued existence of vulnerable communities into the future?

2.3 The Right to Self-government

The modern state of Ethiopia was formed through the incorporation of many previously self-governing groups into the larger society. Before their incorporation into larger state, just by virtue of being an institutionally complete society, each group was building its own nations. After the forcible incorporation of these groups into the central government, they faced the threat of assimilation. Before the official adoption of federal state structure, the Ethiopian successive regimes tried to diffuse a common national identity to its diverse ethnic groups informed by a single language, culture and religion③. Such assimilative pressure is very often, part of the reason for the national minorities to seek their hitherto self-governing status④. Taking these things into account, one may conclude that the state has the obligation to protect their right to self-government. Since they were not facing a threat of assimilation when they were living alone in their own historical places, and since they have not agreed to join the greater state, the burden of ameliorating the assimilative pressure of the mainstream society lies in the state that they are part of.

It is clear that before their incorporation into the larger state, ethnic minorities were developing their respective languages as the living and developing ones for the simple reason that they were not competing culturally and linguistically, so to say, with any other group. In those "old good days" the development of their languages as the living and developing ones was just taken for granted as now is the case with the dominant language. They were using their languages and

① Will Kymlicka, Multicultural Citizenship: A Liberal Theory of Minority Rights.New York: Clarendon Press, 1995:30.

② Ibid, 30.

③ Yonatan T. Fessha, "The Original Sin of Ethiopian Federalism", Ethnopolitics,2017,16(3):234.

④ Will Kymlicka, Contemporary Political Philosophy.New York: Oxford University Press, 2002: 50.

its associated traditions not only as private languages, but also as the language of the traditional court systems and other institutions. Now that they have become part and parcel of a larger society, they are facing the problem of making their language the public language. But since they have not faced this problem at will, the burden of making the language so becomes partly the responsibility of the larger state.

As research findings show, one of the reasons why language communities maintain their distinct existence is because of their geographical isolation from the larger society①. Here, I am not arguing against linguistic integration as succ. As Kymlicka notes, "[I]f taking language preservation seriously means adopting policies that prevent the spread of literacy, block access to mainstream society and economy, then this seems so high a price to pay"②. If minorities are constantly isolated from the mainstream society in the name of preserving their distinct cultural identity, this tends to marginalize minorities from major economic, academic and political institution③.

As argued earlier on, when the state lends support for the dominant group by making the language the language of schooling and the national one, it has already provided the group one of the most important form of support it needs to sustain its distinct existence into the future. In effect, the group's nation-building process goes unabated due partly to the state's inevitable bias in favor of it. Therefore, to ameliorate its inevitable bias in favor of the dominant cultural group, the state needs to provide support for the "societal cultures" of national minorities. This can best be done when the state respects their right to self-government in their historical place. This means that internal boundaries can be drawn so that ethnic minorities who form majority in their locality can have important control on crucial issues that affect their lives. Since this culture is based on shared language and it is territorially concentrated, "encompassing both public and private spheres"④, its sustained existence into the future will be ensured. The complaints that many ethnic minorities have against the majority is not that their right to private use of language is being violated by the majority. Rather, their complaint is that the continued insistence of the majority to see the minority's language not as the language of institutions but as a private language negatively affects the development of their language and plays upon self-esteem. If a language is used across a full range of activities including religious, educational, recreational and economic life, "encompassing both public and private spheres", its continued existence as a living and developing language will be guaranteed. This is precisely why those ethnic minorities who are found in a geographically isolated area have a greater chance of preserving their cultural and linguistic identity than those who have become part and parcel of the mainstream society. Since they have not voluntarily ceded their hitherto self-governing status, their demand to regain this status cannot be dismissed as illegitimate demand. But since secession is not a viable option, this demand should be

① Will Kymlicka, Allen Patten, "Language Rights and Political Theory", Annual Review of Applied Linguistics,2003,23(3):15.

② Ibid, 15-16.

③ Will Kymlicka, Contemporary Political Philosophy.New York: Oxford University Press, 2002):34.

④ Will Kymlicka, Multicultural Citizenship: A Liberal Theory of Minority Rights.New York: Clarendon Press, 1995):76.

respected since they are not demanding anything else than their hitherto existing self-government rule. Thus, if one argues against this demand, the burden of proof lies in him; he has to provide a compelling reason for why this demand should be treated as illegitimate demand.

3 The Ethiopian Federal Experience: State–ethnicity Relations

Taking the ethnic-based federal structure that divided administrative units along ethnic lines into account, one may argue that the claim that there is still an assimilative pressure that threatens the development of disadvantaged languages is not convincing on the ground that they have now important control over their own affairs. The idea is that since this federal structure put in place after the adoption of the constitution of the Federal Democratic Republic of Ethiopian in 1995 grants the right to self-government to regions, zones and Woredas and since this partly means that they have now an important control on crucial issues that affect their lives, the claim that Amharic still poses a threat to the development of other languages cannot be consistently maintained. Article 5 of the constitution of the Federal Democratic Republic of Ethiopia allows the states to determine their respective working languages. Taking advantage of this, five out of the nine regions opted for their respective local languages as the language of government bureaucracy while the rest chose Amharic as their medium of communication for their ethnically diverse people[①]. Taking this into account, one may argue that the claim that there is still an ongoing assimilative pressure emanating from the mainstream society does not hold water since regions have chosen their own respective working languages. And this can help to ameliorate the government's inevitable bias in favor of the dominant group. But this does not seem to be quite right to me. No doubt the structure has played a significant role in ameliorating the stat's inevitable bias in favor of the dominant language. But, we cannot legitimately argue that the threat of assimilation has gone for good for the reasons mentioned above. We should also take into account the fact that although regions, zones and Woredas have important control over their own language, inter-regional, inter-zonal, and inter-Woredas communication take place using Amharic as the medium of communication. Thus, we cannot reasonably deny the state's inevitable bias in favor of the dominant language.

No one in his sane mind argues that state-ethnicity separation is a viable solution to solve Ethiopian political problems. This is partly because the ethno-nationalist questions have been one of the most dominant political question ever since the Ethiopian students movement during the 1970. Since the successive Ethiopian regimes tried to diffuse a common national identity to its diverse ethnic groups influenced by "the image, language, and culture of a single ethnic group"[②], many ethno-nationalist groups took this move as a threat to their continued existence as distinct societies. In Ethiopia as it is the case elsewhere in the world, the previous Ethiopian regimes mis-

---

① Yonatan T. Fessha, "The Original Sin of Ethiopian Federalism", Ethnopolitics,2017,16(3):235.

② Ibid, 234.

judged the durability of ethnic sentiments. They thought that, when suppressed ruthlessly, ethnic groups would gradually lose their ethnic sentiments. But that was not often the case. When the government of Haile Sellassie tried to forcibly suppress the "relatively pacific expression of Oromo identity as the Mecha and Tulema Self-help association"[①], the ethnic sentiments have not diminished among the Oromo as the result. Many writers thus agree that disregard to matters of ethnicity is not a viable option to Ethiopia.

But can this give us a ground for taking ethnicity as the most important factor in dealing with citizens. We cannot deny the fact that we are beings to whom different things matter[②]. So, one may regard his religious or cultural attachments, not his ethnic identity, as primary to the kind of being that he or she is. Thus, one may argue that since individuals may take different things as essential to their identity, the state should not make one of them, i.e., ethnicity, as the most organizing principle of the state as it is the case with Ethiopia. But, I maintain on the contrary that, a multi-ethnic state such as Ethiopia can legitimately take ethnicity as a sole important factor influencing its governing principle for the following reasons. First, although one may take his religious identity as essential to what he takes himself to be and demand the state to make his religion the national one that represents the state as a whole, the state cannot justifiably meet this demand. This is because, for one thing, since there may be members of other religions making the same claim, and since the state can by and large be neutral as far as the religious differences of its citizens are concerned, and since endorsing a particular religion as the national one often leads to bloodshed, such demands cannot be entertained. But, as mentioned earlier on, the state cannot be neutral towards culture and ethnicity. So, the state can legitimately be concerned on the question of how it can reduce its inevitable bias in favor of the dominant language and its associated culture.

The other important factor for taking culture as the most important organizing principle is the fact that, as Kymlicka notes, culture provides a context of choice[③]. The dominant liberal tradition, by taking individuals as mere right bearers, failed to see that meaningful choice requires a secure cultural context- a choice enabling conditions. But here I am not saying that the state can concern itself with any culture that an individual associate himself with. Instead, I am concerned with what Kymlicka calls a "societal culture":

That is, a culture which provides its members with meaningful ways of life across the full range of human activities, including social, educational, religious, recreational, and economic life, encompassing both public and private spheres. These cultures tend to be territorially concentrated and based on a shared language...and they involve not just shared memories or values, but also common institutions and practices[④].

---

① Bahru Zewde, Society, State and History. Addis Ababa: Addis Ababa University Press, 2008:87.

② Charles Taylor, Philosophy and the Human Sciences: Philosophical Papers.Vol.2.New York: Cambridge University Press, 1985:2.

③ Will Kymlicka, Multicultural Citizenship: A Liberal Theory of Minority Rights.New York: Clarendon Press, 1995:76.

④ Ibid,76.

It is if and only when a group's right to self-government is respected that the members can develop their "societal cultures" which is territorially concentrated and is based on a common language. For the reasons mentioned earlier on, the development of this culture will significantly be constrained in the mainstream society where vulnerable groups contact with the dominant cultural group. Since the culture in question encompasses both public and private sphere, its sustained existence is ensured. Unless the minorities' cultures are embedded in the state's institutions, they cannot last long. As Kymlicka, contends: "Given the enormous significance of social institutions in our lives, and in determining our options, any culture which is not a societal culture will be reduced to ever-increasing marginalization."① His argument in favor of building societal culture for cultural groups allows for national minorities to develop their own culture in the place where they constitute ethnic majority. But when members of these groups come to cities to permanently live there for whatever reason, they will inevitably be immersed in "the societal culture" of the dominant group.

Many writers thus agree that we cannot afford to ignore ethnicity as this point in time. But they reject the type of Ethiopian federalism that runs along ethnic lines as divisive and threat to the continued existence of the state and instead suggest "provincial federalism"② as the way out. They argue that the drawing of the internal boundary along ethnic lines may create a sense of "homeland" and exclude "non-members". Part of the reason for their rejection of multi-national federation is the concern that it may further the secessionist cause. They also mention that "provincial federation" allows the right to self-determination of ethnic groups and also creates a common national identity. The idea is that since ethnic-federalism(multi-national federation) as it the case with Ethiopia takes ethnicity as the primordial identity, it significantly negatively affects people's sense of belongingness to the larger state. In effect, they are arguing against what can be called "hyphenated citizenship"③ such as Amhara Ethiopian and Oromo Ethiopian. Under the multi-national federation model that Ethiopia has been following for well over two decades, such identification are not mutually exclusionary goals.

The proponents of "provincial federation" argue for the division of large states such as Oromia and Amhara into smaller administrative units such as Wolaga, Jima, Arsi, Gojam, Gondar, Wollo, etc④. The advantage of such division, they insist, is that the units exercise their right to self-determination and also can cooperatively engage with the other provinces with homogeneous population. This arrangement, they insist, will necessarily ensure their continued existence as distinct societies and reduces the threat of secession to a significant degree. The problem the proponents of "provincialism" have not paid due attention to though is the fact that this arrangement may work well for states with both large population and large territory, but it is very dangerous for

① Will Kymlicka, Multicultural Citizenship: A Liberal Theory of Minority Rights.New York: Clarendon Press, 1995:80.

② Yonatan T. Fessha, "The Original Sin of Ethiopian Federalism", Ethnopolitics,2017,16(3):240.

③ Christian Joppke, "Multicultural Citizenship", in Handbook of Citizenship, ed. Engin Flesin and Bryan S Turner.London: SAGE publications Ltd, 2002:245.

④ Yonatan T. Fessha, "The Original Sin of Ethiopian Federalism", Ethnopolitics,2017,16(3):240.

ethnic minorities that are concentrated on a limited territory.

Since the underlying assumption behind the idea of "provincialism" is the rejection of the drawing of boundary along ethnic lines, while the arrangement allows for the formation of several states with homogeneous population for states with large size and territory, it endorses the lumping together of various ethnic minorities into one province. Thus, the arrangement does not help ethnic minorities exercise self-administration in a meaningful way. This is because "self-administration" worthy of the name ensures that they have important control on crucial issues that affects their lives such as language policy and educational policy. But, under the "provincial federation", there will be different and often incompatible competing interests, say, for example which language should serve as the working one for the region formed by lumping together different ethnic groups. This means that meaningful self-determination cannot be implemented under such an arrangement. It does not also provide mechanisms for genuine representation because people often want to be led by people drawn from among themselves.

Seen from this angle, multinational federation provides mechanisms of genuine representation. As Clapham writes, "For the first time under Ethiopian rule, people from the previously conquered areas of the country were governed by rulers at the local level who were visibly drawn from their own community."① As Isaiah Berlin notes, the quest for self-determination is also a quest for status and recognition. When people are ruled by their own rulers they feel affirmed and respected. Thus the quest for national self-determination as Berlin insists in a different context makes the members of a group,

Complain less today, when he is rudely treated by members of his own race or nation, than when he was governed by some cautious, gentle, well-meaning administrator from outside. I may feel unfree in the sense of not being recognized as a self-governing individual human being; but I may feel it also as a member of an unrecognized or insufficiently respected group②.

When members seek self-determination, what they demand is a right to be guided by institutions influenced by their own culture. The claim that the right to self-determination can be subsumed under the universal civil and political right is wrong because the people in question may feel marginalized "without being deprived of their freedom and civil liberties...when they are governed by a political culture and political institutions imprinted by a culture not their own"③. Only then can "the individual feels that he lives in a community which enables him to express in public and develop without repression those aspects of his personality which are bound up with his sense of identity as a member of his community"④. Thus, the drawing of the internal boundary of the state along ethnic lines can meet the members' demand for recognition.

But if different minorities are lumped together into one province they cannot even meaning-

① Christian Clapham, "Ethiopia" in On the Fault Line: Managing Tensions and Divisions within Societies, ed. J. Herbst, T. McName, G. Mills,London: Profile Books, 2012:157.

② Isaiah Berlin,Four Essays on Liberty,Oxford: Oxford University Press, 1969:157-158.

③ Ibid, 157-158.

④ Ibid, 157-158.

fully agree on crucial issues such as which language should serve as the working language of the province and the language of schooling. If such issues are put to the usual process of the "majoritarian decision making", the local ethnic minorities will be "outbid and outvoted"①, to use the phrase familiarized by Kymlicka, by the local ethnic majority. Thus, the idea of "provincialism" leads to a disastrous consequence for the minorities.

The question then is, if provincialism is rejected as a viable solution to build common national identity, can multi-national federation provide it? There is no doubt that when the internal boundary of the state is drawn along ethnic lines as it is the case with Ethiopia the tendency of people to see their "historic homeland" as exclusively theirs increases. This again may lead them to see minorities within them as strangers, aliens and new-comers(mete)②. Common national identity cannot be built as long as these attitudes exist.

But this mutual disinterestedness is unfortunately the undesirable consequence of multi-national federation. Of course, democratic citizenship cannot be built unless people of a given bounded political community start to see one another as having common national identity. Otherwise, there is no reason why they should be required to sacrifice for their co-nationals. If there is no compelling reason to regard citizens of a given bounded political community as having a sense of belongingness in some sense, one cannot be obligated to pay tax for the government. It is as if I am paying tax to a total stranger with whom I have no acquaintance whatsoever. This is indeed what the Ethiopian federal experience showed us. People were just by virtue of being a member of a particular ethnic group expelled from regions they migrated to as aliens, strangers and new-comers. But it seems to me that it is wise to ask whether this was inherently the problem with multi-national federation. One may legitimately ask whether this happened owing to the fact that multi-national federation has not been implemented in Ethiopia in good faith to begin with. One can ask, if the "divide and rule" policy that many believe had been implemented by the ruling elites for more than two decades is the root cause behind the lack of a sense of belongingness among the general public. If that is the case, which I believe is true, multi-national federation is not something to ignore for multi-ethnic societies such as ours.

As it is the case with so-called vibrant democracies such as Canada, the possibility of mutual disinterestedness cannot be ruled out altogether. However, that cannot in itself be a compelling reason to reject multi-national federation. The rejection of this arrangement in the name of promoting a common national identity is, in a sense, imposing such identity on the people in question. This is because the national minorities' demand, as mentioned earlier on, is to regain their hitherto self-governing status. There is no compelling reason why they should leave such demand when the national majority is engaged in its own nation-building.

① Will Kymlicka, Liberalism, Community and Culture,Oxford: Clarendon Press, 1989:180-181.

② Jon Abbink, "Ethnic-based federalism and Ethnicity in Ethiopia: Reassessing the Experiment after 20 Years", Journal of Eastern African Studies, 2011,5(4):608-609.

4 Conclusion

Ethnicity and state cannot be separated. They have never been and never will be separated. Man is not only a rational animal having two legs, brain, and other empirically given characteristics. Man is also a language using animal, and this is not a mere contingent feature of his existence. His language and culture partly define who he or she is because we are partly what we take ourselves to be. We are a kind of being to whom certain questions are of crucial importance①. We among other things ask, who we are and address that question primarily in terms of people who have special relationship to us such as our parents and children. We can rightly say that "we are the sons and daughters of this man and woman". We may rightly address it saying, "I belong to this clan or ethnic group." And this is not a trivial matter.

We are a kind of being who have a rational interest to see the continued existence of our language and its associated traditions into the future. What differentiates man from non-human things is the fact that we are beings with interests and concerns that cannot be called into question. As Charles Taylor noted, "I cannot ask what my car really is, as it were."② This is true because my car does not have a concern and an interest of its own. But this is not true of human. One of our concerns and interests that cannot be called into question is the rational interest that we have to see the continued existence of our language and its associated tradition into the future. And this interest gets stronger when we compete with other rational beings with different "conceptions of the good". One may legitimately say that "in the old good days" when his ethnic group members were living in a geographic isolation, they were well-off as far as preserving their distinct cultural existence is concerned. But for the reasons mentioned in the text, their continued existence as distinct cultural community becomes uncertain when they happen to meet opposing worldview. If everything is left for "cultural marketplace" they know that they are the ones to lose because of, among other things, their numerical inferiority. Thus their demand that they be provided with their right to self-government to mitigate their cultural vulnerability is not a trivial matter either.

This quest will be even more legitimate if the claimants are the ones who had their own "historic homeland" before their involuntary incorporation into the larger state. In that case, they are not demanding anything extra from the state. They are demanding to rebuild their previous institutions that run, among other things, in their own language. This can only be done when the state endorses linguistic identity as the most important factor in dealing with its citizens. The idea of a linguistically neutral state is a metaphysical absurdity, to say the least. Thus, the Ethiopian state got it right when it endorsed ethnicity as informing the governing structure of the public sphere but got it wrong when it abused it, period.

---

① Charles Taylor, Philosophy and the Human Sciences: Philosophical Papers Vol2,New York: Cambridge University Press, 1985: 2.

② Charles Taylor, Sources of the Self: the Making of the Modern Identity, Cambridge: Cambridge University Press,1989:31.

Addis Abebenet: between Ethnic Nationalism and Pan Ethiopiansim

Tirsit Sahledengil

Abstract: Recently Addis Abebenet is becoming the counter balance to Ethnic Nationalism and the hope to rescue Ethiopia, following the recent political reform since 2018. Indeed many people contributed to the country-wide political reform. But they couldn't agree up on the owner of the victory. In the first few months of the reform, the reformist prime minster Abiy Ahmed, could entertain prompt peace which is dramatically substituted by mass displacement, question of regional disintegration, civil conflicts, and assassinations of high government officials. With all these gloomy scenarios in the country, the emergence of polarized ethnic nationalism has continued to be a threat to the integrated Ethiopia.

Addis Abebenet which is rooted in pan Ethiopianist nationalism has been the middle ground between promoters and supporters of the polarized ethnic politics and the ultra-nationalist base. Thus, this study attempts to explore Addis Abebenet and the type of nationalism it promotes. The central argument of this article also assesses viewpoints of political forces that refer Addis Ababa as a capital city of Ethiopia and Africa and other claim of the capital as a political hub for a particular group. The fact that it is a seat for the African Union and other international bodies of diplomatic missions seems to have been neglected in the debate between the two political forces despite the multi-cultural nature of the town that reflected impacts from globalization. The views of the "true Addis Ababa residents" seems to have no one's attention. To many in and out of the town, *Addis Abebenet* could rescue the disintegration of the country. It is mainly because of the cultural and ethnic mix of its residents and the different political ideologies they promote and the welcoming spirit associated of then to describe them which is a unique psychology ascribed to the residents of the town. The infamous Addis Ababa master plan and the Oromo protests following the master plan issue have contributed to the Oromo's claim of the town as they often refers to it as Finfine. Indeed "Finfine is the capital city of Oromia Regional State". So, raising the question of Finfine is also appropriate and has its ground on the 1992 transitional charter and the 1995's constitution. However, the residents of Addis Ababa have their own identity which could be depicted in Addis Abebenet. Thus, serving as both ethnic and economic center Addis Ababa continued to live with its own contention and contradiction. This paper, therefore, tries to show the proponents of Addis Abebenet, customarily referred to as Ye Addis Abebalijoch and what makes them stand against ethnic-identification but to Ethiopiawinet. I would like to focus the social and cultural arguments to analyze the divided and clarify the contentions accordingly. I also want to focus on the post 1991 development and still I am giving more emphasis on the post 2018 reform. Primary and secondary data sources will be used as the principal sources of information to support the arguments in this article.

Keywords: Addis Abebenet; Ye Addisabalijoch; Finfine; Ethnic Nationalism; Pan Ethiopianism

Introduction

Addis Ababa has been established as a capital city of Ethiopia in 1886 by Emperor Minilik Ⅱ (Tolon, 2008:15). According to Tolon (2008:15) the introduction of eucalyptus tree, the proclamation for legalizing private ownership of urban land in 1907 and the construction of Ethio-Djibuti railway were among the major reasons that contribute for the persistency of Addis Ababa as a capital city of Ethiopia. Addis Ababa sits at an elevation of 7,726 feet above sea level. This makes it one of the highest elevations of any capital city in the world, and the highest in Africa.

The city also found in latitude 9° 03′ N and 38° 42′ E and ranged at the foot of the Entoto range (altitude 2,900 meters) dropping down to 2,300 m in the southern periphery toward the Akaki Plains. The general climate is sub-tropical with an average temperature range of 10 ℃. Beginning in mid-November temperatures are cooler (10~15 ℃) particularly at night and in the early morning, rising to 20~23 ℃. February to May is the warm season with temperatures climbing to over 23 ℃ in the afternoon. June to mid-September is the long wet season when temperatures are often mild (Mulatu, 2013).

Addis Ababa is where the African Union is headquartered, and the Organization of African Unity was once based. It is also the location for the United Nations Economic Commission of Africa. This has given the city political and diplomatic significance in the continent.

It is also the largest city in the country by population. In 1950, the population of Addis Ababa was 392,000. Addis Ababa has grown by 922,914 since 2015, which represents a 4.37% annual change. According to 2007's census which is the latest one, a total population of Addis Ababa was 3,384,569. The city has through recent years seen a robust annual growth rate, and population counts as of 2017 are growing closer to 4 million. The most recent census was scheduled for 2018 to 2019 fiscal year, as security concerns between 2017 and 2018 delayed it. Currently Addis Ababa's population estimated at 4,793,699 from the latest revision of the UN World Urbanization Prospects in 2020.

Addis Ababa is a chartered city and as such, and considered as both a city and a state. It is the largest city in the world located in a landlocked country. As the country's capital, almost all of Ethiopia's ethnic groups are represented in the city. However, the largest groups include the Amhara at almost half the population with 47%. The Oromo people are 19% of the population, and the Gurage people are 16% of the population. The rest of the city is split between the Tigrayan, the Silt'e and the Gamo people. The major languages also reflect the country's major ethnic groups, with Amharic, Afaan Oromo, and Gurage the most spoken mother tongues[①].

Tolon (2008:17) argued possibly the socio-economic and political development of the city could be categorized into four major phases. The first phase is early period, 1886-1935; when the city was being established. The second phase is included a short period of Italian occupation 1936 to 1941. The third and a longer period of modernization under Emperor Haile Selassie Addis Ababa was the capital from 1941—1974. During this period Modern stone houses were built particularly around the palace, and many roads were paved. Other innovations included the establishment of a water reservoir at Gefarsa to the west and the building of a hydroelectric station at Akaki to the south. There were only limited changes in Addis Ababa between 1941 and 1960, but the development has been impressive since then. There was no stringent planned public guidance or control over housing development in Addis Ababa during the first 10 to 15 years after liberation (1940). As a result, most of the housing was built without any permits. For that matter, it appears that as late as the early 1970s, only about a quarter of the housing units produced in Addis Ababa had municipal permits. The socialist period from 1975-1991 is the fourth period of development. In this regard I want to add two more periods regarding Addis Ababa. These are from 1991-2018 and post 2018 periods.

Addis Ababa since 1991

After throwing away the Ethiopian People's Democratic Republic of Ethiopia (PDRE) in 1991, EPRDF established ethnic identity based transitional government which lead the country from 1991 to 1995. The 1991 conference ultimately resulted in the adoption of the "Transitional Period Charter of Ethiopia", ratified by many political organizations which called themselves as liberation fronts. Here it is worth to underline that the ethnic liberation fronts have their own agenda and those who didn't belong to any liberation fronts were not represented in the transition[②]. Accordingly, proclamation no. 7/1992 established "National Self-governments" in January 1992 by dividing the country's state institutions into the Federal Government, 12 ethnic regions and Addis Ababa and Dire Dawa as the two self-governing cities.

Article 3(4) of the transitional law reserved "the special interest and political right of the Oromo over Region 13 Harari and Region 14 Addis Ababa" since both are located within the

① World Population Review, "Addis Ababa Population 2022", 20 September 2021, https://worldpopulationreview.com/world-cities/addis-ababa-population.

② Wekipedia, "Transitional Government of Ethiopia", 19 March 2022, https://en.wikipedia.org/wiki/Transitional_Government_of_Ethiopia.

State of Oromia. The particulars were to be "prescribed in detail by a special law"[1]. Despite the political right of the Oromia region that was displayed in the transitional charter the 1995's constitution appeared with more complicated and ambiguous issue regarding the Addis Ababa city and the Oromia special interest.

The 1995 constitution article 49 attempted to outline the rules regarding Addis Ababa city under 49(2) which said the residents of Addis Ababa shall have a full measure of self-government. Moreover, 49(3) the administration of Addis Ababa shall be responsible for the Federal Government, and 49(4) the residents of Addis Ababa shall in accordance with the provisions of this constitution, being represented in the House of Peoples' Representatives. Finally, 49(5) the special Interest of the State of Oromia in Addis Ababa, regarding the provision of social services or the utilization of natural resources and other similar matters, as well as joint administrative matters arising from the location of Addis Ababa within the State of Oromia, shall be respected. In this regard it is visible that the 49(5) has clear contradiction with the above three statements. Above all Addis Ababa residents are represented in house of people of representative and hold 23 seats but they are not represented in House of Federation.

Another historical incident was that of 2001, when the governing party passed resolution to move the capital of ONRS from AA to Adama, Art. 6 of Revised Constitution of ONRS, Proc. No. 46/2001. The resolution was unanimously opposed by the Oromo people from all corners. The opposition parties, having foreseen that the resolution will be repealed, speculated that the move was intended as a way to split them among ethnic lines by inciting the non-Oromo residents of AA to oppose the return of the ONRS to the Ethiopian capital city. In 2005 election, the party officially announced plan to move the region's capital back to AA, Amendment proc. No.94/2005, Art. 2(3) providing "Finfine" as the capital city of the region. In any event, non-Oromo groups did not oppose the return of ONRS office to AAC. Despite a step to amend the Regional Constitution, administrative power at the top is still taken by Federal Government[2].

According to Proc. No. 94/2005, a proclamation issued to amend The Revised Constitution, Proc. No. 46/2001, and Art. 2(3), "Art. 6, (Adama shall be the capital city of ONRS), has been amended as, Finfine shall be the capital city of ONRS." It may be considered that AA being capital City of ONRS contributes legally to the prolongation of special interest. It also creates an ambiguity of what constitutes joint administrative matters. The immediate reason of revision is, however, a political cover as a means to delay or it is not to fully enforce the Constitution. In this case amending regional constitution seems normal when it has been changed to shift the capital city of Ormoiya regional capital from Addis Ababa to Adama and returning it to the capital, when the ruling party were lost total seat in Addis Ababa during 2005 election.

① OPride Staff, "Oromia Special Interest Law: Who owns Addis Ababa?", 1 July 2017, https://www.opride.com/2017/07/01/oromia-special-interest-law-owns-addis-ababa/.

② of the State of Oromia", 27 August 2015, https://www.abyssinialaw.com/blog-posts/item/1611-constitutional-special-interest-of-oromia.

As to the legal place of AAC and sub-cities the chief legal regimes governing their status are the Charters, AACG Charter, proc. No. 87/1997 and Revised Charter, proc. No. 361/2003. The former one is the first charter of the city. As we can understand from the connotation, the latter one is revision of the former. And as such it commands more authority than the former charter. However, the former is still applicable as long as it does not contradict with the provisions of the Revised Charter. The Revised Charter has created three tiers of governmental system, Art.2(1, 5 and 6). These are the city, sub-cities and kebeles, the latter currently reordered as woredas. If we include the federal government, there will be four levels of governments in AACA. Each AA sub-city is a municipality, Art.30(7) of the Revised Charter. It has legal personality to sue and be sued in its own name. It should act under the central leadership of the city, Art.30(1). The City Council decides the organization or reorganization of the sub-cities.

Regarding significant political event in Addis Ababa City in post 1991, the 2005 election had been a missed opportunity of the city to entertain their vote. During the 2005 election the capital city was the epicenter of opposition political mobilization. It is recalled that EPRDF has almost lost all the parliament seats in Addis Ababa City Council general election during the bloody 2005 election, which claims around 200 lives.

Meanwhile the then Coalition for Unity and Democracy (CUD) has failed to reach agreement and take over the city, which also led to arrest and exile of thousands of its leaders and supporters, including the recently established EZEMA leader Berhanu Nega (PhD).

Since losing the 2005 general election in many cities, the EPRDF, has been following different techniques to increase its number of supporters in urban areas.

The actions taken by the EPRDF also includes, infiltrating its secret agents in higher education institutions, public services and giving priority and promotion for those who become members of the party. Favoring business people associated with EPRDF and migrating thousands of its supporters from rural areas are mainly from the northern part to Addis Ababa in what looks an attempt to change the demography of the city.

Eventually, the opposition succeeded in achieving the ultimate objective of winning all but one of the 138 seats. However, allegations of vote-rigging, primarily in other parts of the country against the ruling party EPRDF, created national-level confrontations and political crisis. Boosted by its overall victory, although contested, to form a government, EPRDF was determined not to lose its hold in controlling Addis Ababa. The then mayor elect of the city, Berhanu Nega, recently revealed that the EPRDF government "refused to hand over" the city administration for the victorious political party (Eyob, 2020:4).

The 2005 election overtly shows controlling Addis Ababa is not only about a control of the Federal city which seems less important to Federal Government that do not have the right to land administration or resource since both are hold by the regional states that have autonomous power. Controlling Addis Ababa is substantial ground control of the country's politics, which is clearly depicted how EPRDF strives to handle the city by introducing new laws of city governance. One of the election-related laws helped EPRDF to restructure the local councils at the national level. EPRDF enacted legislation to exponentially increase the local council seats, from 15 to 300 (Aalen & Tronvoll, 2009). As a result, nearly 3.6 million seats became available in the local councils across the country. The decision put massive pressure on opposition political parties to put up several thousands of candidates to win local government administrations. None of the opposition parties were in a position to mobilize such a considerable number of candidates and to win a meaningful majority.

Another post-2005 Addis Ababa-focused political strategy was establishing different forums. such as the Addis Ababa youth Forum, the Women Forum, the Trade Forum and the Addis Ababa Inhabitants Forum were established in July 2006①. The party was successful in recruiting enough new candidates to represent the party during 2008 by-election (Gebremariam, 2017b). As a result, EPRDF won the local elections across the country with an unprecedented margin and set the ground for the 99 percent control of the federal parliament in the 2010 election. In addition to the legal maneuvering to expand the formal structures of local government, EPRDF also facilitated the establishment of non-formal channels of power that fed into the formal offices of governance. An internal policy document argues that "developmental good governance" is an essential element of transforming rent-seeking-based socio-economic relations in the city into developmental relations. Hence, the government took a proactive action to mobilize and organize the public in the city into zones and development teams (AACA, 2014: 5). As a result, the city government has established 771 zones to facilitate interactions between development teams (18,000 across the city) and the districts through public mobilization, participation, monitoring and evaluation (Eyob, 2020:7).

Ethiopian ruling coalition under EPRDF succeeded in dominating the socio-economic and political spheres in Addis Ababa (2005-2018). The use of developmentalism as a legitimising discourse was actively pursued by EPRDF as a way of offsetting the democratic deficit of the regime, particularly after the 2005 election, which was a clean curve victory for the opposition in Addis Ababa. Similar to other developmental regimes, EPRDF sought to derive legitimacy from what it delivers to the wider public. But the provision of these services also came hand-in-hand with the political mobilization of the target groups. In Addis Ababa, although slums constitute the greater portion of the residential areas, to date, the city has not had a comprehensive slum upgrading policy or regulation until 2017.

Addis Ababa generates a daily 2,297 m^3 of solid waste on average. This is significantly below the capacities of the Solid Waste Management Department of the city, which can collect, and dispose of, as much as 3,000 m^3 of solid waste per day. Unless the estimated per capita generation of solid waste in the city is far below reality, the Department seems to be operating way below capacity. (Tolon, 2008:36).

① Constitutional Special Interest Africanews, "Ethiopia PM moves to resolve Oromia–Addis Ababa boundary rift", [2019-03-09]. https://www.africanews.com/2019/03/09/ethiopia-pm-moves-to-resolve-oromia-addis-ababa-boundary-rift/.

After the scraping of the master plan the protest persisted until the 2018 reform. This by itself shows that the master plan was the immediate cause of the protest, but not the only reason and end to bring nationwide reform. How the city was reestablished in post 1991. How it has been administered under the charter of Addis Ababa. How it has been administered during and after the transition period, as well as after the 2005 election what happen to the city.

Political organizations that have based in the city. All of movements were started in Addis Ababa. However, the movement of the regional people against TPLF since 2015 is totally excluding Addis Ababa Youth. Thus, Addis Ababa Youth was not significantly represented in the reform and they were told that they do not have share in the reform.

The Addis Ababa City Development Plan (2002-2012) had comprised a statutory structure plan, an action oriented strategic development framework and a management reform component. The statutory structure plan had provided an overall framework for the spatial development of the city. The action oriented strategic development plans had prioritized six key urban issues to be implemented in five years (i.e., housing, urban road network and transport, manufacturing industries and large storage facilities, environment, and inner city renewal and upgrading), and proposed implementation mechanisms and financial investment requirements. The rationale for using this combination of statutory and performance oriented plans had been made (Lia, 2017:2).

Addis Ababa during the Eve of the 2018 Reform

Addis Abebe or Ye Addis Abebalijoch are those of who are represented in the article 2(49) residents of Addis Ababa. They are also told to have Amharic as an official language and they are not nations, nationalities or people. Thus, they are not Qero; the Oromo youth, not Fano, the Amhara youth or zerma, or Ejeto, or Yolaga. They are Ye Addis Abebalijoch. According to Ethiopian Dialogue Forum (2017), the Ethiopian Constitution confers authority and sovereignty to "Nations, Nationalities and People" rather than on Ethiopian citizens. As a result, the regional states or have evolved as "sovereign" entities with the powers to define their boundaries and restrict ownership of natural resource, the movement of people, goods, and services. In so doing this constitution hampers the free flow of free and equal Ethiopian citizens with incredible talents, resources, technologies "segregating" them into ethno-regional provinces. Such kind of state structure has been also blamed for its goal as divide and rule.

Moreover, the special interest issue has been criticized for its short coming solution to bring the required democracy and protection of human right for both the Oromo ethnic group and the rest of the countries citizens including the diversified residents of Addis Ababa①.

After 26 years the Oromiya regional state council brought the leaked document of Oromia special interest details with five sections draft proclaimation in 2017. Most importantly

① Ethiopian Dialogue Forum, "Ethiopian Dialogue Forum Statement on Oromiya's special Interests in Addis Ababa". [2017-07-03].https://ecadforum.com/2017/07/03/ethiopian-dialogue-forum-statement-on-oromiyas-special-interests-in-addis-ababa/.

the reinstitution of official name of the city shall be Finfine, making Afan Oromo as official and work language in line with Amharic and many more liberates has been listed in the leaked document. Regarding the special interest proclamation, many civic organizations, journalists, and activists blamed the proclamation as the immediate solution that the EPRDF leadership bring to divert the attention of the Ormo protests across the Oromia region.

Since Addis Ababa residents were not mainstreamed and have exercised their self-administration since the 2005 election, they didn't go through active political participation in the post 2005 election period. Neither they were involved and joined the country wide protest against the ruling of EPRDF, which was led by the coalition of Oromo and Amhara youth and had different aims in different parts of the country.

Addis Ababa after the 2018 Reform

After the reform of 2018 Addis Ababa political fate was still in the crossroad and the infamous master plan and the persistency of the question of special interest, the issue of demarcating boundary between Addis Ababa and Oromia, the release of all political parties all over the country, and the entrance of many liberation fronts and pan Ethiopians political parties pave another paradoxical season to Addis Ababa.

Many Ethiopian youngsters during 1960s students' movement were tribute a lot in fighting for the "land to tiller" and contemporary youngsters also continued the opposition of former students by changing the slogan from "land to tiller" to "land to my ethnic group" (Tedla, 2014). The economic base of early 20th century Addis Ababa was typical of a consumer city, where taxes and tributes were the principal source of income. In recent times, the city has a diversified economy, being the main center of public administration, commerce, manufacturing, finance, real estate and insurance, according to a 2007 UN Habitat study. Thus, authors of the draft master plan highlight their desire to see the transition from an agriculture to industrialized economy as the main aim for the government's urban plans, in the process creating a single economic unit (Tolon, 2008; Mikias, 2014).

According to the constitution, the Ethiopian state is federal in structure. Ethiopia is a "nation of nations" that can be considered a multinational federation. In the language of the constitution, "Nations, Nationalities, and Peoples" are the locus of sovereignty (Art-8) and have the right to self-determination (Art-39). However, Addis Ababa residents were not represented in the constitution in none of the three categories. Such as Addis Ababan are not nations, nationalities and people. They are residents. This means they are excluded from all of the right that nations, nationalities and people are entertaining. This is indeed my own understanding of the constitution. As sovereign entities, they are the "building blocks" that have a co-equal share in the founding of the contemporary Ethiopian polity. As subjects with the right to self-determination, they have, inter alia, the right to a "full measure of self-government" (Art-39(3)). Accordingly, most of these "nations", based on the four-fold criteria "settlement pattern, language, identity, and consent of the people concerned" (Art-46(1)), have established the nine states that constitute federal Ethiopia (Art. 47), one of which is the state of Oromia (Tsegaye, 2015)

Getaun Benti (2002) argued that Oromo was totally excluded from Addis Ababa politics and it is banned from integrated into Addis Ababa economic system. However, this is quite reductionist view since there are significant numbers of people who, identify themselves as Oromo and live in harmony and integration in the town.

Indeed the urban politics and economy needs high level of integration and communication, as it is also true in other part of the world. Additional problem of the article is that it tried to show that the Amhara ethnic group is predominantly control the politics since the establishment of the city. However, Addis Ababa is not made from the so called Amhara people and significantly the economy is controlled by Guraghe, Silte, Gamo, and also other nations and nationalities of the country. Indeed occupational preference and the contribution of ethnic groups' occupational culture are quite significant in this case. Scholars who studied how primordial tribal (or familial) identities were transformed into urban ones justified that there were complex factors which contribute for the transformation of identities in the urban context. The urban center is characterized by a state of anomie, social void and collective behavior tends to be unpredictable. One could argue that the modern social life is characterized by profound processes of reorganization of time and space, coupled to the expansion of disembedding mechanisms which prize social relations free from local (Tarawneh & Mahmood, 2011: 616).

Feyera (2005) mentioned that Addis Ababa is established totally at the expense of the Oromo farmers and disregard the contribution of different internal and external factors including Italian occupation period for the development of the city to urban center. Nevertheless, he doesn't emphasize the existence of non-Oromo farmers. Such kind of ethno-nationalistic representation of the city seems problematic and ethnocentric in my opinion.

In the post 2018 Ethiopia, expansionist nationalism that claimed the territories in other States/Regions by undermining state borders and preparation for war to recover what they claim "the former territory(rist)", evicting people for the simple reason that they do not belong to ethnic group that is dominant in that State/Region, and media that disseminate hate speeches and extreme and radical ideas that provoke conflict have been tolerated. In short, nationalism in post 2018 Ethiopia is going in the wrong direction and reaching at the extreme point where it may pose danger to the lives of Ethiopians. The failure of government to maintain law and order is making its existence irrelevant and leading to the high demand for guns to protect oneself and family and influx of illegal armaments into the country (Assefa, 2019).

Contemporary Addis Ababa politics could be inculcated in crossroad. To some extent, there are tangible conflicts in the town between who called themselves as "Ye Addis Abebalijoch" and other groups who claim the ownership of the city and waiting for the implementation of the special interest of Oromiya. Here I didn't see any problem in both sides of the competent. However, the problem is quite political and the bargaining capacity of the elites who called themselves as liberation fronts and do not give emphasis for national dialogue.

Urban politics has structure of political conflict that is evident in identifying the nature of the politically relevant cleavages which divide people. Political conflict is a variety of different types of contests over social goals and the allocation of public resources. Such contests typically take the form of electoral competition and organized or quasi-organized articulation of interest (Peter,1997). My contention is that the relative importance of various types of cleavages, which in turn imply varying bases for organized or unorganized conflict groups, differs according to the level of jurisdiction. Relative importance may be understood in terms of the frequency with which particular cleavages structure conflict, the pervasiveness of cleavages in establishing or coloring the issues over which conflict occurs, and the relative ability of different types of groups to gain visibility in the political system. In short, particular cleavages important to the structure of urban political conflict are less likely to be of similar importance to the structure of conflict in other arenas.

The 2018 political reform seems new day for many of Ethiopian people which brings them the desired democracy and development. Addis Ababa was not out of such vibe since the first day of the inaugural speech of the new Prime Minister Abiy Ahmed. However, the Oromo special interest has been continued as unresolved question. Oromo nationalists also claim about the Oromo special interest is not that much special and it is their right from the beginning (Tsegaye, 2017). The well-known activist Jawar Muhammed also said in one of his interviews in Amharic with a television channel called Oromo Media Network (OMN) the following.

The issue of Finfine is the central goal of our struggle. Definitely Oromo will benefit from all solutions that will propose to resolve the Finfine case. We will benefit from the implementation of the special interest proclamation. We will benefit from any kind of negotiation that will be held with any party. And finally we will benefit from any violent activity that will take place to answer our question over Finfine. For me telling the Qero to finalize the struggle by resolving Finfine will be more easier than trying to calming and advising them to stop their struggle. Finfine is navel to Oromia (Jawar Muhammed, Interview in OMN, February 2019).

In his argument, however, Jawar remarked that the issue of Finfine is core for Oromo people from all corners, he also remarked that the town has its own characteristics since it is also the seat of Federal state. Thus, even the Oromo nationalists recognize the heterogeneity of Addis Ababa and its inconvenience to practice homogeneous ethnic politics.

On the other hand, the Amhara elites and nationalists attempt to create counter narratives and advocacy for the Oromo nationalists by claiming that Addis Ababa as the center of Amhara state during 14th century. The narrative about "Barara, the Ancient Addis Ababa (1400-1887) Development, Destruction and Reestablishment", a book written by Habtamu Mengiste has got a special attention in the social media. In this regard many Oromo nationalists also criticized such narratives among the Oromo scholars Guluma (2018) was one of them who has attempted to disprove

Addis Ababa as Barara. According to his argument Barara is not Addis Ababa due to inaccuracy of the proponents in locating the exact place of Barara. He also argued that the ancient Babara is located in the northern part of today's Dukem. Second, he raised the negligence of Barara proponents to the Oromo scholars to their arguments. Finally he remarked that Barara is false narratives which has political objective to obscure the Oromiya special interest①.

In the third place some individuals who were organized by Journalist Eskinidir Nega come up with against the contemporary Addis Ababa city Administration, which they labeled it as "illegitimate" and established Addis Ababa Baladera Council known as Balderas. Balderas was initially launched as a civic society to safeguard the political and economic rights of inhabitants of the capital Addis Ababa from "special benefit" claims of the surrounding Oromia Region over the city.

Mr. Eskinder was sentenced for 18 years in prison until the reformist Prime Minister Abiy Ahmed came to power and announced release of all political prisoners in the country.

The promoters of Balderas, including Eskinder Nega and tens of thousands of the inhabitants of Addis Ababa, who denied their vote to the EPRDF during the May 2005 general election, argued that the same techniques of the TPLF-dominated-EPRDF is being pursued by "the reformed EPRDF", which is directly or indirectly working to diminish the political, economic rights and votes of the Addis Ababans by considering the non-Oromo ethnic group people in the city as aliens.

As a result of the above techniques of implemented and being pursued by the ruling coalition, many observers agree that unlike the 2005 general election result or the recent elections in Ethiopia, it is very unlikely for one political party including the ruling coalition to get landslide victory in Addis Ababa②. Balderas Addis Ababa Council was established after radical Oromo ethno-nationalist elements claimed ownership of Addis Ababa. But many Ethiopians were alarmed more when Oromo Democratic Movement issued a statement on March 7 vowing that it will work to ensure ethnic Oromo ownership of Ethiopia's capital.

Balderas advocates that Addis Ababa belongs to all Ethiopians and Addis Ababans, not to a single ethnic group in the country. Prime Minister Abiy Ahmed recently reflected similar position, but in a murky way, against the position of his party, ODP.

Lemma Megersa, the former president of Oromia regional state and Ministry of defense has been blamed also his hidden agenda of changing the demography of Addis Ababa as secret operation to achieve Oromo's question in one of his closed speech which was revealed in social media. Allegations of plots to change demographic composition of Addis Ababa. He says that it is a story invented for character assassination. But it is clear, unlike last year, that he has lost a considerable number of support bases outside of Oromo region of Ethiopia.

---

① Guluma Gemeda, "Barara is not Addis Ababa", [2018-11-22].https://kichuu.com/barara-is-not-addis-ababa/.

② "Ethiopia recognizes Balderas as political party",[2020-01-22].https://newbusinessethiopia.com/politics/ethiopia-recognizes-balderas-as-political-party/.

Indeed no one attempted to give ructions for Lemma's speech which creates more fear and suspicion in the mind of many Addis Ababa residents. Such kind of speeches and rumors about systematic discriminations of Addis Ababa youth from political participation became visible and persistent. It is also possible to remember the recent secret speech of the current Oromia President Ato Shimelis Abdisa, who has talked about the systematic implementation of the Oromo people special interest by making Addis Ababa irrelevant city.

All the overt speeches of political leaders seem against the constitution and the charter which gives self-administrative right to the Addis Abebe. The process of alienating the Oromo ethnic group from the rest of the country's ethnic group as political strategy seems dangerous. Ironically, training the Oromo youth as distinct group that brought political reform in the country is a manifestation of failed politics. Because the Addis Ababa youth is a mixture of all ethnic groups and Addis Ababa is a melting pot for all Ethiopians.

Remembering the pre 2018 reform of the city youth, many of them were persecuted by the government troops following the post 2005 election crises. At that time about 200 youth were killed and more than 4,000 people were detained according to Amenesty international report on November 2005. During that time none of the reports were revealing ethnic disaggregated data. Besides, the post 2005 established Youth Forum didn't aimed to categorize Addis Ababa youth in ethnic bases at least explicitly. However, after the 2018 reform many conflicts were induced between the so called " Qero versus Ye Addis Abebalijoch". In this regard, it is possible to remember the conflict between these two groups during September 2018 by the time the Oromo political leaders were returned to Ethiopia. It has been remembered that the conflict was revealed due to misunderstanding in painting the squares and the roads of the city with flag color. Thus, dichotomizing the city people into different groups seems threat to many of Addis Ababa people who have been living in mixed way and blended from different ethnic groups and identify themselves as pan Ethiopian.

Addis Abebenet: Stateless Nationalism?

Identity is always in the way of transformation and reclaimed. In the world there is no evidence of static identify (Meena, 2007). Studying the identity of two Turkish cities identity transformation to urbanism Bugatti (2013) argued that multicultural societies of Izmir and Salónica, like those in Istanbul, Beirut, and Alexandria, became far more complex regardless of their ethnic-religious sentiment before the cities establishment. According to this author the designation of the city's quarters for only Islamic religion was replaced by a new social-urban interaction where Muslim and non-Muslim elites affected the modernization of the cityscape.

Sometime people try to present ethnic identity as static and uniform. Opposing such type of functionalist approach Frederics (2004), Aborginal women living in urban center argued Aborginals in the urban centers labeled as fake, unauthentic, and nonrealistic. Normally, the word "authentic" is posed in a way that describes someone being more "tribal" or "traditional". These terms can be sued also in any urban context to express non-urban perhaps local or rural urban migrants whose way of life is not integrated fully to the urban system. Frederics also underlined that there is no single urban Aboriginal experience or identity. The experiences are as diverse as the population and include a diversity of experience, need, prospects shaped by gender, education, religion, age and level of human security. This is more or less the same to Addis Ababa urban identity.

Furthermore, the urbanization of the diversification of cities is inevitable and even most strict homogeneous centers were not exceptional from such reality. Thus, Addis Ababa's residents' identity is not also homogeneous and bounded to specific ethnic or religious group. Accordingly, Addis Ababa's urban identity is interpreted as a process of construction that is always in the process of making. Urbanization, as a continuous process of change, is considered a crucial factor in shaping and constructing the self-identity of a group of people. As a result of urbanization, interactions between and among different social groups increase which lead to the fact that identity will be transformed in form and essence (Tarawneh & Mohamed, 2011).

Ye Addis Abebalijod Cijoch idenitity is more or less collective identity and it couldn't be associate with any of ethnic groups' identity. Such kind of collective identity is a product of different demographic, economic and political process.

According to Assefa (2019) the objective of nationalism is developing and maintaining national identity based on the common characteristics such as language, culture, race, history, religion, political goal, territory, or belief in common ancestry and making the group which has the common characteristics free from unwanted interference. Asseffa further argued that the term nationalism is essentially a sentiment of unity arising among a number of people usually of the same territory, sharing a common language, similar history and traditions, common interests with common political association and common ideals of political unity. Thus, some of the definitions of nationalism seems only manifested the original time that nationalism were born that is the French and Britain revolution and the European nation state. But, here my attention is to give highlight on the type of nationalism in Ethiopia and particularly nationalism that is persuade in Addis Ababa.

Based on its foundations, nationalism can be divided into three main types. Such as Ethnic Nationalism: which is a sentiment that creates a sense of belongingness, loyalty, and devotion based on ethnic group's common culture, language, history, territory, and focuses on the preservation of the identity, solidarity, and tradition of the ethnic group and respect of the right of that ethnic group.

The second one is Civic/Social Nationalism which bases on social and cultural ties rather than common descent. In this type of nationalism, outsiders or immigrants can join the social or cultural group by assimilating themselves into the culture, by complying with their living standard, and integrating into that society.

The third one is Official/State Nationalism. This is a nationalism of state including all citizens of the state irrespective of their ethnicity and cultural identity. It is expressed in term of loyalty to the state or patriotism. It is usually taught at state level by government agencies. Official/ state nationalism takes national sovereignty and territory of birth as an outstanding value. There are also other types of nationalisms such as liberal nationalism which is based on liberal values (freedom, equality, tolerance, and rights of individuals), religious nationalism which is based on particular dogmas or affiliation, nationalism of minorities where minorities in a given country who have common interests come together (Assefa, 2019).

Nationalism needs some symbols that support and sustain permanent popular nationalism. Gebrewold (2009:80) argued that imperial and the socialist period, political elites attempted to assemble Ethiopians together through the construction of a sense of "Ethiopianness" designed to surpass ethnic differences, to mobilize the population against external aggressors and to encourage it to sacrifice economic priorities for national unity and identity. Ethnic nationalism emerged right after the EPRDF took power in 1991 (Gebrewold, 2009:88).

Addis Ababa could entertain the political victory of the country ranging from Adwa to the recent Ethiopia Eritrean war victories. It also hosts from the sad news of the death of Prime minister Meles Zenawi in 2012 to the demonstration to support Prime Minister Abiy Ahmed in 2018.

Apparently athletics have performed a key function in the formation of Ethiopian nationalism. Addis Ababa is also important historical place in receiving the winners of International athletics sport in the open celebration since Abebe Bikila who won the 1960 Rome Marathon on his bare foot to the contemporary Heroes Haile Gebreselase, Tirunesh Dibaba and many more figures of Ethiopia. For people who are living in Addis Ababa celebrating such events in public gatherings is vital. Moreover, the ethnic back ground of the winners is less important in the process of adoring the winners. There is also many more football match that pulls all Ethiopian together and Addis Ababa was undeniably at the center of celebrating all victories of the country's sport engagements (Bertu, 2012).

Even though nationalism has got vital position during 1960s and 1970s political movements by students and different liberation fronts, there was no clear demarcation about what kind of nationalisms were really practiced and efficient. However, learning from different struggles in the country 1991 transitional government under EPRDF coalition gave more emphasis for different ethnic groups to practice their own ethnic nationalisms which were really a challenge to non-ethnic nationalists who referred themselves as "pan Ethiopianists". In this regard Article 88 of the constitution gave ethnic groups in Ethiopia constitutional rights to promote nationalism and the government has a duty respect this constitutional right. This by default limit the right of other groups especially those who are referred as residents of Addis Ababa that do not have homogeneous culture to develop, preserve, and promote. Moreover, the constitution give land ownership for nations, nationalities and people of Ethiopia and Addis Ababain became landless and their status became "settlers".

Media Representation of Addis Abebenet

Both social media and main stream media present Addis Abebenet as the mainstream culture of the country. Of course Addis Ababa is a melting pot which boil all cultural elements of the world and give out new identity.

Different generations narrate their memories about Addis Ababa among this one of the prominent TV show on Ethiopian Broadcasting Service (EBS) TV entitled Tizitachin be EbS our Memories on EBS continues reveal the different memories of the people from economic and social aspects. On his weekly program journalist Yonas Kebede attempted to present the memories of old schools, architectures, ruined villages, different governmental and non-governmental organizations which are really manifestations of city developments. From my observation of such media program the journalist attempt to present the memories as they are presented by the primary sources and informants. Moreover, none of the representations has ethnic bases other than sub-cultural representation of events.

Sheger 102.1 FM is the first private radio station in Ethiopia. Sheger 102.1 FM 18 hour all day broadcasting of news, features, programs and music. Sheger 102.1 FM is an independent station for the online generation, connecting those who already have a strong connection with Addis Abeba, Ethiopia. This media is the pan Ethiopianist media with the motto of "long live for Ethiopia". Indeed many people asked about which Ethiopia should live long? But they continued to mainstream the name Ethiopia and Ethiopiawinet in their programs. After the establishment of this Radio station the name Sheger became brand name to different trade activist such as Sheger Bus, Sheger Bread, Beatifying Sheger, are some of the projects that promote the name Sheger. In fact still some journalists and medias blame the reformist prime minister Abiy Ahmed for using the name Sheger instead of Addis Ababa as a deliberate way of avoiding the name Addis Ababa. Many people, who are not comfortable to use the name Addis Ababa also prefer calling the city Sheger.

The role of social media in promoting identity and nationalism is eminence. Regarding social media the prevalence of Facebook in the country as well as in Addis Ababa there are many bloggers, and groups that were created by different groups in face book. Regarding the bloggers most of the political parties which claimed themselves as the proponents of civic politics in the country established groups and invoke their political attitudes. In this regard Ethiopian citizens for social justice party have different blogs such as "Yeshegerlijoch Hibret Leethiopia Andenet".

Moreover, the Facebook groups designated to different villages are still very dominant. In this regard Cherkos children group, Bole children's group, and other so many villages of Addis Ababa groups of social media are visible. Other important media representations of the Addis Ababaian is the football fan associations which are predominantly the football fan associations of Ethiopian coffee club and St. Gorge club who consider themselves as "Icons of the city".

Conclusion

Some people claimed that Ethiopian post 2018 reform is missing its way and now the country is at critical stage of its substantial existence. Whatever, the paradox are still undeniably there is relative freedom to speech and expressing idea without fear. This is article is a manifestation of such freedom. However, here it has to be remarked that Addis Ababa is not exceptional city in the world to be established in the place where some ethnic groups were living.

Moreover, Addis Ababa is not a city that is exclusively established by certain groups. If the meaning if place is very essential and it associate once existence with the burial of umbilical cord. Most of the residents have natural relation with the land of Addis Ababa. Indeed the primordial approach to ethnicity and the purity of the decent group is less irrelevant in the postmodern and post global 21st century in which there are no more exotic people in the world. Thus, the contention over the land seems political game and the deliberate mechanisms that political leaders create to use ethnicity as an instrument to consolidate their power. Finally, I got from one official page which said "we all are Oromo", we all are Amhara, we all are Gurage, we all are Ethiopian because we are interwoven.

References

[1] BERTU D. 2012. Constitutional Special Interest of ONRS//AACA. Present status & future challenges. Mekele: School of Law of Mekele University.

[2] EMILIANO B. 2013. Urban identies and catastrophes: Izmir and Salonica at the end of the Ottoman Empire. Geographical Review, 103(4): 498-516.

[3] GETAHUN B. 2002. A nation without a city (a blind person without a cane): the Oromo struggle for Addis. Northeast African Studies, New Series, 9(3):115-131.

[4] EYOB B G. 2020. The politics of dominating Addis Ababa (2005-2018). Manchester: ESID Working Paper , 148(7) : 4.

[5] FEYERA A. 2005. Urban expansion and the livelihood of the peri-urban agricultural community: the case of Addis Ababa. Addis Ababa: School of Graduate Studies of Addis Ababa University.

[6] MIKIAS M. 2014. A master of plans. https://addisfortune.net/columns/a-master-of-plans/#!.

[7] TARAWNEh F M, MAHMOOD N. Urbanization and social identities in Jordan: the case of Irbid. Journal of Comparative Family Studies, 42(4): 615-635.

[8] TEDLA A. 2014. Ethnic politics and the Addis Ababa Master Plan. https://ecadforum.com/2014/04/25/ethnic-politics-and-the-addis-ababa-master-plan/.

[9] TSEGAYE A. 2015. Why resist the Addis Abeba Master Plan? – a constitutional legal exploration. https://addisstandard.com/why-resist-the-addis-abeba-master-plan-a-constitutional-le-

gal-exploration/.

[10] ADDIS ABABA CITY PLANNING PROJECT OFFICE (AACPPO). 2017. Addis Ababa city structure plan draft final summary report (2017-2027). https://www.data.gov.et/en/dataset/addis-ababa-city-structure-plan-summary-report-2017-to-2027/resource/3b440b02-f227-420b-ba36-ebe63e7dabc0.

[11] ASSEFA A L. 2019. Oromiyaa/Ethiopia: nationalism in Ethiopia. https://kichuu.com/oromiyaa-ethiopia-nationalism-in-ethiopia-by-assefa-a-lemu/.

[12] MEENA R. 2007. Urban denotified tribes: competing identities, contested citizenship. Economic and Political Weekly, 42(51): 59-64.

[13] PETER K E. 1977. Understanding urban politics: a comparative perspective on urban political conflict. Polity, 10(2): 218-240.

Secessionism in Ethiopian Politics

Wuhibegezer Ferede①

Abstract: The world witnessed the processes of globalization and fragmentation. These integrative and disintegrative impulses primarily challenged the modern state as the internal centrifugal forces opt for dissociation within the penetrating transnational forms of association. These twin processes are evident in the Horn of Africa. In this region, there is a move towards greater supranational integration under the auspice of African Union, Intergovernmental Authority on Development and other trans-national political and economic actors amidst of series of complex secessionist movements. Due to the complexity of addressing the genesis, aspiration and accompanying difficulty of managing diverse data set, spatial focus of this study is confined to Ethiopia. Thus, the study analyzed the historical, political, legal, economic, social, ethnic and cultural factors which are relevant to explain the intensification of secessionist impulses in Ethiopia in spite of the adoption of ethnic federalism and the secessionist constitution (Article 39) to contain such political forces using meta data and discourses collected from social media, interviews and public discourses such as written texts, oral texts (speech) and mixed texts (internet chat) available in the public space. The finding indicted that the interplay of the legacy of colonialism, adoption of anti-state Marxist principles, elitism, ethnicization, domino effect of successfully seceded states and the global developments in communication and military technology as main factors for the intensification of secessionist politics in Ethiopia.

Keywords: Ethiopia; Nationality; Liberation; Secession; Politics

Introduction

The world is witnessing the twin processes of universalization and localization which ultimately leads to fragmentation. Gheorghe (2001: 56) has indicated such phenomenon as tendencies of universalization, integration, and at the same time of separation, isolation and autarchism. These integrative and disintegrative impulses primarily challenged the legitimacy and perseverance of the modern state which had been the most sacred human institution.

As a result, the state system has faced challenges both from internal centrifugal forces

① Associate Professor, Department of Political Science and International Studies, College of Social Sciences, Bahir Dar University, Ethiopia.

demanding for dissociation as it is witnessed in Ethiopia, Egypt, Southern Yemen, Scotland and Eastern Ukraine and the need for transnational forms of association (European Union and African Union). The former usually manifested in what is called "nationality question" seeking for autonomy or outright secession. The second challenge is linked to globalization that has posed considerable challenges to the traditional role of the state.

These twin processes are evident in the Horn of Africa. Thus, we witness both trends which call for integration under the auspice of African Union, and Inter Governmental Authority Development and complex secessionist and liberationist movements. With the intent of fulfilling the dream of the founding fathers of Pan-Africanism and for harnessing the advantages of regional integration both African Union and Inter Governmental Authority for Development are working for ensuring integration. However, the region witnessed the birth of new secessionist states and it is vulnerable to further disintegration. What's unfolding in the region is also very pervasive in Ethiopia. After 1960s, the legitimacy of the ancient polity was seriously challenged by ethno-nationalist forces. Waleligne's thesis (1969) became a mantra of those ethno-nationalist forces that saw Ethiopia as a symbol of oppression with the condemnation of its unitary nature which is radically altered with the coming into power of Ethiopian People's Revolutionary Democratic Front.

There are two compelling perspectives pertaining to the establishment of ethnic federalism in Ethiopia. State nationalists argue that it risks state disintegration. The secessionist clause in the constitution and the adoption of federation itself has the impact of secessionist acts by allowing a risk to become independent. The contenders of this line also argue that there is considerable tension or incompatibility between secessionist right and federalism (Ezgi, 2009; Erk & Anderson, 2009).

The liberation front ideologue on the other hand hold that federalism and the rights of nations to self-determination including and up to secession is the lasting solution (panacea) to the nationality question in Ethiopia (FDRE, 1994; Alem, 2005).

Besides, the differing opinion of the two philosophies what one sees on the ground is the increasing risk of disgruntled political forces which have been in military fronts to challenge the existing political arrangement before the recent political openings. Furthermore, localized conflicts are mushroomed. This signals the question of secession is still a living issue that needs scholarly attention.

In addition, whether the roots and the motives of the movements are simple extensions of the nationality question of the past or new demands is not yet ascertained though few studies attribute the root of these problems from internal point of view as simple continuation from the past. Furthermore, most of the studies have hardly examined the domino effect of successful secessionist movements in the region though many African statesmen indicated that the secession of Eritrea will stimulate secessionist movements from Cairo to Cape Town (Donatella, 1993; Ochieng, 2011).

Again, when the region experienced the birth of South Sudan, African leaders have expressed their concern that the division of Sudan would lead to a domino effect. Their fear wrestles on the ground that internationally sanctioned secession and creation of a new state would be contagious and thereby encourages other secession movements in the continent.

Therefore, the fundamental aim of this paper is to analyze the synergy of the exogenous and endogenous factors in shaping the birth and escalation of the secessionist forces in Ethiopia. Specifically, it seeks to examine these forces by mapping historical, political, legal, economic, social, cultural and ethnic factors. Because the investigation of the roots, aspirations and the complex impacts of these political forces and movements deserve a comprehensive scholarly work so that the identification of historic drives and principles that govern the process could be made apparent. In this connection, the paper addressed the following questions: why there are secessionist forces in Ethiopia today or what historical, political, legal, economic, social, ethnic and cultural factors are relevant to explain the secessionist impulses in Ethiopia?

Secessionism in Africa

Notwithstanding the prophesies of some eminent scholars such as Fukuyama (1992) who had declared that the end of the Cold War would usher in the "end of history" that might bring peaceful, stable and cooperative world order, in actual fact, the predictions of the realists of returning towards Hobbesian world where the fragmentation of international order and the emergence of rivalry among atomistic national units became evident (Kupchan, 1998: 134). Thus, international politics has been dominated by inter and intrastate conflicts that led to the collapse of states and the rise of ethno-nationalism. Therefore, at the global level, the end of the Cold War was accompanied by an increase in the number of secessionist movements which sought to establish their own political entities. The following cases are ample examples of disintegration and centrifugal forces.

The separation of Pakistan from India, later Bangladesh from Pakistan and; the disintegration of Yugoslavia along ethno-religious lines; the dissolution of Czechoslovakia into two republics; birth of East Timor; the disintegration of Somali; the birth of Eritrea and Southern Sudan are important examples which show us the potent nature of secessionist movements. We could also include the claims in Egypt at the Sinai desert, Southern Yemen, Scotland, and Eastern Ukraine as contemporary examples of secessionist impulses.

In Africa, the right to exit was established in the 1960s as a decolonization instrument. At the onset, it was enforceable only for restoring justice to nations that continued under the colonial rule in the post-independence period. In line with this prerogative, the UN general assembly has prohibited the recognition of dismemberment and fragmentation of states in its declaration of the Principles of International Law (UN Resolution 1514-XV, 1960).

Accordingly, it allowed ethnic, religious and sub national cultural entities and groups to claim autonomy only within a state boundary. However, the Organization of African Unity was vacillating between these competing rights in practice (Hussein, 2008: 184). Therefore, in Africa secessionist movements which were presented to the global public as analogues to colonial liberation movements eventually assumed the right to exit through the atomization of the mother state.

According Bamfo (2012: 2) secession has become an imminent threat to the integrity of African states, but only few African governments gave recognition to it. Thus, native African governments from the colonial to post-independence period have confronted secessionism to deter the atomization of states. Nevertheless, after 1990s numerous multinational states have disintegrated and became hotbeds of separatist impulses and thus, many aspirants of outright secession come to the forefront. The case can be attested by analyzing the experience in the Horn of Africa which has hosted several secessionist movements and active claims.

Secessionism in the Horn of Africa

The secession of Eritrean and birth of Southern Sudan are worthy of mentioning. Eritreans relentlessly worked to secure their secessionist right by fighting for about thirty years (Wuhibegezer & Emmanuel, 2014). They attained a prominence during the 1974 popular revolution and consummated it in the Post Dergue Period (Bahru, 2008:7).

After secession, Eritrea has also faced a secessionist movement of the Red Sea Afars who are aspiring for establishing the Islamic Republic of Afaria by uniting the Afars in Ethiopia and Djibouti. The secession of Somaliland and the eventual disintegration of the whole of Somalia is another land mark. Again, the Rahanweyn Resistance Army is fighting for an independent state of South Western Somalia. Somaliland has its own secessionist movement called Awdal land in the Western part of the country. Further fracturing continues in the secessionist claim of Azania, part of Juba land.

Hence, the collapse of Somalia as a nation-state with a de facto independence of Northern Somaliland and Punt land shows a reversal towards the Pre-colonial pattern of clan autonomy and calls for a revisiting of the works of ethno-politicians and theorists of nationalism.

The splitting of Sudan into an Arab-Muslim North and Black-Christian South is accompanied by breakaway movements in Beja, Darfur, Kordofan, Eastern Sudan, Nubian and as well in South Sudan.

In Ethiopia, the right of secession has appeared in the academic debate as part of the student politics of the 1960s (Bahru, 2014). Thus, the issue was publicized following the release of Walelligne's article in Struggle which argued about the existence of many nations subsumed with in Ethiopian state nationalism. Due to this fact, he is adored by some as the Lenin of Ethiopia. His thesis received momentum in the post-revolutionary period and became as academic playground for legitimizing the secession of Eritrean (Bahru, 2008: 7), claims from Ogaden (Samatar, 1994, p. 1), Tigray (Alem, 2005) and Oromia (Asafa, 1998).

Conceptual and Theoretical Perspectives

According to Paul and Anke (2002), the word secession is meant "self-cession" implying a decision by a community to break away from a parent state. According to this definition secession is unilateral interruption of bonds and withdrawal from the association, usually the state. Buchanan (2006: 34) defines secession as repudiation of the obligations to obey the state's laws and taking part of the territory claimed by parent state by a group of persons due to certain injustices. Libertarian scholars referred secession as an act of individual liberation from the hegemonic bonds or compulsory ties of the state (Andrei, 2003).

There are two theoretical foundations that try to justify and promote secessionism. The first is called "Remedial Right Only" and the other is grouped as "Primary Right/Choice Theories" (Buchanan, 1997). According to the advocates of a "remedial right only", groups who believe that their right is grossly violated have the right to break away from the union that they belong to. Therefore, secession can be justified only as a remedy of a last resort for persistent and serious injustice (Buchanan, 1997: 34).

In addition, some version of this strand argue that there can be a special right to secede if the state grants the right implicitly or explicitly in the constitution or if there was an agreement/ covenant during the establishment of the association that guarantees secession at a later period of time. However, these theories place significant constraint on the right to secede by making it conditional on the occurrences of serious injustice. The second strand belongs to thinkers who do not put any conditionality for the practice of secession. They argue that a group should have unconditional right to secede without facing any injustice. Secession is not an instrument on a remedial act to mend past grievances.

Analysis of Causes of Secessionism in Ethiopia

As it was indicated in the introductory statement, this part of the paper analyzes how the interaction/synergy of the exogenous forces shaped by dualistic roles of globalization and the domino effect of successful secessionism in one hand, and the internal historical, political, legal, economic, social, ethnic and cultural factors are relevant to explain the intensification of secessionist impulses in Ethiopia.

Historical Causes: Legacies of Colonialism on State Building

The colonial arbitrary dismemberment without any regard for the pre-existing cultural, linguistic and ethnic lines has promoted secessionism (Ottaway, 1982: 20). Herbst (1989) explained that European colonialists ignored basic guidelines for partitioning, take decisions on scanty information about Africa's geography, and divide territories without taking time to consider demographic, ethnographic and topographic imperatives. They simply broke up or clustered people, languages, customs and alliances with little rational guidance from history, tradition, and logic. Hence, we find an ethnic group divided by imaginary line between two or more countries (Ottaway, 1982: 20).

Contrary to this development, nation states were prescribed to the peoples of the Horn as a manifestation of modernity as their colonizing masters. Thus, the rigid territory centric institutions were transplanted (Ottaway, 1982: 15). Ottaway states that the current political tensions and territorial fragmentation crisis facing the sub region trace their origin from the institutionalization of nation state which calls for irredentism, expansionist nationalism, and ethno-nationalism.

Indeed, the frame works of the institutional structure and as well as the philosophical foundation of the nation states is crafted by the European colonial slaughter on the pre-colonial institutional structures of the Horn. In short, what Jackson (1990: 781) termed as "quasi-states" under colonial masters were treated as if they possessed the full attributes of sovereignty, even if they evidently did not. This vividly indicates that sovereignty was used to cover up loopholes under the assumption that these cracks would eventually be sealed and that artificial states would solidify into the real thing.

Again, the post-colonial states in Horn of Africa have been territory centric and territories continued to serve as authentic markers of social identity. Territorial nationalism has burst out of the artificially installed state identity to play in the territorial loss-gain political game (Bahru, 2008, p. 366). This marked a great departure from the pre-colonial modes of social organizations of the African society (Ottaway, 1982: 20) whereby non territorial markers of identity such as family, kinship, religion, tribe and clan ties have been playing central esteem in determining identity. Most vivid instance for such a case is a wandering tribe whose authority structure is completely disassociated from a fixed loyalty to a particular piece of land as we witnessed it among wondering pastoralist (Omar, 1995: 117-122). This fenced mentality which was based on territorial nationalism served as hot bed for irredentism and secessionist movements following the collapse of nation states in the post-colonial period. Therefore, the post-colonial political seismic cataclysm in the Horn was decisively guided by the foundations led down in colonial period and further consolidated by political elites.

Therefore, the haphazard manner in which European powers sliced the continent into colonies makes every country vulnerable for splitting up for myriad of reasons (Bamfo, 2012). The haphazard manner in which nations were created has caused irredentist movement as it is witnessed in the greater Afar, greater Eritrea/Tigray, greater Somalia and Greater Gambela movements. Thus, colonialism instead of serving as a forerunner of globalism in the region, it ended with counter effect at least in producing partition and hysteria.

Modern state building process in Ethiopia is not purely a colonial construct though it was not immune from the diffusion of the ideologies and as well the process of territorialisation. Like in the rest part of the region, the state-building strategy of the Solomonic monarchies in Ethiopia was highly centrist and unitary. The policy of creating unitary state was unfinished business as cultural units resisted the process. Thus, the multifarious groups were not moulded into a fully integrated nation state. Finally, social identities remained in a state of great ambiguity oscillating between assimilation and rejection of the mainstream culture.

Thus, the imperial drive of brining political modernization by instituting nation state which was the order of the day has set in motion the cultural groups guised the question of nationalities. The question was expounded by the students of Haile Sellassie I University College and it has served as sprite of the student politics in the Imperil protest. The grand failure starts here. Its anomalous and mischievous to believe that heavily agrarian feudal state had discrete nations. Following the downfall of the imperial regime the Derge had attempted to addressed secessions impulses through the tents of socialism, but the question persisted till it's down fall in the 1990s.

In the Post Derge period, EPRDF has made paradigm shift and complete departure in the state building strategy by instituting decentralization approach claiming that it will end the vicious cycle of violence and danger of disintegration along with forging one political and economic community. The ruling party has applauded it as novel change that unchartered space of Ethiopia's political history but sections of the opposition viewed it as plot for balkanization of the Ethiopian state (Alem, 2005: 332). Some others also viewed it as unfulfilled promise that served for the perpetuation of the orders of the old days (Asafa, 2001).

Pandora's Box Tragedy of Colonial Boundaries

The political boundaries that we exhibit form the map of Africa are not the making of the people of Africa. According to Ahluwalia and Abebe (2002: 1), African boundaries are the artificial creation of the European colonial powers that imposed to imprison the people in a specific environment to be easily controlled, exploited and oppressed. Thus, the boundaries of Africa which were designed in the European capitals in the last quarter of the 19th century led to the partitioning of more than 200 ethnic groups in the continent (Michalopoulos and Papaioannou 2011: 1).

The independence leaders were informed to keep them intact instead of seeking for reform or restructure their boundaries for they could cause an active social volcano. Accordingly, as it is mentioned on the charter of the OAU, the founding father believed that legalizing colonial boundaries intact minimizes boundary conflicts in the continent.

New African governments tried to adhere closely to the boundaries they had inherited to uphold the principle of *uti possidetis,* which provides that states emerging from decolonization shall presumptively inherit the colonial administrative borders they held at independence (Emmanuel & James, 1993). That understanding has done little to dampen calls coming from some governments to clarify their boundaries with their neighbours, which is a euphemism for getting apiece of territory back (Bamfo, 2012: 38).

Therefore, delegates at the first Organization of African Unity (OAU) meeting in Addis Ababa in 1963 opted to support the inviolability of national borders as one of the organization's core principles. In 1964, the OAU formally backed this principle at the Cairo's Declaration of Border Disputes among African States. The OAU was seeking to avoid opening a Pandora's Box as it sought to discourage groups from making irredentist claims on other groups outside their common border.

When we ask the question why founding fathers of the OAU feared uniting the divided people, immediately after independence or why they inherited boundaries drawn by the colonial masters instead of resorting towards indigenous institutions, the usual answer is to avoid catastrophic boundary conflict. However, the conflicts that have occurred between nations are blamed on the haphazard demarcation of borders (Hughes, 2004). It can be witnessed from the clash between Egypt and Libya in 1977 when Libyan forces occupied Sallum in Egypt. Egypt and Sudan had a dispute over the Hala'ib Triangle. Ethiopia and Somalia fought over Ogaden, whereas Libya and Chad over the Aouzou Strip. Nigeria and Cameroon had disputations over Bakassi, Ethiopia and Eritrea fought for controlling Badme and recently Abyie became a bone of contention between Juba and Khartoum.

Hence, the first generation of African leaders that worked for the decolonization of their continent failed to decolonize themselves from colonial constructs. They remained passive in uniting divided people by unmaking what had been drawn by their colonizing masters. When they stood to establish organization of African unity, they hoped, to bring continental unity, but they become instruments artificial dividing lines. The boundaries of Somali land and Somalia, Ethiopia and Eritrea, Republic of Sudan and South Sudan are examples that show the shift of politics of boundaries of Africa contrary to inheritance. The worse impact of this process is its replication in defining intra state territorial claims of ethnic groups. In Ethiopia claims and counter claims of territories on the basis of real and invented histories became the order of the day. Therefore, the high level boundary conflicts are reproducing itself at local level.

Domino Effect of the Secession of Eritrea and South Sudan

It is very difficult to measure the level of the regional domino effect of the successful Secession of Eritrea and South Sudan on the secessionist movements in Ethiopia. However, the former was very decisive in shaping the political landscape and the constitutionalization process in Ethiopia. TPLF in its early stage was adopting secessionist manifesto to suit itself with the Eritrean question. OLF had also followed the same suit traversed by EPLF (Alem, 2005: 332). By the same token, the birth of the newest state of South Sudan is re activating the Gambela question. In actual fact, the domino effect is facilitated with CNN effect, technology break through that gave birth to various social media outlets, durable vehicles, satellite mobiles, and modern guns.

Abuse and Invention of History

Manipulation and reinterpretation of history is one of the instruments of political socialization in the region. According to Guazzini (2003: 2-3), the political abuse of history by elites has led to revisions and quest for a new approach centred on cohesive trans-cultural encounters that recognizes the significance of the constituents. Moreover, Crummy expounds the encounter as follows.

"... *across the Horn political elites have... used history for narrow ends and have compromised the conditions for scholarly study of history. The recognition of this common experience could be a starting point for a new agenda for the historians of the region, the development of historical consciousness that is broader than... earlier forms. This would start with a re-examination of constituent assumptions and a commitment to dialogue. It ought to also include a critical examination of the burden of the modern state and its absolutist claim, not least to territoriality and absolute borders" (Crummey,* 2003: 129-130*).*

Thus, he called for a new scholarship that re-envisions the hitherto *sacro sanct* historical assumptions and actors along with the conception of modern state. Therefore, a deeper scrutiny of the recent secessionist movement in the region depicts that of historical identities remained a powerful tool in organizing and mobilizing peoples against the state burdened with the historical load wafted by colonial powers. It was the abuse of history that served to explain the colonization of Eritrea by Ethiopia and for the formulation of the black colonization thesis among Oromo elites. Due to the intellectual failure of turning the past politics into binding history till today our distance past is matter of political concern as it is indicated in many of the public discourses.

The practical steps needed for the purification of history from ab/uses is smartly articulated by Guazzini (2003: 11). This exposition prescribes the production, reproduction and dissemination of a truly free, ethical and socially worth historical knowledge capable of educating the new generation about the culture of inclusion and appreciation of difference (ibid).

Socio-cultural Justifications: Elitism

The legacies of colonialism were not the only reasons which are factored in triggering the secessionist movement in the region. Elites had been entrusted the task of envisioning imaginary community modelled after the nation states of Europe. This has ignited elusive passion and fervour of separatism and ultra-nationalism under the banner of a "mythical nation". The elitist political entrepreneurs in the region have been manipulating identities produced by their own craftsmanship of primordialization (Alemseged, 1998: 14; Tronvoll, 2003: 51; Sisay 2009: 121) as a political strategy for securing political legitimacy (Guazzini, 2003: 4).

For this end, they select or forge identities that suit them in defining their interest disguised as the group's interest. In the process, they affect the self-definition of the group, its boundaries and social formation to the extent that its nationality would be completely different from its pre-cursor or progenitor. That I am Oromo, Tigray or Amhara first discourse which has widely diffused into the self-identification discourse in Ethiopia is case in point. The preoccupation of the populace on divisive and politicized identities confers the chance of ideological legitimacy for political elites (Guazzini, 2003: 3). However, some sections of the society remain sandwiched and highly perplexed with the conflicting of values between their traditions and the notions of the political elites (Crummey, 2003: 117).

This phenomenon has complicated the regional globalization process and promotes separatist tendencies. Again, the contingency of forming preference in a community moves parallel to the knowledge production and dissemination usually spear headed by elites but yet most of them convey political interest imbedded in it. This shows the systematic distortion of facts; information and production of wronged alternatives either by politicizing or de-politicizing history and human identity. Thus, elite driven politicization of history and human identity continued to play its role and the way out remain intact awaiting determined harbingers ready to establish the organic past.

Invention of Identities

In spite of the existence of political entities resting on a common and exclusive identity, in most cases secessionist or/and irredentist aspirations in the Horn were rooted upon the invention of an imagined homogenous political community that rest on critical natural resources instrumental for transforming inventions in to a reality in the form of producing a large political community. This disillusioned process is short sighted and mostly failed to stretch its project as far back to the pre-colonial connections and there of the roots of the community will be traced from sagacious and foggy shared origin.

This shows the irony of the project because while Europe, the birth place of nation state went far to trans-nationality, the Horn is staggering to achieve nationality (Crummey, 2003: 117). For realizing the instrumentalist dream, political elites instead of examining the processes that brought about the post-colonial realities, they were preoccupied in construction of divisive walls centred on animosity neglecting pacific interactions.

However, recently there are very few regionalist head starts aspiring for the rectification of the neglected portion of the Horn's veritable and rich past (Lye, 2004: 38-45). Lye and Crummey are some of the articulators of the regionalist vision and aspire for creating shared past and common destiny among the peoples of the Horn by moulding association of sovereignties.

In describing the causes that infuse barricades of interstate interconnections; both of them criticize the betrayal of the intelligentsia against their own society in the production of knowledge on the history, culture and politics with a general tone of regret and exigency (Cummey, 2003,: 118-129; Lye, 2004: 38-45). While Crummy curses the political elites for the dysfunctional states in the Horn, Lye attributed treason of intellectuals as causative for pervasive spatial identity claims of the society. However, Lye couldn't provide us an alternative approach or a means that liberates the mind tricked by elite's and colonizers forgery.

This shows the systematic distortion of facts; information and production of wronged alternatives either by politicizing or de-politicizing history and human identity. Thus, elite driven politicization of history and human identity continued to play its role and the way out for re-constructing links among the societies of the Horn remain intact awaiting determined harbingers ready to establish the organic past of the region.

Political and Legal Explanations

This subtopic tries to address some of the basic political features and legalization processes that had fundamental impacted on the genesis and growth of secessionist forces in Ethiopia.

Ethnicization of Politics

Ethnicity is an elusive and fluid concept which has subjective and objective components. Thinkers in the earlier period of the nineteen century dismissed ethnicity as a form of irrational and false consciousness. Accordingly, Marx and Engel forecast the disappearance of ethnicity with the emergency of the industrial proletariat, but contrary to their view multi ethnic states fractured in the post cold war period and aggravate the intra state conflict (Denis, 2002:459).The view that ethnicity is a transit phenomenon in the process of the formation of modern nations went through a radical revision. Scholars began to argue that it can neither be merely explained away nor ignored for it's with us in one form or another (Dubow, 1994: 355).

There are two perspectives in the understanding of ethnicity. The first is the instrumentalist perspective which conceives ethnicity in a situational, contextual and subjective sense, and the second is the essentialist/primordial view is typified by a tendency to conceptualize identity in static terms. In fact, ethnic identity is not static, but it bears roots in a historically relevant culture. Thus, ethnicity deserves to be treated as a phenomenon more complex than either primordial identity or the flamboyant garb of self-interest (Fardon, 1994: 355).

In addition, ethnic identity is something that is fluid rather than static, an issue which is sometimes used as a justification for negating its authenticity. The most likely approach in dealing with it is to mingle both perspectives in a double move under a creative synthesis. The histories of various ethnic groups in the Horn are needed to be validated whether they are accurate or mythical. The invention of ethnic identity is dangerous as it misses ethnic feeling and it has to be dealt with in its contemporary sphere of implicit relevance (Carr, 1995: 27).

Again, the liberal blue print of nation-building was instrumented through ethnic homogenization and forceful assimilation. This has caused rise of ethno-nationalist movements as they endeavour not to give up their identity (Salih & Markakis, 1998: 7). Thus, the practice of cultural democracy through multi-national decentralized arrangement has gained momentum in multi-national, multi-cultural and multi-lingual societies in the Horn because of the disastrous destruction of the nation state (Crummey, 2003: 123).

Thus, state-driven national unification and the era of centralization have come to an end. The dysfunctions can be inferred from the irony when the architectures of the notion went far into regional union (Crummey, 2003: 118) yet the Horn is still exercising the project of state building in a fashion of making a new wall out of the old breaks.

The above mentioned explanations trace the roots of the ethno-nationalist movement for secession from the problem of the state in legitimizing itself while it went to the process of nation building. Nation building as its indicated in the liberal blue print and the way ethnicity was addressed in the process is argued to be the driver and the embedded cause for the rise of secessionism in Ethiopia. On the other hand, similar to Rok (2002), Abebe (2011: 86) argued that ethnicity has much to do with competitive politics caused by environmental scarcity. It is used by the powerful and/or powerless groups to control the state apparatus and its resources. The later explanation emphasis on the differential impact in resource bestows and the need for state capture as main cause for ethnic based competitive politics which is usually manifested as outright claim for secession after weighting the power balance of the contenders.

The Politics of the Student Movement

In Ethiopia, the right of secession has appeared in the academic debate as part of the student politics of the 1960s (Bahru, 2014). Thus, the issue was publicized following the release of Waleligne's article which argued about the existence of many nations masked in Ethiopian state nationalism thought it was also challenged by many state nationalists in the movement (Ayalewu, 2013)

Due to this fact, he is adored by some as the Lenin of Ethiopia. His thesis has serve as base for legitimizing the secession of Eritrean, the claim from ONLF, OLF, and TPLF in defiance of state nationalists' tent of maintaining de-ethicized unitary state. The question caused a state legitimating crisis and rise of ethno-nationalism which saw Ethiopian nationalism as symbol of oppression, black colonialism and cultural suicide. It has also created impasse between Pan-Ethiopian state nationalists and ethno-nationalists. However, Waleligne and his colleagues understood the state and its ideology in light of Marxism as an institution of oppression which deserves dismantling for ensuring proletariat internationalism. This is tantamount to ideological national treason and self-denial. Surprisingly, the fundamental pillars of EPRDF's state building strategy was shaped by this conviction.

Post-1991 Developments

After the down fall of Derge through coalition of insurgent groups, there was an attempt of instituting transitional charter which called for redefining the Ethiopia state where by equal rights and self-determination of all the peoples to be the governing principles of political, economic, and social life in Ethiopia. What had been chartered out in this transitional charter was later on reproduced in the establishment of Federation and the secessionist constitution. Thus, EPRDF has made an unforeseen paradigm shift in the state building strategy by instituting radical decentralization approach (Andreas, 2013) claiming that it will end the vicious cycle of violence and danger of disintegration along with forging one political and economic community.

It has applauded it as novel change that could transform Ethiopia's political history. However, both the federal arrangement and the secessionist constitution became intellectual and practical challenges. Scholars and some opposition parties criticized that the federal arrangement as primordial tribalism that will provoke ethnic animosity/violence (Alem, 2005: 332); the continuation of Abyssinian domination in a new fashion (Asafa, 2001) and divide-and-rule by a minority group (Vaughan, 2003). Recently, we have also witnessed localized identity questions even in the core of the Ethiopia state. But still EPRDF insisted that it had instituted political modernization that will ensure Ethiopian renaissance by transcending the odds of disintegration. However, if we ask the question why the adoption of ethnic federalism and the secessionist constitution (Article 39) failed to contain such political forces, the answer remains implausible.

The Current Political Reform and Tides of Secessionism

In the common public discourse, the ongoing political reform in Ethiopia is erroneously dubbed as transition whereas transition is the space between one political regime and another characterized by the dissolution of an authoritarian regime and installation of some form of democracy competed with the return to some form of authoritarian rule or the emergence of a revolutionary alternative (Schmitter, 1986:6). In actual fact what is still going on in Ethiopia is political liberalization which implies an easing of repression and extension of civil liberties within an authoritarian regime by embracing pro-liberalization faction.

Liberalization begins with schisms within the authoritarian coalition (Kaufman, 1986). In Ethiopian context, EPRDF reformist team is acclaimed as harbingers the process. This tendency ignores the fact that internal schisms are necessary if an authoritarian regime is forced to liberalize itself. The splits within authoritarian coalitions as a starting point for liberalization do not mean the role of opposition actors or mass protest is void. Some actors within an authoritarian coalition may begin liberalization primarily in response to actors outside the coalition and may co-opt with moderate ones. Again, liberalization begins because reformist actors in the authoritarian coalition want to minimize losses or retain power by deterring radical change.

In this sense, the political reform after grand popular protests, though its unfinished business, has brought optimism and grand confusion in Ethiopia. The seismic political opening which ensued since April 2018, the web of legal reforms created unprecedented opportunity for disciplining the heavy-handed authoritarianism. The reform was also expected to ensure a peaceful resolution of the fundamental contradictions defining the state and the form of government structure by ensuring separation of the state and the government, and the independence of the judiciary.

However, given the top down approach of the reforming process which was expected to went far towards transitional arrangement being supported from below with civic engagement has made the opening process elitist. The grass root participation was important in shaping the path towards democracy and addressing the fundamental question how the democratic space could become more open and integrating in order to strengthen the social cohesion in the country.

The heightened popular expectations towards peaceful and democratic future along with unenlightened moves returned opposition from exile have shadowed the optimism with uncertainty as its manifested from separatist tendencies in interstate relations and continuation of ungoverned spaces in the hands of armed insurgencies. In spite of the warm applaud for the reform in its onset, now the process is twisting between optimism and suspicion. People are asking where we are heading due to the missing of road map for transition.

The aspiration to move from authoritarian rule to the gestation of democracy has been the question for generations and the grand promise of the "reformist groups" is ensuring electoral democracy at any cost. The message from the high politics who are believed to be in the making of Ethiopian transition speaks of democracy, equality, prosperity, security, common interests, justice and fairness. The reality, on the other hand, as lived by the majority is very different, and includes the experience of exploitation, domination, and sustained inequalities.

The optimism that the old order would give away to transition adversely felt and produces frustration, alienation, anger, dissent and pressure from below for the resolution of grievances.

Thought monolithic reality may not be conceived and articulated in precise terms now those who had been championed as reformist are found countering the general quest for structural political change in the country with intent of preventing such sentiments from turning into radical impulses. The logic in the argument of these forces rested on the belief of gradualist and comprehensive change with the inclusion of the old order which was the grand architect of the problem in the country.

Had it not been for the discrepancy between hegemonic optimistic message flooded by millions as it was verified in the mammoth demonstrations in support of the move towards a democratic transition in the country and the lived reality, there would obviously be much less need for the unremitting assault on popular consciousness through misinformation nor would it be necessary to take much account of critiques as the work of isolated individuals who could be dismissed as eccentrics, and who would have no hope of achieving a serious vision. The discrepancy between rhetoric, even when backed by reality as it is lived, does provide a very large terrain for frustration.

Since the onset of the reformist discourse, cautious scholars had been warning about the dangers of gradualist structural political change associating it with the parable of old win in new bottle. Thus, the stalemate has reappeared in the aspiration for peace full democratic transition that would end the centuries old blood shed caused by political conflict. The expectation was the reformist leaders would chart out the road map towards transition to be preceded by all engaging political processes. Neither transitional road map nor its precedents were undertaken rather manifestations of an authoritarian rollback come into the scene. The only grand promise awaiting for concluding that reformist promise is a grand betrayal or genuine move towards democracy is the upcoming election. However, electoral democracy in its minimalistic feature in the context of societal and party fragmentation, unprecedented militarization and elite polarization is improbable.

The examination of the existing models and theories for an elaborated conviction on possibility of attain a transition in Ethiopia has surmount significance. One of the model which is often used for understanding the prospect of success of transition is the comparative political economy model which analyzes structural variables or historical trajectories. In this case, the country's political history indicates set of dread and deadlocks with high propensity of deterring the move forward. The other approach is the rationality-activist model which seeks informed and active population in politics. However, in the Ethiopian case, populist and inorganic elite are drifting the society towards divergent direction. The third actor centric model which seeks elite bargaining for elite transformations through voluntary collaboration or coalition is lacking in the country's present context. The worst is the parochial, subjective political culture in cultural perspective. The most recent approach is genetic model which calls for national unity and conscious action or pact on the part of the top political leadership is also missing. Thus, in light all these parameters, the prospect for realization of the grand promise of the reforming circle is unlikely.

The unpredictability of the future of the state given the high degree of indeterminacy embedded in situations where unexpected events bursting everywhere with insufficient information, hurried and audacious choices, confused motives and interests, and even in definition of political identities have elevated the confusion. Ignoring all these bottle necks, the legacy of the authoritarian past such as the cult of personality not programs, zero-sum politics, the military contestants for political power, ethnicity, weak state capacity and civil society, mix-up of domestic and foreign politics, lack of collective goals, party and social fragmentation are the possible stumbling blocks for the success of the promised transition through electoral democracy. The worst is the election is extended indefinitely due the outburst of the global epidemic. This might lead us to conclude that Ethiopia could experience its six grand failure and resurgence of secessionism became domineering.

Conclusion

The study was focused on historical watersheds without dismissing the hitherto mentioned factors that serve as root for the rise and development of secessionism in Ethiopia. Accordingly, the making and interruption of nation state building has caused intensification of secessionist, liberationist and irredentist ethno-nationalist forces in Ethiopia. A common way to express the later was using the epithet greater. This political cataclysm was further aggravated by the ab/use of history and instrumentalization of social identities. The crux of the matter centred on the binary political impasse between ethno-nationalism and state nationalism due lack state legitimacy.

Hence, there is need for political modernity that liberates the mind tricked by the imprints of colonialism diffused through modern education and haunts the move towards, creating state legitimacy. As its indicated in the discussion above politics of the past remain as it was and serve for legitimizing political claims. Thus, the purification of history from abuses through the production and dissemination professional knowledge is demanding task that awaits experts in the area in lieu of leaving it aside for miseducated squabbling elites. The other prominent curse is the competitive ethnicization of politics that diffuses in to every village and town in Ethiopia for legitimizing real or invented injustice of the past served for promoting separatism. In addition to the internal developments, secessionism in Ethiopia is also fostered by domino effect of the birth of secessionist states in the region and by the new technological breakthroughs such as social media and war fare technologies. Finally, the evaluation of the onset of the current political reform is unlikely to resolve the political contradictions rather it's expected to herald another lost opportunity and failure in addressing the entrenched issues that promote secessionism.

References

[1] AHLUWALIA P, ABEBE Z.2002. African identities: contemporary political and social challenges. Burlington, VT: Ashgate Publishing.

[2] ALEMSEGED A.1998. Identity jilted or re-imagining identity? the divergent paths of the Eritrean and Tigrayan nationalist struggles. Lawrenceville: Red Sea Press.

[3] HABTU A. 2005. Multiethnic federalism in Ethiopia: astudy of the secession clause inthe constitution. Publius: The Journal of Federalism, 35(2): 313–335.

[4] ANDREAS E. 2003. Ethnic Federalism: New Frontiers in Ethiopian Politics// BARNABAS G. First national conference on federalism, conflict and peace building. Addis Ababa: United Printers, 142–172.

[5] ANDREI K. 2003. The constitutional right of secession, in political theory and history. Journal of Libertarian Studies, 17(4): 39–100.

[6] ASAFA J.1998.The cultural roots of Oromo nationalism. Lawrenceville: Red Sea Press.

[7] ASAFA J. 2001.Fighting against the injustice of the state and globalization: comparing the African American and the Oromo movements. New York: Palgrave.
[8] YIMAM A. 2013. The Ethiopian students movement and the national question: theory and practice, 1950-1980. Takoma Park: Ayakew Yimam (Mukhtar).
[9] BAHRU Z. 2008. Society state and history: selected essays. Addis Ababa: Addis Ababa University Press.
[10] BAHRU Z. 2014. The quest for socialist utopia: Ethiopian student movement, c. 1960-1974. Addis Ababa: Addis Ababa University Press.
[11] BAMFO N.2012. The menace of secession in Africa and why governments should care: the disparate cases of Katanga, Biafra, South Sudan, and Azawad. Global Journal of Human Social Science, 12(10): 37-48.
[12] BUCHANAN, A. 1997. Theories of secession. Philosophy and Public Affairs, 26(1): 31-61.
[13] LUCY C. 1995. Ethnicity: a contemporary issue in African politics. Cambridge: Relationships Foundation.
[14] CLAPHAM C. 2000. War and state formation in Ethiopia and Eritrea. Paris: Centre d' Etudes et de Recherches Internationales.
[15] CLAPHAM C. 2002. Controlling space in Ethiopia//JAMES W, KURIMOTO E, DONHAM D L, et al. Remapping Ethiopia socialism and after. Oxford: James Currey Ltd, Addis Ababa: Addis Ababa University Press, Athens: Ohio University Press.
[16] CRUMMEY D. The horn of Africa: between history and politics. Northeast African Studies, 2009,10(3): 117-138.
[17] DENIS D. 2002. Ethnicity and development//VANDANA D, ROBERT B P. The companion to development studies. New York: Oxford University Press Inc.
[18] DONATELLA L. 1993. Eritreans voting on independence from Ethiopia.http://www.nytimes.com/1993/04/24/world/eritreans-voting-on-independence-from-ethiopia.html
[19] Dubow S. 1994. Ethnic euphemisms and racial echoes. Journal of Southern African Studies, 20(3): 355-370.
[20] AMADIFE E N, WARHOLA J W. 1993. Africa' s political boundaries:colonialcartography, the OAU, and the advisability of ethno-national adjustment. International Journal of Politics, Culture and Society, 6(4): 533–554.
[21] EZGI D. 2014. Making secession possible: federalism as a capacity building instrument. http://citation.allacademic.com/meta/p364233_index.html
[22] FARDON R. 1994. Crossed destinies: the entangled histories of west African ethnic and national identities. Journal of Southern African Studies, 20(3): 355.
[23] FDRE R(1994), Constitution of the Federal Democratic Republic of Ethiopia, article 39. http://www.wipo.int/edocs/lexdocs/laws/en/et/et007en.pdf.
[24] FUKUYAMA F. 1992. The end of history and the last man. New York: Macmillan, Inc.
[25] GHEORGHE E. 2001. Contemporary culture: between individualization and globalization. //

Marin Aiftincă(ed.). Culture and freedom: cultural heritage and the contemporary change series, IVA, Africa, Vol.16. Washington, D.C.: Council for Research in Values and Philosophy.

[26] GUAZZINI F. 2003. Guest editor' s introduction: historians and histories of the hornof Africa: toward a comparative view. Northeast African Studies, 10(3): 1-12.

[27] HERBST J. 1989. The creation and maintenance of national boundaries in Africa. International Organization, 43 (3): 673-692.

[28] HUGHES A. 2004. Decolonizing Africa: colonial boundaries and the crisis of the (non) nation state. Diplomacy and Statecraft, 15: 833-834.

[29] HUSSEIN MA. 2008. From tyranny to anarchy: the Somali experience. Trenton: The Red Sea Press.

[30] IYE A M. 2005. Launching of a new and innovative initiative on the horn of Africa//OSMAN S A. Journal of the Horn of Africa, 23: 37-45.

[31] Jackson R. 1990. Quasi states: sovereignty international relations and the third world. New York: Cambridge University Press

[32] ERK J, ANDERSON L. 2009. The paradox of federalism: does self-rule accommodateor exacerbate ethnic divisions? Regional & Federal Studies, 19(2): 191-202.

[33] KUPCHAN C. 2000. After Pax Americana: benign power, regional integration and the sources of a stable multipolarity//Hansen B, Heurlin B. The new world order: contrasting theories. London: Palgrave Macmillan UK, 134-166.

[34] OCHIENG Z. 2011. Will an independent south trigger more secession? http://www.theeastafrican.co.ke/news/Will-an-independent-South-trigger-more-secession/2558-1086282-sq8r2m/index.html

[35] MANSUR A O. 1995. The nature of the Somali clan system//Ahmed A J. The invention of Somalia. Lawrenceville: The Red Sea Press, 117-134.

[36] Ottawa M.1982. Soviet and American influence in the Horn of Africa// RUBINSTEIN A Z. Journal of studies of influence in international relations, New York: Praeger.

[37] PAUL C, Anke H. 2002. The political economy of secession: centre for the study of African economies. http://citeseerx.ist.psu.edu/viewdoc/download?doi=10.1.1.115.7010&rep=rep1&type=pdf

[38] ROK A. 2002. Politicised ethnicity, competitive politics and conflict in Kenya: a historical perspective. African Studies, 61(2): 251-268.

[39] SALIH M, MARKAKIS J. 1998. Ethnicity and state in east Africa. Uppsala: Nordiske Afrika Institutent.

[40] SAMATAR A I. 2004. Ethiopian Federalism: autonomy versus control in the Somali Region. Third World Quarterly, 25(6): 1131-1154.

[41] SISAY A. 2009. Challenges to peace and sustainable development in the Horn of Africa: Case of Ethiopia. Journal of the Horn of Africa, 27: 119-162.

[42] MICHALOPOULOS S, PAPAIOANNOU E. 2011. The long-run effects of the scramble for

Africa. http://www.nber.org/papers/w17620.

[43] Takele T. 2013. The national question (regionalism) in Ethiopia. ESUNA newsletter// The Ethiopian students movement and the national question: theory and practice,1950-1980. Takoma Park: Ayakew Yimam (Mukhtar).

[44] TRONVOLL K.2003. Identities in conflict: an ethnography of war and the politics of identity in Ethiopia, 1998-2000. London: University of London.

[45] UN. 1960. UN general assembly resolution 1514 (XV). [1960-12-14] https://www.sfu.ca/~palys/UN-Resolution%201514.pdf.

[46] VAUGHAN S.2003. Ethnicity and Power in Ethiopia. Edingburgh: The University of Edinburgh.

[47] MEKONENE W. 1969. On the questions of nationality in Ethiopia. Struggle, ArtsIV, HSIU(17).

[48] WUHIBEGEZER F, EMMANUEL A M. 2014. The trajectories of the ethio-eritrean distinct identity construction and the invention of nationalist historiography. International Journal of Educational Research and Development, 3(3): 46-50.

第二部分　发展与变革中的埃塞俄比亚

第二部分综述

在埃革阵执政时期，埃塞俄比亚在经济建设方面取得了瞩目的成绩，但经济上的繁荣和埃革阵的铁腕统治掩盖了埃塞俄比亚日益尖锐的社会矛盾。领导人梅莱斯·泽纳维去世后，埃革阵内部派系之间的权力斗争愈演愈烈，执政党的领导能力被大幅削弱，宗教冲突、民族矛盾等社会问题井喷式爆发。2018 年 4 月阿比·艾哈迈德·阿里（Abiy Ahmed Ali）上台后通过一系列的政治和经济改革，逐步赢得了埃塞俄比亚人民的认可，并形成了以阿比为核心的繁荣党执政团队。至此，埃塞俄比亚正式进入繁荣党时代。随着政局的演变，埃塞俄比亚的政治、经济、社会、外交、医疗卫生等领域都出现了新的发展趋势和变化。

本部分含中英文学术论文 10 篇，主要涉及埃塞俄比亚的政治改革及其影响、安全形势、对外关系、民族问题、宗教问题、女性主义思潮、医疗卫生领域的问题和挑战等内容。相关选题和内容有助于读者了解 2018 年以来埃塞俄比亚各领域的新动态及其原因和影响。

The Current Economic Development Component of the Ethiopia-China Relationships

Messay Mulugeta[1]

Abstract: This study examines the economic development component of the current Ethiopia-China relationships with more emphasis to the post-April 2018 grand political events in Ethiopia. Since the late 1990s, strong economic ties have developed between these two countries, with trade partnership of more than US$3 billion a year, and over US$4 billion Chinese investment in Ethiopia, from a non-existent base two decades before that time. This relationship provides Ethiopia with an unprecedented opportunity to benefit from China's most rapidly growing economy and technology in the world. Given that the African Union is based in Addis Ababa, the current strong Ethiopia-China relationship also has major economic implications for Africa as well. At the same time, it presents Ethiopia with significant challenges, such as the challenges to adapt Chinese technologies to local circumstances and priorities; and to ensure, among others, that the development projects are sustainable and in essential harmony with the environment and socio-cultural variables. On Ethiopian side, untangling the complexities of the challenges to harness the best out of the relationship requires transformative and accountable leaders who are capable of selecting and channelling the opportunities from China.

Keywords: Ethiopia; China; Economic Relations; Foreign Direct Investment (FDI)

Introduction

Ethiopia is a sovereign state located in the Horn of Africa. With a population of over 110 million (CSA, 2018), Ethiopia is the second most populous country in sub-Saharan Africa, next to Nigeria. Ethiopia has created international reputation for its staggering double digit growth for the last decade. The natural resource bases of the country, government's commitment to change the livelihoods of its people, economic collaborations with other countries and regional organizations (such as China, Rok and European Union) and international development agents, relative security and the aspiration of the people to growth have contributed for that growth. Ethiopia is also characterized as a country with growing flow of Foreign Direct Investment (FDI), which reached 2.2

① Associate Professor, College of Development Studies, Addis Ababa University billion USD in 2015/2016 (EIC, 2016), on account of the robust economic growth and the increase in the number of the middle class in the country. Hence, Ethiopia is currently a preferred destination for investors from many countries, the most notable of which is China.

Ethiopia is listed at 165th in the World Bank's list of countries by per capita gross domestic product, i.e. 768 USD in 2017. According to UNDP (2018), poverty in Ethiopia is estimated to have declined from 45.5 per cent in 2000 to 23.5 per cent in 2016. These trends show that Ethiopia is on the right path to economic development though the issue of income inequality is still a major concern. It is also becoming a suitable investment destination for countries that wish to invest overseas, of which Ethiopia-China relations could likely be most successful in this regard.

Ethiopia's fervidness to have well-built economic relations with China is reflected by the frequent visits made by high level government officials to China as well as the enormous involvement of the Chinese companies in Ethiopia's multiple development sectors, the most notable of which are manufacturing; construction; real estate development, machinery and equipment rental; and hotel and resort development. This outcome has been achieved as a result of a number of investment-enhancing measures taken by the Ethiopian government. Those measures include robust industrial parks development undertakings, enforcement of targeted investor recruitment procedures, finance provision, comprehensive investment climate reforms and maintenance of security across the country.

In order to achieve a well-built and sustainable Ethiopia-China economic relationship, the governments of both countries are advised to work towards sincere mutual benefits, as per the FOCAC principles, unlike the case that Ethiopia has been experiencing from most western countries. The relationship is required to be based on the old principle *teaching to fish to feed for a lifetime* not on the basis of *giving fish to feed on for a day*. Though investments should create opportunities from which all parties would gain, Ethiopia, as a least developed country, has to be provided with sufficient opportunity to learn from circumstances that led to China's economic growth and adapt it to its socioeconomic and environmental situations. This, no doubt, enables Ethiopia to bring about sustainable, equitable and eco-friendly development within a few years to come. This scenario hugely benefits both sides as Ethiopia's economic growth improves the livelihood of the people that, in turn, widens China's market in Ethiopia for its manufactured goods. It also builds the purchasing power of Ethiopians to utilize the goods and services supplied by China. In fact, the Ethiopia-China economic ties should be accompanied by the advancement of the Ethiopian youth in targeted vocational and technological skills so as to widen employment opportunity for the youth in Chinese companies in Ethiopia, a condition that helps the companies to make use of the cheap labour. Therefore, for efficient Ethiopia-China economic relationships, which unfold utmost mutual benefits, various issues should be given attention during strategy formulation. These, include, but are not limited to, adequately thought-out joint projects, exchange of researchers, local employment and market opportunities, local skills development, technology transfer, inclusion of local community and the environmental milieu.

Overview of the Current reforms in Ethiopia

It was in April 2018 that the new political atmosphere has begun in Ethiopia as a result of the wide-spread apprising of the Ethiopian people (particularly the youth) discontented of the inequality, joblessness, grand corruption and the general political climate of the country. The coming to power of the transformative government has been warmly accepted by the vast majority Ethiopians, political activists, the academia, neighboring countries, embassies in Ethiopia, NGOs, aid agencies, CSOs, religious institutes and the Ethiopian diaspora. Particularly, the Ethiopian youth accepted the government with great passion and sanguinity.

In fact, it does not mean that there is no resistance to the transformation though it hasn't stopped the government from going ahead swiftly with much-needed politico-economic and diplomatic reforms. Since he assumed power in April 2018, the current government instituted significant reforms and promised much more. The major targets of the reform include political reforms, social, constitutional, economic, foreign policy, military and the security sectors.

In the political reforms, the government has presided over the release of political prisoners from several jails across Ethiopia and the opening of the country's political landscapes. Thousands of the members of the opponent political parts, such as Ogaden National Liberation Front (ONLF), Ginbot 7, Oromo Liberation Front(ONLF) and Oromo Federalist Congress (OFC), were released. Some of these political parties had been designated as terrorist organizations by the EPDRF government and banned since 2011. A few of the released detainees were facing death penalty on terrorism charges. Charges were also dropped for US-based political activists and affiliated satellite television networks such as OMN and ESAT.

The state of emergency (SoE), previously proclaimed against the wide-ranging public uprising and the consequent damages to resources and humanity, was ended two months in advance of the expiration of its six-month tenure. In the same way, the current government announced to amend the anti-terrorism law which was widely condemned as a tool of political repression.

Economic reform is another vital achievement these days in Ethiopia. A case in point is the announcement of the state-owned enterprises (SOEs) to be partially or whole privatized. This is a landmark shift in Ethiopian economic model which used to be a kind of Developmental Sate Model. Giant state-owned enterprises such as Ethiopian airlines and Ethio telecom are targeted for this purpose though there are many other SOEs deemed less critical including power supply companies, railway operation, industrial parks, hotels and manufacturing firms. The intended economic reform, in addition to the shift in the level of the government control over the economy, is considered as a vital measure aimed at improving the country's deteriorating foreign-exchange reserves, which by the end of 2017 were equal in value to less than two months of import value (i.e. only about 3 billion USD), as well as easing its growing external debt load (i.e. estimated at 22.5 billion USD). In the same way, the Ethiopian Diaspora Trust Fund (EDTF) has been introduced very recently aiming at widely involving the diaspora community in the development trajectory of Ethiopia. The fund mainly targets to get one USD a day per person (30 million USD per month) from the estimated 3 million diaspora Ethiopians. The money will not be part of the government budget, but will be administered through its own independent board for vital development and social projects.

The intention to establish an Ethiopian STOCK Exchange together with the privatization of the SOEs is another very fundamental economic reform of the current Ethiopian macro-economic milieu. According to invest frontier (*www.invetsfrontier.com*), Ethiopia is the most populous country in the world without a stock exchange. It is surprising that nothing had been planned earlier than the announcement by the current government in this regard.

Foreign policy reform is one of the most acclaimed improvements in the current Ethiopia under the leadership of the government. In addition to the targeted visits and talks with many neighboring East African and Arabian countries, the port agreement with Djibouti and an end to the Ethiopia-Eritrea conflict are the much-admired achievements in foreign relations in the current Ethiopian history. In May 2018, Ethiopia signed an agreement with the government of Djibouti to take an equity stake and to have a say in the development and management of Port Djibouti. This is a breakthrough achievement for a landlocked Ethiopia for its import-export trade. It is good news for its economic allies (such as China) and helps Ethiopia to attract more investors and trade partners across the world. In fact, shortly before the coming to power of the current government, Ethiopia has taken 19% of the stake in Port Berbera as part of the joint venture with Dubai Ports World (DP World). Agreement was also signed with the government of Sudan granting Ethiopia an ownership stake in the Port Sudan. Ethiopia also reached an agreement with Kenya for the construction of an Ethiopian Logistics Facility at Lamu Port (in Kenya). There is also a possibility to resume using Ports of Massawa and Asseb (in Eritrea) as a result of the current end to the 2-decades old Ethio-Eritrea conflict.

An end to the Ethio-Eritrea conflict, though it was a frozen conflict commonly known as a policy of *no war, but no peace*, an added highly praised achievements of the current Ethiopia. The two countries signed a *Joint Declaration of Peace and Friendship* proclaiming an end to tensions and agreeing, amongst other matters, to re-establish diplomatic relations; re-unite the Ethiopian and Eritrean Orthodox Churches and Ethiopian and Eritrean Catholic Churches; reopen direct telecommunications, road, and aviation links; and facilitate Ethiopian access to the ports of Massawa and Asseb.

Another key promised reform of the current Ethiopian Government is the Constitutional reform. It was announced on 18 June 2018 to set up a commission aimed at reviewing the divisive system of ethnic federalism. In fact, some of the articles of the FDRE Constitution are widely condemned by the group of society across-the-board. One of the most condemned articles, for example, is Article 39 (1) which states *Every Nation, Nationality and People in Ethiopia has an unconditional right to self-determination, including the right to secession*. In general, the current administration in Ethiopia understands that the Constitution is unable to adequately deal with the propagation of localized disputes over which certain ethnic groups are entitled to control certain areas, calling for an all-encompassing constitutional reform.

More in to the Constitution is the announcement to reform the Constitution in such a way that it limits a prime minister to be in office only for two terms. This has been publicized by the Prime Minister time and again to the public that the Constitution must be the foundation of the nation, and allowing a prime minister to remain in power for more than two terms certainly ensures that he/she will acquire too much influence and power within the government. Such is never good for Ethiopia, as it is a dictatorship, not democracy. It is understood that corruption in Ethiopia is already deep-seated in the government system and will only get worse if left untreated constitutionally.

The security sector reform is another vital area of reform these days in Ethiopia. The new Prime Minister declared to the members of the national defense force his intention to carry out the military to strengthen its effectiveness and professionalism, with limited role in politics. The plan includes dissolving the regional militias who in some regions, such as Somali, are accused of violations against human rights. The Prime Minister is also thinking of reconstitution of the Ethiopian naval force which was dissolved in 1996 in tandem with the session of Eritrea with its seaports.

One more breakthrough reform is education policy, which has been condemned for its failure in bring about quality and equity in education sector. In his public address on 20 August 2018, the Prime Minister promised the public that his leadership is working hard to bring about a breakthrough reform in education so as to address the quality and equity problems.

The abovementioned current politico-economic reforms in Ethiopia, no doubt, contribute greatly to the overall favorable socioeconomic and political changes in East Africa in general and Ethiopia in particular. It enhances the cooperation between countries in the region in aspects of security and economic systems. This helps to bring about the overall peace in East Africa, develop areas around Red Sea and invite the global economic giants (such as China) for economic cooperation. In fact, many countries have already flocked to the area for military bases and commercial ports. USA, French, Japan, China, Saudi Arabia, UAE, and Turkey have already established their commercial ports and/or military bases along Red Sea and Indian Ocean in three countries: Eritrea, Djibouti and Somaliland.

Statement of the Problem and the Rationale

Ethiopia-China relations have ancient roots though there was no substantial socioeconomic and political relationship up until the first Ethiopian Cultural Delegation to China in 1956 (Csanadi, 2017). The formal diplomatic relation between Ethiopia and China was established in the 1970s. Subsequently, various bilateral agreements were signed between Ethiopia and China (Damtew and Tsegay, 2017) though it took over two decades to see a strong economic attachment between them.

The Ethiopia-China economic relationship started booming in the late 1990s. The Chinese economic boom particularly starting from the second half of the 1970s (Csanadi, 2017) and the subsequent Chinese aspiration in overseas trade and investment; the accession of China to the World Trade Organization (WTO) in 2001; and Ethiopia's relative peace/security after 1991; and the determination for economic development have paved the way for strong Ethiopia-China economic ties. The economic nexus between the two countries increased unprecedentedly after the elapse of the second millennium. As a result, various Chinese companies are currently investing in various sectors, most notably, in construction and manufacturing sectors, across Ethiopia. However, the contribution of Chinese investment in Ethiopia has not been methodologically and empirically researched, particularly in view of its contribution in job creation, technology and skill transfer, and overseas trade enhancement opportunities for Ethiopia/Ethiopians. The main objective of this research was, therefore, to assess the economic development ties between Ethiopia and China with particular emphasis on the aforementioned variables.

Methodology

Two approaches were used to obtain data for this research. First and foremost, the unprocessed secondary data were obtained from concerned offices of the Federal Democratic Republic of Ethiopia (FDRE) in Addis Ababa, most notably Ethiopian Investment Commission (EIC), Ministry of Finance and Economic Cooperation (MoFEC), and Ministry of Foreign Affairs (MoFA). Websites of these offices were also visited. Secondly, various published and unpublished documents were accessed at Addis Ababa University (Ethiopia) and Fudan University libraries in China. In fact, two Fudan Development Institute (FDDI) visiting professors, Ethiopian scholars who have good knowledge of Ethiopia-China relationships and expertise in different development sectors in Ethiopia were briefly interviewed to clear up some ambiguous views related to the study. Included were also ideas obtained from the visits and expert explanations at various historical and investment sites in China, including Shenzhen Metro Group Co. Ltd. Weidong Chinese Cultural Museum (Beijing), Weidong Cloud Education Group (Beijing), Guangzhou Creative View Optoelectronics Technology, Huawei Technologies Co. Ltd. (Shenzhen), Shanghai Industrial Investment Corporation (SIIC) Greenport Agriculture, and International Center for Higher Education Innovation (ICHEI) under the auspices of UNESCO (Shenzhen).

The data were analyzed descriptively. This involved describing key quantitative circumstances uncovered from the numerical data to look into the prevalence and incidence of related facts and trends. It also focused on providing explanations to qualitative data obtained through field observations and key informant interviews.

Findings and Discussions

A glance at Ethiopia-China relations

Literatures, such as Bräutigam and Tang (2012), Geoff (2014), Muna (2015), Gebregeorgis (2016), and Craig Benjamin (*www.khanacademy.org; www.newafricanmagazine.com*) indicate that Chinese relations with Africa, particularly, the Horn of Africa including Ethiopia, are long-standing. According to Dent (2011), records of Africa-China bilateral trade date back to the 10th century BC, when the Egyptian city of Alexandria started trading with the people who had settled in the present-day China. Evidences also indicate that trade relationship between China and Africa took place at some point during the first period of the Silk Roads Trade (about 50 B.C.-250 A.D.). Gebregeorgis (2016), for example, cited historical sources indicating the indirect contact of Chinese merchants with Aksumite Kingdom of Ethiopia since the Chinese Qin Dynasty (3rd century B.C.) and Han Dynasty (3rd century B.C.-3rd century A.D.) through the Balkh in Eurasia and Parthia in the Persian Plateau. There are also sources *(www.newafricanmagazine.com*; Geoff, 2014; Muna, 2015) that are sure about the indirect trade involvement of China with parts of the Horn of Africa in some point during the Tang Dynasty(618-907). There are substantial sources indicating the contact of Zheng. Zheng, an administrator and diplomat during the Ming Dynasty (1368–1644) in China, with people who had lived in the present-day sub-Saharan Africa centuries before the arrival of the 16th century European (Portuguese) explorer Vasco da Gama. In fact, the relations had lapsed during the period of Western imperial domination until the later half of the 20th century (Dent, 2011; Geoff, 2014; Muna, 2015).

The modern era of Afro-Asian (specifically, Afro-China) relations was thought to have started in 1955, when the Bandung Conference (Indonesia) brought together 29 African and Asian countries. However, trade and investment between Africa and China increasingly built in 1990s, a process principally motivated by China's rapid industrialization and economic development (Dent, 2011). The relationship was officially inaugurated in a meeting of the Forum on China-Africa Co-operation (FOCAC) in 2000 at Beijing. FOCAC was consecutively held in Addis Ababa (in 2003) and Beijing (in 2006). Those FOCAC meetings ultimately devised four fundamental principles, which most likely initiated Africa to welcome China more importantly than its preceding western partners. The principles are sincerity, friendship and equality; mutual benefit; mutual support and close co-ordination; and mutual learning and common paths of development. These principles give good explanations for the fact that China has no interest to compete hegemony in Africa. Taylor's (2006) arguments and my discussion with a veteran FDDI visiting scholar in November 2017 also validate China's interest in Africa is only economic such as market and natural resources, at least for this time, not to create its authority with dominating political influence over African nations. The Djibouti President Ismail Omar Guelleh's official visit to China (22-24

November 2017) and the warm greetings by the Chinese leaders at the Great Hall (Tiantian, 2017) is one of the testimonies for the burgeoning China-Africa economic ties. In fact, it is more likely to speculate China's interest in Africa may expand to peacekeeping and strategic missions at least to protect its massive investment projects and the Chinese workers in Africa in the years to come.

According to the information from the MoFA of Ethiopia, the first Ethiopian Cultural Delegation was sent to China in 1956. This delegation served as a gateway to the socioeconomic and political relationships between Ethiopia and China. In 1964, the then premier of China visited Ethiopia. Consequently, formal diplomatic relation between Ethiopia and China was established in 1970s (Walsh, 2009).

Next to the formal diplomatic relations, various bilateral agreements have been signed between Ethiopia and China (Damtew and Tsegay, 2017). These include, Ethiopia-China Agreement for Economic and Technological Cooperation (1971; 1988; 2002); Ethiopia-China Trade Agreement (1971; 1976); Ethiopia-China Trade Protocol (1984; 1986; 1988); Ethiopia-China Agreement Concerning the Encouragement and Reciprocal Protection of Investments (1998); Ethiopia-China Agreement for Mutual Promotion and Protection of Investment (1988); and Ethiopia-China Agreement for Trade, Economic and Technological Cooperation (1996). All over again, as noted by Damtew and Tsegay (2017), the Ethiopia-China relation has transformed into a more strategic partnership with the establishment of the Forum on FOCAC in 2000. More importantly, Ethiopia hosted and co-chaired the second ministerial meeting of FOCAC, which was held in Addis Ababa in 2003. The China-African Fund, which was founded following the Beijing Summit FOCAC, was established in June 2007 to support Chinese enterprises investing in Africa. The fund serves as a bridge between Chinese companies and African projects. It opened its East African branch in Addis Ababa in 2010 to facilitate the activities of Chinese companies in Ethiopia and Eastern Africa at large. The opening of the branch office in Ethiopia reflects the strong level of relations between the two countries as well as the confidence China has in Ethiopia. Ethiopia is also one of the countries which have participated/shown interest in the Belt and Road Initiative (BRI), which focuses on connectivity and cooperation between Eurasian countries to develop China-centered continental and maritime infrastructure networks in order to expand China's economic and political influence in global affairs, particularly Asia, Europe and Africa (Chin and He, 2016; Csizmadia, 2017; Klose, Pepermans and Wang, 2017).

Even if the cooperation between Ethiopia and China seems to have started with the signing of trade agreement in 1971 (Venkataraman and Solomon, 2015), the economic and political relationships between them was not remarkable until the coming to power of the Ethiopian People's Revolutionary Democratic Front (EPRDF) in 1991 and the accession of China to the World Trade Organization (WTO) in December 2001. Trade between the two countries, for example, started to boom in 2006, the time when China became Ethiopia's largest trading partner. Yet in the span of about two decades, the economic nexus between the two countries increased unprecedentedly. The bilateral trade between the two countries, for example, increased from almost nil before 2005

(Alemayehu and Atnafu, 2009) to over 3 billion USD in 2015 (Venkataraman and Solomon, 2015). This signifies very close level of bilateral relations that Ethiopia has built with China over the past decade compared to any other country in Africa. Generally, China's current fast economic growth and its accompanied increased investment in Ethiopia over the last decades have brought about enhanced performances in economic activities (mainly in construction sector) and technology transfer to the latter.

The various agreements and forums between Ethiopia/Africa and China are expected to further the socioeconomic and political connections between the two countries in times ahead. Mutual support on issues of, for example, culture, trade, investment, agriculture, education, health, human resource development and many more is expected to expand. The visit of the Chinese Premier Li Keqiang (May 2014) can be regarded as another turning point to broaden the economic ties between Ethiopia and China. As one of the key building blocks of the Ethiopia-China ties, Ethiopian Airlines has been playing a high-flying role. The airline has been flying between Addis Ababa and Beijing since the 1970s and currently it flies between Addis Ababa and various cities of China, namely Beijing, Chengdu, Guangzhou, Hong Kong, and Shanghai. In fact, the Ethiopia-China economic relationship is not free of challenges that both parties are required to come to terms with. Many respondents, in both countries, mentioned several predicaments that they observed in the relationship milieu. These include, but not limited to, the enormous trade imbalance between the two countries, low-priced/low-quality goods that Ethiopia is importing from China, poor compensation for investment-induced displaces in Ethiopia, quality of the project outputs (mainly in construction sector), corruption/bribery, the adverse environmental impacts of the projects, and the rights of the daily works.

Chinese economic performance and its investment in Ethiopia: a synopsis

China has achieved rapid economic growth in the past three decade, which branded it as *China's Economic Miracle*. Various sources (Walsh, 2009; Dent, 2011; OECD, 2011; Yuan and Yu, 2014; CSanadi, 2017; Losoncz, 2017; Morrison, 2017; Rippel, 2017) are of the same opinion that the tremendous economic development over a short period (only since the second half of the 1970s) has lifted China to the second largest economic power in the world. China's economy is the largest and most powerful among the new global economic powers: Brazil, Russia, India, China and South Africa (BRICS). According to Losoncz (2017), China's GDP volume at constant prices reached 11.4 trillion USD in 2016; and its GDP per capita at constant prices was 8,260 USD (Table 1). The country established exemplarily giant companies like China Civil Engineering Construction Corporation Ltd. (CCECC), China Communications Construction Company Ltd. (CCCC), China Railway Group Limited, metro companies, manufacturing companies, ICT technology companies, petroleum and chemicals corporations, automotive industries, power plants and agricultural enterprises. It also exceedingly enhanced its magnificent tourist sites such as the Great Wall, Forbidden City, Pearl River Cruise and Weidong Chinese Cultural Museum, as well as amazing modern skyscrapers such as the Shanghai Global Financial Center. With these achievements, China has become a model country for other developing nations in Africa, Asia, Eastern Europe and Latin America, which, in turn, enabled it to highly deepen its economy across the developing world, especially Africa (UN, 2018). According to Dent (2011), it is with Africa that China has established the strongest links mainly for mutual benefits.

Literatures, for example, Chakrabarty (2016); Gedion (undated); Bräutigam and Tang (2012) indicate that Chinese interest in Africa in general and in Ethiopia in particular is driven by a quest for resources and diplomatic support. Chakrabarty (2016) and Gedion (undated) argue that Ethiopia could be a commercial launch pad for Chinese companies and China is also getting diplomatic support from Ethiopia for its international policies and development strategies like the Belt and Road Initiatives. In fact, Ethiopia needs China for economic assistance as an alternative source to the west and generally considered as a role model for Ethiopia to follow. However, there are many challenges that have been visible in the bilateral relationship between the two countries. Gedion argues that, on the economic front, the bilateral relations are imbalanced; dumping of low-price export; underbidding local companies and ideological differences among others. Adem (2012) also put it in plain words the Ethiopia-China relationship as infrastructure for diplomatic support.

By and large, as indicated by Chakrabarty (2016) and Gedion (undated), the overall impact of Ethiopia-China economic relations is beneficial for both countries. Bilateral trade between the two countries expanded rapidly, and China is currently Ethiopia's top trading partner. Ethiopia gained from China's zero-tariff policy on agricultural imports, and there was a dramatic growth in its agricultural exports (such as sesame) to China. China is also a major source of manufactured goods and machinery for Ethiopia. Despite being an agricultural exporter, it has attracted significant volumes of Chinese official financial flows and foreign direct investment (FDI).

Most Chinese investment projects (both private and state-owned enterprises in Ethiopia are found engaged in manufacturing sector (Figure 1), a growing sector in Ethiopia (accounting for about 13.8 per cent of the country's GDP), revealing a gradual structural transformation of the country's economy from agriculture (current GDP share of 38.8 per cent in 2014) to manufacturing sector (EIC, 2016). Out of the total number of licensed projects, 67.6 per cent are manufacturing, 13 per cent are construction contracting projects, 11.6 per cent are real estate, 3.8 per cent are hotel development, and the rest 4 per cent are agriculture, tour operation, mining, and health projects. Of the total registered capital, 61.7 per cent goes to manufacturing, 24.6 per cent goes to construction contracting and the rest 13.7 per cent goes to real estate development, hotel, mining, tour operation and health projects.

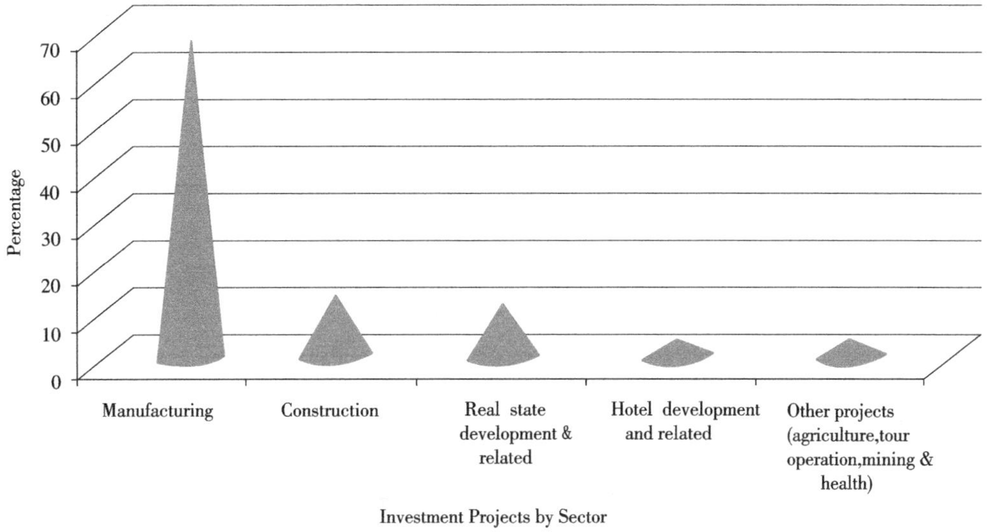

Figure 1　China-origin Investment Projects by Sector in Ethiopia (August 1998-December 2017)

Source: Computed based on unprocessed data obtained from EIC.

China started massive investment in Ethiopia in 1998 (Figure 2). Currently, China is the leading investor in number of projects, employees and foreign capital inflow in Ethiopia (Figure 3). According to the data obtained from EIC, the total number of investment projects licensed between August 1998 and September 2017 is 1,206. It is incredible to perceive that, at the time of this study, 60.3 per cent (that is 728 projects) of the total licensed projects were operational with increasing trend form over the years mentioned above. Of the projects, 24.46 per cent (295 projects) and 15.17 per cent (183 projects) were at pre-implementation and implementation status, respectively. For clarity, EIC characterises projects at pre-implementation stage as licensed investment projects that have not yet started any practical activity; while those at implementation stage are characterised as projects in which practical undertakings, such as construction of civil works, provision of machinery/equipment are underway, but not yet started production of goods or provision of services. The investment projects which have either partially or fully begun production of goods or provision of services are identified as operational projects.

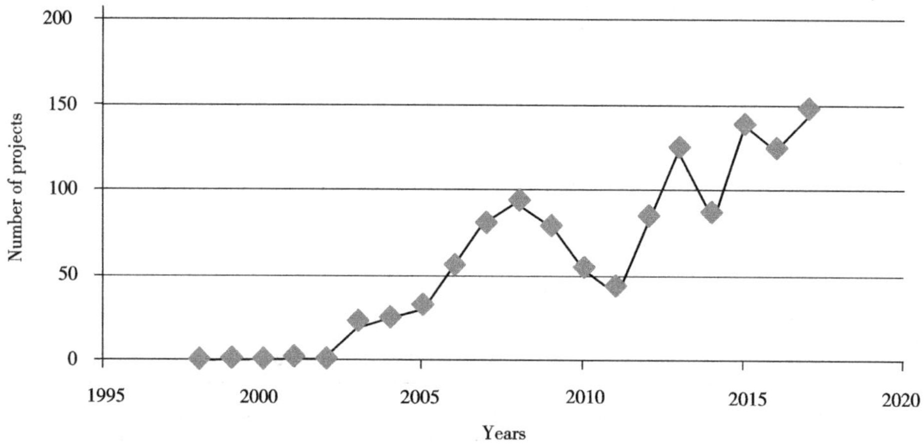

Figure 2　Trend of Chinese Investment Projects in Ethiopia

Source: Computed based on unprocessed data obtained from EIC.

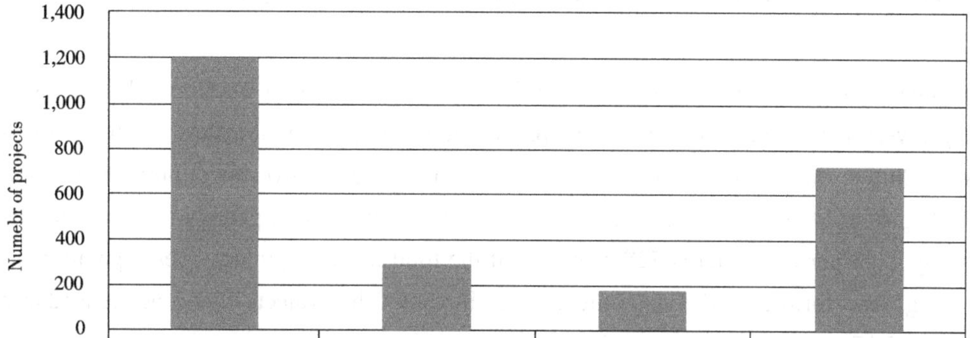

Total	Pre–implementation	Implementation	Operation
1,206	295	183	728

Figure 3　China's Investment Status in Ethiopia(August 1998-December 2017)

Source: Computed based on unprocessed data obtained from EIC.

Regarding the sectoral structure of the investment, out of the total number of licensed projects, 67.6 per cent are manufacturing projects, 13.0 per cent are construction, 11.6 per cent are real estate development, 3.8 per cent are hotel development, and the remaining 4.0 per cent are agriculture, tour operation, mining, and health-related projects. From the total registered capital, 61.7 per cent has been allocated for manufacturing; 24.6 per cent for construction; and the remaining 13.7 per cent for real estate, hotel, mining, tour operation and health-related projects. China's investment in Ethiopia ranks first both in the number of projects and in the registered capital among all foreign investment projects in Ethiopia. This signifies that the prominence of the Ethiopia-China economic relations for various intents and purposes in Ethiopia, such as job creation, technology transfer and economic growth. In case of investment capital, China is still the leading country in the cotemporary foreign investment in Ethiopia, followed by Saudi Arabia, Turkey and India.

In addition to exclusively China-origin companies investing in Ethiopia, there are also Chinese joint venture partners from about 20 countries, such as Australia, Canada, Ethiopia, Finland, France, India, Italy, Malaysia, Netherlands, Sudan, Turkey, South Africa, United States of America (USA) and United Arab Emirates (UAE). The total value of the joint venture investment at all stages (operational, implementation, and pre-implementations) between August 2017 and December 2017 adds up to about 30.970 billion ETB (1.138 billion USD at the current exchange rate). Still, the vast majority of the projects are owned by Ethiopian and Chinese joint companies, constituting about 84.0 per cent of the Chinese joint projects in Ethiopia. With these jointly undertaken business enterprises, China-origin companies are also contributing to Ethiopia's economy in bringing in investors from other countries across the world.

In addition to its current huge contribution in various aspects (such as job creation, foreign currency payment and technology transfer), the Chinese co-investment approach has an enormous role in promoting Ethiopia as a favourable investment destination country. This, no doubt, will help Ethiopia in achieving its long-term vision in the economic sector (NPC, 2016) that is "to build an economy which has a modern and productive agricultural sector with enhanced technology and an industrial sector that plays a leading role in the economy; to sustain economic development and secure social justice; and, increase per capita income of citizens so that it reaches at the level of those in middle-income countries".

Capital inflow

According to the study report by Mileva (2008) to European Central Bank (ECB), FDI constitutes the largest portion of capital inflows in most developing countries in the world. Its contribution in some countries is found to be around half of the total national capital inflows. Beyond adding to existing national capital stock, FDI stimulates investments in other sectors of the host economy through "crowding in" or "spill over effects".

In view of the fore noted supporting fact, Ethiopia is gaining huge amount of FDI as a result of its economic ties with China. As shown in Table 1, China-origin operational investment projects registered between August 1998 and December 2017 in Ethiopia amount to 18.570 billion ETB, equivalent to 682.502 million USD at the current (mid 2018) exchange rate. Similarly, the Chinese joint investment projects (with Ethiopians and other countries) added up to 5.647 billion ETB, equivalent to 207.536 million USD. Altogether, between August 1998 and December 2017, Chinese and Chinese-Ethiopian joint investment amounted to 24.217 billion ETB (which is equivalent to 890.038 million USD).

Table 1 China-origin FDI Sources in Ethiopia (August 1998-December 2017)

Countries	Capital Inflow (only operational projects)	
	In Billion ETB	**In Million USD**
China Only	18.570	682.502
China Joint Investment	5.647	207.536
Total	**24.217**	**890.038**

Source: Computed based on unprocessed data from EIC.

In addition to the operational ones, projects at pre-implementation and implementation levels are also expected to play vital roles in various aspects of the Ethiopian economy. The registered capital by China-origin and China joint investment projects at pre-implementation and implementation stages during August 1998 to December 2017 was about 75.40 billion ETB (equivalent to 2.77 billion USD at the current (mid 2018) exchange rate. This was a very enormous FDI in Ethiopian history and ranks China the leading source of FDI in Ethiopia, followed by Saudi Arabia, Turkey and India. With this, no doubt, China is enormously contributing to the Ethiopian economy in job creation, technology transfer, strengthening the capital stock, and stimulating the national/local investors in every sector through its spill over effects.

Table 2 Licensed Chinese Investment Projects by Their Status in Ethiopia (1998-2017)

Status of Projects	Registered Capital (China-origin & China Joint Investment)	
	In Billion ETB	**In Billions USD at Current Exchange rate**
Pre-implementation	34.870	1.281
Implementation	40.531	1.489
Operational	24.217	0.890
Total	**99.618**	**3.660**

Source: Computed based on data from EIC.

Chinese investment has been rising over the years, particularly between 2006 and 2017 (Figure 4). China and China-Ethiopia joint projects owners invested over 585 million USD in 2009 alone and over 766 million USD in 2017. In fact, the volume of investment decreased in 2011 and 2012; probably because it was this time that the government of Ethiopia set a minimum financial requirement for foreign inventors to initiate investment projects in Ethiopia. Yet, again it started accelerating in 2013 and has been continuing with remarkable pace up to the present time. It is also realistic to look forward that the existing peaceful political and socioeconomic relationship between Ethiopia and China hints at increasing Chinese investment trend during the times ahead, and will be contributing more greatly to the Ethiopian economy in many aspects.

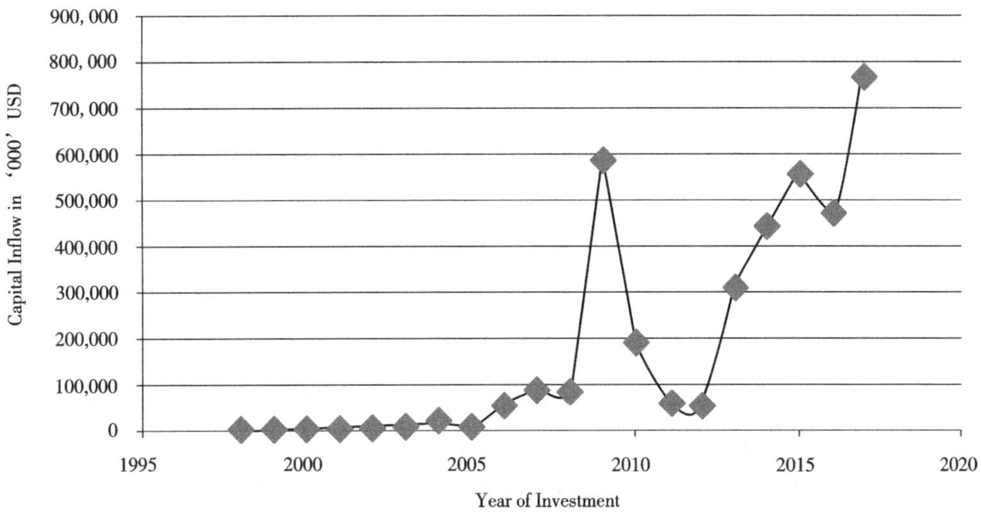

Figure 4 Trend of Capital Inflow from Chinese Investment Projects in Ethiopia

Source: Computed based on data obtained from EIC.

Import-export trade between Ethiopia and China

The import-export trade between Ethiopia and China started shooting up in 2006, the time when Ethiopia's import Free on Board (FOB) value was 663,570,000 USD while the export FOB value was 71,688,000 USD, showing a negative balance of 591,882,000 USD. Ethiopia's import from China tremendously increased and hit a record high in 2015 when the FOB's value mounted to over 6 billion USD (Figure 5). It seems that Ethiopia's export to China is not only lower but it is also slower in progress (with coefficient of variation /CV/ of FOB values over years = 0.51) as compared to the more accelerating importation from China (with the CV = 0.62). This can be an important economic implication for Ethiopia in that it is expected to work hard towards enhancing its export trade and make the best out of its current encouraging relationships with China.

As a key component of Ethiopia-China economic relations, the import-export trade between the two countries plays a vital role for economic transformation in Ethiopia in that, as indicated in the European Commission (EU) "*benefits of trade for developing countries*", "trade strengthens ties between nations by bringing people together in peaceful and mutually beneficial exchanges and as such contributes to peace and stability". Similarly, it "... enhances competitiveness by helping developing countries reduce the cost of inputs, acquire finance through investments, increase the value added of their products and move up the global value chain". UNCTAD (2014:1) also clearly indicates that "...in the post-2015 development agenda, international trade should be seen an *enabler* for achieving a broad range of development goals through promoting inclusive and sustainable economic growth". Particularly, if properly harnessed, the opportunities brought by international trade can be vital for investment stimulation, job creation, efficient resource utilization, technology transfer, innovation, production efficiency and ultimately livelihoods enhancement in developing countries, such as Ethiopia and China.

In view of these realities, the enormous and rising import-export trade amount between Ethiopia and China certainly contributes hugely to achieve the overall importance of trade indicated herein both for Ethiopia and China. It is said to be contributing significantly to the economy in both countries by allowing them to access new markets for their raw materials and/or finished/semi-finished goods, and thereby opening up new production possibilities and technologies for both countries. Though the trade balance is positively skewed to China (Table 3), the vast market in China for Ethiopian raw materials and/or semi-processed goods certainly encourages export diversification for Ethiopia, which, in turn, contributes greatly to job creation and balance of payment for Ethiopian economy. In the same way, the ever-progressing Ethiopia-China trade has an immense role in enhancing the financial capacity of the local enterprises and producers in Ethiopia and enables the Ethiopian people to consume cheaper Chinese products in comparison with overpriced/costly import items from Europe and North America.

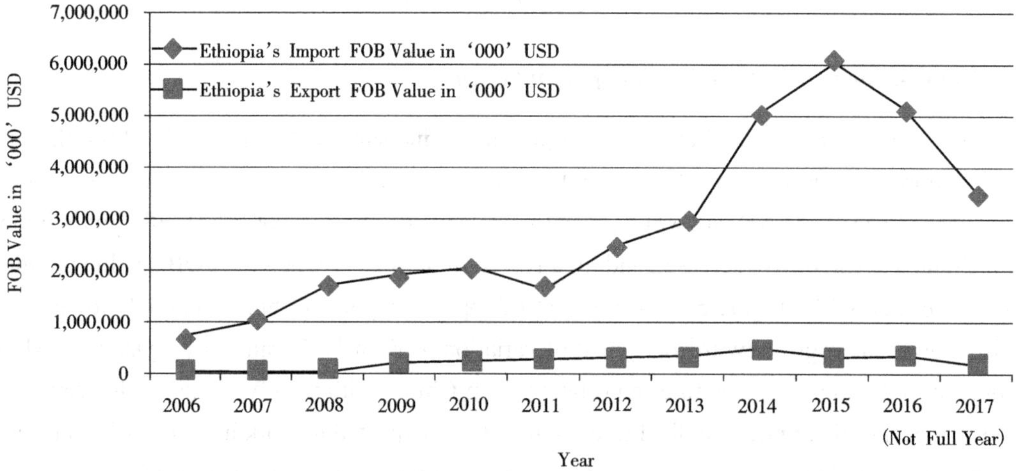

Figure 5 Trend of Import-export Trade Between Ethiopia and China(2007-2017)

Source: Computed based on data obtained from EIC.

Table 3 Summary of Licensed Chinese Investment Projects by Sector and Status(3 April 2018-22 August 2019 in Ethiopia)

Sectors	Total				Operational Projects			
	Ho. of Projects	Capital in '000' USD	Employment (Permanent)	Employment (Temporary)	Ho. of Projects	Capital in '000' USD	Employment (Permanent)	Employment (Temporary)
Agriculture	2	14,451	159		1	377	60	
Manufacturing	200	519,652	47,387	15,134	46	33,311	8,927	2,615

Sectors	Total				Operational Projects			
	Ho. of Projects	Capital in '000' USD	Employment (Permanent)	Employment (Temporary)	Ho. of Projects	Capital in '000' USD	Employment (Permanent)	Employment (Temporary)
Hotels (Including Resort Hotels, Motels and Lodges) and Restaurants	2	4,082	50	190				
Tour Operation, Transport and Communication	1	4,007	50	50				
Real estate, Machinery and Equipment Rental and Consultancy Service	12	136,618	798	2,130	4	679	62	10
Construction Contracting Including Water Well Drilling	17	26,852	1,204	3,218	2	3,276	99	220
Others*	3	4,667	65	1	1	1,140	10	0
Grand Total	**237**	**710,329**	**49,713**	**20,723**	**54**	**38,783**	**9,158**	**2,845**

Source: Computed based on data obtained from EIC.

**Meat Export, Property Management and Maintenance service, Architectural engineering consultancy services*

Conclusions and the way forward

China, as an emerging donor, is not new to Ethiopia and Africa. It has been providing aid to Ethiopia since Emperor Haille Sillasie's time and to Africa since the end of colonial period, at least as long as the West. However, until 1990s the aid flow from China to Ethiopia was very minimal. Unlike the West, China has no conditions on governance, democracy and human rights. China has valuable contributions to make towards Ethiopia's development in the spirit of South-South cooperation, which needs to be understood in the context of the changing global development assistance architecture. The present study indicates that the unprecedented economic relationship between Ethiopia and do have both opportunities and risks. The researcher also recommends policy interventions to minimize the risks and maximize the benefits of the development cooperation, which can be implemented unilaterally by Ethiopia and by China as well as through the cooperation of the two.

The economic cooperation between Ethiopia and China is found to be fundamental for both countries in various aspects. It creates more investment milieu for Chinese investors while benefiting Ethiopia in job creation, efficient use of resources, entrepreneurship, technology and skills transfer and in due course improving the livelihoods of the people. If properly harnessed, the opportunities brought by these activities can be a powerful force for economic development and have a great role to play in promoting inclusive and sustainable economic growth in Ethiopia.

However, the Ethiopia-China economic relationship is not free of challenges. It requires facing and challenging various challenges in order to make the best out of the relationship. One of the key issues to be addressed in Ethiopia is establishing competent, proficient, accountable and transformative leaders who can foresee the fast economic and technological transformations in China and gear up the society to select, adapt and make the best out of it. The leadership in Ethiopia should be able to foresee the technological dynamics in China and align the development policies/strategies so as to catalyse the positive effects of the Chinese investment in Ethiopia. It may be important to focus on identifying the types of national policies/strategies and institutions that would harness the enabling power of Chinese investment projects in Ethiopia, and against that background, design a coherent framework in which the development goals are sustained with respect to the policy mix and conditions required to bring about the desired goals.

Another key challenge that must be adequately met prior to implementation of the projects is related to land tenure systems and human displacement. It is inevitable that investment projects require a piece of land to operate on. Land acquisition, in turn, displaces local people in most cases. In Ethiopia, investment projects have resulted in various disarticulations, livelihoods disruption, family breakages, public violence and even deaths in many parts of the country. Therefore, investment projects that inevitably displace local residents are strongly recommended to adequately compensate the displaces so as to sustain their livelihoods in more sustainable way than their pre-displacement status. In fact, the displaces must be compensated not only for the resources and land use right they are losing, but also for their psychosocial damages as displacement by its very nature results in psychological disturbances and socio-cultural disruptions.

In the same way, the government of Ethiopia has to be proactive to environmentally and socially sensitive investment sectors, such as large-scale agriculture, though Chinese investment projects in this regard are minimal so far. Despite the growing number of works which indicates that "investment in developing countries agricultural sector is among the most efficient ways to reduce food insecurity", some forms of large-scale agriculture entail risks both for host and investing countries. The studies by Zwerg and Arango (2008) and Liu (2014), for example, found that the large-scale land acquisitions contribute to the problems of environmental pollutions and force the destruction of the environment by the poor in order to survive. It aggravates local community's reduced access to natural resources and loss of livelihoods, which are likely to generate harsh local opposition the and irreversible damage to the investment project itself. Even from the perspective of the investor, land acquisition is unlikely to be the most profitable business model due to the high potential for conflict and damage to reputation. In this regard, the government of Ethiopia is required to have a comprehensive inclusive business model as to how investments involve local farmers as business partners, giving them an active role and leaving them in control of their land so as to have the most positive and sustainable effects on local economies and social development. In fact, this requires also strong support from the investing country (China in this case) to establish strong investor-farmers relationship in order to succeed.

More to the point of environment and investment, currently China has outstanding experiences in establishing eco-friendly investment projects that can be adapted to the Ethiopian situations. A case in point is the SIIC Dongtan Low-carbon Agriculture and Eco-City Development Project in Shanghai where close to carbon neutral, recycling, reuse, integration and zero waste dumping technologies have been vigorously implemented to bring increased sustainability for improved economic efficiency and social benefit. In this regard, Ethiopia is expected to fill in the gaps in its policy frameworks to adapt the nature-friendly investment projects of this kind for sustainability and efficiency of the projects which ultimately exceedingly benefit the society at large.

By and large, Ethiopia needs not only to obtain the technology but to learn how to use it to its fullest potential from the incoming Chinese projects. In this context, to effectively leverage FDI as a means to achieve technology transfer and diffusion, Ethiopia needs to establish an effective national innovation system which caters for technology-related activity, supports the development of the absorptive capacities of domestic enterprises and their linkages with Chinese investment projects, and provides a regulatory framework, including a framework for intellectual property that enables the development of a knowledge base and technological capacities in Ethiopia. The coherence between FDI policy and other relevant policies (especially education policy, international trade and/or export-import policy, agricultural development policy, industry policy, technical and vocational education strategy, innovation and technology policy) is important in this regard. Most importantly, the government of Ethiopia is required to enhance its policies and leadership so as to cope with high-tech and dynamic developments in China. Only transformative, accountable, capable and dedicated leadership can sustainably benefit both countries. To bring to a close, as noted by Taylor (2009), Ethiopia cannot benefit from China's investment and technology transfer if the leadership is corrupted and/or incapable to harness the best out of the relationship. The commitment of both countries to social, environmental and transparency standards is also of the essence.

References

[1] ADEM S. 2012. China in Ethiopia: diplomacy and economics of Sino-optimism. African Studies Review, 55(1): 143–160.

[2] ALEMAYEHU G, ATENAFU G M. 2009. China-Africa investment relations: case study of Ethiopia. Mobasa: African Economic Research Consortium Collaborative Research on the Impact of China on Africa.

[3] BAHRU Z. 2002. A history of modern Ethiopia, 1985–1991. Athens: Ohio University Press, Oxford: James Currey, Addis Ababa: Addis Ababa University Press.

[4] BRÄUTIGAM D, TANG X. 2012. An Overview of Chinese agricultural and rural engagement in Ethiopia. https://deborahbrautigam.files.wordpress.com.

[5] FEDERAL DEMOCRATIC REPUBLIC OF ETHIOPIA CENTRAL STATISTICAL AGEN-

CY. 2019. Population projection of Ethiopia for all regions at Wereda level from 2014-2017. https://www.statsethiopia.gov.et/wp-content/uploads/2019/05/Population-Projection-At-Wereda-Level-from-2014-2017.pdf.

[6] CHAKRABARTY M. 2016. Ethiopia-China economic relations: a classic win-win situation. World Review of Political Economy, 7 (2): 226-248.

[7] CHIN H, HE W. 2016.The belt and road initiative: 65 countries and beyond. Hong Kong: Global Sourcing Fung Business Intelligence Center.

[8] CSANÁDI M. 2017. Chinese power structure and its transformation in comparative perspective. Financial and Economic Review, (16): 7-20.

[9] CSIZMADIA N. 2017. Geofusion: mapping of the 21stcentury. Singapore: World Scientific Publishing Co. Pte. Ltd.

[10] DAMTEW R Y, TSEGAY SM. 2017. Developing south-south cooperation: the case of Ethiopia-China economic relationship, International Journal of Research Studies in Management 2017, 6 (1): 75–89.

[11] DENT C M. 2011. Africa and China: a new kind of development partnership// DENT C M. Africa and China relations. London: Routledge.

[12] DUNNING J H, RUGMAN A M. 1985. The influence of Hymer's dissertation on the theory of foreign direct investment. The American Economic Review, 75(2): 228 -232.

[13] ELMSLIE B, WILLIAM M. 1996. Free trade and social dumping: lessons from the regulation of U.S. interstate commerce. Challenge, 39,(3): 46-52.

[14] ETHIOPIAN INVESTMENT COMMISSION. 2016. Ethiopian Investment Report 2016, Addis Ababa: Ethiopian Investment Commission.

[15] FEENSTRAA R C, HANSONB G H. 1997. Foreign direct investment and relative wages: evidence from Mexico's maquiladoras. Journal of International Economics, 42(3-4): 371-393

[16] GEDION G J. 2014. Development assistance from the south: comparative analysis of Chinese and Indian to Ethiopia. Chinese Studies, 3(1): 24-39.

[17] GEBREGEORIGIS A K. 2016. Ethiopia-China economic relations: nature of China's foreign direct investment in Ethiopia (MA thesis). Addis Ababa: Addis Ababa University.

[18] WADE G. 2004. Ming China and Southeast Asia in the 15th century: a reappraisal. Working Paper Series No. 28. Singapore: National University of Singapore, https://ari.nus.edu.sg/wp-content/uploads/2018/10/wps04_028.pdf.

[19] GLASS A. J., SAGGI K.2008. The role of foreign direct investment in international technology transfer//DUTT A, ROS J. International handbook of development economics volumes I and II. Cheltenham and Northampton: Edward Elgar Publishing Limited, 2008.

[20] PEPERMANS A, WANG L, KLOSE S. 2017. An uphill struggle? towards coordinated EU engagement with China's Belt and Road Initiative. [2017-11-27] .https://www.egmontinstitute.be/uphill-struggle-towards-coordinated-eu-engagement-chinas-belt-road-initiative/.

[21] LIU P. 2014. Impacts of foreign agricultural investment on developing countries: evidence from case studies. Rome: Food and Agriculture Organization of the United Nations (FAO) Commodity and Trade Policy Research Working Paper No. 47. https://www.fao.org/3/i3900e/i3900e.pdf.

[22] LOSONCZ M. 2017. The dilemmas of China' s shift in growth trajectory and economic governance. Financial and Economic Review, (16): 21-49.

[23] MILEVA E. 2008. The impact of capital flows on domestic investment in transition economies. European Central Bank Working Paper Series No 871. https://www.researchgate.net/publication/4891001_The_Impact_of_Capital_Flows_on_Domestic_Investment_in_Transition_Economies.

[24] MORRISON W M. 2017. China' s economic rise: history, trends, challenges, and implications for the United States. Washington D.C.: Congressional Research Service.

[25] FEDERAL DEMOCRATIC REPUBLIC OF ETHIOPIA NATIONAL PLANNING COMMISSION. 2016. Growth and Transformation Plan II (GTP II) (2015/16-2019/20) Volume I, Main Text. Addis Ababa: National Planning Commission. https://ethiopia.un.org/sites/default/files/2019-08/GTPII%20%20English%20Translation%20%20Final%20%20June%2021%202016.pdf.

[26] NAYAK D, CHOUDHURY R N. 2014. A selective review of foreign direct investment theories. Asia-Pacific Research and Training Network on Trade (ARTNeT) Working Paper No. 143. https://artnet.unescap.org/publications/working-papers/selective-review-foreign-direct-investment-theories.

[27] ORGANIZATION FOR ECONOMIC CO-OPERATION AND DEVELOPMENT (OECD). 2002. Foreign direct investment for development: maximizing the benefits, minimizing costs. Paris: OECD Publications Service.

[28] ORGANIZATION FOR ECONOMIC CO-OPERATION AND DEVELOPMENT (OECD). 2011. China's emergence as a market economy: achievements and challenges. Beijing: OECD contribution to the China Development Forum. [2011-20-21]. https://www.oecd.org/china/47408845.pdf.

[29] RIPPEL G. 2017 China-rebalancing and sustainable convergence. Financial and Economic Review, (16): 50-72.

[30] TAYLOR I. 2009. China' s new role in Africa. London: Lynne Rienner Publishers Inc., 2009.

[31] TAYLOR I. 2006. China and Africa: engagement and compromise. London: Routledge.

[32] BAI T. 2017. Djibouti president kicks off Beijing visit as China expands interest in Africa. [2017-11-22]. https://www.globaltimes.cn/page/201711/1076682.shtml.

[33] UNITED NATIONS. 2018. World Economic Situation Prospects 2018. https://www.un.org/development/desa/dpad/publication/world-economic-situation-and-prospects-2018/.

[34] UNITED NATIONS CONFERENCE ON TRADE AND DEVELOPMENT (UNCTAD). 2010. Foreign direct investment, the transfer and diffusion of technology, and sustainable de-

velopment. [2010-12-8]. https://unctad.org/system/files/official-document/ciiem2d2_en.pdf.
[35] UNITED NATIONS CONFERENCE ON TRADE AND DEVELOPMENT (UNCTAD). 2015. The role of international trade in the post-2015 development agenda. https://unctad.org/system/files/official-document/cid33_en.pdf. // OECD/WTO Aid for Trade at a Glance 2015: Reducing Trade Costs for Inclusive, Sustainable Growth. http://dx.doi.org/10.1787/aid_glance-2015-en.
[36] UNITED NATIONS DEVELOPMENT PROGRAMME (UNDP). Implementation of the third United Nations decade for the eradication of poverty (2018-2027). [2018-08-06]. https://documents-dds-ny.un.org/doc/UNDOC/GEN/N18/250/39/PDF/N1825039.pd?OpenElement.
[37] VENKATARAMAN M, GOFIE S M. 2015 The dynamics of China-Ethiopia trade relations: economic capacity, balance of trade & trade regimes. Journal of the Global South, (2): 8-25.
[38] WALSH B. 2009. GCSE modern world history[M]. London: Hodder Education Publisher.
[39] YUAN Z, YU Y.2014. China's economic growth under globalization// YUAN Z. Economic transition in China, long-run growth and short-run fluctuations[M]. Singapore: World Scientific Publishing Co. Ltd.
[40] ZWERG A M, ARANGO L C. 2008. The Impact of Foreign Direct Investment on Developing Economies and Environment. https://www.researchgate.net/publication/277121301_The_Impact_of_Foreign_Direct_Investment_on_Developing_Economies_and_the_Environment.
[41] BENJAMIN C. 2017. The first silk road: trade routes connect the vast continent of Afro-Eurasia. https://www.khanacademy.org/humanities/big-history-project/expansion-interconnection/commerce-collective-learning/a/the-first-silk-roads.
[42] MUNA A. 2015. Ethiopia-China ties, 45 years and growing ever strong. [2015-09-27]. http://aigaforum.com/article1/Ethio-China-45years-gettingstronger.pdf.

Political Reform and Consequences for Displacement of People in Ethiopia since 2018

Desalegn Amsalu[①]

Abstract: Interethnic conflicts and internal displacement in Ethiopia are one of the major questions in Ethiopia before and after the event of "political transition" in April 2018, when the TPLF "state capture" was replaced by a reformist Prime Minister Abiy Ahmed. There were 2,895,000 new displacements in the country between January 1st and December 31st, 2018, the biggest global record for the year. While only 10% of the displaced people were because of natural disasters, the rest was due to ethnic conflict. Conflict and displacements also extended into 2019, so that the number reached 3,191,000 amounting to 36% of the global sum. Due to inequality, corruption, and human rights abuses, people in Ethiopia, particularly the youth protested against the ruling coalition party EPRDF which was under the hegemony of the Tigrean People's Liberation Front (TPLF). Series of protests before April 2018 led to a political transition where Abiy Ahmed became a new prime minister from another member of the EPRDF coalition: the Oromo People's Democratic Organization (OPDO), now the Oromo Democratic Party. Despite many prominent and positive political changes that took place in the country under the leadership of the new prime minister, old conflicts that had existed before the transition became further strengthened and new conflicts escalated along various ethnic group borders. The prevalent theory on causes of conflicts contributing to these displacements is the fact that they were induced by political entrepreneurs who sponsor conflicts to create instability. Supporters of the current government argue that members and supporters of TPLF, who lost grip on power, were sponsoring the violence. According to this line of argument, members of the TPLF and its supporters have collaborated with thousands of sacked members from other organizations such as OPDO and the Amhara National Democratic Movement (ANDM) to prevent reform. While the government has returned some displaced people since April 2018, the situation remains uncertain over future displacement incidents due to existing ethnic politics.

Keywords: Internal Displacement; Induced Displacement; Return; Political Reform; Ethiopia

---

① Institute of Ethiopian Studies, Addis Ababa University.

1 Introduction

Internal displacement of people was one of the most noticeable problems associated with the political reform in Ethiopia since April 2018. There were 2,895,000 new displacements between January 1st and December 31st, 2018, the biggest global record for the year. While natural disasters account for only 10% of the displacement, the rest was due to ethnic conflict. Conflict and displacements also extended into 2019, so that the number reached 3,191,000 amounting to 36% of the global sum. People have expressed anger or sorrow, shared confusion or hope, and posed different theories about the causes and thought that the political reform might mean for worse.

The purpose of this paper is to discuss the problem of internal displacement of people in relation to Ethiopia's political reform process since April 2018. Ethiopia has witnessed several interethnic conflicts since April 2018 and several of these conflicts have generated internally displaced peoples (IDPs). Some events became very popular in their magnitude of IDPs and got a wide range of media coverage and relatively immediate attention of the government. Conflicts between Kemant and Amhara, Guji and Gedeo, Oromo and Somali, Gumuz and Amhara, Gumuz and Oromo, Amhara and Oromo and Burayu massacre are selected here for discussion. *Even* though I focus on events after April 2018, often I trace backward to put them in context and to show that they did not indeed appear sporadically following the political reform. Unlike many people might think, the conflicts have some historical roots leading them to the concerned period. Then, I will discuss some effects of displacement, government responses, and theories on causes of displacement. I brief conclusion is given in the end.

The paper originated from a close observation of social and political events in Ethiopia before and after April 2018. I also did fieldwork to conduct interviews with key actors in the displacement process, problem and solution. The paper also benefited from reports by international organizations working on IDPs, such as United Nations High Commission for Refugees (UNHCR), UN Office for the Coordination of Humanitarian Affairs (OCHA), Internal Displacement Monitoring Center (IDMC), and the Relief Web.

2 Major Displacement Events

2.1 Kemant-Amhara

Kemant is an Agaw ethnic group located in northwest Ethiopia in Amhara region, north of Lake Tana with their Amhara neighbors. Originally, they spoke a central Cushitic Agaw language known as Kemant, with alternative names of Agaw, Kemant, Kemantney, Kimanteney, Qemant, and Western Agaw. Ethiopia's 1994 national Census reported that the population of Kemant was 172,327. Of these, there were 4,830 users of the Kemant language, of these again, 1,650 people used it as the first language and 3,180 as a second language (CSA, 1998). Eberhard, Gary, Simons, and Fenning (2019) classified the Kemant language is “nearly extinct”.

The 2007 national population census of Ethiopia, however, withdrew the Kemant from the list of ethnic groups in the country (CSA, 2008). This subsequently became the fuel to a continuous request by the Kemants for re-recognition. The Kemant community members raised the question as to why they were lost in the census. However, the answer delayed and the situation turned into series of conflicts. Following years of quest for re-recognition and self-administration and several documented or undocumented deaths and displacements, the Amhara regional government (ARG) made a decision. On June 10 th, 2015, based on the findings of previous survey studies that the region had conducted at six different times, ARG granted recognition of the Kemant as a “nationality”. The region also granted 42 kebeles in Gondar and surrounding areas a semi-autonomous status for the future Kemant self-administration woreda (Wasihun, 2018:44-45).

However, the Kemant rejected the decision because they believed the decision excluded many kebeles of the Kemant that also had fought for recognition and autonomy and a woreda level administration was not enough. On 17 th September 2017, a referendum was held by ARG to determine the status of an additional eight kebeles. The result of the referendum was that seven of the eight kebeles voted in favor of the existing Amhara administration while one kebele voted to join the Kemant self-administration. However, the Kemant believed this measure by ARG was even not adequate. The struggle by the Kemant continued, in the meantime facing many deaths and destruction of property. In 2018, the regional government reconsidered its previous decision of giving a woreda level administration and passed a new decision that stated “the Kemant will have a Zone level administrative structure” which is a higher level administration to woreda. But, the Kemant still continued to argue that this decision excluded a significant number of Kemant Kebeles who had decided to be part of the new Kemant political administration during their referendum from the so-called New Kemant administration.

Longstanding tensions and sporadic conflict between the Amhara and Kemant communities entered into Prime Minister Abey's period. Conflict spiked in September 2018 across the Central and West Gondar zones of the region, leading to the displacement of 56,000 people as of the 4th week of February 2019 (OCHA, 2019). European Commission (2019) in its ECHO Daily Flash reported on 25 February 2019 reported that clashes over the preceding two weeks in North Gondar had raised the number of internally displaced persons in Amhara region of which 40,000 were related to the conflict between ethnic Kemants and Amharas. Dozens of deaths and extended burning of houses and villages have been reported. Violence and displacement have been occurring particularly since November 2018. Over a thousand ethnic Kemants have crossed the border into Sudan and several hundred have requested asylum.A state of emergency was established for West and Central Gondar as well as Gondar city. Ethiopian National Defense Forces took over control of West and Central Gondar at the request of Amhara region, introducing a ban on weapons on the main roads.

In the meantime, as subsequent sections will show, several interethnic conflicts between

Amhara and other groups in other regions caused Amhara to flee to their region adding more IDP crises in the part of the country. On 15 th February 2019, Amhara region announced that the humanitarian crisis was beyond its response capacity, requesting support from the humanitarian community. Regional authorities drafted a response plan and requesting 18 million USD to support 18,000 households. In March 2019, Amhara region organized a fundraiser in Sheraton Addis Hotel and raised 610 million birr to support internally displaced people that were living in the region. Recent rapid humanitarian assessments have highlighted the criticality of the IDPs' situation and the urgent needs they face in terms of basic assistance including food, shelters, and emergency non-food items.

2.2 Guji–Gedeo

Guji, an Oromo group, and Gedeo are ethnic groups inhabiting contiguous territories in the southern part of Ethiopia. During the imperial régime (1930-1974), both ethnic groups belonged to the then Sidamo Teklay Gizat① . Although the Derg régime (1974-1991) carried out an administrative restructuring in 1987 within the former Sidamo Kefle-Hager (as the Tekaly Gizat was renamed), the two adjacent communities continued to live within the same province (Taddesse 1995: 24).

The restructuring of groups into ethnic-based constituencies in 1995 however affected the two ethnic communities. The then actors in the making of new boundaries incorporated most part of the Guji into the Borena Zone of Oromiya Regional State while Gedeo remained under Gedeo Zone of SNNPR. Later, the Guji Zone was created on September 2002, when the upland *woredas* of the Borena Zone were split apart to create it. This situation created disintegration of Guji and Gedeo into three different zones albeit at various numbers. CSA (2007) reported 975,506 populations for Gedeo while the Guji Zone Education Office (2012) reported 1.3 million for Guji. Out of the total population of Gedeo, 729,955 lived in the Gedeo Zone and 245,165 in the Oromiya Regional State, mainly in Guji and Borena Zones (CSA, 2007). Likewise, there are also significant numbers of Guji living in both Gedeo zone and Borena Zones (Girum, 2011:81, 91).

The re-territorialization seemed to have created new problems. Before 1995, interactions between the Gedeo and Guji communities had been both cooperative and conflictual. The conflicts stemmed mainly from competitions over resources. However, post-1995 re-territorialization transformed the conflicts into border claims which were witnessed first and since 1995 (Girum 2011:81, 91). These conflicts have eroded previous friendly relations. The two communities continued at loggerheads since the problem of defining border has not yet been settled.

In April and June 2018, the outbreak of new inter-ethnic conflict between Guji and Gedeo displaced more than a million people in West Guji and Gedeo, along the border between Oromia and SNNPR regions. The displacement was the subject of wide media coverage. Perhaps because

① "Teklay Gizat", which may be equivalent to a province, was the first level administrative division of Ethiopia during the imperial regime. Teklay Gizat was further subdivided into awrajas or districts.

of the gravity of the problem, both Prime Minister Abiy Ahmed and his Minister of Peace Mufariat Kamil visited the IDPs in their temporary shelter in March 2019.

2.3 Oromo–Somali

The Oromia Region is the largest and most populous state in Ethiopia's federal structure, and constitutes primarily those of the Oromo ethnic group, the largest ethnic group in the country, while the Somali Region, the second largest state by area in the country, primarily constitutes those of the Somali ethnic group. Somalis are mostly pastoralists and Oromos tend to be farmers, as well as pastoralists.

Under the new regional administrative structure, the Somali and the Oromia regions share a long boundary that stretches for more than 1,000 kilometers from the Jijiga highlands in the northeast to the Ethio Kenyan borderlands in the southeast. It has been difficult to demarcate clear borders between the states as pastoral communities cross borders in search of pasture for their animals. This has led to competition, such as for wells and grazing land, over the years, with tens of thousands of people being displaced in some conflict.

According to Herbert Lewis, interactions between the easternmost Oromo and the westernmost Somali began during the 1500s and 1600s as the Oromo were expanding to the north, northeast, and southeast (1966: 35). This means the two groups were competing for about 400 years in their borderlands for water, grazing and agricultural land (Lewis, 1966; Turton, 1975). In 2004, a referendum to decide on the fate of more than 420 *kebeles*, the country's smallest administrative unit, gave 80% of them to Oromia, leading to Somali minorities fleeing those areas.

From December 2016 at the border of the Oromia and Somali regions, the Oromia and Somali communities' territorial tension boiled, notably near the town of Deka, leaving at least 30 people dead and more than 50,000 displaced. The Oromo claim the area is their ancestral land and the Somali families had been brought in from Ethiopian Somali regional state. The situation escalated when the two communities' clansmen started revenge attacks[①]. The clashes involved heavily armed men on both sides in locations all along the border. Schools were looted and civil servants shot in their offices. Residents on the Oromo side also reported widespread rapes. The worst of the violence took place in the area around Negele Borana. More than 100 people died and thousands were displaced in February and March 2016 in the Negele area alone. Oromo activists have claimed much higher numbers[②].

On 20 April 2017, the Oromia and Somali states of Ethiopia have signed an agreement to peacefully solve disputes[③]. However, in September 2017, clashes erupted which killed hundreds

---

① http://goobjoog.com/english/relative-calm-returns-deadly-clash-oromo-somali-communities-ethiopia/

② Gardner Tom (2016), "Uneasy peace and simmering conflict: the Ethiopian town where three flags fly".

③ Oromia and Somali states agree to peacefully solve border dispute, [2017-04-21], https://ethiopianembassy.be/en/

of the Oromo ethnicity and some on Somali side①. Violence also continued along the border between Oromia and Somalia regions, where a spike in clashes displaced up to 500,000 people in the last three months of 2017.

In May 2018, four people were killed and 200 houses burned in clashes②. In July 2018, Oromo militias killed 50 Somalis③. The intensity of the fighting decreased in the first half of 2018, but another 200,000 people still fled their homes and the situation remains highly unstable and insecure.④

2.4 Burayu Massacre

A day after the Federal Police Commissioner Jemal Zeinu thanked, Querro, an ethnic Oromo youth group seemingly linked to regional authorities and Oromo Liberation Front (OLF — a radical ethnic-nationalist opposition party with over 40 years of age), for a peaceful reception ceremony for OLF leaders in Addis Ababa, at least 60 Ethiopians were reportedly massacred in Burayu — a town within Oromo regional state-outside of the capital from 14-16 September 2018. Many others were wounded but the exact figure was not confirmed by government although it admitted that there was "a problem in some Oromia zones". Government-affiliated media estimates of the death toll from the attack are between 25 and 30. The regional police commissioner at the time, Alemayehu Ejigu, said the group responsible for the death of over 60 Ethiopians, in just two days, in Ashewa Meda, Burayu, are "organized hoodlums whose interest is looting".

Gamos and Guraghe's are among ethnic groups that were targeted. Victims of the attack and the killings say that they were told to leave the region which makes the attack a form of ethnic cleansing.

Based on information from social media and other Ethiopian media outlets, one of the victims was a pregnant woman who was rapped and whose husband was killed by the same Querro group a day before she died in hospital in the western parts of Addis Ababa. Verified video footages and pictures widely shared on social media suggest that the massacre exhibited barbaric tendencies. The event provoked outrage of many Ethiopians on social media and demanded the government to protect the safety and security of Ethiopians in Oromo region.

2.5 Gumuz–Amhara

The Gumuz relationship with their Amhara neighbors is the history of troubled relations, as they have the same troubled relations with their neighbors in Sudan. The Gumuz suffered military conquest and slave raiding on both sides of the Ethiopian and Sudanese border (Abdussamad,

① "What is behind clashes in Ethiopia's Oromia and Somali regions?". BBC News. [2017-09-18]. Retrieved [2017-09-25]; "Hundreds' dead in Ethiopia ethnic clashes". *Capital News.* [2017,09,26].https://www.capitalfm.co.ke/news/2017/09/hundreds-dead-ethiopia-ethnic-clashes/

② "Four People killed, Over 200 Houses Torched in Renewed Somali-Oromo Clashes". Halbeeg News.

③ "Oromo militias killed 50 Somalis; displaced hundreds as tit for tat violence spiraled out of control in Moyale - OPride.com".

④ Internal Displacement Monitoring Center (IDMC). accessed [2019-05-05]. www.internal-displacement.org.

1995; James, 1986). The relationship between the Gumuz and their Amhara neighbors was historically a typical frontier relationship in which the latter campaigned for several centuries for territorial integration.

The Benishangul Gumuz (B-G) region shares a common boundary stretching hundreds of kilometers with the Amhara region. As indicated in the above paragraph, in the pre-federal era, Amhara dominance over the Gumuz characterized the relationship between the two groups. The formation of the B-G region has changed the inter-ethnic relationship between the two groups in several ways. The Gumuz inhabit a spiral-shaped territory extending from the former Wollega province in the south to the northwestern (Metema and Qwara) parts of the former Gonder province. Even if their settlement is contiguous, it is feasible to divide the Gumuz country into two; Metekel in the Blue Nile valley of northwest Ethiopia and Dedessa in the former Wollega province. The prevailing administrative division of the BGNRS region somehow follows this division. Hence, the parts of the former Metekel Awraja inhabited by the Gumuz now constitute the new Metekel zone, while the Gumuz of the Dedessa valley organized into the newly created Khamashi zone.

In October 2017, hundreds of Amharas have been forcibly displaced and evicted from their homes in Kemashe Zone, Benishangul Gumuz region. More than 530 ethnic Amhara households (each household has from 2-8 members) were displaced from their land and forced to run away from their homes, fearing for their lives. Many informants believe that the eviction was carried out with active involvements of local authorities who ordered armed militias and other residents to attack ethnic Amharas, according to a statement by the Association of Human Rights for Ethiopia. This attack started in October 2017 continued until the end of April 2018. During the attack 13 ethnic Amhara individuals were killed and at least 50 others were injured. The displaced people were sheltered in Bahir Dar[①].

2.6 Gumuz–Oromo

Similarly, the relationships that developed between the Gumuz and their Oromo neighbors in the former Wollega province were asymmetrical, in which the latter took the upper hand (Ezkieal, 2003; Wallmark, 1981). According to Edossa Tassisa, "the Gumuz of Wollega faced slave raiding and subjugation by the Oromo. The Oromo also divided the Gumuz and their land among different Oromo clans. Hence, some of the Gumuz clans even began to be called by the names of Oromo clans" (Berihun, 2004: 271). Like the Gumuz of Metekel, the Gumuz in Wollega resisted the steady encroachment to their territory by highland farmers and excessive taxation by local Oromo chiefs. They rebelled under the leadership of Abba Tonie (Bambog Kili) during the 1950s (Berihun, 2004:272-273).

The formation of the BGNRS, which led to the re-examination of inter-ethnic relationships

① https://amharanews.com/2018/06/09/commentary-increasing-accounts-of-displacement-violence-against-ethnic-amharas-and-why-solving-it-should-be-a-priority-originally-published-by-addisstandard/

between the Gumuz and their ethnic neighbors, could be considered as a water shade. One important aspect of this change has been the forming of a regional boundary. The prevalence of a wide gap in the boundary imaginations of the Gumuz and their Amhara and Oromo neighbors affected this process. For the Gumuz, their boundary with the latter is starkly clear, though not clearly defined. They believe that all the hot bamboo growing lowlands, which were their ancestral homelands, should be recognized as theirs and assigned to the newly established Benishangul-Gumuz region (Berihun, 2004:265).

It is, however, difficult to translate this notion of boundary into intra-federal boundaries, as there are both Amhara and Oromo settlements on these territories. Additionally, the Amhara and Oromo do not acknowledge this Gumuz notion of boundary. Instead, partly due to their long history of frontier relationships with the latter, the former still 216 Chapter 7 appear to consider Gumuz's territory as open for the expansion of subsistent peasant agriculture. On top of these conflicting notions of boundary, the scattered and sparse character of Gumuz settlement presented them with numerous challenges. For instance, almost all of the Gumuz woreda of the Kamashi Zone is inaccessible directly from the zonal capital, Kamashi. As a result, one has to travel through the Oromia region to reach several of this *woreda*. Moreover, there is no road that directly links the zonal capitals of the Gumuz — both Khamashi and Metekel with the regional capital (Assosa) without passing through the Oromia and the Amhara regions. Furthermore, the Benishangul-Gumuz region remains politically fragile due to the lack of a well-developed inter-ethnic relationship among the five constituent ethnic groups of the region. In this respect, the northern part of the region (the Metekel zone) has stronger economic relations with the Amhara region than the southern part of the region. Similarly, the southern and western parts of the region (Kamashi and Assosa) have stronger economic relations with the Oromia region. More importantly, many of the Gumuz are bilingual, speaking Amharic (Metekel) and Afaan-Oromo (Kamashi and Assosa) in addition to their own language.

In 2008, conflict broke out between the Oromo and Gumuz people in Kamashi and Eastern Wollega Zone. The clash started on Saturday, May 18, 2008, when armed Gumuz crossed over from their regional state to Oromia State and attacked villages before daybreak, residents told Sudan Tribune. Government officials have declined to give the official number of the victims of the conflict so far. Residents said that over 130 people died and about 8,000 people have been internally displaced. People died from both sides of the tribes but eyewitnesses have said, "the attacks were preplanned and nocturnal and the Oromos were caught unprepared; asa result, the majority of the people who lost their lives and whose houses were burned down with children inside were Oromos." Oromos further accused the federal government of manipulating and arming the Gumuz to attack their neighboring Oromo over land claim. The Oromo residents also suspect both the regional sate of Benishangul Gumuz and central government have role in arming and mobilizing the Gumuz to attack them[①] over claims to farmlands[②].

Localized conflict in Benishangul Gumuz region (BSG) and East and West Wollega zones of Oromia region beginning in the last week of September 2018 is believed to have displaced an estimated 191,752 individuals comprising 36,438 households. 36% of IDPs are in collective sites and 64% are in host communities. In BSG 14% of IDPs are in collective sites and 86% are in host communities. Bio Jiganfado woreda, believed to be hosting IDPs, was inaccessible due to ongoing conflict at the time of the assessment[③]. The violence began when officials from Benishangul-Gumuz were killed by unidentified gunmen, said the Walta Media and Communication Corporate, citing the region's communications chief Zelalem Jaleta. The officials were ambushed by the group when they were on their way to Kamash Zone, Benishangul region. They were in a meeting which was held in Assosa and was attended by security officials from Oromia region, particularly West Wellega. The meeting mainly focused on solving security problems in the area. Unfortunately, after concluding the security meeting, the deceased officials were attacked on September 25th, 2018 at a place called Mekabila, Oromia Region. The attackers also burned down two vehicles[④].

2.7 Amhara–Oromo

In October 2017, hundreds of ethnic Amharas who have lived in Oromia regional state of Illibabur zones of Buno Bedelle, Choraa Wereda, Jimma Jilaa, Jimaa Togo, Sotolo Jimate, Sotole Gawaa, Agule, Burle number one, and Chabi areas and in Wellega were forced to flee their homes. Many Amharas from different parts of Wello were relocated to these areas in 1977 following the infamous Ethiopian famine, which particularly hit the former region of Wello, now under Amhara regional state the hardest. Through the long years, the residents have made families and properties in other parts of Ethiopia such as Illibabur zone. To the most part, they have peacefully coexisted with Oromos. But since October 2017, many of them have been targeted in ethnic attacks by some ethnic Oromo groups and were forced to flee fearing for their lives. Seid Shibru recounts what he witnessed in one fateful day in October 2017. He said:

Having been granted approval by the woreda authorities, a crowd of people held a demonstration to demand our expulsion; they were holding knives and swords and were helped by the local police. The next day, they started coming into the households of Amharas and Tigreaans; they killed four Amharas. The altercation led to loss of lives from both Amhara and Oromo sides. Finally, it was the Amhara regional police that came to our rescue; they also helped us secure back some of our belongings. I lived there for 34 *years but came to Wello about six months ago,*

---

① http://www.sudantribune.com/Hundred-killed-during-clashes,27265.

② https://ehrco.org/2008/06/110th-special-report-worsening-situation-of-ethnic-clashes-needs-due-attention/?lang=en.

③ https://displacement.iom.int/reports/ethiopia-%E2%80%94-benishangul-gumuz-east-west-wellega-1-rapid-response-site-assessment-report-date.

④ https://www.thereporterethiopia.com/article/idps-number-rise-violence-hits-benishangul-oromia.

*because I have no guarantee of life there, and the officials refused to ensure our safety*①.

Addisu Arega Kitessa, the then head of the Oromia regional state communication affairs bureau in his message on Facebook, which was written in Amharic, said that "eight Oromos and three Amharas" were killed in Dega and Chora woredas in Buno Bedele zone as a result of a "deliberate attempt by some people who wanted to instigate ethnic violence between Amharas and Oromos." Addisu also blamed the violence on forces "who want to destabilize the regional government." Without giving further details, Addisu also said those responsible were placed under police custody. Other reports from social media activists put the number of death as high as 20.

The second source who spoke to *Addis Standard* on his part said that properties belonging to ethnic Tigrayans were also targeted and "more than a dozen houses and businesses were set on fire." However, he added that the "dead were mainly from ethnic Oromos and Amharas who lived together in the area for decades," he said, sounding upset and with a voice shaking uncontrollably. "Many people have fled their houses and are in hiding right now fearing for their lives." The *BBC Tigrinya* news website reported that coffee farms and businesses belonging to ethnic Amharas and Tigrayans were destroyed.

Similarly, on October 11, three people were killed by security forces during a protest rally in Shashemene town, 250 km southeast of Addis Abeba, in west Arsi zone of the Oromia regional state and three more people were killed in Bookeeti town, west Hararghe zone of the Oromia region in eastern Ethiopia, where more than 30 were also wounded②.

3 Effects

It is really difficult to even attempt to make a complete assessment of the effects of the conflicts and displacement. Complete and genuine data is not available in governmental and non-governmental reports. The government does not genuinely report all damages especially underestimate loss of life, and non-governmental organizations do not have complete and timely access to the problem areas. This section will simply provide some allusion of some effects.

3.1 Loss of Human Lives

The major cost of the displacements, as hitherto stated, is the loss of human lives. Government reports do not show the number of deaths in the course of displacement. Besides, international human rights organizations do not report it. However, results from fieldwork indicate horrendous stories of death. According to Germany's international broadcaster, Deutsche Welle (DW) Amharic, as reported on March 16, 2019, for example, up to four civilians were dying every day due to lack of nutrition, prevalence of water-borne diseases and lack of hygiene.③

① https://amharanews.com/2018/06/09/commentary-increasing-accounts-of-displacement-violence-against-ethnic-amharas-and-why-solving-it-should-be-a-priority-originally-published-by-addisstandard/

② http://addisstandard.com/news-several-people-killed-in-another-communal-violence-in-western-ethiopia/

③ Deutsche Welle (DW) Amharic. Live TV report. Reported on March 16, 2019.

3.2 Displacement

As a result of those events discussed earlier, 2,715,076 people have been displaced in the country until May 2019. While some regions are widely ridden by IDPs, there are others who are not or are less affected. The Somali region has a total of 604,253 IDPs, Oromia， 1,204,036，Amhara 107,097, SNN-PR757,636, BG36,634, and Dire Dawa 5,420 IDPs. See the following Figure 1.

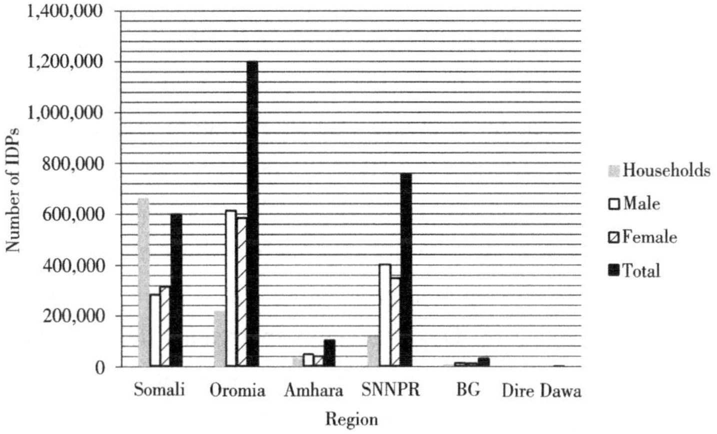

Figuer 1

3.3 Loss of Property and Livelihoods

For the IDPs, displacements did not come alone. Many do not simply get evicted but also lose their land, housing, and property. The IDPs and returnees are exposed to protection risks, suffer constrained access to basic social services, and experience the disruption and loss of their property. The following Table 1 shows reports from the government through the Ministry of Peace.

Table 1

Region	Destroyed Houses
BG	2,814
Oromia	101,975
Amhara	6,404
Somali	-
SNNPR	32,888
Tigray	45,686
Dire Dawa	-
Harari	-
Total	**189,767**

In addition to houses burned completely or damaged, several social service centers were destroyed. A report by the Ministry of Peace shows that 245 schools, 140 health centers, 101 agriculture service, and 58 other social service centers totally 574 social service centers were destroyed.

4 Responses

It is needless to mention that protecting and assisting IDPs is an important social, legal, and political issue. The international law provides that protection of IDPs, from the very beginning of protecting citizens from displacement to giving a durable solution to those once displaced, is the responsibility of the national government (UNHCR, 1998). However, since many of the displacements in Ethiopia or elsewhere in the world are a result of civil conflict and violence, the authority of the central state is in doubt or local authority may not be willing to provide assistance and protection. IDPs suffer from humanitarian assistance from their governments or international stakeholders. Responses to post-April 2018 IDPs in Ethiopia spurred debates. Those on the government side argue that they have tried their own best. Opponents air a flurry of opinions over the social media that the government failed to respond adequately. Lack of responses towards protection of citizens from displacements was one of the areas of critics of Ethiopia's political reform agenda since April 2018.

4.1 Legal Actions

Perhaps the first and immediate action and responsibility of a government in relation people once displaced is prevailing the rule of law by making those involved accountable by the law. The Ministry of Peace report shows that there are 2,537 suspects involved at whatsoever level in inciting displacement. The following Table 2 shows the government report on making people involved in displacement accountable and confiscation of property.

Table 2

Region	All suspects	Captured	Freed	Freed on Advice	Sentenced	Confiscated by government				
						Kalashnikov Rifle	Pistols	Bomb	Bullets	Traditional Weapons
BG	832	832	25	671	136	63	6	2	1,931	207
Oromia	260	138	6	2	89	43	19	2	2,400	171
Amhara	671	65	87	-	-	-	-	-	-	-
Somali	-	-	-	-	-	-	-	-	-	-
SNNPR	754	265	-	-	-	-	-	-	-	-

Region	All suspects	Cap-tured	Freed	Freed on Advice	Sen-tenced	Confiscated by government				
						Kalash-nikov Rifle	Pistols	Bomb	Bullets	Tradi-tional Weap-ons
Tigray	-	-	-	-	-	-	-	-	-	-
Dire Dawa	20	20	6	-	-	-	-	-	-	-
Harari	-	-	-	-	-	-	-	-	-	-
Total	**2,537**	**1,320**	**124**	**673**	**225**	**106**	**25**	**4**	**4,331**	**378**

4.2 Public Awareness Campaigns

Broad public awareness campaign held across different regions. The report in the Table 3 below shows that there were 136 campaigns which involved 854,696 participants. The campaigns were made to raise awareness of the public on the rule of law, peace and reconciliation, and resettlement of IDPs.

Table 3

Region	No. of Conferences	No. of Participants		
		Male	Female	Total
Amhara	65	254,085	155,915	410,000
Oromia	8	59,252	28,643	87,895
SNNPR	31	58,340	13,312	71,652
BG	24	160,540	122,847	283,387
Somali	4	-	-	-
Harari	-	-	-	-
Dire Dawa	2	-	-	-
Tigray	2	1,406	356	1,762
Total	**136**	**533,623**	**321,073**	**854,696**

4.3 Resettlement

Returning IDPs to the place of origin was the major intervention by the government of Ethiopia. Of the total 2,715,076 IDPs, 1,841,312 were reported returned. 391,038 IDPs were returned in Somali Region, 690,956 in Oromia, 56,529 in Amhara, 662,964 in SNNPR, 37,345 in BG, and 2,480 in Dire Dawa (Figure 2).

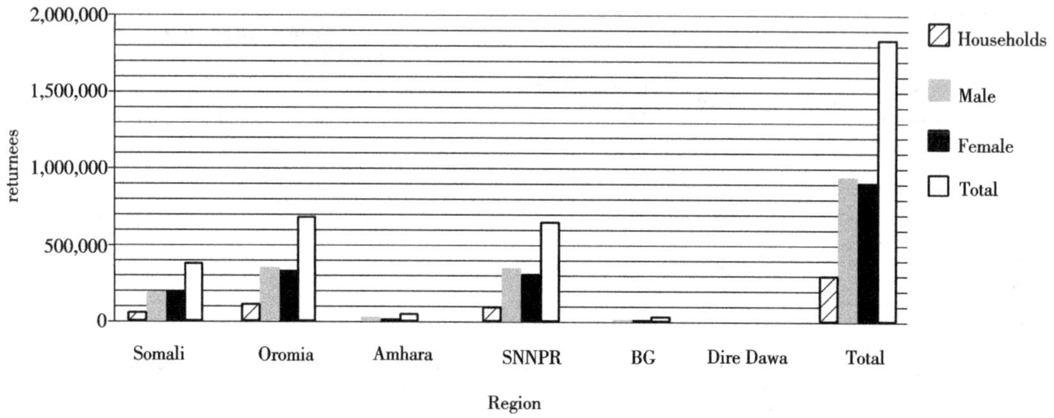

Figure 2

4.4 Reconstruction of Houses and Social Service Centers

Returning IDPs to their original place means that they should have their house reconstructed at least and their property restituted in principle. The government report shows some activities are done in reconstruction of houses and social infrastructure damaged during conflicts (Table 4).

Table 4

Region	Houses reconstructed by the community participation	Social service centers
BG	1,762	-
Oromia	27,253	10
Amhara	2,060	-
Somali	-	-
SNNPR	211	15
Tigray	-	-
Dire Dawa	-	-
Harari	-	-
Total	**31,286**	**25**

5 Theories on Causes of the Conflicts and Displacement

Two arguments are circulated on the causes of the conflict. One argument takes ethnic factors in a literal sense. The conflicts and displacements are the results of interethnic and border conflicts that had been prevalent even before the reform which were suppressed by the pre-Abiy government. A coming into power of the reformist Prime Minister Abiy Ahmed brought waves of hope for democracy, equality, and rule of law. He ended a 20-year conflict with neighboring Eritrea, freed thousands of political prisoners, unfettered the media and appointed women to half the cabinet posts. Parliament also accepted his female nominees for president and head of the Supreme Court. On top of that, he asked a dissident leader to return from exile in the United States to run the electoral commission. Ahmed has also promised to privatize state-owned enterprises. The pace of change has delighted the public at large and pro-democracy activists and thrown more reactionary elements off balance.

According to this line of argument, the opening up of political space has allowed Ethiopians to express long-standing grievances, often over land, border demarcations, access to state resources, and perceived discrimination against their community or ethnic group, without fear of retribution. It seems also that political space also created an opportunity for political manipulators. Local governance and security have sharply deteriorated in many locations. This lack of law and order means there are few constraints on how grievances are expressed. In some places, this has resulted in score-settling, clearing of rival groups from land and housing, and open conflict between ethnic groups-hence with the world-record number of displaced people. It hasn't all been rosy — especially when it comes to the ongoing eviction of ethnic groups in various regions in the country.

However, for many people, this line of interpretation of conflicts and displacement is superficial. The prevalent theory on the causes of conflicts contributing to these displacements is the fact that they were induced by political entrepreneurs who sponsor conflicts to create instability. People who support this line of argument argue that members and supporters of TPLF, who lost grip on power, were sponsoring the violence. According to this line of argument, members of the TPLF and its supporters have collaborated with thousands of sacked members from other organizations such as OPDO and the Amhara National Democratic Movement (ANDM) or the Oromo Liberation Front (OLF) to prevent or deter the course of the reform. Many informants argued that the TPLF and OLF separately or jointly operate to instigate conflicts and displacement.

6 Conclusion

Displacement was a huge social, political and economic problem that posed a challenge against the political reform agenda in Ethiopia that started in April 2018. An immediate question that comes after having such difficult experience is: What is next? Do we expect more displacements or at least how long do we expect these problems to continue in the future? To make the best scenario, even though the problem cannot be completely contained given fragile political conditions in the country which is based on ethnic differences and proliferation of elites that want to exploit the difference, such massive and continuous displacements events, I think, will decline in the future. First, the public seems to be wary of conflicts and displacements and perhaps has taken a lesson from being used as political instruments for political entrepreneurs of orchestrating ethnic such conflict. Second, the circulation of arms seems to be increasing and now the weapons are not only in the hands of those who evict but also among those who are vulnerable to be evicted. Finally, it is expected and we have observed a trend in recent times where the government is discharging responsibility of protecting rule of law and taking measures against those who cause the displacement.

References

[1] CENTRAL STATISTICS AGENCY (CSA). 2008. Summary and statistical report of the 2007 population and housing census. Addis Ababa: CSA.

[2] CENTRAL STATISTICS AUTHORITY (CSA).1998.The 1994 population and housing census of Ethiopia:results for Amhara Region. Addis Ababa: CSA.

[3] EBERHARD D M, GARY F S, CHARLES D F. 2019. Ethnologue: languages of the world. 22ed. Dallas, Texas: SIL International.

[4] EUROPEAN COMMISSION. 2019. ECHO daily flash 25 February 2019: Ethiopia — ethnic violence and forced displacement in Amhara region (DG ECHO, partner organizations). [2019-05-09]. https://erccportal.jrc.ec.europa.eu/ECHO-Flash/ECHO-Flash-List/yy/2019/mm/2.

[5] GIRUM K. 2011. Federalism and ethnic conflict management in Ethiopia: the case of Guji-Gedeo conflict. Addis Ababa: Addis Ababa University.

[6] GIRUM K. 2014. The quest for resolution of Guji-Gedeo conflicts in southern Ethiopia: a review of mechanisms employed, actors and their effectiveness. Ethiopian Journal of Social Sciences and Humanities, 10 (1): 59-100.

[7] Human Rights Watch. 2019. Ethiopia: Abiy' s first year as prime minister, review of conflict and internally displaced persons. https://www.hrw.org/news/2019/04/09/ethiopia-ab-ys-first-year- prime-minister-review-conflict-and-internally-displaced.

[8] LEWIS H. 1966. The origins of the Galla and Somali. The Journal of African History, 7(1): 27-46.

[9] UN HIGH COMMISSIONER FOR REFUGEES (UNHCR). 1998. Guiding principles on internal displacement. https://www.refworld.org/docid/3c3da07f7.html.

[10] WASIHUN B. 2018. The legality of self determination right: the case of Kemant people in Amhara National Regional State. Addis Ababa: Addis Ababa University.

21 世纪以来印度与埃塞俄比亚经贸关系新特点①

杜　英　甘振军

摘要：印度与埃塞俄比亚（简称“埃塞”）作为环印度洋地区大国，历史上就保持着紧密的经贸关系和人员往来。进入 21 世纪以来，双边经贸关系呈现新特点：印度对埃塞俄比亚的投资主要集中在工业和农业领域；快速增长的双边贸易呈现出关系不平衡和不对称；印度奉行多样化援助政策等。21 世纪初期的双边关系是两国关系史上的“黄金时代”，其对中国发展与埃塞的经贸关系具有参考和研究价值。

关键词：印度；埃塞俄比亚；经贸关系；新特点

印度与埃塞俄比亚有着悠久的历史联系。从阿克苏姆王国开始，印度和埃塞俄比亚之间的贸易关系和人员往来至今已经存在了近两千年。6 世纪，印度人与埃塞俄比亚人在阿杜里斯港交易丝绸、香料、黄金和象牙。16 世纪，葡萄牙援助埃塞俄比亚国王，果阿人也来到了埃塞俄比亚。1868 年，为了解救被埃塞俄比亚皇帝特沃德罗斯二世关押的欧洲外交官和传教士，罗伯特·纳皮尔将军率领 3 万英国远征军进入埃塞俄比亚，其中有 1.3 万名印度士兵，而且大部分是锡克教徒。19 世纪下半叶，一些印度商人和工匠定居埃塞俄比亚，居住在印度西海岸的西迪人据说是埃塞俄比亚人的后裔。在意大利入侵埃塞俄比亚期间，贾瓦哈拉尔·尼赫鲁呼吁声援埃塞俄比亚，指出“我们印度对帮助我们在埃塞俄比亚陷入困境的同胞无能为力，因为我们也是帝国主义的受害者，但我们今天与他们站在一起，当美好生活到来的时候，我们希望还站在一起”。1936 至 1941 年，英国派军队应对意大利对埃塞俄比亚的入侵，英军中就有数量可观的印度士兵，如威廉·普拉特将军就指挥了一支由第 4、第 5 印度师组成的部队。

埃塞俄比亚是非洲，也是环印度洋地区的重要大国，埃塞俄比亚首都亚的斯亚贝巴是非盟总部所在地，因此印度注重发展与埃塞俄比亚的友好关系。埃塞俄比亚是非洲国家中少数几个与印度保持友好互利关系的国家之一。在过去的岁月里，尽管两国之间的合作领域发生过重大变化，但目前两国的合作伙伴关系依然紧密。本文首先回顾 1947 年至 2000 年印度与埃塞俄比亚经贸关系的发展历程，分析 21 世纪前 20 年双边经贸关系的特点，其双边经贸关系对中国发展对非经贸关系和新时期中非共建“一带一路”会提供一些参照、思考和借鉴。

① 本文系 2018 年度国家社科基金一般项目“印度与印度洋沿岸东非国家经贸关系研究（1947—2017）”的阶段性成果（项目批准号：18BSS051）。

一、印度与埃塞经贸关系的历史回顾

1948 年，印度在建国的第二年，就与埃塞俄比亚建立了外交关系。埃塞俄比亚是第一批与印度建立外交关系的非洲国家之一。萨达尔·桑特·辛格是印度驻埃塞俄比亚第一任大使，阿曼纽尔·亚伯拉罕是埃塞俄比亚驻印度大使，也是第一位非洲国家驻印度大使。印度通过当地印度裔加强与埃塞俄比亚政府的联系。1952 年，为了庆祝埃塞俄比亚皇帝诞辰 60 周年，当地印度裔捐赠了 74 000 美元，印度政府也提供 2 000 美元建造了亚的斯亚贝巴产妇之家。作为答谢，海尔·塞拉西皇帝给予印度 500 吨小麦作为回礼，而产妇之家也成为埃塞俄比亚首都重要的公共卫生保健机构①。1956 年、1959 年和 1968 年，海尔·塞拉西皇帝三次访问印度，印度商人开始投资埃塞俄比亚的磨坊、棉花等相关产业，在亚的斯亚贝巴建立三家印度和埃塞合资的棉纺织工厂。此外，印度商人还通过建立医院、诊所和其他社会福利设施为埃塞俄比亚人民服务，如 1955 年建立了甘地纪念医院、1957 年建立哈勒尔军事学院等。1965 年，印度总统拉达克里希南访问埃塞俄比亚，印度与埃塞俄比亚经贸关系进一步加强。1969 年，埃塞俄比亚接受印度经济与技术合作项目（ITEC）的资助，在此计划下，埃塞俄比亚从人力资源发展中受益。

1974—1991 年，在门格斯图统治时期，印度与埃塞俄比亚关系恶化。1977 年 8 月至 1978 年 3 月，在埃塞俄比亚—索马里战争期间，印度选择站在埃塞俄比亚一边。1978 年，印度与埃塞俄比亚签署了避免双重征税计划。

20 世纪 90 年代，印度、埃塞俄比亚面临的内外困难推动了双边关系的提升。1991 年，印度国内开始进行经济改革，鼓励对外出口和投资；1998 年，印度强行进行核试验，成为有核国家；1999 年，印度与巴基斯坦爆发卡吉尔冲突。1991 年，埃塞俄比亚门格斯图政权垮台，埃塞俄比亚国家经济陷入破产，又遭受饥荒；1993 年，厄立特里亚脱离埃塞俄比亚独立，埃塞俄比亚成为一个内陆国家，丧失了红海的重要港口阿斯马拉。1991 年以来，印度日益成为埃塞俄比亚的重要伙伴之一，特别是在贸易、援助领域，如货币援助（如信贷额度）和非货币援助（如人力资源开发和能力建设）。印度与埃塞俄比亚贸易额逐年攀升。1992 年，双边贸易额是 1 200 万美元②。

1993 年以来，印度对埃塞俄比亚基础部门的投资超过 15 亿美元，其中 97% 是在农作物种植、水果、蔬菜、鲜花和用于制作饮料的作物领域，其余是动物养殖和采矿业③。1996 年、1998 年，埃塞俄比亚投资委员会先后修订投资表，放松投资限制。印度在埃塞俄比亚几乎所有经济部门的私人投资都在增加。印度是埃塞俄比亚第一大投资国，投资额是 47.8 亿

---

① Sushil Kumar, "India's Development Cooperation with Ethiopia in Sugar Production: an Assessment", http://www.ris.org.in/images/RIS_images/pdf/DP%20198%20Mr%20Sushil%20Kumar.pdf.

② Dr. Suresh Kumar, "The Role of India in Agricultural Development in Ethiopia", [2010-12-01]. http://www.africaindia.org/index.php?option=com_content&view=article&id=48:the-role-of-india-in-agricultural-development-in-ethiopia&catid=34:agriculture-sector&Itemid=29.

③ Belayneh Leta, Belayneh Girma, "Economic relations of Ethiopia and India: Trade and Agricultural Investments after 1991", *African Journal of Political Science and International Relations,* 2017, 11(8):213.

美元[①]。1997年,印度与埃塞俄比亚签订经济合作贸易协定,并建立联合贸易委员会。不过,埃塞俄比亚在印度一直没有投资。

综上,印度与埃塞俄比亚建交以来,双方长期保持友好关系,但其中也有波折。21世纪之前,印度与埃塞俄比亚经贸关系紧密,尽管双边贸易额不高,且保持单向度。埃塞俄比亚积极吸入印度投资,尤其是私人投资。印度对埃塞俄比亚的经济援助也足以维系双边关系,这是21世纪印度—埃塞俄比亚双边经贸关系进入新阶段的基础。

二、21世纪以来印度与埃塞经贸关系的新特点

21世纪以来,印度和埃塞俄比亚之间的关系达到了前所未有的高度。正如埃塞俄比亚总理梅莱斯·泽纳维[②]高度评价21世纪初的埃塞俄比亚与印度关系为"埃印关系的黄金时代"[③]。两国的经贸关系,在投资、援助和进出口贸易等领域呈现新特点。

首先在投资领域,在埃塞已修订投资政策的背景下,印度资本集中在工业和农业领域。2002年、2012年、2014年埃塞政府三次修订投资表并逐渐解除投资限制,吸引印度在内的外国投资者。2005年,在亚的斯亚贝巴印度使馆的支持下, 130人的印度商业论坛成立,鼓励印度人投资埃塞俄比亚,在印度裔社区内,建立对话平台和提供联络机会。2011年,印度是埃塞俄比亚第二大投资国,投资额是47亿美元,实际投资额是20亿美元,共596家公司[④]。2012—2013年,印度对埃塞俄比亚投资是3.0299亿美元。印度是埃塞俄比亚三大投资国之一, 2014年印度对埃塞俄比亚投资额是20亿美元[⑤]。2006年,印度进出口银行向埃塞俄比亚发放了一笔为期20年的6 500万美元的电力项目信贷,并为埃塞俄比亚制糖业的发展提供了6.4亿美元[⑥]。此外,为了增强和升级亚的斯亚贝巴黑狮医院的医疗设备,印度政府提供了一台计算机CT扫描仪和200万美元的贷款。2007年3月,印度外交部部长普拉纳布·穆克吉访问埃塞俄比亚,双方签订《双边投资促进和保护协议》(BIPPA)等五个主要协议。印度外交部选择埃塞俄比亚作为连接非洲国家的泛非电子网络项目的试点国。2008年首届印度—非洲峰会期间,埃塞俄比亚是获得税务减免优先计划的不发达国家之一。2011年印度—非洲论坛峰会上,印度宣布给予3 000万美元支持埃塞俄比亚—吉布提铁路线[⑦]。

印度中小型企业 (SMEs) 是在埃塞俄比亚投资的主力,投资领域是农村电气化和糖业,2010年3月投资额达到45亿美元[⑧]。2015年,埃塞俄比亚为印度企业家购置土地,并提供其他奖励措施和税收便利,以便在埃塞俄比亚建立其他保健设施。

2003年6月至2014年5月, 632家印度公司在埃塞俄比亚共投资约50亿美元。投资

---

① Gedion G Jalata, "Development Assistance from the South: Comparative Analysis of Chinese and Indian to Ethiopia", *Chinese Studies*, 2014,3(1):28.

② 梅莱斯·泽纳维在1991—1995年任埃塞俄比亚总统,1996—2012年任埃塞俄比亚总理。

③ Kishan S Rana Bipul Chatterjee, *Economic Diplomacy: India's Experience,* Jaipur: CUTS Books, 2011:153.

④ Prateeksha Tiwari, "Indian and Chinese FDI in Ethiopia: Nature, Impact, and Challenges", *DU Journal of Undergraduate Research and Innovation*,2015,1(3):129.

⑤ Ibid,128.

⑥ Magdalena Hules, "India's quest for resources in Africa: land grabbing and its implications for India and Ethiopia", http://othes.univie.ac.at/29304/1/2013-08-07_0847522.pdf.

⑦ 同①。

⑧ Kishan S Rana, Bipul Chatterjee, *Economic Diplomacy: India's Experience*, Jaipur: CUTS Books, 2011:154.

的领域有农业、酒花、棉花及纺织品、塑料制品、皮革制品、采矿业和卫生保健等（见表 1）。印度在埃塞俄比亚投资额的 58.7% 在制造业、15.6% 在农业。1993 至 2014 年第一季度，印度对埃塞俄比亚工业部门投资约占印度在该国投资的 54%，对纺织业的投资约占印度对埃塞制造业投资的 46.6%[①]。2011 年，萨拉棉花纤维私人有限公司（Sara Cotton Fibres Private Ltd.）建立了一个轧棉厂，计划对印度出口棉产品[②]。印度公司在埃塞俄比亚还投资食品和饮料加工和制造。自 1998 年印度公司在工业领域投资超过 12 400 万美元，创造了超过 2 500 个长期岗位和 3 000 个临时岗位。2014 年阿兰那集团[③]（The Allana Group）在埃塞俄比亚投资建立一家肉类加工厂。印度还投资埃塞俄比亚的非金属矿产业（如碳酸钾、黏土、盐、石膏），约 37 000 万美元，占整个制造业投资的 14%，建立超过 5 500 个工作岗位（既有临时工，也有长期固定工）[④]。在联合贸易委员会会议上，41 个皮革工业专家为埃塞皮革工业提供培训进行能力建设。印度中央皮革研究所 (CLRI) 与埃塞俄比亚制革厂完成一笔 100 万美元的无水铬鞣技术转让交易。印度中央皮革研究所与埃塞俄比亚皮革工业发展研究所 (Leather Industry Development Institute) 在埃塞俄比亚联合举办了一场研讨会，并将在八家制革厂进行无水铬鞣技术测试，酶脱毛技术已在三家制革厂通过了测试。据报道，制革者对测试结果非常满意，许多制革企业期待进行商业化规模生产测试[⑤]。2017 年，在埃塞俄比亚投资的印度公司主要有 MSP 钢铁能源有限公司（MSP Steel & Power Limited）、阿文德·恩维索废水处理公司（Arvind Envisol）、巴拉吉制造有限公司（Balaaji Manufacturing Plc.）、奥蒂钢铁股份有限公司（Aarti Steel Pvt. Ltd. Co）和索纳利卡拖拉机公司（Sonalika Tractors）。越来越多的印度公司投资埃塞俄比亚的纺织和服装部门[⑥]。2018 年，印度 KPR Mill 公司在埃塞俄比亚默克莱（Mekelle）工业园建立一个新工厂，这是印度第一家海外服装企业，2019 年初，其产品出口美国和欧洲，为埃塞俄比亚创造 700 个工作岗位，雇佣 1 500 名机械工人，为世界市场每天生产 50 000 件服装[⑦]。

表 1　2000 年以来印度公司在埃塞俄比亚投资一览表[⑧]

时间	公司名称	所属国家	生产范围
2000 年	J.J. 科塔里 & 埃塞俄比亚合资有限公司（J.J.Kothari and co.(Eth) LTD）	印度	观赏瓶和罐子
2000 年	J.J. 科塔里 & 埃塞俄比亚合资有限公司（J.J.Kothari and co.(Eth) LTD）	印度	机械化和可灌溉的商品粮作物种植

① “Prospects of India-Ethiopia Investment and Trade Cooperation”, http://www.ipekpp.com/admin/upload_files/Report_3_52_Prospects_2523493963.pdf,p32.

② 同上。

③ 这是印度最大的食品加工和农产品出口公司，包括冷冻肉类加工、水果和蔬菜产品保鲜、咖啡、香料和谷物，产品出口超过 85 个国家和地区。

④ 同①。

⑤ 《印度在埃塞俄比亚推广无水铬鞣技术》，http://www.pelle.cn/news/show-44374.html.

⑥ “India-Ethiopia Commercial Relations”, http://indembassyeth.in/india-ethiopia-commercial-relations-2/.

⑦ Ike Dzokpo, “India’s KPR Mill Opens New Factory in Ethiopia”, [2019-05-15]. https://www.newsghana.com.gh/indias-kpr-mill-opens-new-factory-in-ethiopia/ -.

⑧ Indian Embassy in Addis Ababa & Ethiopian Investment Authority, “List of Indian Companies Invested in Ethiopia”, http://www.ethiopiaembassy.in/Indian%20Investment%20in%20Ethiopia.htm.

续表

时间	公司名称	所属国家	生产范围
2000 年	牛津工业私人有限公司（Oxford Idustries Plc.）	印度 / 埃塞俄比亚	便携塑料袋
2008 年	塔塔埃塞俄比亚公司（Tata Ethiopia Operations）	印度	皮革原料
2012 年	苏里世大理石公司（Souriish Marbles）	印度	大理石

1993 至 2014 年印度在埃塞服务业（如计算机和互联网有关的活动、机械租赁、旅馆业、卫生和社会工作、教育、建筑业、不动产）的投资是 72 000 万美元，为埃塞创造 304 330 个工作岗位①。在亚的斯亚贝巴，印度公司主要从事工程服务、咨询服务、信息通信技术服务、制造业、水管理服务和教育服务②。

2011 年底，埃塞俄比亚政府租赁给外国投资者 80 万公顷土地，印度农业公司从中受益。印度在埃塞俄比亚的农业投资与粮食生产有关，如油籽、豆类、棉花、大米、谷类、玉米、小麦、糖、茶和花卉栽培等，如卡拉图里全球公司（Karaturi Global）在甘贝拉地区租赁 30 万公顷肥沃土地，租期 99 年（见表 2），希瓦集团（Siva Group）租赁 5 万公顷土地③。

表 2　投资埃塞俄比亚农业部门的印度公司④

序号	印度农业公司	土地规模（公顷）	农业作物
1	卡拉图里全球公司（Karaturi Global）	300 000（一期是 100 000 公顷，二期是 200 000 公顷）	棕榈油、谷物、甘蔗
2	JVL 海外私人有限公司（JVL Overseas PTE ltd.）	5 000	棉花
3	绿色山谷农业公司（Green Valley Agro Plc.）	5 000	棉花
4	汉普吉（Hampoorji）	50 000	谷物、油料和香料作物
5	BHO 生物制品公司（BHO Bio Products Plc.）	27 000	谷物、食用油
6	白色田园棉花农场（White Field Cotton Farm Plc.）	10 000	棉花
7	鲁驰·索亚（Ruchi Soya）	25 000	大豆
8	散那提农业种植企业（Sannati Agro Farm Enterprises）	10 000	大米、谷物等
9	瓦丹塔作物公司（Vedanta Harvests Plc.）	3 012	茶叶和套种作物
10	CLC 工业公司（CLC Industries Plc.）	25 000	棉花

① "Prospects of India-Ethiopia Investment and Trade Cooperation", http://www.ipekpp.com/admin/upload_files/Report_3_52_Prospects_2523493963.pdf.

② The Embassy of India, "India-Ethiopia Commercial Bilateral Relations", http://www.indembassyeth.in/eoi.php?id=Commercial.

③ "Who's Behind the Land Grabs",W1siZiIsIjIwMTIvMTAvMTYvMDlfMzhfMDJfMjY5X2xhbmRncmFiYmVycy5wZGYiXV0 (grain.org).

④ "Prospects of India-Ethiopia Investment and Trade Cooperation", http://www.ipekpp.com/admin/upload_files/Report_3_52_Prospects_2523493963.pdf.

"FAQs on Indian Agriculture Investments in Ethiopia", https://www.oaklandinstitute.org/sites/oaklandinstitute.org/files/Ethiopia_India_FAQ.pdf.

Magdalena Hules: India's quest for resources in Africa: land grabbing and its implications for India and Ethiopia, http://othes.univie.ac.at/29304/1/2013-08-07_0847522.pdf.

续表

序号	印度农业公司	土地规模(公顷)	农业作物
11	马刀农业公司(Saber Farm PLC(Saber Group))	25 000	棉花和黄豆
12	翡翠生物技术公司(Emami Biotech)	100 000	麻风树和食用油籽
13	S&P 能源出路公司(S&P Energy Solutions)	50 000	生物燃料、可食用油料作物
14	S&P 能源出路公司(S&P Energy Solutions Plc.(Shapoorii Pallonii))	50 000	粮食作物等
15	阿尔米达哈(Almidha)	28 000	食糖
16	内哈国际有限公司(Neha International Ltd.)	4 000	油籽、大米、小麦类

其次,快速增长的印度与埃塞俄比亚双边贸易存在贸易关系不平衡和不对称。印度—埃塞俄比亚双边贸易增长快。2000—2001 年双边贸易额是 10 800 万美元。[①]2001—2002 年,双方贸易额超过 1 亿美元。2009—2010 年印度与埃塞俄比亚贸易额是 27 200 万美元,2011—2012 年贸易额是 66 000 万美元[②]。由于国际钢价上涨和中国低价商品的竞争,2002—2003 年,印度与埃塞俄比亚的贸易额下降,21 世纪以来,大部分年度印度和埃塞贸易额一直处于增长态势,2015 年双边贸易额达到 12 亿美元,印度成为埃塞俄比亚的第二大进口来源国,仅次于中国[③]。2017 年,双方签订贸易协定。此后,双边贸易额持续走高(见表 3)。双边贸易长期维持不平衡和不对称关系,埃塞俄比亚从印度进口额高于对印度出口额,存在贸易逆差。印度对埃塞俄比亚出口以工业制成品为主,如钢铁、金属制品、药品、机械仪器、纸 / 木制品、纺织品、汽车配件、塑料制品等;进口以农产品和原材料为主,如豆类、毛皮、原棉和皮革。印度是埃塞俄比亚最大食糖进口来源国。2004 年,埃塞俄比亚从印度进口食糖贸易额是 93 万美元,2005 年是 62 万美元,2006 年是 1 093 万美元,2007 年是 2 955 万美元,2008 年是 5 327 万美元,2009 年是 379 万美元,2010 年是 282 万美元,2011 年是 13 300 万美元[④]。

表 3 印度与埃塞俄比亚贸易额(2000—2019 年)[⑤] (单位:美元)

年份	印度从埃塞进口	印度对埃塞出口
2000	8 296 999	65 882 693
2001	18 007 825	99 106 215

① Dr. Suresh Kumar, "The Role of India in Agricultural Development in Ethiopia", [2010-12-01]. http://www.africaindia.org/index.php?option=com_content&view=article&id=48:the-role-of-india-in-agricultural-development-in-ethiopia&catid=34:agriculture-sector&Itemid=29.

② Amsalu K Addis, Zhu Zuping, " Assessment of the Impact of Chinese and Indian Economic Activities in Africa", *China Report*,2019,55(3):248-249.

③ Belayneh Leta, Belayneh Girma, "Economic relations of Ethiopia and India: Trade and Agricultural Investments After 1991", *African Journal of Political Science and International Relations,* 2017,11(8):212.

④ Sushil Kumar, "India' s Development Cooperation with Ethiopia in Sugar Production: An Assessment", [2015-08-08]. http://www.ris.org.in/images/RIS_images/pdf/DP%20198%20Mr%20Sushil%20Kumar.pdf.

⑤ Belayneh Leta, Belayneh Girma, "Economic relations of Ethiopia and India: Trade and Aagricultural Investments After 1991", *African Journal of Political Science and International Relations*, 2017,11(8):213.

续表

年份	印度从埃塞进口	印度对埃塞出口
2002	9 996 833	103 163 051
2003	8 029 491	175 414 047
2004	9 579 348	190 519 257
2005	8 003 268	249 903 429
2006	9 521 289	314 125 781
2007	15 569 207	421 298 888
2008	14 416 051	361 382 539
2009	18 801 131	634 245 253
2010	27 509 833	623 608 487
2011	32 980 239	773 276 100
2012	42 219 447	1 071 945 594
2013	355 333 787	1 224 650 153
2014	53 127 646	1 056 107 230
2015	64 908 691	1 151 498 728
2016[①]	6 840 万	130 000 万
2017	3 041 亿[②]	4 522 亿[③]
2019[④]	9 330 万	82 800 万

最后，印度对埃塞俄比亚多样化援助是双边经贸关系的新特色。21 世纪以来，埃塞俄比亚从 1969 年的 ITEC 计划的人才资源发展中获益。2000 年印度对埃塞俄比亚投资项目三个，价值 270 万美元[⑤]。2007—2008 年，印度提供的培训名额为 25 个，之后培训名额稳步增加。2009—2011 年，印度政府提供了 300 多个培训名额，埃塞俄比亚政府充分利用了上述培训名额[⑥]。2012—2013 年培训名额为 160 人[⑦]。截至 2018 年，在 ITEC 项目下，印度已经接收了 2 732 名埃塞学生[⑧]。

印度的发展援助项目涵盖埃塞俄比亚政府的不同机构。2002 年，两国政府签署了微型水坝和小型灌溉计划合作协定。2007 年签署了科学和技术领域合作协定。同年 7 月，双方

① 此处单位应该是百万美元，特此补充说明。参见：India-Ethiopia Relations(2017 年 9 月)。

② Exports 2020 Country Comparisons, Ranks, by Rank (photius.com), https://photius.com/rankings/2020/economy/exports_2020_0.html.

③ 同②。

④ India (IND) and Ethiopia (ETH) Trade | OEC—The Observatory of Economic Complexity https://oec.world/en/profile/bilateral-country/ind/partner/eth.

⑤ " Inida-Ethiopia Bilateral Relations",[2011-02-21]. http://www.indianembassy.gov.et/FINAl_800by600/bilaateral relation.htm.

⑥ Gedion G Jalata, "Development Assistance from the South: Comparative Analysis of Chinese and Indian to Ethiopia", *Chinese Studies*, 2014, 3(1): 33.

⑦ 参见：India-Ethiopia Relations(2013 年 7 月)。

⑧ India-Ethiopia Bilateral Relations), [2019-05].http://indembassyeth.in/india-ethiopia-bilateral-relations/.

签署了建立部长级联合委员会的协议。2010 年 12 月,联合委员会第一次会议在印度新德里举行。埃塞俄比亚副总理兼外交部长海尔马里亚姆·德萨莱尼出席了此次会议。

印度积极向埃塞俄比亚提供金融援助。2006 年以来,印度对埃塞俄比亚的财政援助逐年增加,印度政府通过印度进出口银行向埃塞俄比亚政府提供超过 12 亿美元软贷款,如 6 500 万美元信贷额度支持哈哥马林·梅佳区建设农村电气化的输变电和配电项目。这是印度对埃塞俄比亚的第一笔贷款。正如印度进出口银行驻亚的斯亚贝巴的一名高级官员所说,印度将贷款与来自印度的设备联系起来,"印度利用这一战略作为进入受援国的技术准入入口,但印度并不要求印度公司和劳动力来到受援国,而是该项目在一定条件下可以接受竞争性投标的设备必须来自印度"①。

2007 年,印度提供 6.4 亿美元贷款支持埃塞俄比亚糖业,这是印度当年在海外最大的投资②。作为印度政府对单一国家首次提供的最大一笔信贷,以支持埃塞俄比亚建立新的制糖工业。这两笔贷款利率是 1.75%,期限是 20 年③。2008 年,印度对埃塞俄比亚糖业给予 64 000 万卢比的金融贷款。2012 年提供 5 亿美元贷款进一步支持埃塞制糖业发展。印度对埃塞 15.4 亿美元全部信贷款中的 12.4 亿美元给予埃塞制糖业。这使得埃塞俄比亚成为世界上获得印度信贷额度最高的国家之一。在埃塞俄比亚,印度发展援助的 78.1% 用于制糖业。项目的总花费是 13.5 亿美元。在完成滕达霍(Tendaho)、翁吉(Wonji)/ 绍阿(Shoa)和芬查亚(finchaa)这三个项目之后,埃塞俄比亚将成为主要的食糖出口国。这些项目将创造巨大的就业机会,预计将有助于埃塞俄比亚经济融合。正如在亚的斯亚贝巴印度进出口银行一位官员所说,"印度正在推动制糖业发展,印度不想从埃塞俄比亚进口糖,我们想复制埃塞俄比亚的经验"④。

三、印度与埃塞俄比亚经贸关系的新动向及启示

鉴于中国在埃塞俄比亚经济发展中的作用日益加强,印度也在基础设施、教育培训等方面加强了与埃塞的合作。印度加大投资来改善埃塞的制造业基础。不过,同中国相比,印度对埃塞的贸易、投资和援助额是相距甚远的,但印度与埃塞经贸关系的发展仍值得中国观察、跟踪和思考。

首先,埃塞俄比亚是印度—非洲论坛峰会外交的积极参与者。2008 年至今,印度共举办了四届非洲论坛首脑峰会,埃塞俄比亚都是该论坛的重要参与国。2011 年 5 月,第二届印度—非洲论坛峰会选择在埃塞俄比亚首都亚的斯亚贝巴举行,会上发表了《亚的斯亚贝巴宣言》和《印非加强合作框架文件》。印埃双方确立到 2015 年印非贸易额达 700 亿美元的目标。非盟组织也积极评价印非合作,表示将尽快设立驻印度办事处。这凸显了印度与埃塞俄比亚的紧密关系。2019 年,印埃两国启动印度—埃塞俄比亚创新技术商业化方案,

---

① Gedion G. Jalata, "Development Assistance from the South: Comparative Analysis of Chinese and Indian to Ethiopia", *Chinese Studies*, 2014, 3(1): 31.

② Sushil Kumar, "India's Development Cooperation with Ethiopia in Sugar Production: An Assessment", [2015-08-08]. http://www.ris.org.in/images/RIS_images/pdf/DP%20198%20Mr%20Sushil%20Kumar.pdf.

③ Gedion G. Jalata, "Development Assistance from the South: Comparative Analysis of Chinese and Indian to Ethiopia", *Chinese Studies*, 2014, 3(1): 28.

④ 同③。

分享在医疗保健、农业、水卫生与环境和林业等领域技术和创新[①]。

其次，埃塞俄比亚是印度泛非电信网络计划、聚焦非洲计划的先行国，是印度与非洲合作新模式的优选国。印度与非洲联盟合作推行泛非电信网络计划，项目所需10亿美元由印方出资，旨在增强非洲的互联网连接和通信，计划实现53个非洲国家之间的互联网连接。2007年7月，印度与埃塞俄比亚之间的“远程医疗网”开通，是泛非电信网络的试行项目。远程教育中心由埃塞的亚的斯亚贝巴大学与印度德里和开普尔的技术研究所合作，远程医学中心位于亚的斯亚贝巴黑狮医院。这两家中心由印度提供213万美元兴建。在埃塞俄比亚负责远程医疗网络的印度政府官员拉坦·辛格说，“我们希望与非洲分享专业技术，希望缺乏医生的地区能与城市医院相连接，进而由城里医生填补那里的空缺”。印度驻埃塞俄比亚大使古尔吉·辛格强调，“印度参加非洲互联网建设与印度企业投资当地矿产资源项目没有关系”。《印度时报星期刊》的英德拉尼·巴格奇声称，“印度模式大不相同，从印度独立斗争和随后印度移民在非洲获得的商业成功，到不结盟运动，等等，印度一直是一个具有潜在影响的国家”。印度宣扬与非洲合作的“新模式”，但仍然延续了发展经济和贸易的路子，真正目的还是推动自身经济发展。印度参与的泛非电信网络计划即为一例。路透社记者巴里·马隆认为，“印度与埃塞俄比亚合作的远程医疗网络确实减轻当地不少负担，也吻合印度加强与富饶非洲的联系并确保市场和能源供应的目标”[②]。

最后，能源和工业原材料是印度对埃塞贸易领域与投资的重点方向。2011年9月，两大印度政府皮革机构中央皮革研究协会(CLRI)和鞋类设计发展协会(FDDI)已经与埃塞俄比亚皮革产业发展协会(ELIDI)作出承诺和安排，两大印度机构将进行技术转让并帮助加快东非国家皮革及其产品出口收益的增长。印度将为埃塞俄比亚提供所有培训和必要的支持，使该国成为全球鞋类和皮革制造业的十大国家之一。目前，埃塞俄比亚国家已经拥有非洲最大的牲畜群。通过中央皮革研究协会(CLRI)和鞋类设计发展协会(FDDI)提供的支持和培训，印度皮革产业已经为350万人提供就业机会，年产值将达34亿美金。这项计划宣布，将在未来3至5年继续对埃塞俄比亚的皮革生产进行投资[③]。据埃通社报道，2011年12月12日，埃塞俄比亚和印度两国农业研究院院长签署了农业科研合作备忘录，两国同意将在农业科研方面密切合作。埃塞农业部国务部长在签字仪式上表示，两国合作开展农业研究，将有助于提高农业生产，推进技术转让，提升两国关系。据了解，两国农业科研合作还包括肉类和奶类开发等领域[④]。印度的中央皮革研究所和鞋类设计和开发研究所一直与埃塞俄比亚皮革开发研究所合作，以提高埃塞俄比亚制革厂和制鞋厂的质量标准。由印度两家机构和皮革行业41名专业人员组成的代表团，于2010年3月抵达埃塞俄比亚，进行为期6个月的项目。该合同由印度提供资金，价值约为100万美元。合同后来又延长了6个月，价

---

① Ethio-India relations: Spirit of solidarity, https://www.press.et/english/?p=18098#.

② 袁原，“首届印度-非洲合作论坛峰会开幕：软实力下真经济”，http://www.chinanews.com/gj/gjzj/news/2008/04-08/1213901.shtml.

③ 印度承诺扶持埃塞俄比亚，http://www.zhongsou.net/%E7%9C%9F%E7%9A%AE%E6%9C%8D%E9%A5%B0/news/13145829.html.

④ 亢升，“印度的大国追求与印度洋非洲国家：认知与行为”，http://www.cnriio.com/news/showit.asp?id=188.

值 80 万美元①。2021 年 2 月 19 日,印度、埃塞俄比亚签署了有关皮革技术协议②。

四、结语

印度与埃塞俄比亚作为印度洋地区大国,历史上就保持着紧密的经贸关系和人员往来。进入 21 世纪,双边经贸关系呈现新特点:印度对埃塞俄比亚的投资主要集中在工业和农业领域;快速增长的双边贸易呈现出关系不平衡和不对称;印度奉行多样化援助政策等。21 世纪的印度与埃塞关系被称为双边关系的“黄金时代”,值得我们对此观察、思考和借鉴。

① Gedion G Jalata,“Development Assistance from the South: Comparative Analysis of Chinese and Indian to Ethiopia”, *Chinese Studies*,2014,3(1):33.

② “India, Ethiopia Sign Agreements on Leather Technology, Visa Facilitation”, https://www.jagranjosh.com/current-affairs/india-ethiopia-sign-agreements-on-leather-technology-visa-facilitation-1613810973-1.

Assessing the Current Peacebuilding Essence in Ethiopia: the Challenges and Prospects

Gubaye Assaye①

Abstract: The protest and riot against the EPRDF government in Ethiopia has been lasting for many years. But the intensity and the turning points of the protest against the government became imminent since 2015 in Oromia region which was initially triggered by Addis Ababa Master plan and 2016 in Amhara Region which was also triggered by arbitrary detention of Colonel Demeke Zewudu. But the main causes for the protest were emanated from the cumulative effects of social, economic and political injustice that prevailed in the country for more than two decades. The persistence of the protest in these two regions became intensified within the past three years which result in the readjustment of power within the EPRDF itself. Soon after PM Abiy Ahmed took power on 2nd April 2018, he promised to make many reforms in political, social and economic aspects of the country. Thus, this article is aiming to assess the type of changes that PM Abiy brought to the reality and their significance in peacebuilding process of the country. To do this, I used his speeches and dialogues that were done by him at various occasions and with different professionals, communities and opposition leaders, and evaluate it with strategic peacebuilding accords. In addition, secondary sources were consulted to address the aforementioned issues. As the study shows, the measures that the prime minister took along the lines of building "national consensus" and creating favorite political space in the country, including the release of political prisoners, undoubtedly brought about pro-Abiy sentiment to even in the opposition quarter. The relatively freeing of media from the government influence is another achievement taken by him. Among others, the most decisive and historical event that made by him is the peace accord with Eritrea which is fruitful not only between the two countries but also it can create stability in the region. And also the idea of unity with in diversity "Medemer" which has attracted the attention of the populace for better future has been framed by him to transcend the persisting ethnic politics of the country. But, now the concept losses its popular acceptance as the result of the continuation of ethnic tensions, conflict as well as the displacement various ethnic groups throughout the country.

Keywords: Ethiopia; Peacebuilding; Medemer; PM Abiy Ahmed; Dialogue

① Faculty of Social Sciences, Bahir Dar University

Meaning of Peacebuilding

The term Peacebuilding first came to being in the 1970s and as defined by Johan Galtung as the establishment of peacebuilding structures to advance sustainable peace by addressing the root causes or underlining causes of violent conflict and sustaining indigenous capacities for peace management and conflict resolution. In 1992 report of An *Agenda for Peace,* UN Secretary General, Boutros Boutros-Ghali defined peacebuilding as deed to recognize and maintain structures which tend to reinforce and coagulate peace in order to prevent setback of conflict (United Nations, 2010). From then on, the definition of peacebuilding has appeared in almost every UN document dealing with the methods of peace operations. For instance, in 2001, the UN Security Council Presidential Statement said that the Security Council is to be aware of the need for short and long-term dealings adapted to tackle the meticulous needs of societies descending into conflict or emerging from it. These actions should focus on fostering sustainable development, the purge of "poverty and inequalities, transparent and accountable governance, the promotion of democracy, respect for human rights and the rule of law and the promotion of a culture of peace and non-violence (Uuited Nations, 2010).

As illustrated by Johan Galtung (1975), peacebuilding means something more positive and dynamic than simply creating stability to prevent violent conflict. Thus, it requires building political, social and economic institutions, and turns around notions of capacity-building, good governance, inclusion economic opportunity and individual well-being. For this reason, in order to incorporate this comprehensive understanding of peace, we need to address the concept of development as part and parcel of peacebuilding (krause and Jütersonke, 2005). Peace-building encompasses a multidimensional task put into practice in the context of emerging, current or post-conflict circumstances and which are overtly guided and motivated by a primary dedication to the prevention of violent conflict and the promotion of long-lasting and sustainable peace. Furthermore, peace-building can be understood as a supplement to preventive diplomacy, peacemaking processes, conflict resolution and peacekeeping operations (OECD, 2005).

Strategic Peacebuilding

The strategic framework is a way to be used to configuration the planning and implementation of operations. In order to have a logical chance of success, peacebuilding has to be comprehensive and coherent. Peacebuilding has three, reciprocally strengthening dimensions such as security, political development, and social and economic development. Peacebuilding should include all three magnitudes at the same time. A sequential approach is not usually logically and practically acceptable (Johnson, 2004). By taking these three dimensions of strategic peacebuilding as the basic criteria, this research article tried to assess the peacebuilding efforts that have been taken by the current government of Ethiopia. This article is aiming to assess the type of changes that PM Abiy brought to the reality and their significance in peacebuilding process of the country. To do this, the speeches and dialogues that were done by him at various occasions were used. The discussions that were conducted with different professionals, communities and opposition leaders were consulted and assessed it with the different peacebuilding accords. In addition, secondary sources were consulted to support collected evidence of primary data in addition to its use as the theoretical base for peacebuilding. The article is guided by the following research questions.

What security reform measures did PM Abiy's government take to address the peacebuilding process?

What political dimension reforms were taken by PM Abiy to enhance the strategic peacebuilding in the country?

What socio-political reforms were underpinned by the current government of Ethiopia to address the existing deep-rooted problem?

1 Security

According to Johnson (2004:16), the security dimension of peacebuilding comprehends the security of a country as well as the security of individual citizens in the country. It incorporates "Disarmament, Demobilisation and Reintegration (DD&R) of ex-combatants". It is a very essential phase for long-lasting and sustainable peace is to be constructed afterwards to a conflict.

"Demilitarization is a process whereby political, societal, environmental, economic, and security issues can be addressed in nonviolent and non-militaristic ways via constructive conflict management approaches". Demilitarization came to be understood as a result of processes centrally located within this interface, along with "disarmament, demobilization, reinsertion, and reintegration (DDRR) and security system reform (SSR)" (Lala, 2011:225). It is the goal of creating a secure environment for achieving freedom from fear and from want. As Alex de Waal notes, the values of militarization affect not just soldiers but all members of society, indicating that militarization extends to other domains than security. De Waal's notion of *demilitarizing the mind* appears to assume renewed meaning and relevance in contemporary politics. Demilitarisation allows for greater understanding of its inherent challenges and potentialities as a tool to promote human security. The idea of addressing the security development nexus seems, however, to be more enshrined in discourse and policy suggestions than in practice (Lala,2011:225).

Within these criteria, the current government of Ethiopia tried to take some steps in the process of disarmament and demobilization of the political rebel groups at least at the initial stage. During his inauguration speech, PM Abiy Ahmed promised to work with any opposition parties including the rebel groups whose base are in the neighbor and abroad. PM Abiy Ahmed ascertains these issues as such.

Ethiopia is a country of all of us and it is our common house. In one country, there will inevitably be differences in opinion. Differences in opinion are not curses. When we are able to listen to each other despite our differences and engage in principled discourse, our differences return dividends in the form of blessings. In a fight over ideas, are solutions. There is strength in cooperation. When we team up, we become stronger. There is no problem that unity cannot resolve, since it builds a nation. The sentiment that "I rather die than see my idea not win" destroys families, let alone nations. What we have is one Ethiopia. Above any political thought, national unity is supreme. We need to, however, underline that national unity doesn't mean oneness. Our unity needs to be one that embraces our diversity and highlights our multinational identity①.

The above speech forwarded by PM of Ethiopia was the first step that indicates his determination to invite the different position parties and work with them. In order to achieve what he promised, the current government of Ethiopia has been taking different measures in releasing thousands of political prisoners and other innocent civilians. In addition to this, the government took a step in widening the political space through making dialogue and consensus with the different rebellion groups including closing of Meakelawi Prison. As the result of this dialogue, there was an assumption that the various rebellion groups abandoned their war mongering ideology and promised to compete via peaceful political principle.

The other attempt that created a favorable environment for the rebel groups to abandon their aim of fighting was the positive step that the parliament took. The Parliament also ruled that the Oromo Liberation Front and the Ogaden National Liberation Front, two secessionist groups, and the "Ginbot 7", an exiled opposition movement, were no longer terrorist groups. From international perspective, PM Abiy visited Cairo in June and secured the release of imprisoned Ethiopians there. In May in Saudi Arabia, he secured the release of around 1,000 jailed Ethiopians②.

Even if the government of PM Abiy Ahmed took a step in bringing the various rebel groups to their home, it lacks the real sense of demilitarization since most of them did not disarmed and reintegrated to the social fabric. Thus, the process and practice of disarmament and demobilization of soldiers have not been done practically since the government did not do the disarmament and demobilization of solders in real terms. This is actually ascertained by the fact that the faction of the Oromo Liberation Front began to rebel and destabilize the country by looting the people's property including National Banks in Oromia Regional State in addition of the killing of different ethnic groups in the country. The peacebuilding attempt of PM Abiy was not practically realized, since the process and implementation of reinsertion and reintegration of solders, and political and other innocent prisoners does not occur. Reintegration of ex-combats, prisoners and return migrants needs ample time, huge human and capital resources. As explained by Johnson (2004) and (Vencovsky,2006:264-266) the economic reintegration is the process of absorbing ex-combatants into peaceful economic structures. This process consists of two phases: reinsertion (interim assistance that meets the immediate needs of the ex-combatants in the period before lasting reintegra-

① Ethiopiaforums, "Ethiopia: Full transcript (in English) of Prime Minister Abiy Ahmed's speech at Millennium Hall", [2018-04-13]. https://ethiopiaforums.com/ethiopia-full-transcript-in-english-of-prime-minister-abiy-ahmeds-speech-at-millennium-hall/.

② Maggie Fick, "Ethiopia offers amnesty to recently freed political prisonersReuter", [2018-07-2/20]. https://www.reuters.com/article/us-ethiopia-prisoners-idUSKBN1KA1U0.

tion structures are established) and reintegration (efforts to durably engage ex-combatants in non-violent economic activities). The failure of reinsertion and reintegration (RR) can negate previous successes of the disarmament and demobilization (DD) phase and hinder the transition to peace or result in increased crime and insecurity, discouragement of other ex-combatants from disarming and substantial re-recruitment. Therefore, the EPRDF government has a lot of tasks and efforts in order to address the above stated problems.

1.1 Control of Small Arms and Light Weapons

Actions to governor the international trade in small arms and light weapons comprise programmes for tapping in devise "national legislation and strengthening international co-operation on the enforcement of such legislation on the basis of international agreements". With the blend of "national legislation and international co-operation" is indispensable for restriction of "illicit trade in, and production and transfer of small arms". In addition, it is crucial to fulfill the fundamental causes of the claim for these arms for the aim of "armed conflict, terrorism and organised crime". After the movement of small arms is governed, the subsequent phase will be to abolish prevailing stocks and establish a structure for voluntary assignments of prohibited weapons in private hands and destroy them forever (Johnson 2004:19).

In this case, the current EPRDF government does not take direct measure to control the movement of Small Arms and Light Weapons since it needs long time to establish the system. But what is important in this case is the government has made different peace and collaborative working atmosphere with the neighboring countries particularly peace accord with Eritrea which is a great achievement for PM Abiy's government. A collaborative talk with the other neighbouring countries is also another important step to minimize the movement of Small Arms and Light Weapon. But practically, even after reform, the smuggling of Small Arms and Light Weapons has been becoming a norm rather than the exception throughout the country.

1.2 Civil and Military Reform

One of the most important steps in peacebuilding determination is the civil and military reform. This is to address the core foundations of conflict and to advance the security of the citizen after conflict circumstances have brought about a higher attention on the security system. The very significance duty in peacebuilding is to warrant that "civil and military security actors are accountable to the civil authorities in accordance with democratic norms and the principles of good governance". Among others, the principal contest is to achieve "transparency and accountability" knowing exactly what amount of the government budget is assigned to military expenditure. This is an imperative part of the efforts to adjust civil and military security to peace situations in its place of a conflict state. It has have tried to attest in many junctures that the extent of military budgets raises difficulties for development co-operation. Ethiopia, Eritrea and Uganda are some of the African countries that have been categorized under such trend (Johnson, 2004:20).

In Ethiopia police, the military, the internal security, the correctional facilities and others within the military-security establishment in the country have been the ones that suffered from a serious lack of public confidence. Reforming these institutions is a vital step towards restoring public trust and stability. It was along these lines that PM Abiy Ahmed started by replacing old-guard veterans within these institutes in a rapid succession. This was done in a respectful manner to ensure continuity in accordance with state protocol and full-honor retirement to the likes of head of defense (etats-majeure), head of security and former Prime Minister. The prime Minister's courageous defense of his reforms in front of the House of People's representatives goes so far as accusing some within the government itself for terrorizing the Ethiopian people, and firing and reshuffling of a series of untouchable civil servants. He promised on laying out a clear policy direction towards good-governance and accountability. Consequently, even state-owned/affiliated media such as EBC/ETC and Fana started broadcasting various rights abuses including in the criminal justice system at least at the initial stage of the reform. Such investigative reporting by the media is paving the way for those in the security and jail systems to be held accountable and brought to justice. But the civil and military reform does not bring security as expected due to the prevalence of violent conflicts and the reform has not been reached every level of the bureaucracy. Thus, the people live under security threat which has negative replica on the development of the country.

2 Political Development

The political dimension of peacebuilding is vital for encouraging and upholding "security and social and economic development". Development cannot be achieved via an oppressive peace. Weak public institutions, corruption, and absence of respect for human rights, a democratic shortfall and the insight that the administrative and political mechanisms are insufficient and/or unreachable are among the basic causes and triggers of violent conflict Jonson 2004.

In Ethiopia, the institutions within which the various functionaries operate are not autonomous. At higher level of the bureaucracy, the positions of different governmental offices have been assigned predominantly in light of an ethnic-based quota system. As a result, the perception held by the public is that bureaucrats are expected to operate in line with their ethnic affiliation rather than in pursuit of the goals of the organization. Moreover, Ethiopian elites have been recruited based on their ethnic and political affiliations so that they are usually accountable to their ethnic and political elites. Because of this, the bureaucratic leaders and high-ranking civil servants in Ethiopia have been involved in widespread corruption. Also, instead of having selfless devotion to common national development causes, civil servants have predominantly been becoming political cadres recruited for the maintenance of the ruling party (Gebremariam, 2017).

In his inaugural speech PM Abiy gave stress on the issue of governance as illustrated here. Corruption is one of the main reasons that have galvanized the grievances of our people in recent years. It is impossible to combat corruption by merely establishing anti-corruption institutions. He asked the people of Ethiopia to do all that can to ensure that Ethiopia won't become a country where one works hard and the others simply steal it away. It is impossible for a people and a country that is busy taking away a wealth that was created yesterday from another and settling scores to move forward. In situation where there is a bigger quiche where everyone can work and become prosperous, Ethiopia will not become one in which one thinks, let alone be obliged, to steal from another. Rather, let us busy ourselves with utilizing the unique opportunities presented to us by the circumstances, coordinating our national capacity, and overcoming our scarcity and shortage mindset. He cited the saying of the famous Indian freedom movement leader, Mahatma Gandhi, once said, "the world has enough resources for everyone's need, but not enough for everyone's greed." In the new path that the PM Abiy's government just charted, we shall work tirelessly day in and day out to combat robbery, wastage of wealth, and fight organized corruption in a manner that will enable all our people to participate①.

It is argued that the personal development of the top leader alone is not enough to undertake a lasting and sustainable change at this critical moment in the history of our country. It is a real that, PM Abiy has a clear vision many including those outside of his party bought in easily. However, transforming his vision into actualities and making a smooth transition to democracy is impossible without having cabinet members, leaders of the various institutions, and departments of his new administration who have well developed personal growth like him. It is true that, a nation cannot go any farther than its collective leadership②.

Without exaggeration, one can argue that the protests of the last three years erased the status quo and allowed the government of Abiy Ahmed to emerge, and embark on a project of serious political and democratic reform. Nevertheless, in spite of the fact that the real hopes, there are still many systemic problems to be addressed. First, there is an urgent need to organize rules for political engagement and participation. Failure to build consensus on the rules of the game could threaten the regime's survival. Second, the conflicts that occur here and there, if not dealt with properly, could turn into a threat to the existence of the Ethiopian state, giving way to possible political regionalism raising its head. Such a scenario has the capacity to plunge the entire region into chaos③.

Based on this premises the PM Abiy took different political and administrative reforms which helped him in minimizing the aforementioned problems at initial stage and there was high expectation from the public that he will appoint the politicians based on achievement and intellectual merit. The ethnic quota system in appointing higher positions of the government persists after the so-called reform. Thus, the issue of corruption, maladministration, joblessness, inefficient bureaucratic system prevailed at alarming rate still now.

2.1 Reconciliation

Reconciliation, in crux, signifies "a place, the point of encounter where concerns about both

① Ethiopiaforums, "Ethiopia: Full transcript (in English) of Prime Minister Abiy Ahmed's speech at Millennium Hall", [2018-04-13]. https://ethiopiaforums.com/ethiopia-full-transcript-in-english-of-prime-minister-abiy-ahmeds-speech-at-millennium-hall/.

② Assegid Habtewold, "Ethiopia: Prime Minister Abiy and a call to build the capacity of key stakeholders", [2018-04-26]. https://ethioforum.net/ethiopia-prime-minister-abiy-and-a-call-to-build-the-capacity-of-key-stakeholders/.

③ Mebratu Kelecha, "Protest, Repression and Revolution in Ethiopia", [2019-01-24]. https://roape.net/2019/01/24/protest-repression-and-revolution-in-ethiopia/.

the past and the future can meet". Reconciliation as chance meeting advocates that space for the recognizing of the past and envisaging of the future is the essential element for reframing the present. For this to happen, people must find ways to encounter themselves and their enemies, their hopes and their fear (Lederach,2014).

"Reconciliation involves building or rebuilding trust and friendly relations between individuals and between peoples and institutions". Attaining long-lasting and sustainable peace be contingent on both "decisions at political level" and on widespread acknowledgment of the peace settlement. Peacebuilding comprises "reconciliation and the promotion of non-violent conflict resolution at every level of society: among political, military, religious and business leaders, and at middle management and grassroots levels". Reconciliation can be encouraged via dialogue and beleaguered schemes, but it has to also be integrated into peacebuilding as a whole. "Healing the physical, psychological and psychosocial wounds inflicted by violent conflict is an important aspect of peacebuilding." (Johnson, 2004: 22-23)

The prime minister of Ethiopia took different measures and techniques in order to bring reconciliation in country. The first measure is his acceptance of the wrong doing of EPRDF government. At his inauguration, he plainly asked forgiveness for his party's wrong deed of the past. His asking of forgiveness at public is unique and the first in Ethiopian government history which develops hope for people in alleviating pressing problems in the near future.

The second reconciliation technique used by the Prime Minister is the dialogue, as he made with the different ethnic groups in Ethiopia. As presented by Svensson, and Brouneus, (2013), dialogue is considered to be indispensable for generating harmonious relationships in multi-ethnic societies which is very pertinent in promoting trust. One common initiative for peacebuilding at the grassroots level is the use of dialogue processes to build trust and peaceful relations. Trust and dialogue are important features of group relationships in the contexts of group-based tension, violence, and ethnic conflicts and are hence a fundamental part of peacebuilding processes around the world.

It is his understanding of the important of dialogue in promoting trust and understanding, PM Abiy Ahmed made regional visits and discussed with the community on matters that are important to them in addressing past injustice and for future better prospects. He also delivered messages of solidarity in languages, customs and clothing akin to the specific regions, raising issues that were taboo in Ethiopian politics yet very reflective of the local need. He started visiting the most affected areas in the last three years of anti-government demonstrations such as Ambo, Bale, Dembi-dollo and Gondar and continued to other regions such as Tigray, Hawassa, and Afar to experience first-hand the state of affairs in the different regions to ensure all voices are heard. His message of peace and unity was delivered in such an out-of-the-box and disarming way that it brought about a tangible impact on the nations and nationalities embraced in the country.

The other dialogue that was taken by him, was the calling up of all Ethiopian to unit and love each other for future development and working together at the rally of Mesquel Square at the day of "Medemer". The meaning of Medemer is very wide and inclusive which is the philosophy of PM Abiy himself. PM Abiy defined the concept of Medemer during his speech at the peace accord of Eritrea as:

"Tender love instead of abject cruelty, peace instead of conflict, and love over hate, forgiveness over holding grudge, pulling instead of pushing. Peace to be the mother of prosperity, one will stay a pipe dream without the other. He asked if two individuals agree on all things then the need for the second one becomes irrelevant since he is not adding anything new. Handled wisely our differences (that) are our assets. What "Medemer" does not like is conflict instead of cooperation, banning instead of accommodation, polemics instead of discussion and acquiring fame through war by killing each other instead of resolution through a healthy debate."①

"Medemer" is simply practicing the principle of inclusiveness. In South Africa, they call their inclusiveness "Ubuntu": ("I am because you are." In other words, you are part of me and what happens to you affects me too.) For Mandela, Ubuntu is the "profound sense that we are human only through the humanity of others; that if we are to accomplish anything in this world, it will in equal measure be due to the work and achievement of others". Abiy Ahmed's "Medemer" has similar connotation with Mandela's Ubuntu. "Medemer" is all about cooperation, collaboration, consultation, common cause, give-and take, partnership, alliance-building, team work, giving a hand up and creating synergy for the common good. In the Philosophy of "Medemer", what PM Abiy Ahmed believes is similar in the decree of Dr. King: Walk together, work together, go to jail together, celebrate together, cry together, laugh together, pray together, sing together, and live together in peace until that day when all God's children — Amhara, Oromo, Tigray, Somali, Gurage, Wolayita, Sidama, Afar and the other 75 or more groups of the Ethiopian family — will rejoice in one common band of humanity②.

The third reconciliation practice is related to the church institutions. PM Abiy Ahmed believed reconciliation is holistic and inclusive. Thus, to accomplish this, he has been trying to solve the religious division. The first step of reconciliation occurred in Orthodox Tewahdo Church. The division in the Orthodox Church back in the 1990s was engineered to serve political purposes. Merkorios, the rightful successor of Abune Teklehaimanot (in 1988) was forced to abdicate by the then new regime, the Ethiopian People's Revolutionary Democratic Front. Abune Paulos, coming from the same Tigray ethnic group as the late Prime Minister Meles Zenawi, was appointed a new head of the church. This injected tribalism in the church. The move was seen by many as a way of keeping this powerful church on a short leash so it would not be a threat to the establishment③.

The church has always mirrored Ethiopian society, including its ills and hopes. Its unification

① Yilma Bekele, "Ethiopia: Discourse on the concept of Medemer (መደመር)", [2018-07-21]. https://ethiopianege.com/archives/6813.

② Alemayehu G. Mariam, "Medemer or not Medemer, That is the Question for All Ethiopians", [2018-08-26]. http://almariam.com/2018/08/26/medemer-or-not-medemer-that-is-the-question-for-all-ethiopians.

③ Mohammed Girma, "How the Orthodox Church in Ethiopia Can Play a Role in Reconciliation", [2018-08-19]. https://ewn.co.za/2018/08/19/opinion-how-the-orthodox-church-in-ethiopia-can-play-a-role-in-reconciliation.

brought hope to the whole nation. This was reflected in the welcoming ceremony of the Abune Merkorios. Lining up to welcome him at the Bole International Airport were not only Orthodox Christians, but also Protestant and Muslim leaders. This shows the magnitude of the impact the church could have if it is able to get its house in order. The Ethiopian Orthodox Tewahido Church is more than just a church. It is a source of philosophy and indigenous innovation such as unique architecture, music and literature. For most of its history, it's coexisted peacefully with the state, with only occasional tension①. Abiy understands the importance of its role in Ethiopian society. He has made it clear that the country needs strong religious institutions; both Islamic and Christian. He has invited them to hold him accountable when he crosses the line, and to make their own contribution in combating corruption and promoting peaceful coexistence.

As cited in Urbain, et al (2008) Johan Galtung, one of the founders of peace studies illustrates the important of art in peace and reconciliation. He affirmed that "Art uproots us into a virtual reality. Art is something that has touched our soul and moved it on". PM Abiy Ahmed conducted discussion with the Ethiopian Artists about the role of art in social engineering. He gave emphasis on the role art on reconciliation and peacebuilding. He encouraged them to use their art to inculcate and sermonize, the issues of unity, harmony and co-existence. Based on this direction, the different artists at the moment give emphasis on unity, harmony and nationality songs which create awareness about the aim of the current government ideology.

In general, the prime minister has not been unsuccessful to reply adequately to these complex crises beyond establishing ad-hoc commissions, including one for reconciliation and the other for administrative boundary and identity issues. The government must move beyond symbolism and empower institutions; particularly the recently established ministry of peace; to deliver local reconciliation efforts that is linked to a genuinely inclusive nationwide peace process and in accordance with the will and interest of various groups②.

2.2 Good Governance

There is also peacebuilding attempt through establishing good governance. Good governance can be manifested through democracy, respect for human rights and sound economic management. The formation of impartial, fair and real judicial institutions with the necessary power and devices for implementing sanctions is a prerequisite for peace and development, and international backing is always important for the consolidation of such institutions. A well an interactively planned development approach needs a least of sureness in the objective implementation of "the rules governing property matters and corruption, violence and other crimes". Out of such main self-confidence it would be problematic to imagine the presence of actual "credit arrangements, economic growth and peaceful dispute settlement mechanisms". (Johnson, 2004:24-25).

---

① Mohammed Girma, "How the Orthodox Church in Ethiopia Can Play a Role in Reconciliation", [2018-08-19]. https://ewn.co.za/2018/08/19/opinion-how-the-orthodox-church-in-ethiopia-can-play-a-role-in-reconciliation.

② Ahmed Soliman & Abel Abate Demissie, "Can Abiy Ahmed Continue to Remodel Ethiopia?" , [2019-04-12]. https://www.chathamhouse.org/2019/04/can-abiy-ahmed-continue-remodel-ethiopia.

The power of darkness that ruled Ethiopia under the TPLF for the last 27 years used and deployed betrayers, corrupt, cunning and fraudulent people throughout the political, economic and social system of the country destroying not only the country but also centuries old social capital of the Ethiopian people. Only light will overcome and dislodge these powers of darkness out of our country and our society. Shining light on such people and clearing them out of the system requires transparency and the full power of the Ethiopian people①.

For PM Abiy to wield the political power of the Ethiopian people in confronting this power of darkness, he adopted a clear policy of transparency in his administration's day to day activities starting from day one. He has been appointing competent and capable people who will clearly articulate his administrations visions, strategies and every day decision making process to the Ethiopian people at least at inception. Therefore, the acceptance speech of PM Abiy should layout clear vision, addresses the concerns of the Ethiopian people his constituency and promises transparency at all levels of his administration by freeing up the state and private media②. To consolidate the practice of good governance, the PM called up all opposition and rebel parties for discussion and dialogue in a round table. He also promised to implement the real accountability of the government and even his promise goes further to limit the power duration of the prime minister.

It is very pertinent to see the current Ethiopian good governance reality via the World Governance Indicators (WGI) for better future. At initial stage, concerning "voice and accountability", there have been some promising measures taken by the administration of Dr. Abiy Ahmed to address the outstandingly bad and inadequacies of his predecessors. One well-known admired instance of the steps taken to promote free and fair elections is the invitation of opposition parties to participate in the upcoming elections with Ms. Birtukuan Midekssa as the head of the Election Board③.

Nevertheless, there are still many worrying issues that would cast doubt on how successfully the current government can create a favorable environment for the people to exercise their democratic rights. The major problems are being the existing divisive ethnic federalism which the constitution that sanctions it as legitimate form of government for Ethiopia. Other factors that certainly will undesirably affect the implementations of the Prime Minister promises are rooted in other indicators of good governance, namely, absence of political stability and prevalence of unchecked violence in most parts of the country, government ineffectiveness, lack of rule of law, and government's inability to control extremist media fomenting hate and ethnic conflicts in the country④.

The absence of a designed transitional roadmap has left these groups indeterminate about their specific roles; and they have been left to engage in sporadic and disjointed activities that are not focused on the immediate tasks of the transitional process. Some are commencement to quarrel over the

① "Unsolicited Advice to the Incoming Administration of Dr. Abiy Ahmed and the Ethiopian People", Kaliti Press, 2018-04-01.

② Ibid.

③ Getachew Begashaw, "Good Governance in Ethiopia with Checks and Balances", [2019-03-28]. https://ethiopoint.com/good-governance-in-ethiopia-with-checks-and-balances/.

④ Ibid.

interim agenda, as they have mainly intended the transition through the views of maximizing their own (group) space and role in the government. Some politicians and activists have called for the instantaneous establishment of a transitional government; these groups support for a fundamental change, irrespective of all the confusion it may involve and others favoured for a smooth and systematic transition to a representative government in the 2020 election①.

Inter-ethnic violence has resulted in nearly three million internally displaced people in Ethiopia and now it is also increasing in alarming rate. In addition, disputes between and within regional states have worsened. The worst has been the Guji and Gedeo crisis, resulting in the displacement of 1 million people, many whose farms and homes have been destroyed and for whom access to humanitarian assistance has been restricted. The security situation has worsened partly because Abiy has targeted Ethiopia's authoritarian security agencies to gain popular support and remove threats to his leadership. Senior officials have been dismissed from their positions or arrested under corruption charges. This has resulted in the TPLF and Tigrayans feeling targeted by the government and has caused a damaging power vacuum②.

The above assertion is supported by one of Ethiopian opposition party called the Ethiopian Social Democratic Party (ESDP). The party has come out to express its dissatisfaction with the government of Prime Minister Abiy Ahmed over the lack of the rule of law and gross human rights violations as follows.

It should be remembered the Ethiopian opposition initially demonstrated an optimistic attitude towards the Abiy led administration, just like the rest of the Ethiopian public. Now, however, the opposition is increasingly expressing its reservations for lack of seriousness in protecting human rights. Beyene Petros, chairperson of the ESDP said: "defending human rights of citizens as a primary responsibility of the government is forgotten." The ESDP pointed out the government authorities are leading in egregious human rights violation. People are also skeptical about the Oromo Democratic Party (the prime minister's own party) and how it is exploiting youth groups like Qeerroo to drive its political agenda. Ongoing displacement of people and violence put people at risk while putting pressure on the limited resources used to assist the affected. The prime minister must move fast and salvage the situation before it escalates. Part of the solution lies in establishing a system of accountability for the gross human rights violation. It doesn't mean aggressive prosecutions, but it can involve establishing a form of inquiry to give Ethiopians a platform to air their grievances, question officials and seek closure as most of the reforms instituted are long-term. According to the ESDP, the federal government lacks the commitment to investigate and punish perpetrators of human rights violations, which includes members of the security agencies and party loyalists③

① G. Teressa, "Analysis: Democratic Transition in Abiy's Ethiopia: Managing the Bad, the Good and the Troubling", [2018-09-25]. https://addisstandard.com/analysis-democratic-transition-in-abiys-ethiopia-managing-the-bad-the-good-and-the-troubling/.

② Ahmed Soliman, Abel Abate Demissie, "Can Abiy Ahmed Continue to Remodel Ethiopia?", [2019-04-12]. https://www.chathamhouse.org/2019/04/can-abiy-ahmed-continue-remodel-ethiopia.

③ Solomon O, "Opposition Party slams Ethiopian Government for Failing to Safeguard Human Rights", [2019-03-28]. https://www.ezega.com/News/NewsDetails/7028/Opposition-Party-Slams-Ethiopian-Government-for-Failing-to-Safeguard-Human-Rights.

Notwithstanding the unreserved backing the government acquired in the first few months of its formation, it is at present facing considerable challenges from various groups, including its once enthusiastic supporters as well as TPLF supporters①. Based on recent events in various parts of the country, the government' s record in this regard is poor at best or tragic at worst. Indeed, it is safe to say that the success of the ongoing reform or the future of the country is heavily dependent on how effectively and genuinely the government addresses these issues②.

It is, hence, critical for the current government to engage pro-reform Ethiopians in constructive dialogue enable vibrant civic societies as watch-dogs, implement unambiguous and ethnic-blind measures to promote national reconciliation, and clamp down on extremist groups that foment inter-ethnic violence and propaganda campaigns. The government should be able to muster all government instruments of peace and security and normalize the political environment in the country.

2.3 The Role of Civil Society and Media in Promoting Peace

As illustrated by Johnson (2004:26-27) backing for national authorities should be complemented by provision to "peace-oriented organizations and institutions in civil society," as well as the media. Peacebuilding ought to incorporate the involvement of civil society actors, devices and developments that encourage peace and reconciliation and avert sustenance from being given to belligerent parties or groups.

Succeeding 2005 notable national election in Ethiopia, the government implemented suppressive actions as the result more than 200 opposition followers were killed by ruthless security forces and about 30,000 were arrested, with the highest opposition party leaders.③. Furthermore, the new laws were articulated to deteriorate human and democratic rights institutions and actors such as the media, civil society and opposition parties④. In this regard, both "Charities and Societies Proclamation" and "Anti-Terrorism Proclamation" were being introduced in 2009 alone. As a result, under the new civil society law, any foreign Non-Governmental Organization (NGO) is banned from engaging in work pertaining to human rights and democratic governance (Bekele, 2012). Also, as per the equivocal and indefinite elucidations of the anti-terrorism proclamation, a number of opposition party members and journalists were trapped so that the basic constitutional rights of freedom of expression and association have been curtailed (Fesseha and Abatewold, 2017).

The newspapers play a crucial role in a democratic society by creating access of information to its citizens, creating an environment for different outlooks and serving as ombudsmen against misuses on the part of the authorities. Unrestricted and autonomous media assistance to safeguard

① Getachew Begashaw, "Good Governance in Ethiopia with Checks and Balances", [2019-03-28]. https://ethiopoint.com/good-governance-in-ethiopia-with-checks-and-balances/.

② Ibid.

③ Leonardo R Arriola, T Lyons, "Ethiopia: The 100% Election", Journal of Democracy, 2016, 27(1): 76-88.

④ Abebe Gellaw, "The shocking level of control that Meles Zenawi has consolidated over media outlets throughoutEthiopia", [2012-05-30]. May 2012, https://ecadforum.com/2012/05/30/abebe-gellaw-oslo-freedom-forum-2012/.

that numerous groups, together with marginalised ones, create access to information essential for making knowledgeable choices (Johnson, 2004).

Ethiopia's government has a long roadway history of restricting autonomous media preventing the rights to freedom of expression and access to information. Since 2005, the government has shut down dozens of publications. Many journalists have been threatened, intimidated, and targeted for politically-motivated prosecutions under criminal or terrorism charges. As a result, many journalists have fled into exile since 2010. In 2017, Ethiopia was among Africa's leading jailer of journalists. The government had also sought to suppress independent diaspora-led media outlets based outside of Ethiopia. Many blogs and websites run by Ethiopians in the diaspora were blocked inside Ethiopia[①].

Substantial development has been made on media freedom in Ethiopia. Within a year, Ethiopia has gone from being one of the leading jailors of journalists in Africa to having no journalists in jail for the first time since 2004. Diaspora media outlets previously expelled in Ethiopia operate freely and journalists report few threats from the government's security services. Despite the progress, there's still reluctance in the media to critique the government or ask difficult questions. Hate speech on social media, especially Facebook, is a serious and growing problem, although the government's proposed hate speech law raises concerns it may be used to stifle legitimate expressions of dissent[②].

According to human development report (2019), however, during a wave of protests in September, the PM Abiy's government shut down the Internet and mobile data in parts of the country where there were demonstrations, restricting access to information. The government also announced plans to pass a hate speech law in December 2019. While hate speech is a serious problem amid growing ethnic tensions, especially on social media, the government should be careful not to undermine efforts to reform repressive laws by drafting a new hate speech law that could be used for the same kinds of abuse. In July, Abiy appointed new members to the boards of the Ethiopian Broadcasting Corporation and the Ethiopian Press Agency, including opposition members. Even now, as Human Rights Watch asserted that it remains difficult to criticize the Abiy government due to pressure from editors and peers.In addition, Human Right Watch suggested that the media law and computer crime law should be reformed to guarantee freedom of expression. While hate speech online is a problem, any potential hate speech law should not unduly limit freedom of expression. There are other approaches that should be considered first, including public education campaigns. Social media companies have a significant role to play in terms of content moderation and public education campaigns.

Generally, the first and most important step that was taken by PM Abiy is guaranteeing freedom of assembly, freedom to form associations and the rights of the Ethiopian people to free ex-

① Human Right Watch, "Ethiopia: Abiy's First Year as Prime Minister, Review of Freedom of Expression", [2019-04-03]. https://www.hrw.org/news/2019/04/03/ethiopia-abiys-first-year-prime-minister-review-freedom-expression.

② Ibid.

press their views and ideas. All medias have been given the free will to collect and disseminate information according to the media law or ethics. Based on these measures, the past injustice and wrong doing of the government have been revealed to the public. It also creates public confidence about PM Abiy' s administration. Thus, PM Abiy' s administration has not be required to do anything except repealing civic society and charities laws and press freedom laws, and removing the repressive government institutions established to control the Ethiopian people.

2.4　Justice and Peacebuilding

Understanding and doing with the matters of human rights exploitation in transitional and post-conflict situations is significant to nurture reconciliation and sustainable peace and stability. Also, justice attempts to know the predicaments executed on the sufferers, and, censoriously, to admit that the wrong endeavor. The purpose is to restore the victims' self-esteem and to reintegrate their condition in society as completely appreciated citizens. This more all-encompassing considerate of justice is principally significant to building sustainable peace (Davis and Unger, 2009).

Taking into consideration past contributions to develop a more just society in the future is very crucial. Creating justice-sensitive institutional restructuring is significant for shielding citizens' rights and develops approachable to the citizens' needs and able to empower victims to turn out to be citizens and grasp public institutions to account. Creating responsible judicial institutions is very important for building democracy, promoting good governance and the rule of law. Knowing that the victims are citizens whose rights to access to resources, services and rights is based on equity, not membership of one powerful group, and a society in which all people are equal before the law, and equally protected and served by the state (Davis and Vnger, 2019).

The injustice and suffering the peoples of Ethiopia faced with in the EPRDF regime is affirmed by PM Abiy Ahmed in his inaugural speech as presented here under;

Our problems are many and don't allow us any respite. Lack of a developed democratic culture, deep-rooted poverty, organized corruption and bureaucratic inefficiency, and lack of good governance have been compounding. It has created a complex and trying challenge for us. It is regrettable that over the last few years many members of our society have been uprooted from their places of residence. They were exposed to displacement and grave loss of life and property. The rights of citizens to freely move throughout the country and make a living have to be respected. Therefore, we will strive to stop these unbecoming practices and ensure that such actions are never repeated again. Let alone facing them divided, our problems demand years of work even working together in love and unison. Accordingly, to make up for lost time and be able to move forward, we will strive forward with a new spirit. All our problems cannot be solved in a single day. However, we can speed up the work we have begun to build a better country for all. There is a strong initiative on the part of the government to build a better country. But we all have responsibilities. Rather than seeing each other as strangers and seeing each other with indifference as members of different countries, we must hold each other' s hands and strive together as actual owners of the country[①].

The above premise of the PM Abiy obviously revealed that there is a need for reforming the institutions and personals to alleviate the uprooted injustice prevailed in Ethiopia in social, economic and political spheres. The Ethiopian people, in the 20th century, kept their independence and territorial integrity by fighting multiple wars including the 1896 Battle of Adwa. The goal of the Ethiopian people' s movement for justice, equality and freedom in 21st century is to establish the government of the people by the people for the people. The Oromo protests and the Amhara resistance which played a central role in the election of PM Abiy as the prime minister are at the forefront of this movement. PM Abiy is well aware and is enthusiasm to fully address the issue of justice by alleviating the past grievance in the future. As a change leader, PM Abiy and his administration should adopt the idea of establishing the government of the people by the people for the people as the central governing idea in transitioning Ethiopia from the 20th century to 21st century.

There may have freshly been a greater patience for protests and a decline in the number of demonstrations in Oromia, however, in the same time period, enduring conflicts have spreading and inter-communal violence in the country has been on the rise. These are possibly encouraged by regional and local power-brokers who are excited to progress their own interests in this period of political change. There is presumption, which Prime Minister Abiy may have helped suppress the crisis in Oromia and contributed to a more restrained security sector, but Ethiopian politics remain contentious. A number of local flashpoints for inter-communal violence. Particularly border disputes between Oromia and Somali are ignited, and other conflicts between Oromo and Gedeo people, conflict in Gondar and Beneshagul-Gumuz regions have been suggesting that Ethiopia can anticipate continued instability[②].

3 Social and Economic Development

Social and economic progress is an indispensable state for permanent and sustainable peace. Conflicts are frequently instigated by huge and mounting "socio-economic disparities, economic decline, inequitable distribution of goods and burdens, and marginalisation of vulnerable groups and geographical regions". Relative poverty is perhaps a further vital source of conflict than absolute poverty. Additional basis of conflict is competition for restricted natural resources. Conflicts can be instigated by greedy leaders and by popular grievances, which may or may not be justified (Johnson, 2004).

The social and economic progress in Ethiopia is characterized by inequality of circulation of goods and burdens, and the society is grieved from relative poverty since access power and resource is overpoweringly occupied by the few elites. Furthermore, in Ethiopia notwithstanding of

① Ethiopiaforums, "Ethiopia: Full transcript (in English) of Prime Minister Abiy Ahmed' s speech at Millennium Hall", [2018-04-13]. 2018, https://ethiopiaforums.com/ethiopia-full-transcript-in-english-of-prime-minister-abiy-ahmeds-speech-at-millennium-hall/.

② Hilary Matfess, "Change and Continuity in Protests and Political Violence PM Abiy' s Ethiopia", [2018-10-13]. https://reliefweb.int/report/ethiopia/change-and-continuity-protests-and-political-violence-pm-abiy-s-ethiopia.

the optimistic progresses in investing relatively enough budget and policy directions to social service there have been significantly compromising quality and standards of those services. Even if there are massive expansions of infrastructures such as roads, railways, power plants, dams and other strategic investments their durability has been below the minimum standards so that they could not qualify the standards of developmental state ideology, which stands for durable infrastructures to ensure sustainable development (Fesseha and Abatewold, 2017).

Thus, the government conducted various institutional reforms in unsustainable and uncoordinated manner. The reform was good beginning but it lacks effectiveness, innovation and continuity. The government failed to create the capable, accountable and modern civil servant based on the level of new economic and social development in the country. This erodes the credibility of civil services that could have been played major role in national transformation (Adugna, 2016).

In his inaugural speech, the prime minister clearly shows the economic and social situations of the country as presented here. Due to the fast growth that our country has achieved over the past years, our successes in poverty alleviation; in building basic infrastructure; in human resource development and the like are visible for everyone. In this regard, the government has taken policy and practical actions to contain price inflation; to stabilize the foreign exchange market; to keep the health of the financial sector; to expand the reach and access of financial services needed for the economy; to generate foreign currency; to encourage savings and investment; to create employment opportunities; to increase the per capita income of the people as well as to reduce abject poverty. To overcome the persisting economic crisis, Abiy Ahmed has unsettled Ethiopia' s state-led developmental model and instead sought to wrestle Ethiopia' s debt and currency crisis by renegotiating Chinese loans, seeking financial and technical support from the World Bank, and courting new investment from the Gulf and Western partners①.

But when one evaluates the socio-economic change that observed in the country since PM Abiy Ahmed took power is insignificant and even become the Worst. As 2019, humanitarian aid ascertained 8.86 million Ethiopians were in need. Economic growth has been hopeful but there have been, border conflicts such as in the Afar-Issa area, and mass displacements in the Oromo-Somali Region boundary area, in Beni Shangul-Gumuz Region, and in the Guji-Gedeo area. Communal clashes have been observed in cities, like in Hawassa, in Moyale, and even in Addis Ababa, where dozens were killed in August 2018 in the Burayyu suburb, causing tremors all over the country. Ethiopia has also recently become the country with the most internally displaced persons (IDPs) in the world②. At the present, the country remains in flux and the trajectory of its transition uncertain. Long-simmering ethnic grievances have been compounded by elite disagreements about a range of issues, including the proper balance of power between the Centre and re-

① Ahmed Soliman, Abel Abate Demissie, "Can Abiy Ahmed Continue to Remodel Ethiopia?" , [2019-04-12]. https://www.chathamhouse.org/2019/04/can-abiy-ahmed-continue-remodel-ethiopia.

② Jon Abbink, "Ethiopia' s Successes Under Abiy Ahmed Constrained by Ethnic Divisions" , [2019-04-04]. https://theglobalobservatory.org/2019/04/ethiopias-successes-abiy-constrained-by-ethnic-divisions/.

gional states and how; or whether; to reform a state-dominated economy. The grievances are coming to a boil, threatening the country's stability and perhaps even its unity①.

Although the economy has been growing for the past ten years, over the past three years, the absence of internal stability and the long-stalled government mega projects were daunting challenges. Furthermore, infrastructure projects demand foreign currency and export capacity did not increase as expected which resulted in a large discrepancy whereby the foreign currency exchange was overcrowded by black market smugglers. As a result of this economic shortfall, jobs have plummeted, especially in the construction sector and the cost of living has increased significantly exacerbated by the increase of unemployed youth. Thus, different activities have been accomplished since he took power to temporarily mitigate internal and external financial crisis.

Undertaking youth unemployment is a critical encounter in a country of 100 million people, with two million young people entering the job market every year. Ethiopia plans to create a million jobs a year through the expansion of its industrial parks and rapid growth in the manufacturing and services sectors. Cognisant of the role of youth in upsetting the previous EPRDF leadership, Abiy has given attention on renovating the capital city instead of rural areas, appealing that "if you can change Addis...you can change Ethiopia". Nevertheless, to decrease Ethiopia's inequalities, transformation have to begin in the rural areas which accounts about 80 per cent of the population②.

As alternative solution to the economic grave of the country, the government has also initiated a cautious move to private sector-led liberalization, with preliminary privatizations intended in the telecoms and logistics sectors. This will be a staged process, starting with regulatory reform and a greater role for business in job creation. Eventually, Ethiopia's many challenges are far more than one leader can tackle alone, and PM Abiy Ahmed must trust in the expertise around him to ensure the support and goodwill generated in his unrestrained first year is not fruitless③.

Even though, the government is paying attention to the educational sector and working hard, particularly with regard to ensuring the quality of education, there is real notice that the country has many home works to do and many activities to be carried out. While the expansion of education is among the commendable achievements of our government, as long as that educational coverage and reach is not supported with quality, the relentless efforts will not bear the fruits that we desire. Accordingly, starting from primary school all the way to the institutions of higher education, the government will redouble its efforts with absolute determination to make all our centers of knowledge to focus on quality. Maximum effort will be made to ensure that especially graduates from our higher education institutions and technical and vocational colleges harvest knowledge that is comparable to their endowment of abilities. To deal with these problems and many

① International Crisis Group, "Watch List 2019–Second Update", [2019-07-17]. https://www.crisisgroup.org/global/watch-list-2019-second-update.

② Ahmed Soliman & Abel Abate Demissie, "Can Abiy Ahmed Continue to Remodel Ethiopia?", [2019-04-12]. https://www.chathamhouse.org/2019/04/can-abiy-ahmed-continue-remodel-ethiopia.

③ Ibid.

others, tried a certain reform but did not crystallize it.

4 Spoiler of Peacebuilding

What is spoiling? The complexities of violent conflict require a broad definition of spoiling behavior, contrary to the generally accepted narrow definition of spoiling in much of the literature. At the core of this broad definition are the activities of any actors that are opposed to peaceful settlement for whatever reason. These actors are either within or (usually) outside the "peace process", and use violence or other means to disrupt the process in pursuit of their aims. Some groups have clear incentives for the continuation of violent conflict or in contesting the nature of peace. Environmental variables (such as nature of peace settlements, the role of external actors, the political economy of the conflict, disputes over natural resources, the influence of significant diaspora groups) give rise to certain types of spoiling activity. Amongst these factors, the existence of powerful groups whose primary intent is economic gain must be addressed by tactics that may be different from conventional conflict resolution methods. It may be unrealistic to bring every armed group into a peace process but this should not be allowed to obstruct or disrupt the process (Newman and Richmond, 2006).

The government of Ethiopia has tried to accommodate the divergent views in peacebuilding process via inviting both internal and external opposition groups to join the change that prevailed in the country. Accommodation of these diverged views to the extreme case helps government to minimize spoilers in the country. For external spoilers PM Abiy Ahmed took a great step in making peace agreements with strategic and historical enemy, Eritrea and make diplomatic negotiation with other neighboring countries. The diplomatic negotiation is not only aimed at Ethiopia but it works to create harmony in the horn of Africa①.

Even if there is success in reducing spoilers from internal and external, there are still some groups or individuals who do not have positive outlook about the new change in Ethiopia. This is generally emanated from their greed of accumulated wealth. These spoilers are generally categorized as those who had been benefited from the past government posts and those who were leading great projects as assigned by the government.

The other and emerging challenges was the advent of NAMA (National Movement of Amhara), a new party in Amhara regional state, and Amhara Democratic Party' s former leadership was forced to turn to a more radical Amhara nationalistic rhetoric in order to try to stem the grass-roots support to NAMA. Whether the new leadership in ADP will continue along the same strategy to desperately try to win the 2020 elections, or reassess its options moving forward, is too early to assess. For sure, they must be hesitant to enter the electoral race under the current circumstances, facing a possible electoral defeat in 2020②.

① Ahmed Soliman & Abel Abate Demissie, "Can Abiy Ahmed Continue to Remodel Ethiopia?" , [2019-04-12]. https://www.chathamhouse.org/2019/04/can-abiy-ahmed-continue-remodel-ethiopia.

② Addis Standard, "Opinion: Putting Humpty Dumpty Together Again: The Restoration of EPRDF?", [2019-03-26]. https://addisstandard.com/opinion-putting-humpty-dumpty-together-again-the-restoration-of-eprdf/.

A deteriorated ADP also indicates a debilitated underpinning for PM Abiy to govern. On the other front, his own ODP (Oromo Democratic Party) is challenged in Oromia, by both organized Oromo opposition and political demands put forward by the Qeerroo. It has been noticeable that if ODP demanded the leadership, they would face complications of balancing Oromo demands expressed by the Qeerrro who brought them to power, with the needed to govern the country that any Prime Minister must exhibit. The ruptures Abiy is presently required to perform, preaching medemer at the federal level, concomitantly as accepting the Oromo question on Addis Abeba and at regional level, is likely not a sustainable aerobics exercise which would take him safely to 2020 and further①.

Conclusion

As indicated in the introduction, the peacebuilding accord of this paper is assessed via three important dimensions that is security, political development, and social and economic development. After long and challenging process, PM Abiy Ahmed made an ascending to power on 2nd April 2018 and tried to take reforms in the aforementioned scopes. He tried to take reforms in security, political, and socio-economic aspects unlike the trend of EPRDF political ideology.

The security dimension of peacebuilding in Ethiopia has been characterized by ill equipped attempts of disarmament, demobilization, and reinsertion and reintegration. The Ethiopian government only did the calling up on the rebel groups to the table and able to discuss about the possible political feature of the country. The security reform did not address the very essential dimensions of any peacebuilding process.

The political development aspect of peace building is most important reform steps that was taken by PM Abiy which guaranteeing freedom of assembly, freedom to form associations and the rights of the Ethiopian people to free express their views and ideas and the releasing of all prisoners without any precondition. PM Abiy's administration also has been trying to repealing civic society and charities laws and press freedom laws, and removing the repressive government institutions established to control the Ethiopian people. And the idea of unity with in diversity medemer which catches the attention of the populace for better future was framed by him to transcend the persisting ethnic politics of the country even if its influence has not been staying for long due to his impotent to implement it in practice. The peace accord with Eritrea is fruitful for not only between the two countries but also it can create stability in the region. But for unknown reason the instruction of the two countries remain at the air after not more a quarter of a year.

The present government of Ethiopia conducted various institutional reforms in unsustainable and uncoordinated manner. The reform was good beginning but it lacks effectiveness, innovation and continuity. The government failed to create the capable, accountable and modern civil servant

① Addis Standard, "Opinion: Putting Humpty Dumpty Together Again: The Restoration of EPRDF?", [2019-03-26]. https://addisstandard.com/opinion-putting-humpty-dumpty-together-again-the-restoration-of-eprdf/.

based on the level of new economic and social development in the country. This erodes the credibility of civil services that could have been played major role in national transformation. Economic growth has been hopeful but there have been, border conflicts in various parts of the country which has also recently become the country with the most internally displaced persons (IDPs) in the world. Inflation has been rising in alarming rate which creates economic disparity between the poor and rich.

In general, at the moment the peacebuilding essence in Ethiopia is uncertain. Even if at initial stage there was hope in addressing security, political, and social and economic reform, it is now remaining only as promise and the actual injustice, insecurity and maladministration continued throughout the country. As the result the government of PM Abiy has been losing its sincerity by the majority of the population.

References

[1] ANÍCIA L. 2011. Demilitarization and human security.// ERIN M, TONY K. Peace, conflict and development in Africa: a reader. Geneva: University for Peace, 225-227.

[2] AYENACHEW A. 2014. The Ethiopian developmental state and its challenges. https://ssrn.com/abstract=2512907.

[3] BEKELE S, REGASSA T. 2012. Democratization in a developmental state: the case of Ethiopia: issues, challenges, prospects. https://www1.undp.org/content/dam/ethiopia/docs/Democratization%20in%20a%20Developmental%20State.pdf.

[4] DANIEL V. 2011. Economic reintegration of ex-combatants//ERIN M, TONY K. Peace, conflict and development in Africa: a reader. Geneva: University for Peace, 264-268.

[5] EDWARD N, OLIVER R. 2006. Peace building and spoilers. Conflict, Security & Development, 6(1): 101-110.

[6] FESSEHA M, ABATEWOLD M. 2017. Ethiopia: a democratic developmental state? ILIRIA International Review, 7(2): 9-26.

[7] HILARY M. 2015. Rwanda and Ethiopia: developmental authoritarianism and the new politics of African strong men. African Studies Review, 58(2): 181-204.

[8] HILDE F. 2004. Peace-building: adevelopment perspective. https://www.regjeringen.no/globalassets/upload/ud/vedlegg/fredsarbeid/peace_engelsk.pdf.

[9] ISAK S, KAREN B. 2013. Dialogue and inter-ethnic trust: a randomized field trial of "sustained dialogue" in Ethiopia. Journal of Peace Research, 50(5): 565-574.

[10] KEITH K, OLIVER J. 2005. Peace, security and development in post-conflict: environment. Security Dialogue, 36(4): 447–462.

[11] LAURA D, THOMAS U. 2011. Justice in peace-building: towards a policy framework for the European Union. https://www.ictj.org/sites/default/files/ICTJ-IFP-EU-Justice-Peacebuilding-2008-English.pdf.

[12] MELES Z. 2006. African development: dead ends and new beginnings(preliminary draft). http://www.meleszenawi.com/wp-content/uploads/2012/11/.

[13] MINISTRY OF FINANCE AND ECONOMIC DEVELOPMENT OF ETHIOPIA. 2010. Growth and Transformation Plan (2010/11-2014/15). https://planipolis.iiep.unesco.org/sites/default/files/ressources/ethiopiagtp.pdf.

[14] ORGANISATION FOR ECONOMIC CO-OPERATION AND DEVELOPMENT(OECD). 2005. Peace-building overview. https://www.eda.admin.ch/dam/deza/en/documents/themen/fragile-kontexte/92802-peace-building-overview_EN.pdf#:~:text=Peace-building%20can%20be%20understood%20as%20a%20supplement%20to,violent%20conflict%20and%20promoting%20lasting%20and%20sustainable%20peace.

[15] TEWELDE G. 2017. The "democratic developmental state" in Ethiopia: origin, challenges and prospect//SONJA J, DAGNACHEW A, BUSHA T. From theory to lived experience. Addis Ababa: Fiedrich-Ebert-Stiftung Ethiopia, 88-104.

[16] UNITED NATIONS. 2010. UN peace-building: an orientation. https://www.un.org/peacebuilding/sites/www.un.org.peacebuilding/files/documents/peacebuilding_orientation.pdf.

Centering "Local Nationalism" through Political Liberalization: the Case of Gambella & Somali

Eyob Asfaw①

Abstract: More often than not, the political history of Ethiopia has recorded a variance balance sheet on discourses of nationalism. Also, the federal restructuring of the Ethiopian state brought either local nationalism to overrides civic nationalism or "pseudo self-government". As a result , ethnic nationalism was on the rise against the nation building (Kefale, 2009). To its discredit, the ethnic federalism has decentralized all-embracing civic nationalism into very localized "local nationalism" compelled the regional elites to fiercely fight for power struggle at the local level. Fast forward, the ascent of prime minister Dr. Abiy Ahmed to the helm of power in April 2018, has ushered in a process of political changes which has raised hopes of a democratic transition and a prospect to avert the discourses of nationalism. As a consequence of the reform measures overtaken by Abiy Ahmed and "Team Lemma", Ethiopia is entering a process of change that some have likened to Huntington's waves of democratization. Notwithstanding to their divergent orientation of nationalism, opposition parties in exile, rebel groups and media run by Diaspora have returned to Ethiopia since the month of April 2018. On the other hand, the prime minister, in his inaugural address to the House of People's Representatives (HoPR) and subsequent speeches, coined the "medemer" ideology (to mean "synergy") which he later published it as a book, has struck a chord with sections of the public. Imperatively, this popular ideal of "medemer" is unilaterally prescribed to became a panacea for the ever divided political groups without according political pluralism of any sort and enabled the ruling coalition to form monolithic "Prosperity Party". Through the prism of what Kjetil Tronvol characterized "EPRDF" as infamously re-ideologized in 2000, "medemer" became another bazaar of re-ideologizing the polity to the end of democratic deepening. This paper, through employing qualitative data collection and interviewing key informants, will delve into the modalities of how the dividends of the recent political liberalization resulted in centering local nationalism towards Ethiopianist narrative by historically marginalized regions such as the Gambela and Somali. Also, the merger, alliances and principled divisions in local oppositions, capability to negotiate national icons, trading-off

① Eyob Asfaw(eyob.asfaw@aau.edu.et) is currently a lecturer of Moral & Civic Education at Addis Ababa University.

language policy, moderating historical injustice, overcoming local rivalry and negotiating electoral constituency determines the prospect of centering local nationalism. At last, the paper pinpoints on how actors and stakeholders ought to consider reinvesting the capital gained from political liberalization for exerting the right balance on the discourses of nationalism.

Keywords: Pan-Ethiopianism; Local Nationalism; Medemer; Political Liberalization

1 Introduction to the 2018 Democratic Transitions of Ethiopia

The ascent of prime minister Dr. Abiy Ahmed to the helm of power in April 2018, has ushered in a process of political changes which has raised hopes of a democratic transition (Lefort, 2018) and juxtaposed to end the polarization of contending nationalism (Yusuf, 2020) . As a consequence of the reform measures overtaken by Abiy Ahmed and "Team Lemma"[①], Ethiopia is entering a process of change that some have likened to Huntington's waves of democratization (Huntington, 1991). So far, opposition parties in exile , rebel groups and media run by Diaspora have returned to Ethiopia in the months since April 2018. The prime minister, in his inaugural address to the House of People's Representatives (HoPR) and subsequent speeches, coined the "medemer" ideology (to mean "positive plus or synergy") which has struck a chord with sections of the urban public and also drawn the support of political actors who were previously at enmity with the government (Lefort, 2018) . Imperatively, this popular ideal of "medemer" is became a glue for the ever divided political groups without according political pluralism of any sort. In light of what Kjetil Tronvol characterized EPRDF as infamously re-ideologized in 2000 (Tronvoll, 2011) , this became another bazaar of re-ideologizing the polity to the end of democratic deepening. To the dismay of his constituency of Oromo, Abiy's prescription becomes to march towards national unity. Debatably enough, his policy and action also served towards attracting the political field under construction by virtue of the political liberalization. Henceforth, previously outlawed parties such as Patriotic Front-Ginbot 7 Movement for Justice, Democracy and Freedom, Ogaden National Liberation Front (ONLF), Oromo Liberation Front (OLF) , the Amhara Democratic Force Movement (ADFM), and the Tigraian Alliance for National Democracy (TAND-led by Aregawi Berhe) are among others. Activists in exile that are not formally affiliated to any political party such as Jawar Mohammed and Tamagn Beyene have also returned.

This article will dwell on the following questions.

What is the prospect of the post April 2018 political liberalization for centering local nationalism?

Does the ideology of the ruling party, i.e "medemer" philosophy , valuable to center local nationalism of Gambela and Somali regions.

What are the opportunities, challenges and prospects of centering local nationalism through

① Team Lemma is a metonym coined after the Oromo Democratic Party, to represent the reformist of the EPRDF contesting the reactionary groups within the party. Abiy is argued to be a member of "Team Lemma" quite before his ascendancy to the post of Ethiopian premiership.

"oppositional nationalism"?

What lessons can political actors draw to recapitalize the political liberalization for centering local nationalism?

In sum, drawing from key informant interviews and desk review, this article will delve into the modalities of how the dividends of the current political liberalization can be harnessed by historically marginalized regions such as Gambela and Somali; how actors and stakeholders ought to consider reinvesting the capital gained from Gambella and Somali under the banner of Ethiopianist narrative.

2 Theoretical Framework

From the onset of Ethiopian socialist revolution, the ideology of "Ethiopia First" of the Ethiopian military government ruled from 1974 to 1991 with mixed legacy of maintaining national unity and suppressing local nationalism without due negotiation of the divergent narratives. It is also pertinent to point out that the current transition is occurring in a context defined by instability and the polarization of diverse ethno-nationalisms which some interpret as an outcome of the past 27 years of Ethiopian Ethnic federalism. In this endeavor, Dunkwart Rustow argued that Democratic transitions, inter alia requires national unity (Rustow, 1970). Fukuyama also recently forwarded that "liberal democracy" in the twenty first century ought to pass the litmus test of identity politics of various sorts (Fukuyama, 2018). Perhaps, Fukuyama is always known to alarm Democracy enthusiasts as to how best to insulate democracy from nationalism. For him, nationalism is totally either completely at odds or counterproductive for democracy (Fukuyama, 1994). Though ideology often assumed in tandem with class differences and political economy, this article contends that it is sine qua none to explain its correlation with nationalism and political liberalization (Fuche, 2000).

3 Origin and Evolution Contending Nationalism in Ethiopia

To date the Imperial Ethiopia prior to the 1974 revolution, the nationwide nationalism was obviously nationalistic without moderation to recognize the local diversity. Furthermore, in the wake of 1974 Ethiopian Revolution, Mengistu's call for Itiyopia Tikdem (to mean "Ethiopia first!") was assumed as an ultra-unionists at the expense of local nationalism (Tareke, 2009). Tareke (2009: 39) reminisces that Mengistu, upon the establishment of the Military Committee, meant "Ethiopia First" to preach virtue, honesty, selflessness, and love of the motherland. To the favor of the revolutionaries, the intelligentsia was able to wage nationalism through that banner. Ironically enough the eventual protracted blood shade was in contradistinction to the slogan's longer version which says "Ethiopia first, but without bloodshed" (Itiopia tikdem yale minim dem). Henceforth, it is not unanticipated when the actors at the negotiation table of the 1991 transition briskly contended as the ultra-centrists ideology has gone away with the military/socialist regime before 1991 (Gudina 2004: 33).

Fast forward to 1991, Since the Ethiopian state was restructured as Federal Democratic Republic of Ethiopia (FDRE), Ethiopian politics has oscillated between the two contending narratives of centralist/Ethiopianist nationalism versus sub-state ethno-nationalisms (Vauhgun, 2006). In the Ethiopian federal system, historically marginalized and economically less developed regional states such as Afar, Somali, Benishangul-Gumuz and Gambella are officially classified as emerging regions. As a result, the post-EPRDF regime was totally a U-turn for the balance sheet of nationalism. The fact that the post 1991 state restructure employed ethnicity as an organizing device has undoubtedly played counterproductively for the development of countrywide citizenship (Allen, 2006; Gebrewold, 2009). Looking at the counter-productivity of the ethnic politics, political pundits blacklisted the EPRDF as anti-nationalists.

Also, it was a norm than exception to criticize EPRDF for making neither full hearted nor genuine ethnic empowerment (Kefale, 2009; Markakis, 2010:288). As a result, high level peripheral regions were taken as apprentices with degrees. It is irony that highlander deputies were placed to back regional presidents through their required skills and experience under the guise of self-administration. To the dismay of local nationalists, instituting "Department of Regional Affairs" under the Prime Minister's Office as oversight body to distantly watch the regional activities since 1995.

4 Pre-political Liberalization Era and Local Nationalism

4.1 The Gambella Periphery in Brief

Against the aforementioned background, it is not uncommon when one finds the Gambella as a periphery (Markakis, 2010). The demographic composition of Gambella regional state informs the politics of the regional state. In Gambella a key aspect of the local political dynamics centers on the divide between natives (ethnic groups considered indigenous to Gambella) versus highlanders (a catch all term in Gambella used to refer to Oromo, Amhara, Kambata) and the "Highlander" to comprise their version of "others" drawn from Ethnic Oromo, Amhara, Kambata regional minority (Feyissa, 2006: 245) . However political contestation is complex and layered as rivalry between native groups such as the Nuer (40 %), Annya (27 %), Mezeneger (10 %), Opo, nd Komo over economic resources and political influence in the regional administration has occasionally led to violence (Feyissa, 2006).

Political groups and actors in Gambella have had negligible political impact on politics at the center and have confined their resources and actions to seeking more decentralization. In this context it is critical to point out that one aspect of the political dynamics in Gambella i.e. the rivalry between the Nuer and Annya has larger regional implications in terms of the interlinkages with the conflict and political contestations in South Sudan.

Perhaps, noting the counter-productivity of the ever divided nationalism, Obang Metho (Gebrewold, 2009: 88) "*the Anuak addressed the Oromo Community in Minnesota on* 08 *April* 2007 *saying "If Woyane (to mean Tigray Peoples Liberation Front) Can Unify,* Why *Can't We?*". In his remark, he was over-zealous to mobilize collective oppositional nationalism indifferent to Anuak, Nuer, Majangir, Opo, and Komo diversity, against the ruling party.

Although, the span of 27 years ranging from 1991 to 2018, the ruling coalition Ethiopian People's Revolutionary Democratic Front (EPRDF) embraced only four organizations, namely Amhara, Tigray, Oromo & South. However, political parties, who used to govern the regional states of Afar, Gambella, Somali and Benishangul-Gumuz remained to be satellite party under the banner of so called PDO's. The parties retained the status of "allied" parties were constantly estranged from central policy planning. For Markakis (2010: 281) self-administration has been taken as a major step forward in the periphery. The assumption is their countless diaspora, intelligentsia and elites would vie for power share in the affairs of local government, with the accompanying perquisites of power, social status and economic privilege. As a consequence, none of political movements from the "emerging regions" has exerted influence or power at the center in real terms. The governing party in Gambella regional state i.e. Gambella Peoples Democratic Movement (GPDM) is a regional party and is a site of intra-party power rivalry between Annyaa and Nuer. None of the multiethnic parties registered by the National Electoral Board of Ethiopia (NEBE) has individuals from the peripheral regions in its leadership.①

In appraisal for the reform, the recent leader of the region-Omod Ojulu reiterated that "for the preceding 27 years it was not unusual when the periphery was constantly implementing ready-made proposals by the central government". In his opinion, it was symptomatic for the ever peripheralised region. Since the Ethiopian federal restructure, the peripheralisation can neither evolve for real autonomy nor solves the dependency syndrome. To the dismay of the fan of regional autonomy, Young (1999) underscored that the EPRDF coalition party at the center assigned advisors from the core of Tigray Peoples Liberation front that ever-problematizes the peripheralisation (Young, 1999: 343). Asnake Kefale (2009) also noted the defunct Organization for Regional Affairs (ORA) to be succeeded by Ministry of Federal Affairs. Yet, the peripheralisation proved to be multi-layered throughout its evolution.

For Kefale (2009), the peripheralising of emerging regions has resulted for trivial power rivalry, insecure minority protection even in a very unconstitutional manner. Their peripheralization were also illustrated by their continual inability to confront the political ideology of the center (Kefale: 2004). As per Merara Gudina (2004) regionalization policy and the proliferation of PDO's (Peoples Democratic Organization), i.e Gambella Peoples Democratic Organization, was often criticized for pseudo-pacifism of the region which assumes to balance power between the

---

① Interview with Sebsibe, Yosef, on 1st October 2018, held in Addis Ababa, Ethiopia. Currently there are more than 62 political parties out of which only 20 of them are registered as Multi-national parties.

center and region in a very disguised manner (Gudina, 2004).

4.2 The Somali Region in brief

"Moderating Rectifying Historical Injustice": From its outset, old manuscripts such as Wayne (1903) Said, Somali resentment against the central government brew starting from the time of Menelik II at the end of 19th century. Comparatively speaking, Menelik is neither demonized as other local nationalists do such as Oromo and Wolaita nor celebrated as the ultra-centerists do such National Movement of Amhara (NAMA) and Ethiopian Citizens Party for Social Justice (EZEMA) do①. However the Somali local nationalists claimed the re-interpretation of Ethiopian history against the common portrayal Ahmed ibn Ibrahim al-Ghazi (1506-1543) as invaded (commonly known as "*Ahmed Gragn*") . An informant boldy claimed that as he was originated from Somali "he is Brave and deserve celebration".②

Secondly, the perceived marginalization by the center after the Ethio-Somali war during the Dergue Regime also contributed for the longevity of Somali nationalism (Tareke, 2009) .

Historically, no Somali were represented at the state structure. An informant disclosed that, "down the line from imperial regime to the military government no known Somali were placed neither at the Ogaden nor at the central government. I only remember an uncle of mine who is Somali was placed at Dire Dawa city." ③

Also, the fact that much of the Ogaden region , during the Dergue Regime was highly militarized as a response to secessionist or irredentist movements throughout the region, especially, after the Ethio-Somali war of 1977 caused by the invasion of Siad Barre under his ambition to establish the Greater Somali through unifying Ethnic Somalis found in the whole horn of Africa. (Tareke, 2009)

Principled Alliance, Merger and Fracture of Somali Local Nationalists

Abstractly, the periphery of the Somali region was not resolved other than being re-constituting the marginalization (Kefale, 2009). As a result of the marginalization, WSLF (Western Somali Liberation Front) and lately ONLF (Ogaden National Liberation Fronts) were known to stand in brute insurgent war against the central government (Ali, 2019). The latter declared itself as a grassroot social and political movement founded in August 1984 but waging violence. Initially, it was a splinter group WSLF founded by six men led by Sheikh Ibrahim Abdalah Mah, a graduate of Bin Saud University in Mecca (WSLF) (Markakis, 2010) .

---

① Interview with Hasen Malin, (Deputy Chairman, ONLF and Office Head of Addis Ababa branch) held in Addis Ababa on 23rd Sept emper, 2020. The informant claims ed that Menelik didn' t entered Somali instead the Somali region was perceived to be ruled by the local society.

② Interview with Hasen Malin, (Deputy Chairman, ONLF and Office Head of Addis Ababa branch) held in Addis Ababa on 23rd Sept emper, 2020. Ahmed gran engaged in expansionist war against the Central Highland kingdom during the medieval period until he was won by Emperor Gelawdiwos. Interestingly, he hed a statue on Mogadishu build by brothers in Somalia but in the Ethiopian border Ahmed Gragn was thought as an invader.

③ Interview with Elias Mohammed, a central Committee of Prosperity Party and advisor to the Office of Somali Prospety Party, held in Addis Ababa on 13rd September, 2020.

For WSLF, their war was fought under the banner extreme nationalism against the backdrop of reintegrating with the greater Somalis or to secede from the Ethiopia. Exceptionally, in post-1991 a group appeared to register themselves as a moral inherit of WSLF but perceived as a mere coopted party without strong constituency ①.

In general, to our dismay, actors of local nationalism are criticized for non-meaningful faction politics for the past half a century at least. Since 1991, the Narsullah-WSLF (Western Somali Liberation Front) , the Issa and Gurgura Liberation Front (IGLF), the Horyal (Gadabursi clan organisation), the ONLF, the Al-Ittihad al-Islam and several smaller Somali political organisations . In gross evaluation made by Sandra Joireman and Thomas Szayna (1997), only 6 percent of Somali were represented at the level of Council of Ministers of the federal government which qualifies what Arend Lijphart (1977) dubbed "power sharing agreement". Indeed, for critics such Semir Yusuf (2020), such power sharing arrangement as typical forms of consociational (non-majoritarian) democracy in a highly diverse and divided societies is one of the weakest solutions of centering local nationalism. Arguably, the peripherization redirects the potential political competition from Somali into Local nationalism to be exercised in a fierce local battle. Consequently, as Asnake Kefale (2003) rightfully argued that,

"The clans in the Somali region appear to play the functional role of competing ethnic groups in multi-ethnic regions."

The EPRDF government facilitated the merger among 14 small parties to form ESDL ("Ethio Somali Democratic league" commonly known "the League") against the backdrop of the dominance of ONLF. Perhaps the merger was quintessentially perceived as a continuum of what Gudina (2004) dubbed PDO's syndrome. The functioning of ESDP widen the division as its move didn't differ the Ogaden clan with ONLF (Asnake, 2003: 139). To discredit hardliner ONLF, EPRDF coerced ESDL to form SPDP (Somali People Democratic Party) by accommodating liberal elements of ONLF②. By virtue of the volatility of the Somali politics, in less than eight years the region reshuffled eleven regional presidents much of it were orchestrated by the federal government.

Fast forward to the rise of the Abdi Illey③ (who ruled the region constantly from 2005 to 2018) , his stature comprises watershed moment in the dynamics of Somali local nationalism explained (Asfaw, 2019). Rather his local government is often explained to overshadow the saga of local dictatorship with his tricky style of clientalist-patronage capitalized upon the ossification of "pseudo-self-government". His dictatorial tendency were marked in his unpopular divisive

① Interview with Somali Prosperity Party representative and a senior politician from ONLF held in Addis Ababa in September 2020.

② Interview with Elias Mohammed, a central Committee of Prosperity Party and advisor to the Office of Somali Prospety Party, held in Addis Ababa on 13 September 2020.

③ His official name is Abdi Mohammed Oumer. Perhaps "Illey" is the name of the sub-clan in which such customary nomenclature locally identifies the bearer replacing surname. As one one informant shared "Illey" is marginalized sub clan from the whole clans found among the Somali. According to him, it is speculated that hias authoritarian brutality originated from inferiority complex due to the perceived marginalization.

re-organization of local governance structure. Also, his infamous "Heego" organized as a defunct hooligan youth groups, was secretly organized by the former Somali region exercise violence at a contingent aided by the Special force of the regional government. His regime can be narrated as follows.

Disguising Local Autonomy for Plundering Regional Resources:

It is not uncommon to hear a rumor among political pundits as the TPLF oligarch and military generals created cliques with Abdi Illey for plundering the regional resource and scramble for contraband. The struggle of local nationalism was to race for economic and political justice at their own region. As an informant said "let alone for struggling to be represented at the center, the whole regional administration was lost to be ruled by advisors and military generals of Tigray People Liberation Front"① . Abdi Illey's authoritarianism has borne smear struggle by the insurgents such as ONLF. By then, The ONLF was also agitated by both the unionist camp and the regional co-opted Somali representative led by Abdi Illey.

Pseudo Local Nationalism: It is not uncommon to hear the allegation against Abdi Illey for engaging in unscrupulous warfare with Oromia regional state under the disguise of border dispute②. As Bonsa (2017) noted that he disguised the border conflict to serve the TPLF's interest of proxy war against the Oromia Regional State as a vengeance for the then "Oromo Protest".

5 The Genesis of Medemer and Its Implication for Centering Nationalism

In a day of live streamed ordination before the House of Peoples Representatives, Abiy addressed the parliament in an exceptional way which catches away the public to be conciliatory of the contending perspectives on the Ethiopian Politics. His excerpt said "We Ethiopians live as Ethiopians and died to compose 'Ethiopia'".

Abiy's remark surprised all of the Ethiopian political commentators. Be it his supporters or enemy, the remark contained resonance of a nationalist variants. Undoubtedly, he seems to be convinced that his "Ethiopia" is not started in vain as if there is no background history to compose the nation and to glue them for a political community. In another token, it meant that when someone dies, he would join the league of ancestors. And that Ethiopia is live also the deceased "Ancestors" to serve as enigmatic aura for the subsequent generation, by way of charting the continuity of imagining Ethiopia.

Imagining Ethiopia in the fashion of Benedict Anderson (1983) dubbed "nations are nothing but imagined community". Henceforth, the live Ethiopians can't miss the requisite incentive to imagine Ethiopia composed of "Ancestors" land.

A caption goes over virulent showcasing Abiy's excerpt in a moment of celebrating anniversary of SEPDM (a sister party within the ruling coalition) , Repeatedly he was shown

① Interview with Elias Mohammed, a central Committee of Prosperity Party and advisor to the Office of Somali Prospety Party, held in Addis Ababa on 13 September 2020.

② Ibid.

when he was saying, in a literal sense like , "we had two option" . The first option is either to get positive plus (Medemer) and be accommodated. Or else to went trivial and end our communal life. So all of us undoubtedly opt for the first choice Abiy appeared smoothly one of the rare leader that the African states used to have. Medemer, to mean "getting plus to be accommodated" was one of the known & engaging narrative other than its popularity.

Since then Abiy made all of his eventual policy and practice to be parceled within the rhetoric of medemer as an anti-dote to the ever divided fabric of the society. Abiy realized medemer through his round of visit right after his public oath. He started his first round of visit to Jigjiga, and he went back to address the people in Tigray in Mekele. And in later of hid days he had a protracted work visit to all the regional capitals, including Semera, Assosa, Gambella, Hawassa and also the town of Wolkitte. The busy itinerary schedule of Abiy, indeed impacted positively to credit him with tangible output. Courageously he distanced himself from the old narrative of EPRDF's "Revolutionary Democracy", as he also out rule it altogether in his book (Ahmed, 2019). Perhaps there are clear gestures when he pended the narrative of "Developmentalism"[①]. More importantly, he publicly announced the retirement of the old ideologue of the party such as Sebhat Nega, Abay Tsehaye, Bereket Simone, Kassu Ilala and others to appeal for new dispensation[②]. Against this backdrop, one can note that medemer is continuity of re-ideologizing EPRDF, as Kjetil Tronvol infamously characterized EPRDF in 2000. By virtue of medemer , the ruling party enter into another bazaar of re-ideologizing the polity to the end of democratic deepening. Perhaps its practical impact on local nationalism and its interplay with regional elites is the attempt of this paper to address.

Although rendering a thorough explanation of medemer is not the intent of this article, we can contextualize from his book in a manner towards the analytical exercise of centering local nationalism. In his conceptualization, medemer entails the nuance of three inter-related concepts, namely "Mesebseb" (to mean "collection"), "Makabet" (to mean accumulation) and "Makemachet" agglomeration. In "Mesebseb", it is implicit to understand that local nationalism became sources of disunity other than unification through civic identity. On page 35 he put "common destiny" and self-motivation as the two fundamental the bigger "Medemer" ideal and on page 47 prioritizes unequivocally "national unity" as opposed to divide sovereign nationalism. Moreover on page 50 "Medemer" is dubbed as a prescription to broker/reconcile extreme nationalism. Hence, through the sub-ideal "Mesebseb", he meant. Inter alia, the philosophy is meant to collect divergent and divided local nationalism.

---

① Interview with NEBE officer who attended the three days long EPRDF general conference. On the conference it was anticipated, but went defunct, the EPRDF may consider an ideological shift. However, four of the constituting parties remained with their own old narrative to pend the change of "political ideology". For now the congress decided, after tough debate, to continue with "revolutionary democracy".

② The post-Meles EPRDF used to have the feature of "old comrade" and "younger comrade". The façade was to ensure policy and ideology continuity other than meaningful renewal. However it was an expedition to maintain the power grab under the disguise of policy continuity.

6 Challenges and Opportunities of the Current Political Liberalization for Centering Nationalism

6.1 Gambella Periphery

The Role of Agency: The influential activist Mr. Obang Meto, Annya by origin, is also part of the wave of Diaspora returnees to Ethiopia. Mr. Obang is also the Executive Director of the Solidarity Movement of the New Ethiopia (SMNE). In the aftermath of his return to Ethiopia after twenty eight years of exile, he conducted several round of discussions in the Gambella with youth representatives (Addis Admas , 1st October 2018). The event is about a precursor to a more comprehensive attempt to institutionalize dialogues as a tool to resolve inter-ethnic and intra-ethnic animosity under the Ethiopianist banner . The advocacy charity group that Mr. Obang is leading has supposedly set its sight or being registered as a locally based group aspiring to mobilize people around Ethiopia under Moto that is "No One is free until all are free!" ①

The SMNE-Movement is planning to organize a series of dialogues and negotiations within the Gambella and also in the rest of the country. The movement is not yet a party, and the trend is a source of lessons for actors, activists, politicians amidst the political transition within Ethiopia (SolidarityMovement.com).

Right after Obang's visit to Gambella, the region has showcased a youth protest demanding the perceived "medemer" wind of political reform would be blown also within the periphery. After the tension happened the regional authorities has attributed the cause to Obang visit to the region provoked the youth for protest. In reply, Obang also reiterated that the youth protest were inevitable as he perceived the region lags behind the "medemer" ideal and were yet far from the nation-wide political reform. Fast forward, the regional ruling party — Gambella Peoples Unity Democratic Movement (GPUDM) began to hold Gimgema/ Evaluation on which the chair and deputy resigned from their office. Accordingly, Omud Ujulu became the new chairman and Anguanaya Jacken is the new deputy-chairman. Though the succession is yet to prove as a promising momentum to be aligned with the nation-wide political reform(Borkena.com).

At the risk of overstating the role of agency, Obang Meto's trajectory showcases the impact of an individual from historically peripheralized regions as an actor and force for pushing for a unitarian political system in a context where the historically peripheralized regions have tended to produce movements aiming for greater autonomy or independence.

Silencing Dissents and Political Opposition: On August 2020, the EZEMA party (unionist)

---

① Meto Obang (2018) Interview with the author 27th October. Addis Ababa, Ethiopia. Mr. Obang elevated SMNE movement from its predecessor Anuak Justice Council after he was provoked by the post-2005 political repression and his personal encounter with a taxi driver in Ethiopian corner of Washington DC agitated him as if Obang was not a mainstream Ethiopian. All of those incidents caused him to strive to prove "No one will be free until all are free" & "Humanity before Ethnicity" to be treatable only through "New Ethiopia".

announced that its members more than 32 are detained by the Gambella regional government. Despite the party made a good gesture to include native peoples from the region, it has become a victim of the dissent faced the regional government. Against the appeal to end intimidation of party members by forum of political parties through their "common code of conduct" the problem on dissenting thrives to be formidable challenges in inter-party relations. Silencing dissent was even worse for local parties such as Gambella People Movement for Justice, Peace, Freedom and Democracy[①]. Ironically enough, silencing dissent incentivizes neither for centering local nationalists nor parties and activist of Ethiopianism (Ethzema, 2020).

Overcoming Local Power Rivalry: The power rivalry in Gambella persisted in post 2018 political liberalization. As an informant share that "When Abiy came to power the ethnic entrepreneurs was mocking as Nuer resembles the looser Tigray and Anyua resembles the gainer Oromo". By way of giving an ethnic dimension of the 2019 power reshuffle among the ruling GPDM (Gambella Peoples Democratic Movement), an intra-party perception has built as Annya ethnic group dominates which eventually degenerated into rivalry through intra-ethnic cleavages within the party . At last, the regional president over reacts by incarcerating oppositions as for the alleged assassination attempt in August 2020[②] .

6.2 The Somali Region Case

The post 2018 political liberalization has helped the promising pacification of Somali regional politics. In the aftermath of the Abiy Ahmed ascent to power in April 2020 he made his first official trip to Somali region as a marker to end the two year long skirmishes on broader dispute. The informant discloses that.

"Initially Abiy made a good gesture to embrace the administration of Abdi Illey for which Abdi Illey reacted positively. Perhaps within the following day I saw Abay Tsehaye (TPLF old guard) with suspicious mission to abort Abiy's initiative through convincing Abdi Illey to remain rigid against the reform measures of Abiy. The outcome Abdi Illey's disagreement was bitter when he forcefully orchestrated a tragic violence through the aid of his Special forces and Heego."[③]

Restoration of Peace through Insurgent Local Nationalists: One can enumerate that the closure of Jail Ogaden (Grave Detention for Perceived ONLF), the welcoming of ONLF, ensuring border and regional security (Bedil , 2019). Right after their arrival to home, ONLF unequivocally praised the welcome and attributed the conciliatory/reformist tendency of PM Abiy Ahmed[④]. As a

① Interview with the Senior Party leader of "Gambella People Movement for Justice, Peace, Freedom and Democracy" on 28th Sept ember 2020.

② Ibid .

③ Interview with Elias Mohammed, a central committee of Prosperity Party and advisor to the Office of Somali Prospety Party, held in Addis Ababa on 13rd September 2020.

④ ONLF Official Website (Accessed 12 September 2020). It has to be recalled that ONLF signed a peace agreement with the government led by Prime Minister Abiy Ahmed in Asmara, Eritrea on October 21st, 2018.

clear gesture to loosen its previous hard line tendency, ONLF vowed to unilaterally declare cease fire. The post-2018 political liberalization bore fruit for the local politics in centering local nationalism. For the past two years, ONLF and The Somali Regional government led by Mustafa Omer held several talks on the regional affairs.

Short-lived Pseudo Local Nationalism: In august 2018, right before he was removed for Somali region presidency, Abdi Illey was provoking secession at the state legislature through intimidating the members to vote for his motion until his attempt was interrupted by the federal defense force①. His motion for secession was basing under the façade of the newly found Petroleum would make self-sufficient until aborted by the Defence forces. Notwithstanding with his stature as unreliable advocate of separatist actor unable to outmaneuver the reputation of ONLF, his alleged unilateral bid for succession doesn't meet any of Donald Horowitze's (1985: 285) prerequisite for succeeding in secession bid.

Post Abdi-Illey administration led by the Somali Democratic Party (later merged in Prosperity party) embraced "medemer" in full heart. As an informant disclosed that.

"Medemer has got an indigenous ground as the Somali proverb says 'IJJEG Handugha' (to connote 'the mutual pulling of two hands is a futile exercise'). Hence the only option for all of us is to appeal to the sub-ideals of medemer, i.e. to agglomerate, accumulate or collect"② (emphasis added).

In contrary to extremist's local nationalists, Mustafa made a different departure by way of marking centering local nationalism. By virtue of his progressively centrist tendency, he openly publicizd as he changed the victimhood narrative through his rhetoric that was challenged by Somali nationalists from both prosperity party and ONLF alike③. Accordingly, he often shared rhetorically the Somali people were mocked by previous elites by portraying Amhara as a historical enemy.

Correcting Divisive Decentralization: To the worst of its weakness, Abdi Illey introduced a decentralized governance without any prior study which ended up with 11 zones (third tier governance structure) and 100 woredas (fourth tier governance structure). An informant reveals that:

"The scheme was totally divisive. There were kebeles (fifth tier of governance) which were organized to administers 304 households illogically. At the same time there were kebeles which administer up to 1,500 households" (emphasis added).

The Abdi Illey's asymmetric local governance restructuring was deviant to what Aytenew

① Interview with Somali Prosperity Party representative and a senior politician from ONLF held in Addis Ababa in September 2020. It has to be recalled that right from his secession attempt his special forces entered into skirmishes which led to the death of 58 people, and the bodily of 266 people, the burning of churches by Heegoo and Abdi Illey's special forces until the federal forces stabilize the region in the following days and arrest in custody of Adbi Illey. By then, throughout the unrest Heego was observed publicly to raise up the flag of the greater Somali in the middle of JigJiga city as a unilateral declaration of Irredentism.

② Interview with Elias Mohammed, a central committee of Prosperity Party and advisor to the Office of Somali Prosperity Party, held in Addis Ababa on 13rd September 2020.

③ Interview with Somali Prosperity Party representative and a senior politician from ONLF held in Addis Ababa in September 2020.

(2014:322) characterized "decentralizing asymmetrically to manage ethnic diversity or administrative convenience". Therefore, as antidote to Abdi Illey' s divisive decentralization, Mustefa abolished the incorrect decentralized structure and revised the region to comprise 80 woredas and 9 zonal administration.

Trading-off Language Policy: In 2019 the announcement of the Education road map (Ministry of Education 2019) manifested body building exercise for local nationalism for various regions. Despite rejection by extreme local nationalists, Mustafa Omer contended that his administration would keep to teach Amharic language at the primary school within the bound of his region. Boldly, he justified " Teaching Amharic Language for Somali Children would eventually incentivizes our move for representation at the central government". This was remarkable for a very politicized contentious environment for revising language policy than ever before.

Negotiating the Electoral Constituency: In general, the Ethiopian electoral system and the electoral map has left the local nationalists to be cornered than moderated. An informant compares as follows.

"The fact that only 23 Somali elected representatives are arranged to represent in the House of Peoples Representatives makes the constituency below the general provisions of the electoral law' s provision of every representative covers a constituency of not more than 100,000 electorate."①

The fact that the electoral map is asymmetric to give a constituency for Tigray region by 38 elected representative to enter the parliament adds a salt for the discontent of Somali local nationalists. The skewed electoral map also persists after the recent liberalization just like what Beza Desalegn (2018) argued that the objection of the House of Federation to revise the map based on Census and population projects disadvantaged the Somali people. At last, the National Electoral Board of Ethiopia was subjected to reintroduce an electoral map which allotted more than 23 seats for Somali out of the total of 547 seats in the lower house-parliament but the remapping proposal still awaits the approval of the upper house.

Undoubtedly, the new proposal of revising the electoral map is intended to enhance better Somali representation as per their demographic dividend. Consequently enfranchising the Somali people to be represented by at least 55 elected representatives with fair share of electoral constituency will play role to center the polarized orientation of local nationalists② .

Negotiating the National Icons: On September 20th Mustafa had appeared on a sudden visit to one of the branch found in Jigjiga City (capital of Somali region) to commence the new national paper money introduced by the National Bank of Ethiopia and admonishing the latent departure of the money as the new money note contained the camel image which symbolized the pastoral community found in Afar and Somali. Ever since, it is not uncommon when the political pundits

---

① Interview with Elias Mohammed, a central committee of Prosperity Party and advisor to the Office of Somali Prospety Party, held in Addis Ababa on 13rd September 2020.

② Ibid.

and local nationalists lament on the exclusionary tendency of the money printed and the coin minted as a mere carrier of the dominant culture. For Marten Lutz and Kula Nancy C. (2008), through embracing cultural diversity via paper money carries far beyond economic value as an integrationist force for the nation (Somali Communication, 2020). In pursuant to Lutzetal (2008) the new national paper money is a recipe for the perceived lack of representation across many national frontiers.

Unhindered Demobilization and Reintegration Programs: Right after the pact with former insurgent groups such as ONLF, one of the agreements was to productively demobilize former ONLF insurgent and reintegrate them the job that seems half accomplished to the dismay of local nationalists. Though initially only 600 former were safely reintegrated to the Somali region special forces, the rest of demobs face again to the Somali government after seemingly wasting the 75 thousand birr per head which was intended to resort to peaceful life. As an ONLF informant disclosed that:

"With Struggle with meager resources, we finally seem to retain them by assigning some of the them as a full time cadre in our party structure from regional to woredas level. Otherwise, we fear they can be approached by extremist group such as AlShabab through capitalizing their resentment. We need to be cautious that the demobs didn't yet experienced a life other than warfare."①

In nutshell of successfully easing local nationalism and conflict transformation in Somali region, the attempt to reintegrate former ONLF combatants to pass the litmus test of what Philip Stibb (2012) qualified "challenges of demobilization and reintegration".

Balancing Inter-Party Relations: In favor of centering local nationalism, there is no moment than the past two years the relation between the Somali Prosperity party led by Mustefa Mohammed and ONLF has got peaceful and productive discourses. However some formidable challenges seem outstanding in which the regional government would not tolerate the party flag of ONLF through the regional party offices. Once Mustefa also alleged for labeling "ONLF is clan based entity" (Abdulahi, 2020) as retaliation ONLF defiance to Mustefa's replacement after the removal of Abdi Illey. For ONLF, In the recent days there is no way Ogaden connotes the clan rather the term evolved to represent the whole Somali ethnic group and at times appealed to unify the clannish divided society in their own way.

Managing Regional Diversity: Against the background of inability to fully materialize minority representation neither for the native marginalized groups (Bantu and Sheikash clans) nor for people from other regions, such as Amhara and Guraghe (Kefale, 2009), Mustefa Omer and oppositions vowel frequently to ensure better minority representation. As to Arendt Lijphart

① Interview with Hasen Malin, (Deputy Chairman ,ONLF and Office Head of Addis Ababa branch) held in Addis Ababa on 23rd Sept embtr 2020. The informant draws an analogy with how Oromo Liberation Army resorted to violence against the backdrop of the government that didn't keep its promise to reintegrate them. The informant believes that they escape the possibility of resorting to violence by former insurgents with a very small margin.

(1977) , such move towards consociation arrangements at the regional power sharing faced the dilemma of balancing the elites competition and demographic pressure.

7 Implications of Ethiopianist Narratives for Ending Crisis in Gambella & Somali Periphery

7.1 Gambella

Practically speaking, the discourse of Ethiopian nationalism is not alien to Gambella in so far as large numbers of Nuer and Anuak volunteered to fight in the Ethio-Eritrea war (Young, 1999; Feyissa, 2006).

The phenomenon of a Diaspora Anuak activist articulating an Ethiopianist narrative and the local Gambella peoples membership into unionist party such as EZEMA party is far from being a matter of an individual' s political positioning and belief. The instrumentalization of the Ethiopianist narrative and to dilute the perennial Anuak vs Nuer rivalry and positing it as an antidote debunks the assumption that automatically posits the Amhara and Tigray as the traditional sponsors and guardians of Ethiopian identity.

The rich resources in Gambella and its historical marginalization from the political center have allegedly facilitated corruption and embezzlement in the region in different forms.(Gebremedhin, 2017). Gambella' s experiences in this regard support the thesis articulated by Anwar Shah et al who argued that federal systems unless precautionary measures are in place, tend to be more susceptible to corruption (Shah and Boadaway, 2009). Against the aforementioned background, the political capital and potential inherent in the adoption of an Ethiopianist narrative by a famous political activist from Gambella should not be underestimated. The impact at its simplest could be twofold in that it could destabilize the binary divide between the Ethiopianist and ethno-nationalist narratives, and at the same time by bridging the divide between center and periphery reduce if not detering corruption and exploitation of the region' s resources.

The prosperity party prescribes medemer ideal, inter alia, a means to terminate clannish rivalry and relaxing extreme local nationalism. The Somali peoples predominantly engaged on pastoralism, traditionally a race to access to land mandatorily requires evoking one' s clan identity[①]. This is coterminous with what Ernest Gellner (1983) argued that nationalism is an exercise of pre-industrial society towards state formation.

7.2 Somali

In a similar observation with the aforementioned case of Gambella' s and Somali' s Mustefa cloaking towards centrist tendency could be treated as far beyond than individual affairs. Since

① Interview with Elias Mohammed, a central committee of Prosperity Party and advisor to the Office of Somali Prospety Party, held in Addis Ababa on 13rd September 2020.

he assumed the office of presidency of the Somali region it was not uncommon which punditsed speculate that he might one of the very few candidates who would ascend to deputy chairmanship of the Prosperity Party. Undeniably, his rhetoric was applauded among the Amhara elites(once perceived as dominant group) and other Ethiopianist camps.

Celebrating Victory Days at the Dismay of Local Nationalists: The Somali nationalists felt discontent when the government celebrated the Karamara victory in 2019 as a victory over Somali invaders in 1977 as opposed to the characterization of Karamara that was one of the latest national war, according to the Historian Gebru Tareke(2010), for which the whole country has entered in full scale. In informant pointed out as the government made a mistake to celebrate Karamara without assessing its meaning for the Somali context. He remembers, by then,

"Our brothers has fought against the Military government of Mengistu under the banner of WSLF. And our brothers too deserve celebration. As an exit, it would be one of the agenda to be discussed on national dialogue." ①

In the words of the informant we can note the following;

"the pro-unity camp, due to its excessive focus on unity and its negligence of ethnic rights, makes us despise the very idea of unity and Ethiopianism." ②

8 Conclusion

In Sum, for the political actors aspiring the end of the Gambella and Somali conflicted, it is high time to consider capitalizing on Ethiopianist seeds from the Gambella and Somali soil. Deductively, such a u-turn of nationalist narratives can be a beginning to an anti-dote for what Horowitze (1985) called "decentralized ethnic conflicts in Federal structure". In turn, it is a recipe for flattening the obstacle for democratic transition.

According to the conventional wisdom, the key weakness of most of the existing multi-national parties in Ethiopia is their weak social base amongst the non-Abyssinian peoples. Abiy Ahmed's medemer philosophy, the movement led by Gambella's Mr. Obang and the leadership style of Somali president — Musefa Omer is a welcome corrective to this situation and heralds the possibility of a multi-national Ethiopianist narrative and centering local nationalism. Ethiopianist political parties should furthermore consider expanding their membership and opening up their leadership to individuals from the historically marginalized regions. Also, the merger, alliances and principled divisions in local oppositions, capability to negotiate national icons, trading-off language policy, moderating historical injustice, negotiating electoral constituency determines the prospect of centering local nationalism. These steps will undoubtedly assist in healing the divide between competing and seemingly antagonistic narratives in Ethiopia and will also facilitate the democratic transition.

---

① Interview with Hasen Malin, (Deputy Chairman ,ONLF and Office Head of Addis Ababa branch) held in Addis Ababa on 23 Sept 2020.

② Ibid.

References

[1] LOVISE A. 2006. Ethnic federalism and self-determination for nationalities in a semi-authoritarian state: the case of Ethiopia. International Journal on Minority and Group Rights, 13(2/3): 243-261.

[2] AHMED A. 2019. Medemer. Los Angeles: Tsehai PubAalen, Lovise, lishers.

[3] ANDERSON B. 1983. Imagined communities: reflections on the origin and spread nationalism. London: Verso.

[4] ASFAW E. 2019. The role of non-state actors in Ethiopia' s political reform. Tianjin: Tianjin University of Technology and Education.

[5] AYTENEW Z. 2014. Local government in Ethiopia: advancing development and ethnic mianorities. Nomos Verlagsegesellschaft: Baden-Baden.

[6] DESALEGN B. 2018. Challenges of ethnic representation in Ethiopia and the need for reform[J].Mizan Law Review, 12 (1):1-28.

[7] FEYISSA D. 2006. Decentralization as ethnic Closure, with special reference to declining negotiated access to natural resources in Western Ethiopia. Africa Development Special Issue: Decentralization and Livelihood in Africa, 31(2): 243-260.

[8] FUCHS C. 2020. Communication and capitalism: a critical theory. London: University of Westminster Press.

[9] GEBREWOLD B. 2009. Ethiopian nationalism: an ideology to transcend all odds. Africa Spectrum, 44 (1): 79-97.

[10] GELLNER E. 1983. Nations and nationalism, Oxford: Blackwell.

[11] GUDINA M. 2004. The state, competing ethnic nationalisms and democratisation in Ethiopia. African Journal of Political Science / Revue Africaine de Science Politique, 9(1): 27-50.

[12] HUNTINGTON S. 1991. Third wave of democracy: democratization in the late Twentieth Century. London: University of Oklahoma Press.

[13] HOROWTIZE D. 1984. Ethnic groups in conflict. Berkeley: University of California Press.

[14] KEFALE A. 2009. Federalism and ethnic conflict in ethiopia: a comparative study of the Somali and benishangul-gumuz regions. Netherlands: University of Leiden.

[15] LIJPHART A. 1977. Democracy in plural societies: a comparative exploration. New Haven and London: Yale University Press.

[16] MARKAKIS J. 2010. Ethiopia: the last two frontiers. London: James Currey Publisher.

[17] MARTEN L, KULA N C. 2008. Meanings of money: national identity and the semantics of currency in Zambia and Tanzania. Journal of African Cultural Studies , 20(2): 183-198.

[18] MINISTRY OF EDUCATION. 2019. Ethiopian education development roadmap (2018-2030)：an integrated executive summary. Addis Ababa: Ministry of Education.

[19] RUSTOW D. 1970. Transitions to democracy: toward a dynamic model. Comparative Politics , 2 (3): 337-363.

[20] JOIREMAN S, THOMAS S. 1997. Identifying potential ethnic conflicts. New York: Rand Corporation.

[21] TAREKE G. 2009. The Ethiopian revolution: war in the Horn of Africa. London: Yale University Press.

[22] Tronvoll K B. 2011. The Ethiopian 2010 federal and regional elections: reestablishing the one-party state. African Affairs, 110(438): 121-136.

[23] Vaughan S. 2006. Ethnicity and power in Ethiopia. Edinburgh: University of Edinburgh.

[24] SWAYNE H. 1903. Seventeen trips through Somaliland and a visit to Abyssinia. London: Rowland Ward.

[25] Shah A, Robin B. 2009. Fiscal federalism: principles and practices of multi order governance. Cambridge: Cambridge University Press.

[26] Young J. 1999. Along Ethiopia's western frontier: Gambella and Benishangul in transition. The Journal of Modern African Studies, 37 (2): 321-346.

[27] YUSUF S. 2020. Constitutional design options for Ethiopia: Managing ethnic divisions. Johannesburg: Institute of Security Studies.

[28] ABDULAHI H B. 2020. An Ogadeni feud and Somali folktale. https://www.ethiopia-insight.com/2020/05/10/an-ogadeni-feud-and-somali-folktale.

[29] BADEL A, MOHAMED-TAQWIM. 2020. Somali Region's two years of transition: successes and shortcomings. https://addisstandard.com/viewpoint-somali-regions-two-years-of-transition-successes-and-shortcomings/.

[30] BONSA J. 2017. History repeating itself in the Horn of Africa: is the crime in Darfur being replicated in eastern and southern Oromia Regional State of Ethiopia? https://addisstandard.com/analysis-history-repeating-horn-africa-crime-darfur-replicated-eastern-southern-oromia-regional-state-ethiopia/.

[31] FUKUYAMA F.2018. Can liberal democracies survive identity politics. https://www.economist.com/open-future/2018/09/30/can-liberal-democracies-survive-identity-politics.

[32] KEFFYALEW G. 2017. Gambella's failed commercial agriculture & Tigrean investors. https://ethiopiaobservatory.com/2017/01/02/gambellas-failed-commercial-agriculture-tigrean-investors-tplf-nepotism-lawlessness-corruption-sebhat-nega-rooting-for-land-grabbers-unequalethiopianity-is-the-challenge-in-2017-pa/.

[33] BORKENA. 2018. Gambella region president Gatluak Tut resigned, says EPRDF. https://www.borkena.com/2018/10/25/gambella-region-president-gatluak-tut/.

[34] LEFORT R. 2018. Pacified politics or risk of disintegration? a race against Ethiopia. open democracy. https://www.opendemocracy.net/ren-lefort/pacified-politics-or-risk-dis-

integration-race-against-time-in-ethiopia.
[35] MOHAMED-TAQWIM B. 2019. Somali region's two years of transition: successes and shortcomings. https://addisstandard.com/viewpoint-somali-regions-two-years-of-transition-successes-and-shortcomings/.
[36] PHILIP S. 2012. Challenges to disarmament, demobilisation and reintegration. https://www.e-ir.info/pdf/26301.

埃塞俄比亚女性主义思潮发展历程与影响

李炜婷

摘要:虽然女性主义最早被认为起源于西方国家,是西方国家女性民主意识的觉醒,但是对于非西方国家的女性而言,女性解放运动往往是"被隐藏起来的历史",就一些非西方地区和国家而言,一定程度上来说女性主义已经以某种形式存在了,甚至有的部落仍旧保持着母系社会的制度,只是没有形成像西方国家成体系的理论和派别。然而从宏观角度来看,女性主义思潮在这些地区仍旧局限于非主流群体内,尤其对于埃塞俄比亚(简称"埃塞")这一高度宗教化的国家来说,现任领导人在女性问题上所做的改革未能彻底改变埃塞俄比亚大众女性的地位和生存情况,可以说是"精英层面的实验",女性主义思潮仍旧被视为是对传统文化和宗教教条的冲击。

关键词:埃塞俄比亚;女性主义;思潮

一、埃塞俄比亚的女性主义思潮的发展历程

非洲国家的女性主义运动与西方国家在一定程度上具有相似性,但更多的是差异性。从一些斗争目标来看,比如女性参政权或者女性实现个体自由等具体权利方面一致;但是在宏观层面上的运动属性、运动目标和具体背景等方面差异较大。对于西方国家来说,女性主义运动相对独立;而非洲国家的女性主义与民族主义密切相关,通常依附或从属于民族主义。非洲的女性主义运动在19世纪初的殖民统治时期就已经出现,她们是反抗殖民统治与奴役的先驱,例如尼日利亚的伊格博与伊比比奥族(Igbo and Ibibio)妇女战争,但是没有形成女性主义运动体系,非洲女性更偏向于在男性主导的团体中发挥作用,或者是参加男性主导的民族主义斗争,被笼罩于非洲国家民族主义构建的框架之下,而非自发组织起来为性别平等和女性权益而奋斗。因此,从某一程度上可以解释为什么非洲国家在国家独立或者民族解放时并没有形成两性平等的社会,即便是社会主义国家,也未能实现女性解放——非洲的女性主义仍旧是民族主义主导,根本出发点在于国家利益与政党形象以稳定社会,并非从女性的角度出发。

从非洲大陆这一大背景看,大部分国家的女性主义所奋斗的目标偏向于马克思主义女性主义的主张,指导精神更偏向于后殖民主义,更加力图从西方的理论体系和影响中划分出来,建立属于非洲语境的女性主义。津巴布韦女性主义学者 Shereen Essof 的观点就是偏后殖民主义的例子,她曾表示女性主义是西方国家的舶来品,并非源于非洲,也并没有扎根于非洲,而且是一种"资产阶级"现象,对于非洲女性来说"没有实际的价值或意义"。当"第一世界"女性为社会权益、政治权利和性别歧视作斗争时,往往忽视了"第三世界"地区的女

性的处境。她们不仅需要为其自身争取经济、教育、社会和政治权利，除此之外更需要与西方殖民残余的殖民统治与当地根深蒂固的传统宗教和文化抗争。对于女性主义在非西方地区的发展，必须承认“种族、阶级和文化上的差异”，非洲的女性主义与西方的女性主义不同，所关注的是“面包、黄油和权利”问题。西方国家女性不必争取与男性平等的受教育权，并且具有经济自由与经济活动权利，不存在“满足温饱”的就业问题。但是在非洲大部分国家，女性仍旧缺乏教育，弱势就业群体庞大，有的地区仍旧需要与割礼和童婚等问题作斗争。尼日利亚女性学者 Amina Mama 指出，非洲女性不需要照搬西方的女性主义，我们可以引入这一精神，然后将这种精神变成我们的，变成具有非洲意义的女性主义——这就意味着非洲女性需要从本就较为脆弱的女性主义基础上发展适合非洲语境的女性主义。因此，非洲的女性主义发展不仅要关注自身，更要与西方的外来价值观进行界限划分，强调个体差异，使得女性主义在非洲国家发展面临基础薄弱与推进艰难的问题。

埃塞俄比亚的女性主义较非洲其他国家来说，具有较高的教育水平和组织度，但其运动的最终目标是服务于政党，无法脱离宗教文化，成为隐形的存在。由于殖民主义的迫害和父权制宗教的引入，使得原本就游离在社会文化边缘的女性更加被排挤在资源之外，缺乏系统的教育，因此女性主义运动在非洲其他被殖民国家的组织性不高，更易被传统父权势力熄灭。与非洲其他国家不同的是，埃塞俄比亚是唯一一个没有被殖民主义浸染过的国家（除了被意大利侵略的短暂时期以外），因此殖民主义在埃塞俄比亚遗留的毒害和宗教迫害程度较低。20 世纪 70 年代的以学生为代表发起的女性主义运动就展现了较高的教育水平和组织纪律。但是当时埃塞的女性主义者始终无法脱离政党的影响，最终是为其政党上台而服务，从而限制了其发展，也未能真正实现女性解放与独立。在早期的神话传说和王朝统治中，不乏精英女性统治者和军队领导者，但由于后来父权制宗教的引入，导致女性的地位与古代截然相反。包括近代历史上有若干个女性组织成立并且在当时的时代背景下发挥了女性的力量——武装部队妻子协会和埃塞俄比亚女青年基督教会（Armed Forces Wives Association and the Ethiopian Young Women’s Christian Association）、埃塞俄比亚妇女福利协会（Ethiopian Women’s Welfare Association）等，但是在文献和历史记载中几乎没有任何研究，埃塞学者 Abraha Girmay 就曾表示，女性在埃塞历史上对国家的建设、发展和民主化进程中发挥了很大作用，但这些作用都被埋没，变成了无形的存在。比如埃塞历史上著名的阿达瓦战役，女性就在这场战役的前线与后方发挥了至关重要的作用，但这些被湮没在对领导战役和参加战役的男性的描述之中。因此，父权制宗教的引入是埃塞乃至大部分非洲国家女性被贬低的主要原因，被排挤的社会活动导致女性的低教育程度，而低程度的受教育水平又直接导致非洲国家女性运动的低成效，但是埃塞较高教育水平的女性主义运动在父权制思想和政党控制的双重枷锁下也未能真正解决女性问题。

（一）埃塞俄比亚的古代女性统治者

在埃塞早期历史记载中可见的女性形象都为少数的统治者或精英层面，并没有描述大众女性或者普遍意义的“女性”文献，并且当时的社会情况缺乏文书记载，多为世代相传的口述历史和神话传说。这些精英女性有的作为直接统治者或者其男性后代的摄政者统治国家或者国家的部分地区，有的率领军队解决国家冲突，即便在后来以男性为中心的主要社会话语系统中,也将这些女性描述为“能干的、有影响力的统治者”,勇敢又能武,经常指挥军队作战。有相关文献记载在整个非洲都存在母系社会,女性可以当选酋长与争夺统治权。最早古时的埃塞统治者也为女性,其中在 *Kebra Nagast*(ክብረ ነገሥት),或称《国王的荣耀》(*Glory of the Kings*)神话中的示巴女王(Queen of Sheba 或 Makeda)就是具有代表性的一位。示巴女王定居在厄立特里亚海岸,是当时的“埃塞俄比亚”的统治者。在她访问以色列的时候,皈依了以色列国王所罗门的犹太教,并且与国王结婚,婚后生有一子 Menelik I(也称“Ibn-al Malik”,意为“国王之子”)。之后当孟尼利克一世回去探望父亲时“将圣柜偷回埃塞俄比亚”。自这次事件以后,国王宣布只有他的直系男性后裔才拥有王位继承权和国家统治权。这一条法规在历史中的实行情况没有详细记载,但是即便如此,国家统治权仍未被男性垄断,在此之后依旧有女性统治或摄政国家。

当时的女性领导者不仅有卓越的领导统治力,更有向权威挑战和独立思考的能力,甚至能够向宗教挑战。如 Falasha 族领袖的女儿 Judith 王后,有传说她在杀死了当时的皇帝后篡位,统治了埃塞俄比亚将近 40 年的时间。在其统治期间,她几乎将统治范围内的基督教毁灭,后来的基督教教士和作家将其描述成“恶魔”和“反基督的叛乱者”。从一定程度上来讲,当时女性的绝对地位并非女性主义的作用,而是在当时的社会背景之下,女性与男性之间并不存在差异,是否有能力领导或者统治决定于个体,而非性别,因此也就不存在女性主义之说。

(二)泰图皇后的女性主义先河

除了以上民间和神话传说中寥寥几位女性统治者或领导者的描述以外,埃塞历史上对于与女性相关的记载和研究少之又少,这也间接地反映了埃塞从历史上便存在深刻的父权制思想,因此若要研究埃塞女性是从何时开始处于被压迫和奴役的状态,可以说无从考究。由于父权制宗教的介入和统治,女性便被压迫与无视。自确立东正教成为埃塞的政治宗教与阿姆哈拉民族的统治地位确立时期,就是女性受压迫之时。阿姆哈拉文化极度推崇等级制度、崇尚权威,而在这一社会等级制度中,女性身处最低一级,男性对于女性来说即是“绝对权威”;无独有偶,父权制思想的宗教文化更加剧了这一观念。

在埃塞的女性主义历史中,首次出现争取女性权益的是泰图皇后,从一定程度上来说,泰图皇后开启了埃塞女性主义的先河。从客观角度来看,泰图皇后的一些政策和行为虽然不是以保障女性利益为目的,仍旧是从巩固国家权力的角度出发,并且具有一定的争议性;但是不可否认她先导性的做法的确符合女性主义的一些理论与精神。由于她没有自己的孩子,于是通过安排亲戚或者表兄妹的婚姻,利用他们与其他统治者建立联盟。她会毫不犹豫地强迫解除稳定的婚姻,或强迫她的亲属离婚并与她选择的女子或男子再婚。虽然这一做法在后来被认为是利用婚姻作为巩固权力的牺牲品,但是考虑到当时的社会背景,没有稳定的国家环境便没有稳定的家庭环境,因此某些程度上来说这一行为可以理解。

虽然具有一些争议性做法,但是泰图皇后对于婚姻和女性教育方面提出的一些主张确是女性主义的先驱。首先是她对于女性婚姻改革的主张。由于埃塞根深蒂固和非常普遍的童婚文化习俗,婚姻总是由父母和 / 或亲属在双方不知道的情况下进行安排。她从与外国女性的接触中观察到,婚前男女双方相识相知的过程很重要,有利于婚后的感情发展,她提出这种方式应该在埃塞俄比亚复制；同样，女性在离婚后应该获得离婚赔偿金。其次，她意识到了女童教育的必要性，于 1907 年 10 月发表的一份公告中谏言皇帝将女童教育纳入教育体系之中。虽然泰图皇后的这些主张在当时的世代背景下具有异常的超前性，但是这些主张没有被真正实施，童婚依旧延续，并且在公告发布后依旧没有女童接受教育。种种迹象表明，泰图皇后开始思考许多与女性有关的问题，但是可能缺乏能力或条件来进一步解决这些问题。

（三）海尔·塞拉西（Haile Selassie）时期的女性主义

在海尔·塞拉西时期，外敌的入侵使得女性开始自发组织在一起并进行抗战活动。这些协会由受过教育的精英女性主导，发起的活动和协会组织目的也主要与自身权益相关。在 20 世纪 30 年代之前，海尔·塞拉西（Haile Selassie）皇帝禁止埃塞任何形式的政治和民间组织活动，他对社会中任何有组织的团体都非常警惕，担心他们会演变成一种竞争性的政治力量。但随着 1935 年意大利入侵威胁的逼近，导致社会民间一些协会相继成立，如埃塞俄比亚红十字会（Ethiopian Red Cross Society）和埃塞俄比亚爱国协会（Ethiopian Patriotic Association）。在这些协会中，精英妇女（主要是来自皇室女性，如海尔·塞拉西皇帝的女儿）主动成立了自己的女性分支机构。他们的主要目的是动员女性参加即将到来的抗意卫国战争。Tenagnewerq 公主（海尔·塞拉西皇帝的女儿之一）成为协会的名誉主席。Tsehai 公主于 1935 年在其母亲 Empress Menen 的支持下，发起了第一个全国性的妇女组织，称为“埃塞俄比亚妇女志愿服务协会”（Ethiopian Women’s Volunteer Service Association），第二次世界大战后，其名称改为埃塞俄比亚妇女工作协会（Ethiopian Women’s Work Association, EWWA)。这一协会同样也是鼓励女性从事与战争有关的活动。尽管这是当时“较为先进”的女性组织，鼓励女性从家庭中走出来，仿佛有自由主义的味道，但它没有强调女性的问题，也没有努力改善女性的权利。由于这些协会通常由皇室成员建立或领导，因此所成立的协会不仅没有挑战皇帝的法律和政策，更没有激发女性的政治意识或鼓励女性领导，只是停留在给予女性微弱的“自由活动”与“参与感”的表面，实质依旧是利用女性为皇室与国家政治服务。

（四）学生运动与女性主义

随着马克思列宁主义的传播和受教育群体的增加以及学生运动的快速发展，使得社会开始公开表达对政治统治和社会问题的不满，比如民众的弱势地位和人对人的剥削、教会对人的迫害和剥削等。学生运动的积极发展可以说标志着埃塞马克思主义女性主义思潮的广泛蔓延，并形成具有代表性的激进运动，是埃塞女性主义发展的一个重要的里程碑，受过高等教育的女学生开始在社团与社会中发挥其重要作用。在 20 世纪 50 年代，开始有女性学生能够进入高等教育学府的大门：1954—1955 年，有 5 名女学生；到 1960 年，有 40 名女学生；1960—1970 年，接受高等教育的女性人数进一步增加到 356 人。随着 20 世纪 60 年代末埃塞学生运动激进化，当时的男性学生认为女性同学被学校行政部门误导并故意保持无知状态，不能成为他们运动斗争的有力参与者，因此他们发起了一场“反对无知和剥削的斗争”，鼓励女学生“抛弃旧的观念和价值观，以适应 20 世纪埃塞俄比亚的要求”。男学生鼓励女学生参与社会变革运动的意识培养过程极大地助长了一些女学生的激进行为，亚的斯亚贝巴大学学生会（University Students Union of Addis Ababa，USUAA）在竞选演讲中也谈到了“解放女性”的事业，敦促女性为自己的解放而斗争。这导致这些女学生更加积极地参与各种学校和社会活动，其中活跃的代表性人物如Martha Mebratu，她在与当时激进的埃塞俄比亚学生运动的其他革命成员一起劫持一架埃塞俄比亚客机的过程中被埃塞俄比亚政府军杀害。她在劫机事件的前一天留下了一条信息（写于1972年12月7日），后来被称为“玛莎宣言”（The Martha Manifesto）。与此同时，前往其他国家学习的埃塞留学生在20世纪60年代成立了各种学生组织，例如欧洲埃塞俄比亚学生会（Ethiopian Student Union in Europe，ESUE）和北美埃塞俄比亚学生会（Ethiopian Student Union in North America，ESUNA）。同埃塞国内一样，这些海外的学生组织了不同主题的学习小组，如国家问题研究小组、妇女问题研究小组、青年问题研究小组、土地分配问题研究小组等。正是国内外学生的活跃，使得女性问题在这一时期开始被作为一项较为独立的问题对待。

可以说埃塞的女性主义开始向前推进与学生的活跃运动关系紧密，而学生们大多受到马克思列宁主义的社会主义思潮影响。许多在国外留学的埃塞学生也将西方的女性主义思想带回了埃塞，但没有相关文献说明这些留学生曾经在其所在国家参加过女性主义运动或有过相关活动的经验，因此由学生发起的女性主义运动缺乏组织性与可持续性，女性主义思潮依旧没有在埃塞本土广泛传播。当时，所有关于社会主义国家女性解放的主张都集中于将她们从剥削性劳动中解放出来，并引导她们从事另一种没有剥削的劳动形式。其目的不是将女性从劳动力中剔除，而是将劳动力的政治观点从资本主义转变为社会主义。受这一理论影响，当时的女性主义将两性不平等问题全部归于“阶级”，急迫地希望将女性从经济压迫和人身自由方面解放出来，但是未能看清埃塞女性问题的根本原因在于父权制的意识形态，当时学生认为独立对待的女性问题，仍旧是困于政党之争和国家政治改革的框架下，这一时代背景下的女性更偏向于“政党分子”，而非“女性主义者”，因此也未能真正解决女性受压迫的源头问题。

（五）德格政权下的女性主义

20世纪70年代初，埃塞的政治过渡标志着君主制度的瓦解和社会变革时代的开始，从理想层面上来说，若是在变革时期能够针对女性问题进行一些改革或者行动，那么也许女性问题会比现今的实际情况有所提升。但是埃塞的女性问题并没有乘上这一“东风”，军事政权以国家控制限制了女性任何争取自身解放的空间或自由。德格政权虽然宣扬社会主义大旗进行土地所有权改革，女性第一次被写入埃塞的法律之中也是在德格政权期间（1987年的《德格政权宪法》规定女性在各个层面都享有平等的权利，包括经济、政治和社会层面）；但其中央集权统治未曾改变埃塞深刻的等级制度，进一步加深了阿姆哈拉文化的统治地位——于1987年的宪法中规定阿姆哈拉语为官方语言。其间的“红色恐怖”更是将女性解放问题彻底扼杀，“仅仅知道如何阅读和写作以及年龄在20岁或20岁以下就足以定义潜在的或积极的‘反革命’。当局甚至制定了一项法律，授权逮捕8至12岁的儿童”，这意味着包括许多女性在内的整整一代埃塞俄比亚知识分子被消灭。“红色恐怖”成功地将女性，甚至有革命精神的男性置于国家控制之下。巨大的恐惧在埃塞人民心中烙下了深刻的创伤，一些原本活跃的女性主义运动成员也不得不放弃自己的事业，到国外寻求庇护，再也不敢采取任何形式的活动或者发表任何的个人言论。德格政权期间，在国家指导和管控下建立了一个埃塞俄比亚革命妇女协会（Revolutionary Ethiopian Women's Association，REWA）。该协会的目标群体是 15 岁以上的女性，并且有具体的任务和目标，而这些任务和目标与女性解放和促进她们的利益无关，目的是教育她们并向她们灌输国家的政治意识形态——当被教育的女性返回家庭后，能够向她们的孩子进行再教育，从而让被灌输的意识形态以家庭为单位进行传播，另外就是提高女性的经济生产活跃度，并且建立考勤登记系统。

在德格政权期间，这一协会使得埃塞的女性第一次有机会组织起来，并且跨越文化和民族的界限，其影响也并非全部都是负面的，就积极影响来看，许多女性因为加入协会而学习了基础的阅读书写能力，协会一定程度上培训了女性的职业能力，有的女性甚至后来创办了属于自己的企业；但该协会建立的初衷决定了负面影响大于积极影响。例如，由于埃塞当时处于与叛乱分子和游击队持续作战的状态，因此急需物资和食物。在 REWA 的领导下，埃塞的所有女性承担了向政府民兵提供食物、干粮等物资补给的责任，并规定了配额和配给量，这一强制性要求迫使女性不仅要在家庭中承担家务劳动，还要额外担负物资补给的配额量。另外，虽然女性在一定程度上接受了最基础的教育，但是教育女性的最终目标依旧是服务于政党，因为她们能够阅读竞选材料和政治口号或法令，当教育程度满足政党需求后，后续教育便无关紧要，另外 REWA 也从未向传统的陋习提出质疑或尝试改变。

德格政权对女性生活的专制和集中控制的程度可以被定义为一种新的剥削形式，完全服务于德格政权的政治意识形态，而这种意识形态也远非任何形式的社会主义。“解放女性”仅仅是一个由独裁者塑造的政治工具，并由 REWA 进行控制与监督。虽然其打着“没有妇女就没有革命”等社会主义口号，但是政府的 20 名部长中没有女性，只有 1 名女性副部长。女性组织在德格政权下未能延续学生运动掀起的浪潮，也失去了其独立性，中央集权统治对埃塞的女性主义套上了沉重的枷锁，埃塞女性的基础生存条件与被父权制排挤的现实并没有得到任何改善，所有“善待”也都只是表面文章，实则是统治者新的控制方式。

（六）埃塞俄比亚联邦民主共和国与女性主义

1991 年德格政权垮台后不久，埃塞俄比亚新政府批准了一项国家妇女政策，并设立了妇女事务办公室（Women Affairs Office，WAO）。最高级别的 WAO 隶属于总理办公室，联邦一级的每个政府部门中都有 WAO。此外，权力下放的国家还允许设立地区妇女局，并赋予其宪法授权。但是同样的，新政府下的女性问题仍旧无法逃脱一直以来的宿命，成立的 WAO 面临预算和资源不足的问题，有的甚至没有办公空间和相应的办公设施，她们只不过是埃革阵（EPRDF）的政治和体制结构中“考虑女性问题”的一种象征性姿态。不过可以肯定的是，自向正式民主政治体制过渡以来，在埃塞俄比亚的确出现了一些女性民间社会组织。埃塞俄比亚女律师协会（Ethiopian Women Lawyers Association，EWLA）是这些团体中第一个建立的，同时也是最著名的。EWLA 是一个非营利性宣传团体，由一群女律师于 1995 年创立，旨在通过法律制度捍卫女性权利，提高公众对女性困境的认识,并致力于促进两性平等的改革,其成员已扩大到法律领域以外的其他专业的男女,专业成员约有 300 人。总部设在亚的斯亚贝巴,并设有 6 个分支机构。其官方发布的组织宗旨是:

“促进女性的经济、政治和社会权利,并为此协助她们得到《埃塞俄比亚联邦民主共和国宪法》和相关人权公约赋予她们的权利。”

EWLA 有一系列的活动,并与许多不同的团体合作,成员们不仅向贫困女性提供法律援助,而且还通过各种培训举措努力提高女性认知,包括开展埃塞女性问题研究,进行法律援助和游说大众女性等。自成立以来, EWLA 进行了若干项研究,涵盖了影响女性及其权利的大多数法律。其研究侧重于“有害传统习俗”等问题,以及联邦修订的《家庭法》对女性权利的影响。1996 年, EWLA 向联邦和地区立法机构提交了《家庭法》修正案草案,但直到 2000 年 7 月才最终颁布了新的《家庭法》。

然而,在 2005 年全国大选之后,梅莱斯·泽纳维(Meles Zenawi)总理几乎立即通过了一项禁止所有公众集会和示威的禁令,并且通过了一项新的法律,即《慈善机构和社团登记和管理公告》(*The Proclamation for the Registration and Regulation of Charities and Societies*),将海外捐款占其预算 10% 以上的民间社会组织归类为“国际”非政府组织。法律确定了非政府组织不能开展工作的领域,其中之一就是性别问题。EWLA 已被执政党重新定位为一个政治威胁,可能是因为它直言不讳地批评现行立法,并质疑执政政权对保护女性权利的承诺。由此,埃塞的女性主义组织发展又再一次被执政党所遏制。

虽然阿比上台后,颁布了具有历史变革性的女性政策——其内阁成员 50% 为女性,但是正如 Jon Abbink 所说的,“埃塞俄比亚的政治文化还没有摆脱其专制主义、精英统治和庇护的历史遗留……政治制度被重新构建,成为一种回归旧模式的新世袭治理……”纵观女性主义在埃塞的发展历程,无一不是被镇压在执政党与父权制文化之下,形式主义的女性政策始终无法从政党利益中分离开来。阿比领导下的新政府是否能改变一直以来的女性主义“梦魇”,能够切实地从大众女性的权益和待遇角度出发改善性别不平等的问题,并且能够从精英女性层面延伸至大众女性层面,而不仅仅是利用女性问题建立政党形象,一切都需要时间和具体事件来进一步验证。

二、埃塞俄比亚的女性问题现状

目前,埃塞俄比亚政府已经加以重视女性问题及倡导性别平等,特别是在政治赋权方面;同时一些地区相应实施了一系列有利于女性发展的项目,例如在应聘条件同等的情况下优先录取女性;也有一系列的政府及非政府组织来维护和推动女性权益及地位,外界各国际组织也对埃塞的女性问题给予格外关注,例如联合国妇女署、联合国儿童基金会、联合国教科文组织等。但是埃塞具有以男性为中心的社会文化传统,这种文化导致女性从历史上来说更类似于“男性附属品”。虽然女性现已登上了政治舞台,种种权益也较之前有了保障,但从实际情况上来说,发达城市与农村地区之间发展不均衡,埃塞较欠发达地区的女性地位仍旧较低、宗教化程度深,其中主要体现在较高层次的受教育机会和社会经济地位,经济地位和经济能力的低下决定了女性在社会层面以及家庭层面的低决策权。另外,埃塞女性还在人权保护、教育培训以及就业等方面面临一系列的问题。

（一）性别平等综合表现提升，但主要由于“政治赋权”“一家独大”

世界经济论坛发布的《2020年全球性别差距报告》中显示，埃塞在性别平等问题方面做出了一定的努力，在所有被调查统计的153个国家中，埃塞俄比亚综合指数排名第82，相较于2006年首次实施调查的100名有了较大改善。但从细化的具体数字来看，可以说埃塞性别差距指数的提升与其国家内女性参政从政率等政治赋权方面的提高呈正向关联。女性的政治赋权指数从2006年的61名跃至2020年的16名，说明女性在埃塞政治体制内的参与度有了绝对性的提升，这在非洲地区国家之中独树一帜。然而若从经济与教育等民生和基本权利方面来看，埃塞女性与男性相比仍旧处于较弱势状态。女性在受教育度方面与男性相差较远，主要表现在初等教育之后的阶段；进而再观察女性在社会生产活动中的活跃度与参与度发现，虽然女性的受教育程度低于男性，但仍旧保持着与男性基本相同程度的活跃度与参与度。就业者在市场中的就业情况与其受教育背景息息相关，女性较低的受教育程度与较高的经济生产参与率一定程度上说明女性大多参与的是较低层次的体力劳动或回报率和稳定性较低的工作，经济地位和经济能力的弱势又会衍生出在其家庭内较低决策权的问题。

（二）社会精英层面与优质资源利用方面依旧为男性主导

埃塞男性与女性人口数量基本持平，且劳动力占总人口的比重也几乎相同，结合表1的细化数据来看，女性的经济参与度为77%，几乎与男性的87.8%持平，这一指数在全球范围内也处于较前的排名（52名）。但若同时横向与其他指数进行对比参照来看，埃塞女性的高经济参与度与活跃度并没有为她们带来同等效益的经济收入和社会经济地位，女性多从事兼职工作（见图1）和非正式工作，在社会层次较高的政府官员级别和管理层，女性数量仅为男性的一半；在公司创业等方面，女性所有权或女性为主要管理层的数量分别只有16.5%和4.5%。尤其是在专业技术方面，埃塞女性从业者占比名次在153个国家中排名129，说明所谓的社会精英层依旧为男性所主导，女性在专业技术方面获得的机会与教育程度远不及男性。在受教育程度方面，综合指数为0.850，排名在140名，说明男女受教育均等方面存在严重不平衡现象。但其子条目显示，初等教育和中等教育阶段，男女比例较为平均，主要影响平均指数的是高等教育阶段，女性所接受的高等教育占比还不及男性的一半。综合女性在经济层面与教育层面的相关数据来看，在基础阶段，埃塞女性和男性所享机会较为平均，然而上升到较高一层便出现严重分化，例如女性在大量从事经济活动，但较高层次和专业的社会职位均以男性为主（主要因为女性的较低教育程度决定了其工作的层面较低，无法进入到精英层）；女性虽然在基础教育阶段与男性享有同等机会，但上升至高等教育阶段，接受高等教育的女性远远少于男性（主要因为女性较男性有较高的辍学率，一部分是因为家庭经济条件不支持，一部分是因为有的女性选择结婚生子照顾家庭）。因此，从一定程度上来说，埃塞的社会经济与教育的优质资源依旧主要由男性占有。

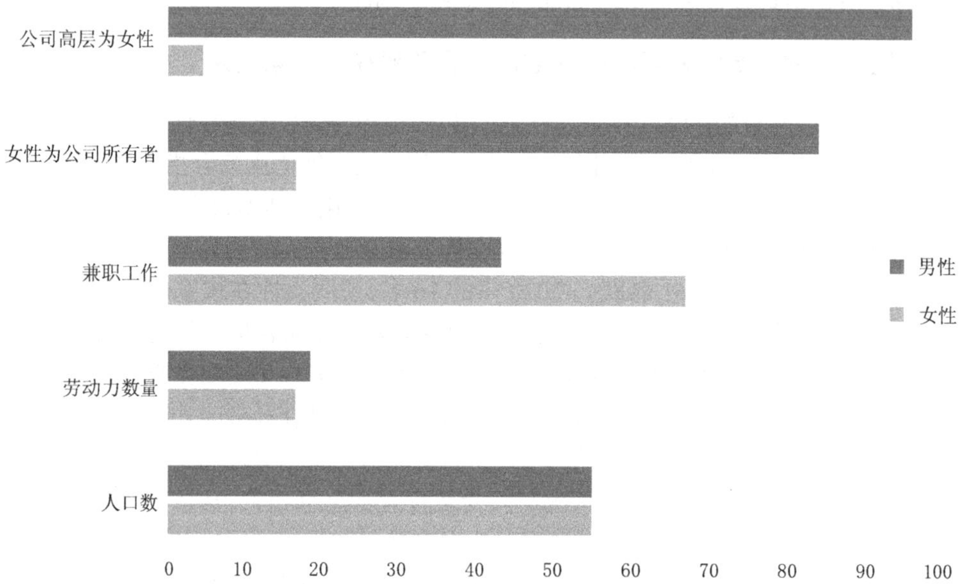

图 1 埃塞俄比亚女性与男性劳动工作情况

* 表格来源:根据世界经济论坛(World Economic Forum)《2020 全球性别差距报告》数据整理而得

表 1 《2020 年全球性别差距报告》中埃塞俄比亚国别细化指数

	排名	得分	女性	男性
经济活动参与	125	0.568	—	—
劳动力参与率(%)	52	0.877	77.0	87.8
立法委员、高级官员及管理层占比(%)	103	0.361	26.5	73.5
专业技术人员(%)	129	0.484	32.6	67.4
受教育程度	140	0.850	—	—
识字率(%)	135	0.750	44.4	59.2
初等教育入学率(%)	135	0.928	81.5	87.7
中等教育入学率(%)	120	0.968	30.3	31.3
高等教育入学率(%)	141	0.483	5.3	10.9
政治赋权	16	0.427	—	—
议会女性占比(%)	21	0.633	38.8	61.2
部长级女性占比(%)	11	0.908	47.6	52.4

* 表格来源:世界经济论坛(World Economic Forum)

(三)埃塞俄比亚女性的政治赋权提升

埃塞的第一个议会于 1931 年建立,当时的参议院和众议院都是由男性成员组成,女性不仅不可能成为议员,更无法参与政治活动。德格政权时期,虽然给予了女性一些政治权利,一定程度上将女性的政治赋权纳入宪法体系中,但范围和程度具有局限性,女性仍旧被排除在主流政治体系以外。女性的政治赋权的明显提升阶段是在1991年埃塞过渡政府(The Transitional Government of Ethiopia Charter)时期,在该过渡政府下建立的下议院中,26名成员中有3名为女性,可以说是埃塞女性赋权问题上具有历史性的时间节点。除此之外还颁布了国家妇女政策(1993年),并建立妇女相关事宜的部门(Women's Affairs Offices, WAO),且州级别的政府下也成立了相应级别的具有宪法赋权的妇女事务办公室。埃革阵一直以来在女性权益及女性赋权方面保持了相当高的活跃度和非常积极的态度。2006年大选期间,埃革阵对性别平等和女性权益方面做了相当大的工作,包括《国家性别平等行动计划》(National Action Plan for Gender Equality, NAP-GE, 2006-2010)的颁布,政策上将女性参政和其他权益方面纳入整个社会公共系统之内,但其具体实施效果与影响还未盖棺论定。

自2018年4月阿比·艾哈迈德上台以来,他对埃塞的政治系统大刀阔斧地进行改革,其中就包括任命萨赫勒—沃克·祖德(Sahle-Work Zewde)(女性)为总统,另外还有首席法官、新闻秘书以及一半数量的内阁成员等重要职位,这对于埃塞本国甚至非洲大陆来说,都是颠覆以往的举措。阿比直接肯定了女性在国家建设方面所做出的贡献,如果不给予为这个国家奉献的女性们肯定,那么埃塞就不可能真正地实现民族复兴。如果不认同女性的作用,那么民族身份和民族认同便毫无意义可言。正如其所宣讲的精神一致,阿比将新政府中10个命脉部门的职位都交予了女性领导人,例如和平发展部、国防部和劳动与社会事务部等。

可以说女性在埃塞的政治系统内的赋权道路以积极态势发展,女性担任国家总统以及政要职位是埃塞女性地位颠覆性的转折点,新的国家政策以及对女性的政策倾斜仿佛将从以往的"表面性"逐渐转向"实质性",长远来看对于埃塞本国的政治与社会发展来说也许会产生积极影响。从政治层面来说,正如Lovenduski在其阐述女性在任何一个国家政治生态内的作用时一样,女性登上政治舞台可以发挥其正义性与差异性作用。一方面大众观念里认为女性相较于男性而言,出现腐败问题的概率较低,面对社会问题时能够展现更多的正义性;另一方面,女性由于生理、精神和人生经历,在处理女性、儿童和青少年问题上能有更强的共鸣与共情能力,因此能够更好地解决相关问题,并且与男性政要长久以来的固有形象产生强烈反差,差异性会使女性在政治体系内发挥其独特的作用。社会层面来说,女性担任国家政要可以为社会上的女性树立形象,激励大众女性和青少年女性,已经有相关研究表明女教师的存在会改善女学生的学习成绩,并且教师会影响学生的人生规划——更多地接触女性科学家、工程家或者政治家等专家学者,会对学生的职业选择与学习意愿产生一定影响,促使学生在相关领域从业。但是作为对传统"男权"体系的政治结构与社会结构的冲击,究竟女性政要在解决埃塞国内民族矛盾和提升女性权益方面是否会发挥理想中的作用,另外,政治赋权的提升是否真的是从提高女性的相关权利出发还需要事实和时间去验证。

三、埃塞俄比亚女性主义思潮的影响

不论对于西方国家还是发展中国家,还是欠发展国家来说,女性为其政治权利抗争从一开始的选举权演变到后来的参政权,都是改变女性社会地位的重要途径,也是女性相关权益提高的集中表现,更是女性向传统父权制社会结构和运作方式挑战的方式。随着越来越多的女性参政,在埃塞的政治生态内可能会产生滚雪球效应,使得越来越多的女性参与到政治系统之内,但同时女性问题与执政党的利益环环相扣,非"脚踏实地"的政策看似光鲜亮丽,但同时问题重重又危机四伏。

(一)女性主义思潮与埃塞俄比亚政治生态的关系

首先,女性主义思潮和埃塞的政治生态形成了一定的相互作用关系,即女性主义在埃塞的传播提高了女性的自主意识,使得女性在从政参政方面拥有更宽阔的渠道和更高比重的配额,并且能在国家发展和政策制定方面有一定的参与权和决策权。反过来,从国家高层做出的姿态在一定程度上对女性主义思潮的进一步发展起到推波助澜的作用,容易在埃塞社会内加深渲染思潮氛围,在女性主义思潮发展的过程中会辐射更广,理论上最终发展趋势有利于埃塞女性生活质量与社会地位的提高,这也是人权保障与先进文明的具体体现。

其次,与其说埃塞俄比亚的女性主义思潮会对埃塞的政治生态系统产生影响,倒不如说在现今阶段以及短中期之内,女性主义在埃塞的发展现状是埃塞政治生态的反映。虽然埃塞的女性问题看似正在以一种良好的趋势发展,但埃塞的女性地位存在地区间巨大差异、书面与实际脱钩的情况。目前埃塞政府实施了一系列的措施和法律来提高女性的地位和权益,在较发达的城市和地区,似乎已经逐渐向"平权"靠拢;但高度的政治宗教化使得根深蒂固的父权制依旧难以动摇,各项政策的落地性有待商榷,书面上的立法措施和实际情况存在脱节,为女性而呐喊的声音与现实进行比对后更像是"政治装饰"——是执政党从国家政策需求和维护政党利益出发,其根本目的并非是从女性的根本需求出发,对于父权政治的埃塞政府来说,女性问题从根源上来说是"需要解决",而非"为了解决"。对于大众女性来说,更多聚焦于关乎切身利益的"维权",关注的是日常生活和基本权利,但面对实际情况又无力改变,女性主义思潮对于大众女性来说还在意识蒙眬状态,即有这一方面的意识,但是若要她们坚定这一意识并为之抗争的概率并不高;对于精英女性来说,无论是天生条件具备还是后天自身努力,女性主义在这些人身上已经得到体现,从政参政一定程度上可以推动关于女性的各项政策,为女性发声,但已经开始实践女性主义的这些精英女性是否可以颠覆以往深入骨髓的父权制政治还未可知。

(二)女性主义思潮在埃塞发展的潜在问题

由于埃塞社会正处于由传统向现代过渡的阶段,因此不论是在社会经济发展还是意识形态方面都存在一定的矛盾性。对于埃塞来说,女性主义思潮虽然在政治赋权方面有了较其他非洲国家来说更为先进的表现,在大众女性的基本权益方面有了进一步的改善,但从整个国家层面上来看,女性主义仍旧有着其"理想与现实"和"传统与现代"的矛盾性。加之埃塞本身政治系统内严重的腐败问题,女性主义思潮的发展和对政治以及整个社会的正向影响也面临着挑战。

1.“配额制”与“特殊制”

阿比领导的新政府对于女性配额制的采纳表明了国家政府对女性问题积极正向的态度，在政治和公共部门任命女性领导的确会增强女性的政治领导力并影响政策决策结果。但是必须考虑到的是有机会上升到“领导管理”和政治体制内层面的女性，最基本的前提是接受过高等教育。虽然说在首都亚的斯亚贝巴或其他较发达城市中，女性的受教育情况较好，但不能以偏概全；从全国范围内来看，埃塞的实际情况仍旧面临女性受教育层次较低和辍学率较高的问题，高等教育层次的女性数量仍旧只有男性的三分之一。由于城市与农村地区发展的极度不平衡，在这种配额制下当选的女性从政者更有可能来自社会背景优越的阶层和家庭，或者是所谓“上层社会”中男性从政者的亲属，加之埃塞政治与社会体制内不可忽视的腐败问题，这种趋势可能会演变成天生优势的女性的特殊事业通道，使得实际情况游离在原本旨在平衡全社会女性权益的初衷之外。

2.“支持”与“阴谋”

另外，以全球范围内的女性主义传播视角来看，女性主义若在埃塞真正落地开花，还需要警惕西方的价值观渗透，以及外来势力打着女性主义旗号进行的政治干扰，甚至是恐怖主义活动。因为女性主义这一理念从根本上来说的确起源于西方国家，埃塞甚至非洲大陆的女性主义都或多或少地受到西方女性主义的影响——无论是理论影响还是著作影响，也容易通过此种方式受到西方国家价值观的被动输入，例如过度宣传自由主义引发社会动乱等问题。另外，沙特一直在以资金方式资助“女性主义组织”，有相关数据表明超过 350 个欧美大中型女权组织都受到沙特等中东国家资金支持。虽然女性主义目前仍旧是非主流思潮，但是所谓的“女性主义”组织的国际间合作很可能夹带极端主义与恐怖主义，例如欧洲极端女权组织“红色卓拉”，鼓吹消灭白人和亚裔男性，世界的统治权应交给女性和穆斯林。该团体创立于 1977 年，之后与基地组织勾结，逐渐发展成恐怖主义组织。到 1996 年，该组织已在欧洲制造了多起恐怖爆炸行动。因此，埃塞的女性主义需要在其发展过程中警惕极端主义的出现以及西方“自由民主”的价值观侵略。

3.“传统”与“现代”

埃塞仍旧是以传统观念为主导的社会，传统文化在大众层面扎根较深，女性主义思潮的发展可以说是“现代思想”与“传统思想”间价值观念的碰撞。现今，即便是在基本已经实现两性平权的发达国家，女性在政治决策层的任职数量仍旧远远低于男性。在参政参选过程中，“女性”这一“性别”是把双刃剑，无论是从生理性别还是社会性别来说，都无法摆脱固有的传统观念——女性应该在家庭事务或子女教育上付出更多的时间和精力。如果正向来看，女性在某些问题上的确可以收获更多的“好感”，在处理相关事务时也有更多的经验；但也存在相应的反对意见，认为女性如果投身于政治，那么其对家庭的贡献必定很少，这样“不顾家庭”的女性是否真的能为大众女性发声，她们所做的决策是否真的能了解大众女性的需求。因此，女性领导者在发挥其领导角色时，是否能真正引起大众女性和普遍社会的认可仍旧是未知数；进一步来说，若未来在某项重大问题上出现了失误或负面效果，“女性领导人”也许会被“女性”所“反噬”，演变为“成也女性，败也女性”的局面。

"Enabling Women": Philosophical Foundations for Gender Equality and the Roles of Females in the Political-Public Spheres in Ethiopia

Eyasu Berento Assefa

Abstract: Issues of gender equality and enabling women are essential aspects of social justice that transcend the fundamentalist feminist movement and signify holistic moral imperatives and metaphysical issues, semi-pragmatic programs of promoting feminine values for human equality. The conceptual dichotomy of "Men-Women" is a problematic social construct of patriarchal socio-political mentality manifested in "subject-object" relationship between males and females and thereby shackles the opportunity of females' decision making statuses. As an immediate response to this problem, this paper intends to philosophically examine the challenges and prospects of feminism and gender equality in Ethiopia. Qualitative research method is used from critical social theory approach to analyze the historical and contemporary contradictions of perceiving females in Ethiopia and examine the roles of feminism to challenge the gendered status quo in the political-public spheres. It is concluded that we can derive important lessons from the wisdoms of philosophers and Ethiopian experiences for enabling women to females' participation in political-public spheres in Ethiopian context. Hence, besides "short-term" affirmative actions for females as victims of historical injustices, and against extreme separatist feminist movements, we need to look at genuine philosophical (metaphysical) foundations for long-term agendas of enabling females as stakeholders of decisions for all-inclusive sustainable development goals in Ethiopia.

Keywords: Enabling Women; Feminism; Gender and Sex; Humanity; Philosophical Foundations of Gender Equality

1 Introduction

The genesis of feminist movements is attributable to female's oppression by patriarchal thinking of culture constructs and political dictatorships of masculinity driven values. The assumption that females are lower than males in reason, science, morality and physical capacity traced back to the religious and philosophical thoughts of the ancients. The judeo Christian claim that Eve was responsible for the original sin of human race welcoming Serpent' s offer of the "leaf of wisdom" (Genesis 3: 2-3).Females are assumed to be weak to be deceived, irrational and passionate compared to males who are aggressive, powerful, patient and rational.

The same claims about the inferiority of women are witnessed from the words of the wise philosophers. Plato (1997) argues that the relation between men and women is the relation between superiors and inferiors. He further argues that women and children to be common properties for the guardians. This is one of the great mistakes of the Noble man among philosophers according to Cicero (1999). For Aristotle, males are more properly situated to lead and control than females who are weak and incomplete (1984).

There is an ancient translation of the Ethiopian Version of the Oedipus story. The main character of the story, Sekendes the wise was asked many questions related to metaphysics, human nature, cosmology, society, culture and astrology. Among others he was asked "What is woman?" In his replay, women are characterized as evil, causes of disaster, beast and constantly intent upon destruction (Sumner, 1985: 187).

This personal opinion about women seems unexpected from the man attributed the title of "Sekendes the Wise". But such claims are not uncommon from the arguments of philosophers. For example, St. Augustine accuses Eve responsible for the religious claim of the original sin of human beings. Man/Adam was led astray because of the woman given to him; "who was of small intelligence and who perhaps still lives more in accordance with the promptings of the inferior flesh than by the superior reason... that through her the man became guilty of transgression" (Brown,2019).

Another medieval period church scholar St. Aquinas argues that females are the reasons of perfection in the universe. His claim on females is interpreted that femininity is the complementary attribute of nature to masculinity. For him, grace and knowledge can be given to women though they are not allowed to teach publicly, but of privately. But by virtue of intelligence and leadership quality man should lead woman. "[g]ood order would have been wanting in the human family if some were not governed by others wiser than themselves. So by such a kind of subjection woman is naturally subject to man, because in man the discretion of reason predominates" (Question 92, Article 1, 2006).

While Schopenhauer considered women as a midway between children and men (Ramakrishnan Parthasarathy), the 19th century existentialist philosopher, Nietzsche, had strong hatred to women who argues that they are "not yet capable of friendship: women are still cats, and birds. Or, at best, cows" (Nietzsche, 2006, p. 41).It is such views of the influential men that contributed to the development of misconceived approaches towards women in the church.

Ethiopian women are subjected for ill-conceived cultural, religious, political and social exclusions. Their place in the society is denigrated and they are deprived of their participation in the political and public spheres. Studies on the cultures, religions and different traditions in Ethiopia reveal that women are victims of the patriarchal system (Riot, 2004; Bimer and Alemneh, 2018; Burgess, 2013; Jeylan, 2004; and Abreham, 2007).

These and other views from philosophy, culture and religions contributed to the oppression of females and the evolution of patriarchal socio-political orientations. Considering women as incapable and subordinate creatures to men is deep rooted and highly entrenched in the mind of both males and females as objective truth and pose undesirable consequences on the lived experiences of females. The subordination of women by men led to responsive counter feminist movements. The primary emphasis of this study is these ideological and practical problems.

This study tries to tackle two problematic orientations in the relationships between females and males: demystifying the socially constructed traditional contradictions that suppress females and critical reflection on the possible discontents of extremist feminist movements. By incorporating arguments from the values of femininity (example female care ethics and maternal thinking), it is argued that we can employ feminine values to enrich the practical successes females' participation in political and social, decision making and human development goals. Thereby, the feminist movements in Ethiopia and elsewhere can play this double role.

The objective of this study is to promote human development that assures females' decision making beyond the political orchestrations of gender equality for short term affirmative action measures.

The research questions include:

What is gender equality?

What are the philosophical, religious and cultural bases of gender based injustices and females' oppression?

What lessons can be taken from feminine values, the thoughts of philosophers and Ethiopian experiences?

Which feminist movements can best fit to Ethiopian contexts to ensure sustained participation of females in the political-public spheres?

How can genuine gender equality be attained for effective actualization of human development?

Methodology, as a philosophical analysis, is qualitative research method is employed from the critical social theory perspective to reflect on the contradictions of cultural, social, political and religious assumptions that resulted in gender based discrimination as well as the stereotyping separatist problematic feminist movements which are dangerous to societal solidarity and females themselves. Critical Social Theory is the 20th century interdisciplinary approach to disclose the contradictions in the public assumptions, politics, religion, technology and culture; and an attempt for solutions from different perspectives (Freeman, and Vasconcelos, 2010; Harney, 2017). As an aspect of critical social theory, intersectionality is used to articulate the multifaceted geneses (gender, poverty, illiteracy, culture) of females' oppression. "As a critical theory, intersectionality conceptualizes knowledge as situated, contextual, relational, and reflective of political and economic power" (Atewologun, 2018: 1).As the way out from such contradictions, the research employs hermeneutics and intercultural approaches. Intercultural philosophy is a quest for dialogues between cultures and different wisdoms for the sake of mutual enrichment (Bekele, 2005); and hermeneutics is a philosophical approach on the interpretations of foreign literature, culture, history and philosophy (Hacker, 2007; Eguale, 2003). Hence, critical social theory is used from philosophical perspective to critically reflect on the public and professional discriminations of females in Ethiopia. Interculturalism and hermeneutics are used to recommend on how the different culture traits can contribute promoting gender equality in Ethiopia and how modern institutions can hermenutically introduce the arguments of feminisms in line with the time tested indigenous knowledge systems (IKSs) in Ethiopia.

2 Conceptual and Theoretical Frameworks

2.1 "Gender Equality" Beyond Feminism and Affirmative Action

Though the philosophical foundations of such ill-conceived assumptions are not distinctively describable, the problem of gender inequality have pervasive socio-political and economic consequences that affect the lives of females in developed and developing societies. Proponents of gender equality argue that gender based oppressions emanate from the wrong conception of natural differences and manifestations of sexual variability between females and males. Such nature based and socially constructed problematic power relations between females and males lead to different forms feminist movements.

The historical development of feminism is divided into three waves. The first wave comprises movements from late 19th century to early 20th century with the themes of equality of women, the right to property and formulation of divorce laws. The second wave (1960s to 1990s) is broader in scope and the themes include the freedom of all women throughout the globe, women's class struggle across the world which is radicalized in its later stages. The third wave (1990s to present) is more radical and influenced by the postcolonial and postmodern thoughts (Kroløkke et al, 2005). Some add a fourth wave of feminism.

A brief summary of the different kinds of feminist movements include following parts. (1) Radical Feminism: radical feminism attempts for 'absolute liberation' of females from males' domination. These feminists argue that females' oppression is deeper and harsher than any form of oppression and it demands revolutionary measures. (2) Liberal Feminism: as the name indicates it is most acceptable form of feminism that demands the equal participation of females in the socio-political arena. (3) Marxist and Socialist Feminism: this form of feminism is similar with Marxist politico-economy philosophy which argues that females' oppression is similar with the social class based oppression and the liberty of females is part of the social revolution against capitalist orientation of the patriarchy. Both Marxist and liberal feminism have almost similar intentions and approaches to the oppression of females. Their difference is that liberal feminism suggested legal measures and reforms to minimize gender based injustices within the institutions, while Marxism quests a radical change in the system of production (Reiner, 2008). (4) Cultural Feminism: according to cultural feminism, there are really differences between men and women and the values of women are special and should be incorporated into the laws, strategies and institutional arrangements so as to foster the quality of life, world peace and stability. They argue that women are more kind and gentle than men and "if women ruled the world there would be no wars".

There are diversified forms of feminism varied according to the cultural and political contexts. What is common to all feminist movements is the thesis that women are victims of historical injustices due to patriarchal world views; and this oppression should be ruled out.

While the feminist movements played significant roles in liberating women from socially constructed impositions, some forms of feminism are problematic both for the development of females themselves and the socio-cultural and religious values of humanity. On the one hand, the separatists' claims for lesbianism and other forms of homosexuality, stereotypes to males and attempts to absolute independent of females are untenable claims of feminist movements. On the other hand, the feminist movements driven responses to gender based injustices resulted in the feeling of resentment from females and sense of inferiority to be supported as well as the problematic attempts to identify females with males. For example, uncontrolled attempts to of gender equality appear in the form of "social genetic engineering" producing the psychological personality of manish women and boyish girls, where the mind is not in absolute communion with the biological and physiologically feminine nature. Reflecting on this problem Storozhuk and Goian (2017:209) wrote as follows.

Moreover, the boys' system of education is often taken as the standard one. In other words, girls are brought up in a boyish way. We seem to be doing everything to bring up necessarily a "mannish" woman. The latest achievements in the field are judo and karate classes. However, the girl still will become a woman with characteristic to her genetic program — "a woman as mother", "a woman as the keeper of the fire", "a woman as wife". Unfortunately, she will not become a woman "in a pure form". The system of education manifests itself — there appears some kind of creature with dual origins: "half-woman — half-man".

The danger of such contradictions within the feminist assumptions and governmental and nongovernmental responses to the historical injustices is that they are producing abnormality in the minds and personalities of the females as an extension of traditional patriarchal assumptions. The myths of gender equality and affirmative action, therefore, are manifested in such problematic forms of affecting and hiding the real natures of femininity by implicit adoption of masculinity. They turn to identify females with males than cultivating their nature, disabling feminine qualities than enabling their hidden potential (Ibid). Gender equality appears in a perverted form of sameness that overlooks the feminine characteristics. But, "to be respected as an equal should not mean being reduced to sameness, which purported sameness has historically reflected the characteristics of the dominant group" (Held, 2006:153).

Genuine comments on female's equality can be taken from the arguments of philosopher' s like the ancient Roman Philosopher Cicero, 17th century Ethiopian philosophers Zara Yacob and Wolde Hiwot and contemporary feminists like Simone de Boveaur. Cicero was one of the ancients who defended for the rights of women. "And that law itself, which was passed in the interest of men' s utility, is highly injurious to women. Why should a woman not have money?" (1999: 65). Zara Yacob and Wolde Hiwot criticized the patriarchal tradition of Ethiopia and openly advocated women' s equality with men (Sumner, 1985). There are feminists from the philosophy schools who demand the genuine foundations of gender equality. For example, after a detailed analysis of the historical, biological, mythical and psychological bases of female inequality, the bifurcation between the males and females as the self and the other, Simone de Beauvoir (1956), argue for the genuine equality between males and females.

Such claims from the feminists and philosophers lead us to the analysis of genuine equality agendas and search for the values of femininity that advance the solidarity in the social arena. Integrating feminine and masculine behaviors can produce a good human personality proper of the public and political spheres. But what are the feminine behaviors to be appropriated in the public sphere?

2.2 The Values of Femininity

What type of feminism is healthy and desirable? The feminism that is desirable in contemporary world is the one that promotes sustained peace, inclusive and serve as a response for the historical and contemporary challenges of females in the patriarchal social orientations. By pragmatic extension, the feminism that is desirable is the one that can promote and cultivate the famine values which are relevant to handle all forms of discriminations.

The feminist movement that aspires to the equality of women based on the experiences of females similar to the experiences of males will lead to the healthy communication between females and males. Such experience "is the lived experience of feeling as well as thinking" (Held, 2006: 23) and the practical interaction with others, responses to the environmental and personal impressions. Such experiences of women must have visible implications in the public sphere like the male' s decision making status in the social paradigm. There are arguments that stress the feminine values as the bases of care, compassion and sympathy that have positive contributions for world peace and cultivation of morality. Two important philosophical arguments are proper candidates for this discussion on feminine values: Care Ethics and Maternal Thinking.

Care Ethics: Advocates of care ethics argue that promoting feminine characteristics into the values of ethics and the like will contribute for the success of feminist cause and world peace

(Keller et al, 2003).Their attempt is to change the problematic assumptions that neglect the values of feminity like care and compassion in moral and legal theorizations.

Feminists do not seek to simply replace men with women in the existing positions of power determining how society will develop, they seek to change the way these positions are thought about and structured. The ethics of care seeks to change dominant normative evaluations and recommendations (Held, 2006:152).

This form of feminism by extension will contribute to the development of society where are equality is guaranteed regardless of differences in ethnic, religious and racial lines. Advocates of ethics of care "seek an ordering of society along cooperative lines that foster mutual trust and caring" among males and females (Held, 2006:152).

According to Held, the grand narratives in theorizing morality and law did not consider the experiences of females. Instead they are based on the males' experiences as manifested in the public sphere. In doing so they cannot be the right candidates in contemporary morality and legal frameworks. In commenting on Kantian categorical Imperative based on universal reason and calculative Utilitarianism (Held, 2006:24) argued that "affectionate sensitivity and responsiveness to need may seem to provide better moral guidance for what should be done in these contexts than do abstract rules or rational calculations of individual utilities". This claim is a feminist extension of ethics of care as the foundation of morality for example. Ethics of care can be among possible alternatives for contemporary theorizations in morality, social and political affairs.

The ethics of care is a deep challenge to other moral theories. It takes the experience of women in caring activities such as mothering as central, interprets and emphasizes the values inherent in caring practices, shows the inadequacies of other theories for dealing with the moral aspects of caring activity, and then considers generalizing the insights of caring to other questions of morality [and social solidarity] (Held, 2006:26).

Hence, such feminine behaviors and values have social dimensions, political aspects and equality and rights advocacy functions. Advancing feminine values will contribute for the progress of gender equality within and pragmatic integration of these values to our pressing problems.

Maternal Thinking: Mothering is central to the experiences of most if not all women. The emphasis on the practical life forms and emotions of women will lead us to think on the patterns of life females lead. It is at this juncture the other feminine value emerged, Sara Ruddick's (1995) theorization of "maternal thinking". There is a sacred moral practice in mothering that can contribute for global justice and equality, world peace and integration. The lived experiences of females show us their approach to family, the friends, the needy and the sick in the form of care. But the mother's lived experiences are manifested in the highest practical form of the ethics of care that combines the maternal thinking of care and the practice of raring the child; a special form of affection to one's own offspring.

It is such feminine values which are excluded in the history of philosophy, literature and jurisprudence. Besides the culture based and patriarchal orientations that suppress females' participation and gender equality, the epistemological tradition also denied the lived experiences of females'. Hence, feminist movements are expected to challenge the deep rooted exclusions of feminine characteristics and experiences and promote the opportunities of women to have their own voices in the public spheres. And they are in the burden of prove to show the real relevances of feminine values.

That is why I argue that beyond the politically engendered forecasting of affirmative action and uni-linear ill sighted gender equality manifested in females' abnormal imitation and identity to masculine characteristics, we should promote the feminine values that fill the gaps of the masculinity driven global mentality to solve the pressing socio-political and environmental problems. At the heart of such philosophical search for the harmony of the values of femininity and masculinity, there is an aspiration for the manifestation of mental flexibility and psychological androgyny of individuals to fill different contexts for the sacred end of reverent to humanity — humanity in its broader connotation and denotations. It is at this ontological spot that true gender equality will be actualized. I will deal with these arguments after a brief analysis of the Ethiopian experiences of feminism and roles of women.

3 Ethiopian Experiences: Challenges and Prospects for Females' Leadership

"Despite hegemonic gender discourses which place Ethiopian women in the private sphere of the home, there is a long history of women's presence in the public, political sphere." (Burgess, 2013*: 107)*

3.1 The A priori Intersectionality of Women's Oppression in Ethiopia

Single study like this cannot deal with complete picture of the place of women in Ethiopian history, culture, religion, social, political and economic participation and recent feminist activism against the deeply entrenched oppression of women. But it is the very conviction of the writer that contemporary debates on gender studies, policy and practice in Ethiopia should be informed from the views of the historical, cultural, religious social and political experiences of the country. The Ethiopian women, like women in other developing countries with poor economic and democratic culture, are subject to interrelated, multilayered oppressions. According to Burgess, "[w] omen in Ethiopia face multiple civil, political, economic, social, and cultural problems" (2011: 169).The patriarchal thinking gives little or no place to the participation of women in decision making. Developments in the political arena and economic activities further victimize women. As an African predicament, Ethiopian women are victims of the colonial experiences responsible for liberating struggles. They are highly affected by the continued internal clashes and revolutions of 20th century Ethiopian political upheavals. Recent discourses in the mainstream Ethiopian politics put women in precarious situation compared to men. For example, women in Ethiopia are victims of polarized elite based ethnic political discourses and subsequent violence based displacements.

In short, women in Ethiopia are at the intersection of such complexities of dehumanizing past and present scenarios in the nation.

As for the categorical gender based biases, Ethiopia is not exceptional that females are oppressed by male dominated tradition. Although the songs and the proverbs claim the values of motherhood, femininity is often assumed to be the negative quality used as insult, ignorance, cowardliness and weakness. Though recent developments in the politics and legal frameworks stress the equality of females, the deep rooted misconceptions are retained in the public spheres. The mythical, historical, cultural and religious based deep entrenched claims about "evilness" and weakness of females are tantamount to the practical suppressions of females by males. Such wrong views are not only promoted by males, females themselves have their role in sustaining the *status quo*(Riot, 2004; Bimer and Alemneh, 2018; Burgess, 2013; Jeylan, 2004; Abreham, 2007). But can we find a falsification for this grand narrative on the weakness and incapability of females? What can the Ethiopian tradition inform us about the roles of females and their role in the political, social, religious, and cultural arena?

3.2 The Place of Women in Ethiopian Tradition

Although, women in Ethiopia are denied equal opportunity, there are symbolic representations from women who play significant roles. The two sides of our history and tradition should be analyzed so as to enable women and incorporate feminine values to enrich our praxis of genuine policy implementations. The question to be addressed here is "what are the best experiences from the cultures, politics, religion, folk wisdom, literature and general tradition of the Ethiopians that promote feminine values?" Arguing from example, we can trace the role of women and the contribution of feminine values through the narrative of selected prominent women figures. But it is to be noted that these are far from the complete representation of holistic contribution of females. A book published by Women's Strategic Development Center (2012) gives us better understanding on the contributions of women in Ethiopia.

Women in culture: The Oromo Gada system promotes feminine values through the contributions of the Atete. Many scholars who studied the Oromo culture argue that Atete is the group of women that is a symbol of peace and good neighborhood. The Atete ritual, according to Jeylan (2004), is the gathering of women to appease Waaqa (God, Allah) in the times of atrocities. Besides this religious role, the Atete play significant roles in protecting the rights of women in the society. As the assumption is that women are nearer and have strong link with nature and Waaqa, they are intermediary agents between Waaqa and men; thereby men are dependent on women (Asmerom, 1973). For Aba Gada Workineh, the very beginning of Irrecha, a thanksgiving day of the Oromos, is the commemoration of Atete's planting of Odda tree for the memorial of her dead son and the symbol of peace among the family (2003). According to my personal experience, practice of the Atete women is similar to the Duberti of the Rayan women who play significant roles in reconciliation procedures of killing by pleasing the victims, by praying to God to prevail peace and in times of recurrent drought to bring fertility.

Women in politics and war: The history of Ethiopia informed us that significant number of women played prominent roles in wars and politics (Minale, 2012). The legend of Queen Sheba in the Kebre Negest (2000) is one of the determining forces in main stream political philosophy of Ethiopia. With its own problematic and mythical sides that are subject to criticism, it played significant roles in sustaining state strength and restoring peace in the times of state upheavals. The woman is known by her love of wisdom and impressed by the wisdoms of King Solomon. She went to attend from his wisdoms of ruling, to take experiences of leadership. The story goes that according to the dictates of nature she conceived from the king and begot a baby who determines the fate of Ethiopian politics for the next two millennia. Leaving the oral tradition, we can take lessons from her love of wisdom, leadership qualities, and the time tested sophisticated place and the swimming pool (Mai Shum) near to Axum City are witness of the material prosperity of the nation in her time. Though detailed study recommended, at the center of Solomonic dynasty in Ethiopia there is a woman who can be a good example of leadership.

The roles of Mintiwab in the political life of Emperor Tewodros are exemplary of women' s therapeutic roles in the success of their husbands. Her unreserved advices shaped the political behavior of the king for good as much as her lost jeopardized his success (Marsedin, 2009). Emperess Taitu' s role played in the battle of Mekelle is an exemplary intelligence of women, while Shewareged Gedlie is one of the unforgettable names to our memory in handling internal guerilla fighting by providing food and clothes, leaking information to the patriots. Women have played significant roles in the TPLF' s struggles against Derg (Yewubmar, 2001) and women are playing prominent roles in politics and socio-economic activities.

Females in literature: While the literature gives little attention to the roles of females, one of the liberal figures in the literature is Haddis Alemayehu' s Novel *Love unto Grave' s Seblewongel*. She is a revolutionary symbol of the uncritical tradition that oppresses female's decision making. Birhanu Zerihun's Zerfeshewal is portrayed to represent the ruling women and hence an oppressor. The representation of Woizero Zerfeshiwal in Birhanu Zerihun's three volumes of Novel *Maebel* and Woizero Asegash in Dagnachew Worku' s *Adefris* portray the place of high-clash oppressor women in the Ethiopian tradition of "Feudalism" .

3.3 Feminism in Ethiopia

Despite the above prominent figures in the traditions, feminine values and females rights are overlooked from the public sphere in Ethiopia. Prominent women figures like Yodith (Alelign, 2012) and Empress Menen Liben Amede (Solomon, 2012) are defamed and others are overlooked. Hence, Ethiopia has its own history of feminist social movements started before the emergence of western feminism. The first recorded bold claims for gender equality and females' rights are found on the 17th century treatises of philosopher Zera Yacob and Wolde Hiwot. Both philosophers argue for the equality of men and women in marriage and social life. Zera Yacob openly opposed the idea that a wife is a maidservant of her husband and argued for voluntary marriage. "I do not wish her to be my maidservant, but my wife; husband and wife are equal in marriage; we should not call them master and maidservant; for they are one flesh and one life" (Sumner 1985: 248). Wolde Hiwot argues for the equality of all men. Directly addressing on the equality of wife and husband in marriage he advises the husband to help his wife be happy in marriage and sex (Ibid).

In the Ethiopian written tradition of philosophy there is a book known as *The Book of the Wise Philosophers (Angare Felasfa)*. Despite there are passages that despise the nature of women as badness (Ibid: 114); and bad women as destructive forces (108) there are passages that suggest the equality between men and women. In seemingly religious precept, the husband is advised to consider his wife as one of his body and his own soul. "Consider your wife as one of the organs of your body. Man and wife are one body." (104) "Consider your wife like your own soul, for she is the origin of your children." (120) A man who respects his wife is likened to angels. As a life giving agent, the wife is considered as a symbol of productivity and natural beauty. "A man without wife and children resembles a fruitless tree that grows alone the way." (119).

The first feminist movement known in Ethiopia is the Gurage woman Yeqaqe Wordwot who fought for the rights of women. 150 years ago, Wordwot openly and publicly opposed the anti-females' cultural laws and mobilized females for this purpose (Desta, 2012; Endalegeta, 2008). According to Jeylan's analysis, in the Arsi Oromo, women have their own social organization as a kind of solidarity "that provides women the impetus to participate in village councils and the cultural vehicle to mobilize en masse against mistreatment by men". (2004: 107) Unfortunately, this cannot help them free from patriarchal oppression emanated from their own cultural views and external religious expansions (Christianity and Islam) (Jailan, 2004; Abreham, 2007). Throughout Ethiopia there are traditional females associations of different forms (like Idir, Mahber and Equb) that contributed for the rights and wellbeing of females. But these associations at grass root levels lack strong public agency to influence the public sphere (Burgess, 2013).

According to Burgess, Ethiopia women are not totally forgotten in the public spheres. Though they are not able to have strong hand and louder say, there are individual females visible in the politics and different females' associations in the Empirial, Derge and EPRDF regimes. While the Empirial and Derg regimes' associations led by the elite and political superintendents to boost the consolidation of power, EPRDF's democratization promises show comparative freedom of associations. Females associations and gender equality are part of EPRDF's political programme. As such the right of females is constitutionally guaranteed rights. Article 35 of the EPRDF Constitution states the rights and equality of women. Other apolitical women associations like Ethiopian Women Lawyers Association (EWLA, founded in 1995), first civil society organization for women's rights, have a profound influence on the awareness of gender equality and legislature. But the association was victim of legal reforms and closure of political space following the aftermaths of contested 2005 elections.

EPRDF and its core member party TPLF have no good record of freedom of expression and association. As part of the struggles against the Derg women of Tigray and Ethiopians play prominent roles. TPLF, first as a military insurgence did not accept the participation of women. Latter in mid 1970s recruited women soldiers and organized female fighters' associations. According to deep analysis of Yewubmar (2001) and lived experience narrative of Aregash (interview to Yonas Belay, 2006) (both former TPLF female soldiers), TPLF in its history was so oppressive to the rights of women. One of the debates in the battle field was the negative impacts of feminism for the success of the struggle. Accordingly, females were not able to contribute in leadership and female fighters committee and associations were under systematic control of the top military and political leadership.

Another related feminist movement Setaweet (of Women) established in 2014 is a culture conscious articulation of feminism in Ethiopia with its business group PLC. As its prime visions, the movement "particularly engaged with investigating Ethiopian languages and cultures as avenues of equality" believing "in constructive dialogue and a collaborative work culture (Samrawit Alemayehu 2018: 34)."

There is little village around south Gondar known as Awra Amba established by an individual named Zumra. The norms of the village are that there is no job based division between males and females. Though it is not sophisticated and articulated feminist movement, the assumption that men and women can work together and share responsibilities in any activity contributes to the equality of women.

The Ethiopian village of Awra Amba is well established community with a truly extraordinary life style, especially in terms of equality between men and women, community spirit, absence of religion, honesty, hard work, democracy and even ecology. A ferment for emancipation (Joumard,2010: 1).

EWLA, Setaweet, Network of Ethiopian Women's Association (founded in 2003 and focus on women rights, women empowerment, and gender equality) (Bimer and Alemneh, 2018), ministry of Women and Children Affairs and similar feminist activism played significant roles in influencing the legal and institutional apparatuses to assure gender equality, avoid wrong cultural practices like female genital mutilation (Burgess, 2011: 171). But given the deep rooted intersectionality of problems of females, the feminist movements, legal and institutional arrangements, and bad democratic culture government promises cannot assure the actualization of rights of females. Hence, feminism in Ethiopia is at its infant stage and shackled by the complex political, religious, cultural, economic and social predicaments (Burgess, 2011; Burgess, 2013; Riot, 2004). Strong commitment and contextually situated feminist precepts can be recommended for successful feminism in the nation.

4 Lessons for Ethiopian Feminism and Females' Leadership: a Reverence to Humanity

Feminism in Ethiopia can be criticized for its confinement to urban areas and its vocabulary is for "liberated" females. One may ask what the rural woman is benefited from the so far successes of feminism and how she can understand its failures. Though we may not confidently criticize feminism in Ethiopia in its infancy stage, one may precept for its extension to the rural areas and deal with real life problems than being an outpost of Western separatist problematic feminist movements. Hence, this juncture, the study prioritizes on how to advance the role of feminism in the political-public spheres in Ethiopia. Feminism in Ethiopia is expected to deal with two fundamental problems: the issue of gender and the problems of leadership. As such the precepts, influences and intellectual outputs of any feminism in Ethiopia should contribute to liberate the oppressed women, and men, to challenge the oppressive anti-human public sphere, political arena and socio-economic contradictions. What kind of personality is demanding Ethiopian politics and public sphere and which feminist movement can contribute such personality?

As for feminist movements, we may consult the strong sides of each movement and our epistemic foundation for feminism must be enriched by the IKSs in Ethiopia. Liberal feminism is advised to be integrated to deal with gender based problems in Ethiopia through legal reforms, policy implementation and strategic measures (Bimer and Alemneh, 2018). Riot (2004) inclined to cultural feminism as reformative tool to deal with the oppressive cultural, religious and political attitudes. Besides these, Marxist feminism can be used to rule out the class based economic exclusions of females. One core issue that the Ethiopian feminism should deal is on how we can integrate feminine and masculine behaviors to produce a higher form of human personality that best fits for political leadership and influencing the public agency of public sphere. We can adopt Tesfaye and Yohannes' (2019: 9) argument in favor of androgyny in the public sphere. "Androgyny is the state of being able to access both gender categories to suit different situations". Accordingly, "within this conception of human subjectivity, a biologically male person may display feminine attributes and vice versa".(Ibid 18) Such human subjectivity whose aggressive masculinity is tempered by compassion and maternal thinking of femininity can contribute for the unfolding of world peace and human development. Hence, informed from non-western tradition, like eastern thoughts Taoism, such "a conception of humanity subjectivity that transcends traditional gender polarities/categories" (Ibid 18) can be one of the primary roles of feminism in Ethiopia.

Any feminist movement and female participation in Ethiopia should be cautious of the dangers of extreme feminism. Uncontrolled and stereotyping feminist movements are against the cultural and religious traditions of Ethiopians. While feminism is important voice of the oppressed females in Ethiopian tradition, any feminist movement, program and policy implementation should be informed from the philosophical foundations in global thought and folk wisdoms of the rich culture traits in Ethiopia.

What kind of female leaders are we demanding? This is a broad issue. An attempt to answer this question entails, on the one hand, a philosophical articulation of females' epistemology, ontology and moral-psyche; and on the other hand, a critical investigation of the culture of politics in Ethiopian history and the complexities of contemporary politics in Ethiopia. But from the above discussion it can be commented that short term affirmative action oriented participation of females based on mere calculation of the balance cannot be effective. The patriarchal political system in Ethiopia is characterized by war and aggressive political decisions. The masculine character driven decisions in the political arena cannot be effective in maintaining sustained peace and harmony in the nation. Hence, it can be suggested that people who can exert their qualities, in a right balance between feminine values and masculine characteristics are the right candidates of leadership in Ethiopia. When females are nominated for top leadership in the regional and federal offices, it must be on the merit of their quality to handle the complex nature of politics in Ethiopia with effective emotional intelligence backed up by the values of masculinity and femininity.Informed from philosophical thoughts, feminist movements, folk wisdoms and exemplary symbolic women, experiences of tradition, Ethiopian feminism can boost the role of women in political-social spheres. Agendas of gender equality should produce self-confident females and males, who live their proper feminine lives at their home and private lives and best fit for the professional demands of their society in the political-public spheres.

5 Conclusion and Recommendations

Different interrelated issues are raised above. Feminism and gender equality are inseparable issues. Contemporary political economy cannot be thought without proper participation of females and genuine form of feminism based on the sacred objectives of attaining inclusive human wellbeing than separatist, revolutionary, emotional and stereotyping extreme movements.

5.1 Conclusion

It is concluded that though there are feminist movements majority of women in Ethiopia are still victims of sustained oppression and alienation. Feminism in Ethiopian soil needs to be informed from internal experiences, national realities, global wisdom and future aspirations. Any genuine feminism in Ethiopia should entertain philosophical foundations and the experiences of best exemplary figures in the tradition as well as the folk wisdoms that promote the place of women in society, social solidarity, and by extension ecosystem wellbeing.

5.2 Recommendations

How could be effective participation of females become practical in the lower and higher levels of political decision making and leadership in Ethiopia? The following points are recommendations from the above discussion.

Scholars and feminists should consult rational and genuine comments on gender equality and feminism in science, philosophy, culture and religion throughout the world.

Any feminism in Ethiopia should be culture conscious so as not to contribute for the cultural crisis and anti-religious and cultural claims of feminism that affects the psychosocial and personal wellbeing of the whole community in general and females in particular.

The foundation for females' participation in leadership and decision making should be based on the conviction of incorporating feminine values and enriching our discourse for the practical success than mere short term affirmative action and political propaganda for the balance of female member in the higher political position.

The whole community, especially males should be aware that the participation of females and gender equality is part of the humanitarian responsibility of all for all inclusive and genuine sustainable human development; and Further research from interdisciplinary perspectives on systematic articulation of feminist movements in Ethiopia will reveal possible challenges and future prospects of feminism in Ethiopia and its roles in political-social spheres.

References

[1] ABBA G. 2011(2003 E.C.). ገዳሥርዓትእናየተደበቀውየኦሮሞሕዝብታሪ[The Gada System and hidden history of the Oromo people]. Addis Ababa: Finfine Printing & Publishing [ፊንፊኔማተሚያናፕብሊሺንግኢ.ማ].

[2] ABBA PHILOP. 2000(1992 E.C.). ድለክርስቶስሠምራወተአምራቷሃ [Hagiography and miracles of Kirstos Semra]. Addis Ababa: Tesfagebre Selassie Publishing House [ተስፋገብረሥላሴማተሚያቤት].

[3] ADUGNA M. 2020. The role of women in the politico-military affairs of Ethiopia (1270-1855)//WOMEN'S STRATEGIC DEVELOPMENT CENTER (WSDC). Women's universal contribution. Addis Ababa: Women's Strategic Development Centre.

[4] SAMRAWIT A. 2018. The Setaweet way: an articulation of Ethiopian feminism. https://surface.syr.edu/cgi/viewcontent.cgi?article=1197&context=thesis.

[5] ALEMU A. 2007. Oral narrative as ideological weapon for subordinating women: the case of Jimma Oromo. Journal of African Cultural Studies, 19(1): 55-80.

[6] ASCHALE A. 2020. "Yodit Gudit"—the defamed queen of Ethiopia//WOMEN'S STRATEGIC DEVELOPMENT CENTER (WSDC). Women's universal contribution. Addis Ababa: Women's Strategic Development Centre.

[7] YEWUBMAR A. 2009(2001 E.C.). ፊኒክስ ዋሞታምትነሣለትያልተቋጨውየትግራይሴቶችገድል [The rebirth of the phoenix unfinished struggle of Tigrian women]. Addis Ababa: Fareast Trading PLC.

[8] ATEWOLOGUN D. 2018. Intersectionality theory and practice. https://oxfordre.com/business/view/10.1093/acrefore/9780190224851.001.0001/acrefore-9780190224851-e-48

[9] BARNES J. 1984. The complete works of Aristotle. Princeton: Princeton University Press.

[10] YONAS B. 2014(2006 E.C.) የትግራይ ህዝብ ሽፍቶቹናወያኔዎቹ [The bandits and fighters of people of Tigray]. Addis Ababa: Yonas Belay Abebe.

[11] BROWN M V. 2019.The “woman” of Augustine of Hippo. https://www.cbeinternational.org/sites/default/files/hippo.pdf.

[12] BUDGE E A W. 2000. The Queen of Shaba and her only son Menyelek (Kĕbra Nagast). Cambridge, Ontario: Parentheses Publications.

[13] BURGESS G. 2013. A hidden history: women’ s activism in Ethiopia. Journal of International Women’ s Studies, 14 (3): 96-107.

[14] BURGESS G. 2011. The uneven geography of participation at the global level: Ethiopian women activists at the global periphery. Globalizations, 8 (2): 163-177.

[15] CHO S, CRENSHAW K W, MCCALL L. 2013. Toward a field of intersectionality studies: theory, applications, and praxis. Signs, 38(4):785-810.

[16] FEDERAL DEMOCRATIC REPUBLIC OF ETHIOPIA. 1995. Constitution of the Federal Democratic Republic of Ethiopia. https://www.refworld.org/docid/3ae6b5a84.html.

[17] COOPER J M, HUTCHINSON D S. 1997. The complete works of Plato. Indianapolis, Cambridge: Hackett Publishing Company.

[18] DE BEAUVOIR S, 1956. The second sex. London: Lowe and Brydone (Printers) Ltd.

[19] ENYEW B E, ALEMENEH G M. 2018. Liberal feminism: assessing its compatibility and applicability in Ethiopia context. International journal of sociology and anthropology, 10(6): 59-64.

[20] FREEMAN M, VASCONCELOS E F S. 2010. Critical social theory: core tenets, inherent issues//FREEMAN M. Critical social theory and evaluation practice. New Directions for Evaluation. (217): 7-19.

[21] EGUALE G. 2011(2003 E.C). የከፍተኛትምህርትዘይቤ[The philosophy of higher education] . Addis Ababa: Artistic Publishing Company(አርቲስቲክማ ተሚያድርጅት).

[22] GIRMA S. 2020. Menen-the ill-famed empress: a new historical reading of Sahle Sellasie Berhane Mariam’ s warrior king//WOMEN’ S STRATEGIC DEVELOPMENT CENTER (WSDC). Women's universal contribution. Addis Ababa: Women’ s Strategic Development Centre.

[23] GUTEMA B. 2005. The need for intercultural approach in African philosophy//BEKELE G, SMITH D. African philosophy at the threshold of the new Millinium. Addis Ababa: Addis Ababa University Printing Press, 203-314.

[24] HACKER P M S. 2001. Wittgenstein and the autonomy of humanistic understanding. http://www.phps.at/texte/HackerP2.pdf.

[25] HELD V. 2006. The ethics of care: personal, political, and global. Oxford: Oxford University Press Inc.

[26] HUSSEIN J W. 2004. A cultural representation of women in the Oromo society. African

Study Monographs, 23 (3): 103-147.

[27] JOUMARD R. 2010. Awra Amba, an Ethiopian utopia. http://local.attac.org/rhone/article.php3?id_article=1489

[28] ENDALEGETA K. 2008. የቃቄወርድወትእምቢታ [The rebillion of Yeqaqe-Wordwot]. Addis Ababa: Atafather Printers[እታፍዘርአታሚ ዎች].

[29] KELLER J, NELSON S, WICK R. 2003. Care ethics, service-learning, and social change. Michigan Journal of Community Service Learning, 10(1): 39-50.

[30] KROLØKKE C, SØRENSON A. S. 2005. Three waves of feminism: from suffragettes to girls//KROLØKKE C, SØRENSON A. S. Gender communication theories and analyses: from silence to performance. Thousands Oaks: SAGE Publications, 1-23.

[31] LEGESSE A. 1973. Gada: three approaches to the study of African society. New York: The Free Press, Inc.

[32] DESTA L. 2020 (2012 E.C.) . የቃቄዎእድወትየሴቶችመብትትግልንቅናቄአንትሮፖሎጂያዊእይታ[Yeqaqe-Wordwot's feminist movement from anthropological perspective]//WOMEN'S STRATEGIC DEVELOPMENT CENTER (WSDC). የሴቶችሁለንተናዊአበርክቶ[Women's universal contribution]. Addis Ababa: Women's Strategic Development Centre.

[33] MARSDEN P. 2008. The barefoot emperor: an Ethiopian tragedy. London: Harper Collins Publishers.

[34] MESELE T, YOHANNES A. 2019. Critical discourse analysis of gender conceptions in preparatory Tigrigna language textbooks. Journal of Educational and Behavioral Sciences (JEBS) , 2 (1): 15-31.

[35] NIETZSCHE F, DEL CARO A. 2006. Thus Spoke Zarathustra: a book for all and none. New York: Cambridge University Press.

[36] REINER T. 2008. The philosophical foundations of gender equality in liberalism and Marxism: a study of Mill and Marx. Twenty-First Century Society, 3(1) 13-30.

[37] ALEMU R. 2012 (2004 E.C.). የኢህአዴግቀይእስክርቢቶ [The Red Pen of EPRDF].

[38] RUDDICK S. 1995. Maternal thinking: toward a politics of peace. Boston: Beacon Press.

[39] AQUINAS T. 2006. The Summa Theologica. http://www.documenta-catholica.eu/d_1225-1274-%20Thomas%20Aquinas%20-%20Summa%20Theologiae%20-%20Prima%20Pars%20-%20EN.pdf

[40] STOROZHUK S, GOIAN I. 2017. Gender existence: correlation between equality and identity. Philosophy and Cosmology(18): 208-218.

[41] SUMNER C. 1985. Classical Ethiopian philosophy. Addis Ababa: Commercial Printing Press.

[42] THOMPSON D. 2001. Radical feminism today. London: SAGE Publications.

[43] WALBY S, JO A, SOFIA S. 2012. Intersectionality: multiple inequalities in so cial theory. Sociology, 46 (2): 224-240.

[44] WOMEN'S STRATEGIC DEVELOPMENT CENTER (WSDC). 2020 (2012 E.C.).

የሴቶችሁለንተናዊአበርክቶ[Women’s universal contribution] ሕብረቀለምማተሚያቤት. Addis Ababa: Women’s Strategic Development Centre.

[45] DAHNACHEW W. 2012. አደፍርስ [Adefris]. Addis Ababa: Rhobal Pringting House (ርኆቦ ትማ ተማሚያቤት).

[46] BIRHANU Z. 1972. ማዕበል: ዋዜማ፣መባቻማግስት (Maebel: eve, down and aftermath] . Addis Ababa: Ethiopian Scribes Organization [የኢትዮጵያመ ጸሐፍትድርጅት].

[47] ZETZEL J E G. 1999. Cicero: on the commonwealth and on the laws. New York: Cambridge University Press.

The Contested Hydro Hegemony in Eastern Nile Basin and Ethiopia's Political Liberalization

Wuhibegezer Ferede① & Mohamed Salih②

Abstract: This paper attempted to analyze the reciprocate influences of the Nile politics following the inauguration of the Grand Renaissance Dam project and the ongoing political liberalization in Ethiopia. In the last two decades, Ethiopia was painted as if it were the rising star through massive transformation projects for resuming its glorious past, the renaissance but critiques were arguing about the growth of social fragmentation, politicization of identity and consolidation of authoritarianism and tyranny. Thus, the sooner the Arab spring swept Northern Africa, EPRDF has launching the Grand Renaissance Dam linking it with developmental imperatives. However, Egypt has reacted for such development by sending popular diplomacy and later on resorting towards the age old water war discourse. Eventually, suspicion and diplomatic wrestling was made between the two states. Amidst this, popular discontent against the authoritarian minority rule and unbearable economic cost of living was bursting in the two populous regional states of Amhara and Oromia. This has ended with bloodiest confrontation with the government whereby in some cases the movement was pointing it figures towards the middling of Egypt in Ethiopian internal affairs. After series of state of emergency declarations and continuous popular protest, groups from the ruling party have heralded the need for political liberalization in Ethiopia. Hence, this paper addressed the intricate link between the political liberalization process in Ethiopia and the hydro politics of the Nile following the inauguration of GERD project in a continuum using data set from field and online interviews, key informant interviews, archival materials, documents, online data bases, discourses and narratives.

Keywords: Ethiopia; Egypt; GERD; Nile; Political Reform; Protest

① Associate Professor, Department of Political Science and International Relations, Bahir Dar University, Ethiopia.

② Emeritus Professor, Politics of Development both at Erasmus University Rotterdam and the University of Leiden in the Netherlands.

1 Introduction

This study focused on analyzing the delicate link between Egypt's policies and strategies to assume, maintain and consolidate its position in the Eastern Nile and political developments in Ethiopia after the GERD project . The study argues that the construction of Grand Ethiopian Renaissance Dam (GERD) exemplifies Ethiopian contestation of Egypt's historical hydro hegemony whereby the later has been publicly declaring in televised speech to use all options in countering the developments in Ethiopia.

In spite of some verbal contestations, until recently the hegemonic relations that privileged Egypt have remained intact. Egypt' s hegemonic posture has frustrated Eastern Nile states efforts aiming at the realization of efficacious water regime remain as a Nile Utopia. However, Ethiopia has openly contested the established negative, oppressive and consolidated hegemony through the construction of the GERD and its active engagement in the Nile Basin multi lateral deal. This move have be applauded as game changer and historic . However, the country has faced an Arab spring of its own and the GERD project delayed indefinitely. Therefore, this study aims analyzing the interplay of the domestic and water politics in the Eastern Nile basin with focus on the GERD project and the political liberalization process in Ethiopia.

1.1 Statement of the Problem

The anomalous mix of tyranny of abject poverty and the resource wealth (De Waal, 2009; Petros, 2010) inspires anyone who has a stake on the Nile Basin to ask the question why this naturally and strategically rich region became a realm of poverty. The later can be attested without going far distance in history over a glimpse on the 1970s and 1980s Ethiopian famine, the 2011 regional drought and 2016 Elnino induced famine.

This irony incites to carry out a critical examination by going beyond the normative explanations and established theories to unearth the detrimental force that figured out the paradox. The dictum of Herodotus that "Egypt is gift of the Nile" has reigned as conceptual and practical hegemony in the basin. For centuries, Egypt claimed to be the only wife to Nile while it is married with other ten riparian states. Thus, in spite of its trans-national character the utilization of the Nile River has been exclusively controlled by Egypt.

Beside for maintaining the statuesque, Egypt has invested all its labor in preventing the emergency of balancing or counter hegemonic power in the basin but recently tensions have surfaced as most riparian states have openly defied the status quo(Hanke, 2013). In this sense, Nile has been a focal points of state-centric water conflict studies undertaken by prominent scholars such Waterbury (1979: 2002). The central theme of most of studies was primarily revolved around the question whether water scarcity would lead to cooperation or violent conflict and basically shaped with the fact that the focus of most of the hydro-political research since the 1980s was centered on whether water scarcity will lead to conflict or cooperation (Jacobs, 2006: 2) till the development of the silent conflict or the continuum approach in 1990s.

In this regard, following the inauguration of the Grand Renaissance Dam project, the media was overloaded with narratives about the capricious, untidy and occasionally stormy Ethio-Egyptian relation over Nile. However, most of the discussions ignored the fact that the potent interstate relation was embarked on ever since the pharaonic times elapsing for centuries conditioned by the ebbs and tides of the exchange of water with religion, sporadic conflict and European imperialism. Therefore, as Ethiopia moved towards the construction of the dam, by rerouting the Nile flow and its parliament ratified an accord that replaced the colonial deals, there was heightened expectation about outbreak of war and, many scholars had predicted that Egypt may use the hard water diplomacy to react to the diplomatic and security developments in Ethiopia.

Ethiopia's rerouting of the Blue Nile to make way for GERD construction was counted as "a unilateral move" that risked a regional war (World Bulletin, 2017). Salman, a former advisor to UN International Fund for Agricultural Development and an expert on African water resources claimed that the rerouting of Blue Nile could lead to a regional war for Egyptian radical militants and political figures "might use the dam project as a pretext to attack Ethiopia ." (ibid)

On the other hand, the impossibility of war between the two was predicted based on the belief that Ethiopia has gone through period of building internal capability that could effectively manage Egypt' s interference. However, few others argue that Egypt may resort to use the combination of the two strategies. Thus, the understanding of the recent developments in the basin seeks the investigation of the hegemonic foundation and the prospect of power reconfiguration.

However, the neo-Malthusian position which argued on the direct link of population growth and natural resource scarcity that would lead towards violent environmental conflicts or water wars (Starr and Stoll, 1988; Ohlsson, 1995) is now contested. In his rigorous study, Wolf (1998) has dismissed the neo Malthusian notion of water war. This study has served as watershed for charting out optimistic history which took cooperation as an inevitable phenomenon in water relations (Ohlsson and Turton, 1999). The reason that clouded the optimism is the identification of many destructive but largely silent water conflicts that lie between the much feared water war and lauded water cooperation (Mirumachi and Allan, 2007; Zeitoun and Warner, 2006).

Furthermore, the Eastern Nile Basin is engulfed with protracted internal popular struggles for democracy since the onset of the Arab spring. Ethiopia and Sudan are still under massive popular demands for political change. While domestic politics and international relations tend to be separated in the issue of managing international rivers, they increasingly influence each other (Warner and Zawahri, 2012).

Thus, how the political reform Ethiopia could impact and be impacted by the Eastern Nile politics is the preoccupation of this study. Thought, the heightened tension between Ethiopia and Egypt following the inauguration of the GERD project was tentatively transformed through tripartite diplomacy, the onset of the popular protest that heralded the ongoing reform was attributed to the middling of Egypt in Ethiopia internal affairs. The death of engineer Semgnew Bekele, killing of Dangot cement factory manager, and the METIC grand corruption are assumed to have links with intricacies of the Nile Politics. However, the GERD crisis which was commenced with the death of the chief engineer and corruption by METIC signals the making of the counter balancing process. Thus, this study examined interplay of the political change in Ethiopia and the hydro hegemonic transition in the Basin through Gramscian and neo Gramscian approach using GERD project as case study.

1.2 Research Questions

Is there an interplay between the ongoing political reform in Ethiopia and the Eastern Nile politics?

What are the imperatives for Ethiopian open contestation of the statuesque as it's manifested in the GERD project?

Is there a prospect for hegemonic transition in the basin following the regional geo-political changes?

1.3 Objective

Analyze the interplay of the political change in Ethiopia and the hydro hegemonic transition in the basin following the commencement of GERD project.

2 Review of Related Literature

This section examines the literature in regard to Nile hegemony for there are diverse ways of understanding water related issues and political transition. Accordingly, scholars have designed multiple approaches as per the issue to be addressed. Frey and Naff Power (1985) have developed the interest matrix while Lowi (1993) come up with the theory of hegemonic cooperation. In line with the Neo-Malthusian conviction on population growth and resource stress, one of the proponents of the scarcity thesis, Homer-Dixon (1999) has come up with the idea of environmental determinism.

While Gleick (2001) analyzed the instrumental role of water in conflicts by regarding it as a means and target of conflict, Wolf (2011) has designed water conflict prevention approaches with conviction of the impossibility of water wars. Turton (2002) has also designed hydro political complex theory with securitization approach while Allouche (2005) elucidates the foundations of hydro-nationalism. However, this study will be basically rested on the concept of hydro hegemony with due emphasis on Gramscian and neo Gramscian approach.

2.1 Conceptualizing Hydro Hegemony

Hydro hegemony which is the focus of this study is water power politics primarily at the level of international river basins (Zeitoun and Warnerb, 2006: 435) achieved through water resource control strategies such as resource capture, integration and containment which are usually executed through coercions, treaties, knowledge construction and set of other tactics that could be injected into the society by exploiting the fertile ground created by power asymmetries (ibid).The existence of power asymmetry and weak international water institution serve as enabling agents for the implementation of the controlling strategies.

According to Lustick (2002), hydro hegemony is a more subtle ways of gaining compliance from co-riparian through coercive (force or direct threat of force); utilitarian (bribes, trades of services) and normative agreement, conscious belief that it is in line with the subordinate's best interest to comply, and hegemonic ideology. Out of the aforementioned compliance producing mechanisms, the concept of ideological hegemony was articulated by Antonio Gramsci (1971). Accordingly, ideological hegemony is rested on the conviction that beliefs manufactured by the hegemon provides more efficient mechanism for eliciting compliance than normative appeals to state laws and institutions (Lustick, 2002: 23).

He further argued that the influence of hegemonic beliefs made compliance with the statuesque a normal or common sense behavior and deviance from such order is regarded as insane or crime (ibid). This is similar to the process of the creation of what Engel has referred "alse consciousnesses" that served to keep the working class from recognizing and rejecting their oppression (Heywood, 1994: 85).

The methods of hegemonic influence or compliance creation approach depend on the capacity of the hegemony to persuade the subordinate actors to accept not just its authority. Thus, in addition to coercive utilitarian and normative agreement, a conscious belief that it's in line with the subordinate's best interest to comply and concomitantly reinforcing the legitimacy of the hegemony are used to produce compliance (ibid: 438). In this sense, hegemony is defined as the introduction of a new morality in conformity with a new conception of the world (Gramsci, 1971: 366).

Hence, the use of soft power of attraction and persuasion (Nye, 2004) to secure effective consent of weaker states is the main approach which will be used in the analysis of the case in the Eastern Nile Basin (Warner and Zawahri, 2012). The classical conception of hegemony which emphasis purely coercive measures highly marginalized the pervasive role of the consensual aspect in forming and sustaining hegemony (Agnew, 2003). Thus, in the consensual view hegemony both conflict and consensus are fused together (Haugaard, 2006:10).

Table 1 Conceptual Framework

1. Persuation	*·Water treaties and institution* *·Cultual Controls:religion and rituals; water myths and ideologies* *·Controling political and educational system* *·Civilizing mission movement* *·Material concessions/aid differential*
2. Cohesion	*·Banning access to aid* *·Water technology superiority* *·Intervention/aggression* *·Proxy war/supporting liberationist groups* *·Territorial claims and resource capture*
3. Integration	*·Pan Nilism* *·Unity of the Nile Valley* *·Regional integration*

2.2 Theories Hydro Hegemony

2.2.1 The Original and Revised Framework of Hydro Hegemony

The structural (deprivation) and physical (natural) scarcity of water calls for a critical re examination of water relations. Besides to scarcity and its concomitant impacts, the conventional analysis of water relations has ignored the role of power asymmetry in generating and sustaining "silent water conflicts." Thus, challenging the preexisting position about the possibility of having effective cooperation under asymmetric context, the frame work of hydro hegemony was designed to provide analytical paradigm for re-examining hegemonized basins. Thus, the framework of hydro hegemony (FHH) is an analytical framework devised to study how hegemony and power asymmetries can influence trans-boundary water politics (Zeitoun and Warner, 2006; Cascão and Zeitoun, 2010).

Since its appearance in 2006, the FHH has informed a vast body of literature addressing the role of power and discourse in hydro politics. Among others, Zeitoun and Mirumachi (2008), Daoudy (2009), Dinar (2009), Water Policy (2008), Zeitoun et al. (2011, 2017) have contributed to expand the water discourse to a more critical perspective. FHH approach goes beyond the conflict-cooperation dichotomy, pointing at the need for power analysis to understand asymmetric trans-boundary interactions whereby some of it is applied to the Nile basin case (Zeitoun and Warner, 2006; Zeitoun and Mirumachi, 2008; Cascão 2008; Cascão and Zeitoun, 2010a, 2010b; Zeitoun, Mirumachi and Warner, 2011; Zeitoun et al., 2014, 2016). Here below is the original and the revised frame work of hydro hegemony.

Table 2 The Original Pillars of Hydro Hegemony (*Zeitoun and Warner,* 2006: 451)

3 Pillars of Hydro Hegemony		
Riparian Position	Power	Exploitation Potential
Upstream/downstream	1st Dimension: Military & Economic	Infrastructure Technical Capacity
	2nd Dimension:Active Stalling & Incentives	
	3rd Dimension: Securitization & Sanctioned Discourse	

Table 3 The Revised Pillars of Hydro Hegemony (*Cascão and Zeitoun,* 2010: 32)

Hydro Hegemony Four Pillars of Power			
Geography	Material Power	Bargaining Power	Ideational Power

As its indicated here above, the original framework was focusing on the three pillars of hydro hegemony namely riparian position, power and exploitation potential where as the revised framework broaden the power pillars into four, viz, geography, material power, bargaining power and ideational power. While the concepts and analytical tools proposed by the RFHH have proved valuable to analyze the discursive constructions and the invisible forces that can influence hydro politics, yet a more in depth theoretical discussion is needed to illuminate how the concepts of power and hegemony interact. For addressing such limitation, a new analytical framework named as the circle of hydro hegemony on the basis of neo Gramscian notion of hegemony by disregarding power as the centre of its structure was designed. This approach serves for understanding power in hydro politics in which the various forms of power are connective in the function of hegemony. Thus, the application either versions of the framework of hydro hegemony in this study is inappropriate for its focus is investigating how consent and compliance mechanisms were manufactured for constituting the foundations of Nile hegemony using Gramscian and neo Gramscian approach.

2.2.2 Gramscian and Neo Gramscian Theories Relevance to Hydro Hegemony

The central focus of Gramscian view on hegemony rests on consent creating mechanisms. In fact, he analyzed the concept in Italian setting where there was an ethnic based relation of exploitation. In Gramscian understanding, building hegemonic supremacy is a prerequisite for any actor that demands for ruling (Gramsci, 1971). The idea of a "third face of power" or "invisible power" has its roots partly in Marxist tradition about the pervasiveness power of ideology, values and beliefs in reproducing class relations and concealing contradictions (Heywood, 1994: 100).

Gramsci, took this idea further in his widely influential notions of "hegemony and the manufacture of consent" (Gramsci, 1971). He argued that the capitalist state constituted from two overlapping spheres, a political society which rules through force and a civil society which rules through consent (Baran, 2012:311). In Gramscian analysis civil society refers the public sphere where trade unions and political parties gained concessions from the state, and the sphere in which ideas and beliefs were shaped and hegemonic ideologies reproduced in cultural life through the media, universities and religious institutions to "manufacture consent" and legitimacy (Heywood 1994: 100-101). This notion refers to intellectual dependency on the knowledge fabric of others camouflaged with compliance producing tactics.

Gramsci's insight about how power is constituted in the realm of ideas and knowledge and expressed through consent rather than force have inspired the use of explicit strategies to contest hegemonic norms of legitimacy extending to epistemic revolution and protest on educational system.

The critical theory of hegemony was primarily developed by Robert Cox (1981, 1983) basing on the work of his predecessor Gramsci (1971). Building on Cox's contributions a series of diverse neo Gramscian perspectives have emerged in International relations (Morton, 2001). The development of a neo Gramscian perspective by Robert Cox is rooted in the rejection of mainstream positivist IR approaches.

The concept of hegemony in the critical approach is understood as an expression of broad based consent which is manifested through the acceptance of ideas backed by institutions and material provisions. In this approach, the primary actors in the construction of hegemony are believed to be social forces which had leading role or preeminence within the state. Cox's (1981: 129) critical theory does not take institutions, social and power relations for granted rather it questions their origins and the process of changing. It analyses how existing orders emerged and how dominant norms, institutions and practices were established. The identification of the aforementioned characteristics is not an end by itself rather a starting point for the identification forces for developing emancipatory project for a new and just order. Unlike, the neo-realist hegemonic stability theory, the neo Gramscian perspective broadens the domain of hegemony by encompassing configuration of material power, the prevailing collective image of world order including norms and a set of institutions which administer the order with a certain semblance of universality (Cox, 1981: 139).

In this approach, hegemony is more of consensual order and its establishment within a historical structure is constituted through relation of production, the forms of the state and global order. The social relations of production is the starting point for analyzing the operation and mechanisms of hegemony (Cox, 1987:1-9) and it refers the production and reproduction of knowledge, social relations, morals and institutions that are prerequisites to the production of physical goods (Cox, 1989: 39). Thus, examining how production and reproduction of knowledge, social relations, morals and institutions were initiated developed, consolidated and sustained as instruments of Nile hegemony is one of the preoccupation of this study.

The second factor is the consideration of historical construction of various forms of state and the social context of political struggle. Here the utilization of Gramscian notion of state and civil society as it is mentioned here above is important. For him the state is conceived as both public sphere (government, political parties, and military) and sphere of civil society (church, media, education) through which hegemony functions (Gramsci, 1971: 261). In neo Gramscianism, ideas, understood as inter subjective meanings as well as collective images of world order, material capabilities, referring to accumulated resources, and institutions, amalgams of the two elements are compliance creating mechanism.

The conventional explanation about the foundations of the Nile hegemony was centered on realist explanation rooted in classical international relations theory. Thus, Gramsian and neo Gramsianism both as theory and methodology deviates from the normative approaches rather the focus is on critical understanding hydro hegemonic configuration in the Eastern Nile Basin. Unlike the above mentioned framework of hydro hegemony and classical international relations, this theory enables to have a critical investigation of the process and strategies of consent and compliance manufacturing for assuming and sustaining hegemonic position in the basin and why Ethiopia and other Eastern Nile states failed to contesting it effectively for centuries.

2.2.3 Counter Hydro Hegemony

As it is stated here above whatever consent and compliance creation mechanism are employed, total pacification of society is impossible rather there appears counter hegemonic process against the establishment. This implies that the consent or compliance for the hegemonic relation is not immune from any form of disobedience or resistance. However, the resistance displayed against the hegemony cannot emerge out suddenly rather it goes under a process of historic bloc formation (Gramsci, 1971). This approach is important for explaining recent move of Ethiopia in contesting the establish Nile hegemony through the construction of the GERD project and mobilizing multi lateral engagement.

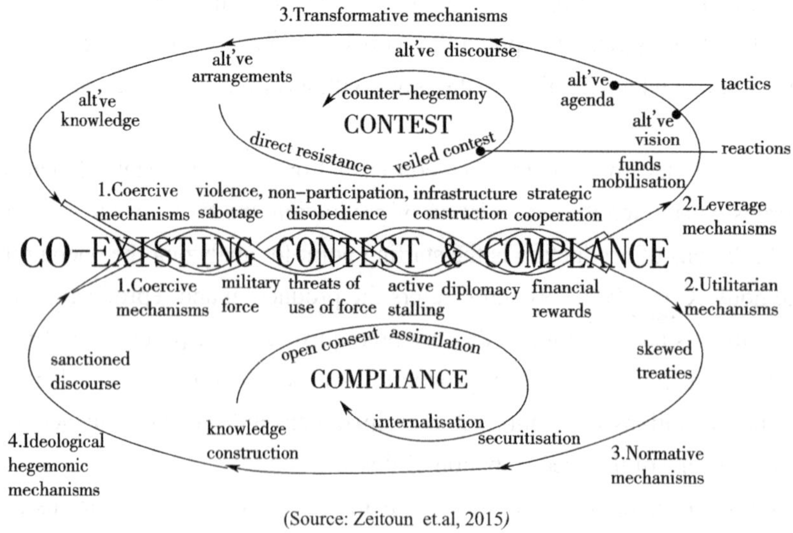

(Source: Zeitoun et.al, 2015)

Figure 1 Dynamic Transboundary Water Interaction

2.3 Political Transition

In this section clarifying the misconception between political liberalization or reform and transition is demanding for its commonly misused in the official public speeches. Political reforms aim at opening the democratic space for civic participation and involving comprehensive reforms of the state institutions and the constitutional, legal and policy frameworks which shaped the relationship between citizens and the state.

However, political transition implies regime change and often associated with the transition from authoritarianism to democratic, competitive political systems. The ongoing political reforms in Ethiopia is not a political transition for it hardly aim at dismantling the state institutions created by the EPRDF rather to reform these institutions within the confines of the current political developments.

The second important issues that needs further elaboration is why political reform is demanded in contemporary Ethiopia. This idea will serve for clarifying the imperatives/ drivers of the reform. Thought the most frequent answers to the above issue is linked merely to internal developments, the quest for democracy in protest of authoritarian minority rule, its link with the intricacies of the water politics of the Nile aftermath of the GERD project is highly sidelined. In reference to the former the reform is attributed to two major related factors: economic shocks combined with mismanagement of the economy along with political issue as a response to internal pressure. Politically, the demand for reform that made the government yield to internal pressure is not the classic revolt of the opposing political elite. It is preferably the revolt of the earth trodden, excluded, unemployed youth and the peasantry, who would probably be the least to reap the economic dividend of the political reforms.

However, for an elaborated identification of the root and the determinants of the ongoing reform process in Ethiopia, examining the existing models and theories has surmount significance. One of the model which is often used for understanding the prospect of success of transition is the comparative political economy model which analyzes structural variables or historical trajectories. In this case, the country's political history indicates set of dread and deadlocks with high propensity of deterring thc move forward. The other approach is the rationality-activist model which seeks informed and active population in politics.

The populist and inorganic elite are drifting the society towards divergent direction and the third actor centric model which seeks elite bargaining for elite transformations via voluntary collaboration or coalition is deem crucial thought its lacking in the country's present context. The worst is the parochial, subjective political culture in cultural perspective. The most recent approach of understanding is genetic model which calls for national unity and conscious action or pact on the part of the top political leadership. This is also lacking. Thus in all models of analysis of prerequisites of transition, the current context of the country is lacking behind and the prospect for realization of the grand promise of the reforming EPRDF circle is unlikely.

The unpredictability of the future of the state given the high degree of indeterminacy embedded in situations where unexpected events bursting everywhere with insufficient information, hurried and audacious choices, confused motives and interests, and even in definition of political identities have elevated the confusion.

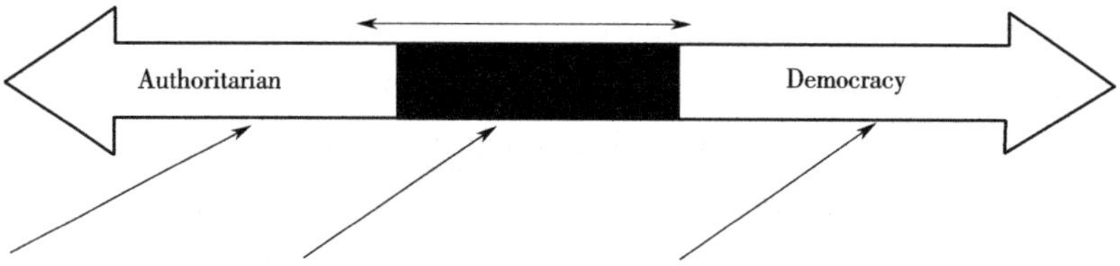

Figure 2 Optimism and Confusion: Where are we heading?

3 Methodology

This study will be grounded in the theoretical framework of Gramscian and neo Gramscian approach in analyzing the hydro politics of Eastern Nile politics in connection of the domestic politics of Ethiopia.

3.1 Methods

The study uses Gramsian and neo Gramscian methods emphasizing on Cox' s critical discourse analysis along with document analysis.

3.2 Data Sources

3.2.1 Archival, Document and Audio-visual Data

Data was extracted from correspondences of Haile Sellassie reserved in Institute of Ethiopian Studies library in Addis, declarations and proclamations, water conventions and decrees such as 1999 UN convention, hidass office bulletins, TV broadcasts, online magazines, past interviews, televised speeches, and press statements.

3.2.2 Field and online Interviews

Semi structured interviews was conducted with members of the GERD diplomacy from Ethiopia, Sudan and Egypt; the academic and political elites, diplomats and political analysts.

3.2.3 Online Data Bases

In this case, online data from global water treaties data base from UN treaty collection; WATERLEX, WATER TREATIES, are used for elaborating the legal commitment of countries in the Basi*n*.

4 The Interplay of Grand Renaissance Dam and the Political Reform in Ethiopia

This section focused on analyzing the rational for the launching of the GERD project from Ethiopian perspective, it's expected benefits, the anti-GERD protest from Egypt, Ethiopian reaction and the future prospect. It attempted to address the debate on why Ethiopia launched the GERD project in 2011 by breaking centuries old silence and how these developments could impact the political reform process and vis versa. It is then followed by a short description of the project and its expected benefits. This portion explains how the project is expected to address the predicaments or how it was legitimized with the popular expectations. The finally section deals about the anti GERD opposition from Egyptian elites and political circles along with the reaction from the Ethiopia.

4.1 Rationale for the Inauguration of the GERD Project

"... centuries of impoverishment curtailed our development and restricted us from exercising our right to use the resources of our own rivers. Now, we are close to opening a new chapter..." Henceforward, nothing can stop us from exercising our rights. So, the first message is that we not only have a plan, but we also have the capacity to assert our rights. The second message we want to send is that the intention to exercise our rights to use our own rivers is in order to fight poverty (Grand Millennium Dam, 15th April 2019).

The most striking question that deserves a non partisan analysis is why Ethiopia decided to launched the GERD project in 2011 waiting in silence for centuries. In fact, the drivers that forced Ethiopia for launching the dam are contested even among Ethiopian scholars leave alone Egypt. The arguments centered on whether the inaugural was really a development driven as in the statements of the government or politically motivated project designed to escape the Arab spring which was the order of the day. Therefore, before dealing with the official inaugural of the project, analyzing the precedents or why Ethiopia seeks for launching the GERD project is very important.

Accordingly, Ethiopia espoused historical explanations that attributes the initiative since the Imperial period and the contemporary development imperatives as its indicated in the inaugural speech cited above. The historical justification which is corroborated with archival sources from the Institute of Ethiopian Studies library addressed that the GERD project was identified as one of the feasible site of hydro electric power generation since the Imperial Era. The Imperial government has made a declaration to develop water resources as it's indicated in the statement made by Emperor Haile Sellassie on 2nd November 1957 which reads as follows.

"... we have already explained that plans are under construction to utilize our rivers as an essential step in the development of agriculture and industry, it is of paramount importance to

Ethiopia, a problem of the first order that the waters of the Nile be made to serve the life and needs of our people now living and those who will follow us in centuries to come... it is Ethiopian's sacred duty to develop the great watershed which she possesses in the interests of her own rapidly expanding population and economy. To fulfill this task, we have arranged for the problem to be studied in all its aspects by experts in the field (Ethiopian Observer, 1958:93)".

In 1927, Ethiopian diplomatic mission to the United States under the leadership of Worqeneh Eshete had negotiated a contract to build a dam on the Blue Nile River. Accordingly, Ethiopia reached an agreement with J. G. White Engineering Corporation of New York, and a number of engineers and experts came to study the feasibility of building a dam over Blue Nile. Therefore, GERD is continuation of preceding historical process aimed at building water harvesting infrastructure contesting the hegemonic arrangement in the Basin.

By the same token, aftermath of their independence and the regaining of the Suez Canal, the next hard slog of the nationalist leaders of Egypt was ascertaining the question of water security through what they referred as the "Nasser Pyramid". With some limited agreement with the newly independent Sudan, Egypt went ahead with the design and the construction of the Aswan High Dam using the assistance both from the West and former USSR.

Ethiopia as a counter reaction went ahead dealing with the United States Engineering firm, Balton Hennessey and Partners, to conduct the first comprehensive survey over Blue Nile. Hence, the first preliminary survey for possible water projects in the Blue Nile and Sobat basin consisting of stream flow, soil type, hydro electric power generating potential, land use, dam site, and irrigation capacity was worked out from 1958-1964 with the assistance of US Bureau of reclamation. Ultimately, four potential hydropower sites with a capacity of three times greater than the Aswan High Dam were identified and the GERD was one of those proposed sites of the time.

In 1962, a German engineering team also carried out further studies on the Blue Nile River. In short, a number of studies, and round table discussions related to the establishment of water infrastructure over Blue Nile were made but none of them were put in to effect due internal constrains and external challenges. As it's indicated here below, Egypt was always determined to keep Ethiopia under constant pressure, so that it would not threaten the continued flow of the Nile water.

Thus, Gamal Abdel Nasser retaliated against Haile Selassie's initiative by supporting armed insurrections of Eritrea (Eritrean question and the Nile) and lastly meddling in the 1974 "induced revolution" along with US. It with this understanding that in a recent interview with one of the prominent editor, Eliase re-coined the 1974 popular upsurge as induced revolution referring to externally driven change. Again, in the 1970s Sadat threatened war over Ethiopia against the construction of a Dam over Lake Tana. The main question is thus, why Egypt became successful in deterring the Imperial and Socialist water project initiatives in Ethiopia?

The second and the most frequent explanation that used to justify Ethiopia's determination for the construction of the GERD project has to do with the alarming developmental imperatives that required high energy production given the magnificent water resource potential (Harris, 1995; Virginia, 2001:7). The great rivers gave the country a cliché name such as the water tower of East Africa. However, these rivers drain out of the country contributing insignificantly to the national wealth. Primarily due to lack of technical and finance capacity compounded with the hydro political wrangling with Egypt, the country failed so far from using them. As a result, its citizens have been suffering from chronic poverty while they stand on rivers that moo and roar year round.

However, the diminishing marginal productivity of traditional rain fed agriculture; alarming population increment and the concomitant deterioration in standard of living threaten the survival of its citizens and put the country at a grave junction. For instance, 83% of its population lack access to electricity and the majority rely on biomass fuel (Global Water Forum, 2013). Worst, its energy demand stretched more than double where as the country lacks water storage facilities and as a result it' s described as hostage to its hydrology.

According to World Bank Report (2006), the cost of hydrological variability in Ethiopia is estimated to be over one third of its annual GDP. Hence, the bank recommended an increased investment in multi-purpose water infrastructure such as hydropower production facilities, irrigation systems, and storage capacities that would make Ethiopia more water resilient.

Thus, the above mentioned juncture calls for pressing duty and determination to exploit its water resource potential in order to put the country on a path of sustainable growth. In repose to this tight spot, first Ethiopia has started building small scale water projects. After building its internal capacity, on 2nd April 2011 the GERD project with the reformed installed capacity of generating 6,750 MW and with faith that the expense will be mobilized from internal funding was officially inaugurated.

Hence, the GERD project is part of a wider scheme by the Ethiopian Government to expand its hydroelectric power generating capacity (Block and Strzepek 2010) and part of the response made to the rising energy demand (MWE, 2016) which has been growing at an average rate 32 per cent per year from 2011-2018. Therefore, the GERD could seen as a response of fulfilling the energy demands of the state following the emulation of the East Asian developmental state model, which requires state capacity in the provision of infrastructures. In short, GERD and the entire hydro electric power producing projects are linked with Ethiopia' s move towards the contested state lead development.

The second millstone is the aspiration to be a regional energy supplier to Djibouti, South Sudan, Keneya, Sudan, Yemen and Europe. After the sacred statuesque was practically challenged by the Ethiopian initiative, the government of Uganda has also commenced the construction of 600 MW Karuma Hydropower Plant (HPP) and associated transmission Lines (Karuma Interconnection Project) on the White Nile having contractual agreement signed with the Sino-hydro Corporation. Generally, it' s significantly justifiable for Ethiopia to use the water of the river to meet its development goals for which increasing power supply is demanding. However, given its coincidence with high days of the Arab spring, opposition political groups and some sections of the society were hesitant to the project thinking that it was means of public attention diversion from political engagement for change.

4.2 The Promised Benefits

The GERD project was launched at Guba 45 KM East of South Sudan in 24 April 2011 with faith of its cost would be covered through internal funding. The dam was expected to generate 6,750 MW and expected to have volume of 60 billion meter cubic.

The project was attracting the popular attention for it is associated with the age old aspiration of generations for uplifting the country's economy. Thus, the main question here is "Do the promises of the project hold water or are they likely to be deferred dreams?"

"... among the concerns we factored in when we made the decision to build the Nile Dam with our own resources, was to avoid any negative consequences for our neighbors and indeed to offer positive benefits for all of them. I would dare to say that nothing can provide a better testimony of our deepest commitment to forge a lasting partnership between all the Nile Basin riparian countries than the building of (GERD). On this occasion, therefore, we, the peoples of Ethiopia, call upon all the peoples of the Nile Basin to turn over to a new page of cooperation and solidarity. As we in Ethiopia build this dam with the aim of eradicating poverty, let it be known to all that it will also stand as an expression of our commitment to the benefit of all the countries of the Nile basin ." (Grand Millennium Dam, 2019)

As its espoused in many public forums and governmental statements, the GERD project is expected to have interwoven effect on Ethiopia economy especially in fueling growth by associating it with studies that indicate a unit percent increase in energy supply resulting in increasing economic growth by at least one percent. The energy supply is also expected to facilitate the application of modern technology for transforming the agricultural sector and bringing a structural change in the industrial sector. The project is also expected to serve for mitigating climatic shocks, as buffer zone for the expanding Sahara desert and a useful corridor for wild life.

According to the technical documents of the project and the Ethiopian electric power corporation (EEPCO), GERD will add 6,750MW to the existing energy supply and create a reservoir area of about 1,680km^2 and 15m depth which adds a new opportunity for the fishery sector of the nation and neighboring countries.

In the short run, the project has created an employment opportunity for about 15,000 citizens. In the future, it is expected to have mega employment opportunity that will have further trickle-down benefits in the economy (EEPCO, 2013). Beside, energy export is expected to diversify export earnings and reduce the shortage of foreign reserve with estimated value of one $billion in a year. Up on the successful completion of the project, the country will be able to generate foreign currency by supplying climate friendly energy to other countries (reducing carbon emission). According to the study from Addis Ababa University, GERD could generate around $1 billion in a year (Yilma, 2013) that would be a very helpful income for addressing the existing trade balance deficit.

In this regard, GERD is the beginning not the end of the projects which Ethiopia planed to construct in the basin. In order to achieve its long term goal of being regional energy supplier, Ethiopia initiated a 25 years master plan for building hydroelectric dams along its 12 river basins (Huffington post 2018). Therefore, the experience gained from the GERD is expected to be harnessed for the completion of the forthcoming energy generating projects. Moreover, the implication of construction of the GERD is not merely process of arresting water for producing energy rather it' s the signal for reinstituting the new Ethiopian self and new ideational power by consolidating the sense of invincibility in contesting the statuesque. Creating sense of the possibility of doing other forms of projects and technological transfer is, therefore, other fundamental contribution of GERD project.

Thus, GERD is taken as seal of all the battles that the country had ever fought even more remarkable than the battle of Adwa, where by Ethiopia has gained military victories and economic defeats, in boosting the tide of Ethiopian nationalism. As in the heroic move during Adwa, currently the mass from every village is mobilized with discourse of invincibility of Ethiopians in harnessing all the penny for finalizing the GERD project so that it will serve as an emblem of national pride.

The developments in Ethiopia for the GERD project have resemblance to the mobilization made in Egypt for the Aswan High Dam. At the conclusion of the Aswan High Dam in 1964, Nasser in his speech with the intention of further stringing up Egyptian nationalism espoused as "here are joined the political, social, national and military battles of the Egyptian people, welded together like the gigantic mass of rock that has blocked the course of the ancient Nile. Its waters now spill into the largest lake shaped by human kind and which will be an everlasting source of prosperity". (Waterbury, 1979:98) In fact, the High Dam discourse was deeply entrenched in the overall Egyptian political psyche and hence it' s referred as an agent for the birth of a "psychological state" (Ibid: 116) In a similar token, GERD is symbolized as unifying national pyramid, flagship project for fermenting the tide of Ethiopian nationalism in the national media. However, the basic question is how the government succeed in convincing citizens about the expected benefits of the dam in addressing the wide spread developmental predicaments given the internal political legitimacy crisis?

In addition to its benefit for Ethiopia, the GERD expected to provide many positive effects for the downstream countries. This was made clear in the inaugural speech which states that "the benefits accrue from the dam will by no means be restricted to Ethiopia. They will clearly extend to all neighboring states, and particularly to Sudan and Egypt". Therefore, the GERD reservoir is expected to regulate the downstream flow so that Sudan and Egypt would have the opportunity for sustainable water outflow. The regulated flow plays a considerable role in reducing the recurring flooding risks, harvest loss due to shortage of water during critical growing periods. It will also boost under-performing downstream hydroelectric power plants capacity. Furthermore, the GERD is expected to trap sediments which would otherwise be carried downstream stream.

The transformational role of the dam on East African economies from water intensive sector to industry and for accelerating regional economic integration is also very immense. Above all, GERD promotes the sub regional power interconnection for stimulating the regional economy. Ethiopia is exporting large amounts of clean power across East Africa starting with Djibouti and Sudan. Djibouti has started taking 70%-80% of its energy demand from Ethiopia. The 283 KM Ethio-Djibouti transmission line which enabled Djibouti to import up to 60 MW of electricity was officially inaugurated in October 2011. Electricity is costly in Djibouti compared with the rest of East Africa and even Arab League member states, making its capital, Djibouti City, one of the most expensive cities in the Arab world. Thus, this interconnection is estimated to provide Ethiopia at least $1.5 million per month, sustainable use of Djibouti port as main gateway and eased Djibouti's reliance on fossil fuel power plants and generators.

Furthermore, the planned energy interconnection to Kenya will be one of the largest African regional electric highways. It is designed to carry between 400 MW and 2,000 MW. The construction and development of the Ethiopia-Kenya electric transmission line could bring Ethiopia closer to the East African community. It would also make Kenya, which has the region's largest industrial base, the largest buyer of Ethiopian power eventually amounting around 400 MW, and could allow Ethiopia to export up to 1,600 MW to countries further South. In 2012, the Ethiopian Electric Power Corporation signed its fourth power export agreement with South Sudan, to be undertaken in two phases (MWE, 2013).

In general, as it is mentioned it in the earlier sections of this study, the country has an estimated potential capacity of 45,000 megawatts (MW) of energy from hydro alone, and this makes the country to be the center of an emerging energy exporter across the region. Ethiopia, a member of East African power pool which aims to connect the power grids of at least nine countries including Ethiopia, Kenya, Rwanda, Uganda, Burundi, Tanzania, Democratic Republic of Congo. Sudan and Djibouti, is contributing its renewable energy to the rest of the countries in the pool. The Ethiopian Electric Power Corporation (EEPCo) has designed a power sector strategy aiming to boost generating capacity to 37,000 MW by 2037 where by the surplus power is scheduled for export to the pool. The regional energy lead inter connection is important for economic and security interdependence. Are all these broken promises or deferred promises that await the finalization of the project? Can the GERD really generate all these promise or are they merely opium?

4.3 Contradicting Visions: Egypt's Anti GERD Protest and Ethiopia's Reaction

This part of the study attempted to address why the protest against GERD project emerged and examine whether the concerns raised were real or imagined. Contrary to the out pouring of popular support for GERD in Ethiopia, the inaugural has quickly drawn indignation from Egypt (World Politics Review, 2019). Though Egypt vehemently rejected the authenticity of the information, Wiki Leaks had disclosed the message of Egypt's ambassador to Lebanon who stated about his country's intention to attack GERD in its inception (huffington post 2012). However, the strongest protest has come to the front following the rerouting of the River which was announced on 28th May as part of the construction process. This event has led into outrageous verbal assault, sabotaging and informal declaration of war. Here instead of narrating the verbiage of the protesting politicians, it's important to review all the concerns raised in due course of time.

4.3.1 Fear of Reduction in Nile Flow/Securitization of Nile Water

The review of written and oral discourses along with online interviews indicated that most of the protests were rooted in anticipated fear of reduction in the volume of water reaching Egypt. For instance, Egyptian authorities have contested its construction with a claim that it would drastically lower the volume of the Nile, which could in turn reduce cultivation of farmland up to 25% (Guardain, 2017). Accordingly, they claimed that they are at a state of about 10bn kilo liters water deficit that would be worsen into catastrophic crisis after GERD. Bahaa Alkoussey, the former chairman of Egypt's national water research centre, claimed about the possibility of crossing the Nile on the back of a camel after the completion of the GERD. This heightened fear could be associated with what the American scholar has referred as water stress phobia.

Let alone the ordinary citizens who were indoctrinated with imagined catastrophic water scarcity following any new development in Ethiopia and the instrumentalist politicians, intelligence experts also share this worry. Jay Radzinski and Nimrod Asulin, senior analysts and intelligence managers at Max security solutions, a geopolitical risk consulting firm, stated that the construction of GERD is a zero-sum game, and Egypt would face crippling water shortage just two years after its completion. Thought the engagement of think thanks in influencing the GERD debate is worthy, the provision of unfounded data and lopsided conclusions as it's witnessed here above rather served for flaring up the conflict.

Hani Rislan, director of al-Ahram: Political and Strategic Research Center of African Unit argued that the project will cost Egypt $4 million revenue loss in agriculture, unemployment of 2 million families, compromising the potential of the Aswan Dam and the submerging of Khartoum due to dam site selection defect.

However, these claims lack empirically grounded argument for the GERD is non water consumptive project and hence, it will not pose significant harm to the water level. Moreover, according to the finding of Lemperiere (2013), the availability of the Nile water could be increased by 30% if certain cooperative measures are taken. Therefore, the claim is merely rested on water stress phobia than actual risk.

4.3.2 Loss of Controlling and Leveraging Power

There is also a fear in Egypt that the large storage capability of the dam of valuable Nile water in the hands of upstream Ethiopia. This claim failed to understand about the jarring energy strain and the cost of being hostage to its hydrology. It is basically rested on the undeclared interest of keeping Ethiopia in chain of poverty trap while Egypt used to milk its own cow. This is equated with the underdevelopment and development narrative of Gunder Frank. The premise is rooted in the misperception that negates economically strong and politically unified Ethiopia. Cairo's real concern centered on the idea that the more Ethiopia gains political and economic clout, the lesser would be Egypt's say on the politics of Nile basin. They presumed the shifting of the balance of diplomatic influence in favor of Ethiopia following GERD. But for Ethiopia this is a relic of 19th century zero-sum thinking where one nation's gain was thought to accrue only at the expense of another. Hence, while Ethiopia's position is shaped by the conviction of regional integration, Egypt is tied with untenable claim.

4.3.3 Fear of Dam Collapse and Pollution

Some others such as Alkoussey claimed the dam would cause more pollution, harming fishing farms and devastate the farming community. Ala al-Zewahiri stated that the dam is constructed on an unfavorable location between two mountains which would cause faults, dam collapse and the submerging of Khartoum. The Egyptian geologists claim that dam site is prone to tectonic activities and higher chance for dam collapse is annulled by Ethiopian experts who revealed the fact that the area of the project was away from the tectonic activity of the rift valley rather the project site is a place where igneous rock mountains are predominant, making it least susceptible to tectonic activities.

4.3.4 Political Motivated Conspiracy

Abbas Sheraky argued that the dam is intended for political consumption and that the amount of megawatt it produces is way beyond Ethiopia's need. In a similar token, Messrs Radzinski, Nisman, and Asulin who are senior analysts and intelligence managers at solutions, reiterated about the impetus of political ideology and foreign conspiracy as a foundation of the project.

The protest includes theory of conspiracy that attributes foreign plot as agent for the initiation of GERD using the internal instability in Egypt as a facilitator. This mind set is still intact as it's reflected in the Egyptian wave of thoughts which attribute the inauguration of the Ethiopian GERD project to the Judeo-Christian plot underestimating Ethiopia's capability to run the project by itself. The Israelization or Americanization of any upstream water project is common discourse among the Egyptian main stream society. Some Egyptians argued that the government of Ethiopian was instructed by the MOSSAD and CIA for constructing GERD to cripple Egyptian move in defiance of the Camp David deal. Some others attribute it to global power dynamics that pulled out Egypt from the game due to its internal instability. Adul Malak Ouda (2002), attributes the changes taking place in the Nile Basin to the intervention of the G-20 powers. According to him, the capitalist economic and military competition has turned Africa in a position of a satellite region where by the competition in the Nile Basin became fierce owing to US big push for the control of the geo-strategy and resources in the Basin.

Accordingly, the Nile basin preferred as a perfect center for American strategists for military command and operations. Furthermore, the USA intends to check Chinese interests in Africa. The competition between France and the USA in the fields of trade, investments, and culture, education, and arms sales has also sharpened to a blade's edge. In regard to the issue of resource, the Nile River Basin hosts Africa's most valuable fresh water which is highly demanded for curving the potential global water stress. Basing their argument on these assertion, some Egyptians trace the inspiration of the establishment of the GERD as concomitant response for the failure of Egypt in competing with the G-20 renewed interest in the continent following the financial crisis and rise of China factor as alternative source of funding to water projects.

However, attributing the mega project to plots of G-20, China, CIA, MOSSAD, Turkey, Israel or any external event than internal development interest has to do resurgence of racist assumptions that undermines the capacity of Ethiopia. Constructor is Saline not china-us support Egypt than Ethiopia. In order annul all of the aforementioned unwise claims, elaborating the foreign policy pillars of the two countries and dynamics of their diplomatic engagements has profound advantage for understanding the GERD relation scenario. However, 'the concerns are bereft of empirical ground but guided the unscientific misperception or fortune-telling (Guardain, 2019).'

Generally, the foundation underneath of all these arguments is basically rested on the latent or undeclared interest of keeping Ethiopia in chain of poverty trap, for dictating stronger Ethiopia will be impossible for Egypt. Accordingly, the development of Ethiopia is assumed as a basic agent that could undermine the progress of Egypt. The rise of Ethiopia is seen as rise of threatening counter hegemony. This mind set is shaped by the unequivocal understanding of the historic water injustice and the concomitant fear of revenge.

4.4 Ethiopia`s Reaction to the GERD Protest

The first question that might strike our mind is how Ethiopia reacted to the anti GERD protest. In spite of the aggressive and outright opposition bursting out in Egypt, Ethiopia's reaction to the move was primarily centered on consolidating its internal military and intelligence capacity. It has also labored highly to dispel fear of aggression coming from Egypt while the later was trying to have air basis both in Sudan and Eritrea claiming to veto the GERD project. Legitimizing the regional benefits of the project and aggressive economic diplomacy with core premises of energy lead regional integration was also perused in its effort for sidling Egypt from the orbit of African diplomacy. Besides, it has officially assured to avoid significant impact downstream riparians. For such end, it has allowed the establishment international pancl of experts and tripartite technical team. The later has opened the way for tripartite diplomacy. Here below is review of some of the reactions that Ethiopia made following the anti GERD protest.

4.4.1 Capacity Building

In the pre GRED period capacity building preparations were made in building proactive defensive military and intelligence capability which served as primary source for dispelling entrenched fear and for building ideational power. However, due to entrenched corruption practice, there is loophole of establishing regulatory mechanism of financial flow so as to curve the economic dimension of the battle. The failure of giving priority for strengthening internal cohesion through basic democratic reforms and failure of deterring the emerging Islamic brother hoods aspiration for creating its replica in Ethiopia might take Ethiopia at a cross road of either swimming ever or sinking for thousands of years.

4.4.2 Continental and International Diplomacy

In the continental diplomacy, Ethiopia has highly labored for the last three decades for representing the African voice. Moreover, its economic diplomacy which is tailored on promoting regional integration was welcomed for promoting intra African trade and for the revival the economies of the continent at large. Thus, Ethiopia has framed all rounded interconnections with the conviction of stimulating its economic growth with support of the comparative gains from its neighbors. In this regard, it has given due attention for the development of roads, railways, aviation and energy infrastructures with a view to enhance meaningful regional integration with South Sudan, Sudan, Kenya, Somali and Djibouti. This is very instrumental for deepening regional market integration as per the guiding principles of AU which aspires for establishing a continental free trade area. Thus, Ethiopia had out maneuvered Egypt's zero sum move in Africa through its fitting economic diplomacy which is pillared on collective decision and mutual benefit making. But, its relation with its neighbors has not yet reached at point of no return. Hence, Egypt will continue to buy off some of the weakest and less stable neighbors.

Therefore, Ethiopia needs a critical and integrated diplomatic response to the ferment in South Sudan, political forces of "Somalia" and Khartoum. There is a tough task of establishing an interface between the pillars of its continental diplomacy and the dynamics of the international political alignment. In this regard, the country has to take lessons from diplomatic twists of the cold war era. The siding of Sudan with Ethiopia on the GERD issue has been marked as remarkable achievement in the public discourse in Ethiopia. However, the ongoing unrest following the recent coup could complicate the politics of the Dam.

4.4.3 Circumventing Financial Deficit

Economic war and aggressive move of halting foreign aid and loans is one of the basic instrument of Egypt with the dual intention of creating constrain of financing of GERD project and for obtaining loophole of intervention in local affairs with the guise of local discontent due to heavy economic burdens. Egypt has been lobbying against Ethiopia and Ethiopia has been unable to get access to fund from the IMF and World Bank to finance mega projects which have the potential to lift millions of Ethiopians out of poverty. Ethiopia has now decided to finance the Great Ethiopian Renaissance Dam using its own sources. Owing to its influence in the Arab world, it has labored to perpetuate hostility and suspicion towards Ethiopia. Egypt has also more or less succeeded by using its influence as leader of the Arab world in blocking Ethiopia from obtaining aid and loans from other sources to exploit the water resources of the Nile. Egypt's belief has been that Ethiopia, mired in poverty and embroiled in endless conflict, could not develop the basin on its own, and that with the opportunities for aid and credit closed, Ethiopians will have no choice but to sit and watch the river flow.

Hence, to curve out the danger of deficit spending, the GERD is highly integrated with the local economy. In such a way, instead of the expected crisis, the project could serve for further stimulating the economy. The country's financial weight is also accepted to be elevated by promoting culture of saving along with the government's endeavor of raising funds through increasing revenues and careful expenditure. The effort of promoting local saving needs to be backed with relentless struggle against corruption and illicit transfer of money outside the country. See challenges-corruption and finical deficient

Legitimizing the benefits of the GERD for the nation and the continent

4.4.4 Tripartite GERD Diplomacy

The Ethio-Egypt GERD diplomacy was characterized by intermittent engagement, wrestling, fallout and Impasse. Thus, analyzing the tides of Ethio-Egyptian GERD diplomacy is important for illuminating the details about the unfounded outright stands of Egypt towards the project. When Ethiopia re-initiated the Nile project to accomplish its unrealized dream over Blue Nile, President Hosni Mubarak did the same as his antecedents.

Mursi again fall in the same realistic trap while he aired the idea of "defending each drop of Nile water with Egyptian blood" in the recent televised Nile row. Morsi warned that "all options are open" to challenge Ethiopia's Nile project. Ethiopia through Haile Mariam responded that "nothing" and "no one" will stop the dam's construction. He downplayed the prospect of conflict, saying Egypt leaders won't go to war unless they go mad. After the announcement of the building of the dam, Egypt started trying to put pressure on Ethiopia through continental diplomacy and psychological warfare.

The inaugural of the GERD project and tabling of CFA was followed by sending of high level delegation to Addis and Uganda. There was also request for technical and environmental studies of the project from Hussein Al-Atfy, the Egyptian Irrigation Minister. He warned that that Egypt would resort to pressure the international community or even consider military action.

Ethiopian Minister of Water and Energy told the parliament that Ethiopia made two bold decisions concerning the dam namely postponing the ratification of the agreement by a year to accommodate Egypt's request for buying time until an elected government was in place and letting experts including from Egypt and Sudan to inspect the Dam.

Due to the stubborn position of Egypt, ultimately Ethiopia's parliament unanimously endorsed the new Nile River Cooperative Framework Entebbe accord already signed by five other Nile River countries amidst of verbal jousting following the rerouting of the Nile. This shows the bold move from Ethiopian side in spite of the declaration of psychological warfare from Egypt. Thus, in those days many were predicting an immediate outbreak of war while established scholars on the area blatantly ridiculed the proposal. Do the Egyptian televised protest strengthened or disturbed Ethiopia? What were the next diplomatic processes? Was there resort from established coercive diplomacy and psychological warfare to actual water war?

4.5 EPRDF's Promises: Electoral Democracy and Mega Dam

The principal aim of this part of the article is to highlight the connects between the ongoing political reform of Ethiopia, and the age old Nile politics. The reform though its unfinished business and premature to be hailed as unprecedented development, yet it has brought optimism and opportunities of practical relevance. The seismic political opening which ensued since April 2018, the web of legal and administered directives, regulations and policy frame created unprecedented opportunity for disciplining the heavy-handed tactics and arbitrary detention orchestrated by the security and intelligence.

It has also created an opportunity for a peaceful resolution of the fundamental issues defining the national question and the future form of government structure ensuring the separation of the state and the government, the separation of power and the independence of the judiciary. However, given the top down approach of the reforming process which is expected to went far towards transitional arrangement needs to be supported from below with civic engagement.

The later is important in shaping the path towards democracy and addressing the fundamental question how the democratic space can become more open and integrating in order to strengthen the social cohesion in the country. Furthermore, the end of the protest and return of opposition from exile have generated both optimism and confusion.

The heightened popular expectations towards peaceful, prosperous and democratic future along with unenlightened moves have shadowed the optimism with uncertainty which can be grasped from interstate relations, federal government and regional states relations and the viability of the reform to stretch towards transition. In spite of the warm applaud for the EPRDF's reform in its onset, now the process is twisting between optimism and suspicion. People are asking where we are heading due to the missing road map for transition.

In fact, in the common public discourse the reform is dubbed as transition where as transition is the space between one political regime and another characterized by the dissolution of an authoritarian regime and installation of some form of democracy competed with the return to some form of authoritarian rule or the emergence of a revolutionary alternative (Schmitter,1986:6).

In actual fact what is still going on in Ethiopia is political liberalization which implies an easing of repression and extension of civil liberties within an authoritarian regime by embracing pro-liberalization faction. As liberalization begins with schisms within the authoritarian coalition (Kaufman, 1986) those EPRDF reformist teams are acclaimed as harbingers of the promise to democracy. This tendency ignores the fact that internal schisms are necessary if an authoritarian regime is to liberalize. The splits within authoritarian coalitions as a starting point for liberalization don't mean neglecting the impact of opposition actors/mass mobilization. Some actors within an authoritarian coalition may begin liberalization primarily in response to actors outside the coalition and may co-opt with moderate groups. Liberalization begins because actors in the authoritarian coalition who initiated liberalization want to minimize losses/ retain power by deterring an all our radical change.

The aspiration to move from authoritarian rule to the gestation of democracy has been the question for generations and the grand promise of the reformative political liberalization is ensuring electoral democracy at any cost. The legacy of the authoritarian past such as the cult of personality not programs, zero-sum politics , the military contestants for political power , ethnicity weak state capacity and civil society mix-up of domestic and foreign politics, lack of collective goals, party and social fragmentation are the possible stumbling blocks for the success of the promised transition. However, all the attributions are entirely confined to the internal challenges sidelining the regional and global challenges. In this case, the examination of the political history of the country, indicates that the birth of democracy was either procrastinated or aborted due to the intricacies of the Nile politics. Now in the 21st century the Nile basin has entered a new chapter since the Arab spring and the inauguration of GERD. Thus, the question that seeks deeper scrutiny both from the lessons of the past and contemporary manifestations is understanding the link between domestic political process in Ethiopia and the Nile politics with focus on GERD project.

In a dispassionate study on the country's past, we find that every single Bishop from the See of Alexandria was serving as political pope. Thus, to control the secular affairs of the state and as well the religious beliefs of the peoples, these religious figures associated themselves with the palace men.

Besides, they were entitled with the ultimate power to decide on the legitimacy of the political figureheads that can rule the country. Ethiopian Monarchs were anointed by Coptic Bishops who were even held sway in courts. Thus, they were serving both as political and spiritual representatives (Paulos, 2005:243). As they do the blessing for the coronation of kings, the popes were also active in unmaking them. They instigated protests against rulers of the country such as Tewodros IV and Leji Iyassu using the church as epicenter of the protest. Thus, disguise themselves in the question of the church, the Egyptians were intervening in the internal political affairs of Ethiopia.

For instance, after the defeat of Dejjach Wube at the battle of Deresege, the captive Abune, Abune Selama, was affiliated with Tewodros IV and blessed him in his coronation in return for enforcing the Tewahido doctrine, but this mutuality weakened and ultimately Tewodros found himself beset in an opposition spearheaded by priests under the tutorship of the Abune (Paulos, 2005:46).

Though in most cases the church opposition against Tewodros IV narrated as internal contradiction between the modernization project of the state and the church resistance against the program, the opposition was initially an outside driven and initiated by Abune Selama, the agent of the Egyptian policy, in response to Tewodros' s obsession against the them and suspicion about the diversion or damming of the Nile as part of his economic modernization program.

Though Tewodros IV come up with a strong belief of defeating the "undefeatable" and attain the state power by crushing the squabbling noble of the era of princes by dint of his power, yet he couldn' t escape the established trap for securing political legitimacy through the blessing of the Egyptian Abune. This engrained mentality of the reigning kings that valued this blessing for the attainment of political legitimacy than the will and the aspiration of the people has cost the country high due to internal strife to capture the throne and the Abune.

Generally, the long annals of Blue Nile revolved mainly around the idea that by controlling the river, Ethiopia could deprive Egypt of its life-blood neglecting its reliance on the Coptic Church as the source of Patriarchal authority. The Egyptians were suspicious of progressive leaders such as Atse Lalibäla (Bairu, 2000:160). In fact, they were protesting against the legitimacy of the Zague dynasty since its inception. Thus, water-cross exchange mutuality has faced decisive blow during the Zagwe dynasty as they challenged the foundations of the Solomonic legend. The fear about diverting the river and the eventually increment of his glory is rooted in this antipathy. However, the Blue Nile was out of the reaches of the Zagwe Kingdom. It was initially incorporated and Christianized during the reign of Atse Amdätsion (Henze, 41; Bairu,160). The emperors of the Solomonic dynasty, especially Dawit II, Yéshaq and Zäŕya Yaéqob went on asserting Ethiopia' s control of the river as a tool in their intercontinental relations. They also worked to cement this concept of mastering the Nile in religious terms, identifying the Abbay with the Biblical Gion. Following the end of the Zagwe rule and the accession of Yukuno Amlak to power in 1270, Egypt has refused to send Bishop backing Sultanate of Yifat. This shows the shift from Christian solidarity to Islamic Alliance.

4.6 Current Status and Future Prospect

The GERD diplomacy was characterized with ebbs and tides with intermittent interruptions. Thus at every episode of interruption, predictions towards continuation of water diplomacy or resorting towards water war were made since the commencement of the GERD. For instance, when Ethiopia rerouted the Nile flow and its parliament ratified an accord that replaced the colonial deals, there was heightened expectation about outbreak of war and, many scholars had predicted that Egypt may use the hard water diplomacy to react to the diplomatic and security developments in the Ethiopia.

The pessimistic hydro political experts from Middle East have described Ethiopia's rerouting of the Blue Nile to make way for GERD construction as "a unilateral move" that risked a regional war. The new myth of doing things perfect by conquest was expected to be applied by hasty political leaders of Egypt that would ended with fatal collision with Ethiopia. But the test from the psychological warfare proved Ethiopian invincibility to the new myth as it can be inferred from the rejection of the late Prime minister has about the possibility of deterring a threat by Egypt on the building of dams and other water projects in Ethiopia. The impossibility of war between the two was predicted based on the belief that Ethiopia has gone through period of building internal capability that could effectively manage Egypt's interference.

Egypt is well aware of the danger of the simplistic calculation of deflecting internal turmoil by declaring aggression on Ethiopia. It's very clear for them that such a decision will be futile not only in terms of stabilizing the internal turmoil but also in coordinating and mobilizing the internal resource for countering the counter offense of Ethiopia for self-defense. Therefore, the possibility of direct aggression for thwarting the GERD project has no any strategic rooms. Besides, the recession of the economy, the decline its tie with the West and the rise of the China factor in the Nile is taken as deterrence factors of the war over the GERD.

Actually, Egyptian leaders have regularly issued threats to deter Ethiopia from completing the project, without much success. Meanwhile, Sudan, has sided with Ethiopia, heightening uncertainty in Cairo over the future of Nile water sharing. The former have attempted to substantiate their argument citing the consistent rejections of the two Nile Basin countries to sign CFA. Despite various prophesies that issued Nile River as major sources of conflict in the region, many analysts argue that the Nile water would continue with its integrative role.

Given this conditions there are still possible scenario that could explain the forthcoming situation between the two states. The first scenario draw lesson from a historical precedent linking with similar event that had taken place in Sudan in1950s. For couple of years, the two were dealing about water sharing but finally Egyptian sponsored military coup changed the terms of the agreement in favor of Egypt. Hence, if Ethiopia failed to give due attention to the internal political stability through a democratic transition, failure in the ongoing process, the possibility of creating coup guising through election fraud in 2020 could serve as basic tool to be backed by the fermenting political Islam. Thus, the implication of the current political process of the country on GERD project and the hydro politics of the Nile is detrimental.

4.7 Conclusion

The geopolitical changes in the basin such as the political liberation in Ethiopia and the construction of the GERD project are highly intertwined with the Nile politics. Its impact on the domestic process is surmounting. Reforming the state institutions and the legal, administrative and policy frameworks which contributed to the political anomaly is believed to be the utmost preoccupation of the political liberalization process. However, for the political reform process to be successful, government and major political forces (civil society, media, women, youth, professionals, workers and peasant associations), must go beyond the normative rhetoric by creating institutionalized channels for citizens' and civic organizations to participate in debating and making submissions to various reforming committees rather than espousing top-down proclamations and directives.

The second utmost engagement is the evaluation of the Civic spaces Reforms namely

Media Reforms for creating vibrant media; Civil Society and NGOs Reform; Electoral System reforms for indicating best electoral system fit for contextual reality of the country and Judicial System Reform. Ethnic Federalism, the Constitution, developmental state and which democracy meant revolutionary, liberal social, procedural substantive are still the sacrosanct and sacred cows of EPRDF.

In spite of the fact that the harmlessness of the GERD project to Egyptian and Sudanese water interests has been identified both by international experts and local tripartite technical committee, the contest is still moving thought the causes of the protest against the project from the Egyptian side and the reaction of Ethiopia are incompatible. Ethiopia argued the Egyptian protest against the dam is baseless and politically motivated but Egypt had set of reasons about the possible impact of the dam on the life of its people. Thus, these categorical contentions needs to be settled through rigorous and inclusive non partisan study.

References

[1] ARON T. 2008. The political economy of the Nile Basin regime in 20th century. Lewiston, New York: Edwin Mellen Press.

[2] CASCÃO A E. 2008. Ethiopia-challenges to Egyptian hegemony in the Nile Basin. Water Policy, 10(S2): 13–28.

[3] CASCÃO A E, ZEITOUN M. 2010. Tactics to counter hegemony in transboundary river basins. London: London Water Research Group.

[4] COLLINS R O. 1990. The waters of the Nile: hydropolitics of the Jonglei Canal, 1900–1988, Oxford: Clarendon Press.

[5] COX R W. 1983. Gramsci, hegemony and international relations: an essay in method. Millienium, 12 (2): 162–175.

[6] DANIEL K. 1999. Egypt and the hydro politics of the Blue Nile River. Journal of North East African Studies, 6(1-2): 141-169.

[7] GRAMSCI A. 1971. Selections from the prison notebooks of Antonio Gramsci. New York: International Publishers.

[8] HAGGAI E, ISRAEL G. 2000. The Nile: histories, cultures, myths. London: lynne Rienner Publishers.

[9] HOMER-DIXON T F. 1994. Environmental scarcities and violent conflict: evidence from cases. International Security, 19(1): 5–40.

[10] DE STEFANO L, JACOB D P, SPROLES A E et al. 2017. Assessment of transboundary river basins for potential hydro-political tensions. Global Environmental Change, (45): 35-46.

[11] LUSTICK I S. 2002. Hegemony and the riddle of nationalism: the dialectics of nationalism and religion in the Middle East. Logos, 1(3) (Summer): 18-44.

[12] MARCEL K. 2007. Geo-politics and geo-economics//MARCEL K, MUNA N, MECHTHILD N

et al. The hydro politics of Africa: a contemporary challenge. Newcastle: Cambridge Scholars Publishing.

[13] MARK Z, JEROEN W. 2006. Hydro-hegemony — a framework for analysis of trans-boundary water conflicts[J]. Water Policy, 8(5): 435-460.

[14] MIRUMACHI N. 2013. Securitising shared waters: an analysis of the hydropolitical context of the Tanakpur Barrage project between Nepal and India. The Geographical Journal, 179(4): 309–319.

[15] NASR H; NEEF A. 2016. Ethiopia' s challenge to Egyptian hegemony in the Nile River Basin: the case of the Grand Ethiopian Renaissance Dam. Taylor & Francis (Routledge) Geopolitics, 21(4): 969-989.

[16] NYE J. 1990. Bound to lead: the changing nature of American power. New York: Basic Books.

[17] Ohlsson L. 1995. Hydro politics. conflicts over water as a development constraint. London: Zed Books.

[18] ROBERT W C. 1981. Social forces, states and world orders: beyond international relations theory[J]. Millennium: Journal of International Studies, 10(2): 126-155.

[19] SELBY J. 2005. Oil and water: the contrasting anatomies of resource conflicts. Government and Opposition, 40 (2): 200-224.

[20] TAFESSE T. 2001. The Nile question: hydropolitics, legal wrangling, modus vivendi and perspectives. Munster: Lit Verlag.

[21] TERJE T. 1992. The management of water and irrigation//DOORNBOS M et al. Beyond conflict in the Horn: prospect for peace, recovery and development in Ethiopia, Somalia and Sudan. Trenton: The Red Sea Press.

埃塞俄比亚医疗卫生的发展与面临的挑战

姚苗苗 王一鸣

摘要：近年来埃塞俄比亚（简称“埃塞”）是非洲政治、经济和社会发展领域的新星，卫生事业也取得了令人瞩目的成绩，现已成为非洲大陆卫生事业发展的典范。埃塞政府致力于为每一个埃塞公民争取合法的健康权益，完善医疗保健系统，努力扩大医疗覆盖体系，改善埃塞国民的健康；筹建各级各类医学人才队伍，充实从中央到基层的医疗机构；改进疾病预防控制策略，改善民众健康质量，提高卫生总体水平；源源不断的外来援助为该国卫生事业发展提供了大量资金。然而，埃塞国内政局频繁快速变迁，城乡卫生供给的巨大鸿沟以及国际援助的大量同质化供给等，给该国卫生事业的进一步发展带来了巨大的挑战。

关键字：埃塞俄比亚；医疗卫生；国际援助

一、埃塞俄比亚的医疗卫生发展现状

埃塞俄比亚是非洲第二人口大国和自然增长率最高的国家之一。近年来，埃塞在经济、政治和社会领域的成绩有目共睹，作为重要的社会服务部门，卫生领域成就斐然，一跃成为非洲医疗卫生发展典范国家，人民健康权益明显提升。埃塞近年来医疗卫生领域的发展主要表现在以下几个方面。

第一，医疗服务可及性提高，医疗服务的供给范围和覆盖人口不断扩展。目前，埃塞全国 92% 的人口能够享受到各类医疗服务，重大疾病的防控取得可喜进展。艾滋病毒 / 艾滋病（HIV/AIDS）感染率、产妇和婴儿死亡率分别下降了 90%、67% 和 69%。（见表 1、表 2、表 3）

表 1 埃塞俄比亚 HIV/AIDS 控制概况

	2001	2012	2013	2014
HIV/AIDS 死亡人数（每 10 万人口）	148.0	51.0	48.0	
HIV/AIDS 在 15 至 45 岁成人中的流行率（%）	1.9	0.8		1.2
HIV/AIDS 发病率（每 100 000 人）	185.0	22.0		23.0

（来源：世界卫生组织，埃塞俄比亚 2016 年卫生统计概况）

表 2　产妇死亡率

	1990	1995	2000	2005	2010	2015
产妇死亡率（10 万个活产）	1.400	1.200	990	740	420	353

（来源：世界卫生组织，埃塞俄比亚 2016 年卫生统计概况）

表 3　儿童死亡率

	1990	2000	2015
5 岁以下儿童死亡率（每 1000 活产儿童死亡人数）	614	146	59
婴儿死亡率（每 1000 活产儿中出生至 1 岁死亡的概率）	122	90	41

（来源：世界卫生组织，埃塞俄比亚 2016 年卫生统计概况）

第二，医疗卫生总支出不断增加（见表 4），卫生基础设施从中央到地方有了根本性的全面改善。埃塞卫生机构的数量从 1 515 家增至 19 506 家，其中 205 家为医院、3 256 家为医疗中心、16 025 家为医疗站点。接下来埃塞政府拟继续将医院增加至 800 家。除卫生基础设施的支出不断增加外，埃塞俄比亚在减少产妇、新生儿童的死亡率以及重大疾病防控方面的卫生支出也在不断地增加。

第三，培养了大量的医务人才，为民众提供安全便捷的卫生服务。为了提供高质量的服务，埃塞政府努力培养医务人才充实医疗卫生体系，医务人员的数量和比例在不断增加。埃塞现有各级医师 86 382 人、职业医生 3 257 人、护士 29 550 人，每年可培养约 13 000 名医学院学生。

表 4　埃塞俄比亚卫生支出概况

	2003	2004	2005	2006	2007	2008	2009	2010	2011	2012	2013
政府卫生开支占政府开支总额的百分比	9.2	10.1	11.2	11.5	12.50	11.9	13.9	14.50	16.40	16.4	16.40
自费支出占卫生总支出的百分比	36.1	35.4	30.60	33.50	35.20	38.50	38.80	39.0	33.70	35.7	35.4
政府人均卫生开支 (PPP① int. $)	13.00	14.00	17.00	18.00	21.00	20.00	23.00	29.00	38.00	37.00	42.00
人均卫生总支出 (PPP int. $)	24.00	25.00	28.00	33.00	38.00	38.00	42.00	52.00	60.00	61.00	69.00
卫生总开支占国内生产总值的百分比	4.70	4.30	4.30	4.60	4.80	4.40	4.40	4.90	5.20	4.90	5.10

（来源：世界卫生组织，埃塞俄比亚 2016 年卫生统计概况）

二、埃塞医疗卫生发展的原因所在

为了保障每一个埃塞人的健康权，埃塞规定国家有义务发布政策和分配日益增加的资源，向所有埃塞人提供公共卫生服务。因此，近几年埃塞卫生部提出了一项全面、明确的卫生部门战略计划，试图在 2015—2035 年这 20 年间，实现全民健康的覆盖。因此，为了促进医疗卫生的发展，埃塞政府不断做出努力，希望减少死亡率和预防传染病。具体来说，主要

① 购买力平价（Purchasing Power Parity，PPP）。

表现在以下几个方面。

第一,完善医疗保健系统,努力扩大医疗覆盖体系,改善埃塞国民的健康。

埃塞地广人稀,为确保偏远地区人口的日常医疗保健,埃塞政府致力于建立完善的从基层到中央的医疗保健系统。埃塞政府所制定的保健政策的核心是确保保健系统的民主化以及权力下放,大力发展保健的预防与治疗体系,确保埃塞人口各阶层都能获得保健服务,并促进私营部门和非政府组织参与保健部门的工作,努力改进埃塞国民的健康,特别是孕妇与新生儿的健康。在埃塞政府实施的保健系统中,最突出的是采用了三级保健系统,其特点是县保健系统为第一级,包括一个初级医院(人口覆盖率为 6 万 ~10 万人)、保健中心及其附属保健站。第二级是覆盖人口 100 万 ~150 万人的综合医院。第三级是覆盖人口 3.5 万 ~500 万人的专科医院。营利性的私营部门与非政府组织在扩大保健服务覆盖面和利用方面发挥了重要作用,使得埃塞的保健系统得到了加强,并加强了公共、私营、非政府组织在该国提供保健服务方面的伙伴关系。

第二,大量医学人才的培养和成长,帮助埃塞建立起从中央到地方的较为完善的医疗卫生体系。

卫生人力资源整体数量不足、城乡地区分布不均、临床专业配比失衡、基层人才流失严重以及高级专业人才缺乏曾是埃塞典型的卫生保健障碍。卫生人力资源是卫生系统的核心环节,对整个卫生体系的正常运转起到至关重要的作用。为了能够应对所面临的危机,埃塞政府在其卫生部门发展规划第三阶段中,提出了以初级卫生保健为基础的卫生人力资源发展策略并明确了其发展目标:培养并招聘 30 000 名农村社区卫生工作者,并确保每 2 500 名居民拥有至少一名服务于基层的卫生工作者;培养并招聘 5 000 名医士;将全国每年医学专业毕业生由 250 名提高到 1 000 名左右;将助产师与全国人口比例提高到 1 : 6759。通过近几年的发展,埃塞的卫生推广工作人员的人数也从 2.4 万人增加到 3.8 万人,护士人数从 1.6 万多名增加到 6 万多名,医务人员从 2 000 多名增加到 6 700 名,卫生站从 700 个增加到 3 000 个,医院从 93 个增加到 311 个。

第三,疾病预防控制的策略不断改进,帮助人民改善健康质量,提高卫生总体水平。

在疾病的预防上,埃塞政府采取多样化手段控制疾病传播,提高医疗质量。在传染病方面,埃塞政府大力控制传染源头,减少传染病的传播和流行。通过有质量保证的医学诊断方法,来确保早起病例的监测;通过实施各级公共卫生应急管理核心程序,加强流行病监测;确保艾滋病毒检测试剂和用品的供应,为慢性艾滋病毒 / 艾滋病护理和治疗创造机会。而在疟疾的预防方面埃塞政府作出大量的努力,由于疟疾主要通过蚊虫来传播,所以埃塞政府为了减少疟疾的发病率以及传播率,政府向疟疾流行地区的家庭分发了几千万个驱虫蚊帐,在室内喷洒药物以控制疟疾的传播媒介。他们还通过卫生工作者在卫生站或家访期间对埃塞民众进行基本的诊断和治疗,这些做法降低了疟疾的发病率以及人口的死亡率。通过社区宣传和大众媒体提高公众对预防疾病重要性的认识,并加强社区动员和男性的参与。在非传染病方面,建立控制非传染性疾病的项目管理和协调结构,对非传染性疾病项目实施宣传、社会动员,发展和维持同其他国家建立的控制非传染性疾病的伙伴关系与协作。

第四,国际社会的持续关注和投入让埃塞卫生事业获得持续不断的外来支持。

埃塞是国际援助集中的国家,其中卫生是国际援助关注的重要领域,国际援助是医疗卫生事业发展的重要源头。数据显示，2014 年国际援助占卫生部门总支出的 49.9%。国际社会对埃塞卫生方面的援助主要为卫生人员交流、派遣援外医疗队、人员培训、援建医院、赠送药品和医疗器械等。

自 2001 年埃塞政府发布可持续发展减贫方案以来，大量的国际援助机构和经济合作与发展组织（简称“经合组织”，OECD）国家关注埃塞的发展方案，埃塞持续十多年的时间成为接受 OECD 国家政府开发援助（ODA）最多的国家，2003—2007 年，国际援助占埃塞卫生支出 67% 以上，成为卫生领域最主要的资金来源。埃塞接受的卫生援助主要来自于 10 个多边机构、22 个双边援助者和 50 多个国际非政府组织的支持。埃塞的卫生保健发展计划（HSDPS）是国际援助最重要的流向。

（一）美国对埃塞的援助

1. 帮助埃塞改善卫生系统

由于埃塞训练有素的保健人员数量不足，卫生基础设施有限，资金、设备及医疗用品的短缺。美国致力于通过加强人力资源、扩大卫生筹资方案、增加保健商品和基本药物供应来改善埃塞的卫生系统。具体的措施主要有以下几个方面。首先是卫生部门的筹资改革：通过改革和体制化的可持续卫生筹资和制度，以及基于社区的健康保险扩大风险分担机制，提高平等获得基本卫生服务的质量。其次是领导、管理和治理：加强卫生管理系统，促进对埃塞卫生工作人员进行协调和认可的在职培训。再次是药品供应管理：建立一个安全、可靠、可持续的药品供应链管理系统，以采购、储存和分销必要的药品和其他产品。最后是加强卫生人力资源：解决卫生人力短缺问题，提高职前教育、在职培训和人力资源管理制度的质量。

2. 帮助埃塞减少孕产妇、新生儿和儿童的死亡率

埃塞是世界上孕产妇死亡比例最高的国家之一。美国国际开发署（USAID）与埃塞政府进行合作，从不同的层面入手，试图减少埃塞孕产妇、新生儿和儿童的死亡率。例如，在埃塞推广全面的妇幼保健方案；USAID 支持在家庭、社区等不同层面不断增加如熟练助产护理和必要的新生儿护理及治疗服务，特别是向医疗服务薄弱的地区提供这些服务；扩大免疫接种、早期鉴定以及患病儿童的护理和治疗的覆盖面，等等。

3. 帮助埃塞制订预防、治疗艾滋病的可持续方案

在埃塞，艾滋病毒的总流行率为 1.5%，在城市中的感染率为 4.2%，这一比率在很大程度上是由于大多数高危人群缺乏意识和行动能力所致。美国总统的艾滋病紧急救援计划（PEPFAR）美国国际开发署则从不同的层面帮助埃塞制订了预防、治疗艾滋病的可持续方案。首先在预防方面，针对弱势少女的艾滋病毒的预防，要制定有助于减少艾滋病毒传播的社会规范，避免弱势少女嫁给年长、离婚或移民到埃塞的男子，从而减少艾滋病毒的传播。其次在治疗与护理方面，设计并建设符合埃塞政府要求的保健中心，并加强对艾滋病毒高发区的医疗设施的建设和资金投入，保证艾滋病毒感染者的治疗与护理。最后在粮食和营养技术援助，对埃塞国家与区域两级提供营养培训方面的技术援助。为感染艾滋病毒的患者及其受影响的成人和儿童提供治疗性和补充性喂养，提高没有粮食保证的艾滋病毒感染者的营养状况和生活质量。

(二)中国对埃塞的援助

中国作为世界舞台中的一支重要力量,也在对非援助中发挥着自身的优势。而在众多对非援助项目中,中国的援非医疗队在其中扮演者重要角色。而援外医疗队则是指向受援国派遣医务人员团队,无偿提供部分医疗设备和药品,在受援国进行定点或巡回医疗服务。

中国也向埃塞派遣了自己的医疗队, 1974 年至今,中国卫生部委托河南省卫生厅 20 批援埃塞医疗队。中国派遣的医疗队对埃塞的医疗卫生发展发挥了重要作用。中国医疗队员在埃塞开展的援助活动大致可以分成三类。首先,对埃塞开展医疗技术援助,主要是培训当地医护人员,传授先进的医疗知识。在这里,医疗队员开展医疗讲学和手术演示,不仅培养与考核了当地医生,也为其培养了医护人员。其次是直接面向需要救治的非洲普通民众,医疗队在埃塞建立了专门的疾病诊疗中心和临床诊室,以弥补当地医疗人员不足的状况。最后是参与特定的救灾和疫情防御项目。 在医疗队的一些临床实践中,援非队员也同样培训当地医疗人员,提高了当地医生的医疗水平,留下了一支带不走的医疗队。医疗队员通过示范观察、主题报告讲座、技术培训和学术交流共享等方式积极培训当地医护人员,这都大大促进了埃塞的医疗卫生发展。

(三)联合国儿童基金会(UNICEF)对埃塞的援助

1. 以社区为基础改善埃塞妇女与儿童的营养健康

UNICEF 帮助埃塞在社区层面建立一个强大的支援系统,并提供安全饮水和卫生设施,改善个人卫生以及改善母亲的营养状况,用以确保儿童获得更好和多样化的饮食,防止儿童的营养不良状况。2011 年, UNICEF 利用加拿大政府提供的 5 000 万美元赠款,在埃塞阿姆哈拉、奥罗米亚等 100 多个地区开展了一个改善儿童和妇女营养状况的项目。这个为期 6 年的项目后来又延长了一年,其目的是改善儿童、少女和哺乳母亲对保健和营养服务的认知,并增加供水和卫生服务的提供。该项目以社区为重点,努力扩大营养活动的范围和覆盖面。该项目为向社区提供安全用水而打井,鼓励家庭建造或改良自己的厕所。在项目结束时进行的一项调查表明,儿童发育迟缓的比例从 40% 下降到 35%,体重不足儿童的比例从 22% 下降到 17%。

2. 开展以社区为基础的新生儿护理战略

尽管埃塞已设法大幅度降低了 5 岁以下儿童死亡率,但新生儿死亡率的下降速度要慢得多。每 1 000 个出生的婴儿中有 29 个死于可预防的原因,如早产、出生窒息、败血症和肺炎等感染引起的并发症。而新生儿死亡人数在 5 岁以下儿童死亡人数中也占越来越大的比例,几乎占 44%。在 UNICEF 的支持下,埃塞政府于 2012 年建立以社区为基础的新生儿护理战略(CBNC)。CBNC 旨在增强健康推广工作者的能力,例如使他们掌握在怀孕、分娩和产后提供妇幼保健服务的技能。健康推广人员也接受培训,以识别和治疗新生儿的严重的细菌感染或败血症,并在定期探访期间,他们在保健站和住家为患病儿童提供治疗。这些健康推广工作者在开展工作时积累了大量的经验,能有效地识别村里的患病儿童,并完成自身非常重要的工作,这也有助于为其他地区的工作开展提供有效的经验。

这些在某种程度上带有浓厚的人道主义色彩的援助活动,使得埃塞的卫生体系得到了良好的建设，帮助埃塞在医疗人员、设备、技术、服务等方面得到了完善。另一方面，国际社会对埃塞的援助，弥补埃塞国内资金、技术以及专业人员的不足，对埃塞医疗卫生体系的发展来说无疑是一个大大的助推器，在一定程度上减少了埃塞在医疗卫生发展道路上艰难探索的时间，加速了埃塞国内医疗卫生体系不断完善的进程。世界各国为埃塞提供医疗援助，使得埃塞解决了一些医疗卫生难题，改善了当地医疗状况和劳动力素质，为吸引外资创造了稳定的投资环境。

三、埃塞医疗卫生发展面临的挑战

近年来，埃塞的医疗卫生取得了堪称不俗的成绩。然而，在埃塞未来医疗卫生系统完善的道路上依旧困难重重，离埃塞实现全民健康覆盖的目标依然任重道远。从目前来看，埃塞医疗卫生发展所面临的挑战有以下几个方面。

（一）埃塞国内政局不稳，政策的持续性受到挑战

埃塞国内不稳定的政治环境，使得埃塞国内的政策方针不能得到很好的落实，从而放缓了埃塞全民健康覆盖的计划，影响埃塞医疗卫生体系的发展步伐。在埃塞拥有大多数人口的奥罗莫族和阿姆哈拉族，长期遭到占人口少数的提格雷族主导的政府边缘化，使得长期处于强政府体质下的埃塞的种族矛盾不断激化，国内部分地区局势持续动荡。持续的反政府示威活动的不断蔓延加之族群之间的冲突，导致埃塞许多人丧生和流离失所，带来了巨大的人道主义挑战。地区间的冲突也使得安全饮用水、粮食、药品无法按时送到流离失所者营地，进一步加剧了流离失所者的健康问题，这也无疑增加了埃塞的卫生部门的压力。埃塞国内局势的不稳定无疑削弱了国际投资者的信心以及国际社会对埃塞的援助，可能引起埃塞在卫生政策的实施中，缺乏国际资金的支持。

（二）埃塞城乡医疗卫生的水平和质量差异明显

埃塞环境卫生尽管实现了较大改善，但是国家内部存在着明显的不平等现象，城市与农村地区的医疗卫生设施存在着巨大差异。由于埃塞国家的资金、技术、人才的限制，大多数的医疗卫生设施的改善是从城市着手，在城市的卫生服务大幅改善的前提下，埃塞政府才会考虑如何改善农村地区的医疗卫生设施现状。在农村地区由于医疗设备的落后，很难确保对早期疾病的检测与预防，而且包括艾滋病毒在内的一些疾病的检测工具和仪器供应不足，一些疫苗和注射器材等用品也极其短缺。在农村地区不仅医疗卫生服务不完善，而且大多数农村地区的传统观念根深蒂固，割礼等传统习俗以及大量不卫生的生活习惯增加了疾病滋生和传播的概率。同时，农村地区的环境卫生也有隐忧，如农村居民的安全用水、人畜粪便的处理率较低、清洁工具供应不足以及废物管理系统的不完善，严重影响农村地区的卫生服务水平和质量。

（三）埃塞的医院以及保健站医疗设施服务存在大量的弊端

埃塞的分级医疗保健制度在非洲国家中首屈一指，提高了基础医疗服务的可及性，改善

了基层民众的卫生保健服务。埃塞政府虽然在城市中建立了不同等级的医院以及在大量社区设置了保健站,并雇用了大量的卫生推广人员来改善农村社区的医疗落后的现状,但是在医院、保健站中均存在大大小小的问题。

第一,一些医院或者保健站建立起来后,无法配套充足的医疗服务力量,有些医疗服务站建立起来甚至连一名医生都无法保证,这类基层医院和保健站实质上形同虚设。

第二,一些医院和医疗保健站无法提供24小时的服务,且一些保健站和社区的卫生推广人员在接受培训时,所学到的知识有限,缺乏专业性,在宣传疾病预防与应对紧急状况时,就会显得技能不足,甚至有时无法应对紧急医疗事件。

第三,由于人手不够和技能不足,基层医院和保健站的病人不得不等待较长时间,耽误最佳治疗时间,病人的隐私有时无法得到有效保护。

第四,一些保健站和卫生推广人员由于资金的不足以及援助资金链的断裂导致后续工作无法落实,在一些地区成了空壳子,无法达到预期效果。

(四)大量国际援助重复性关注同类问题,对于一些关注度较低的问题缺少持续性的关注

埃塞是世界上最重要的受援对象,大量的援助者带着援助来到埃塞,援助的严重碎片化导致埃塞不得不与大量的援助者协调,一大笔资金不得不用于与援助者展开协调。除政府组织外,埃塞2006年拥有30多个双边援助者和14个多边援助者机构。大多数的双边援助者在援助市场中所占的份额极小。2006年,54%的ODA来自30多个援助者,其中12个援助者的援助总额仅占埃塞接受ODA总额的0.87%。而不同援助者提供的援助并没有系统的规划,大多数的援助者均通过不同的支付渠道支持多个不同的项目,面对毫无逻辑和秩序的不同援助,埃塞政府不得不抽调大量的人力物力来管理和接受这些不同的援助,并在运营中根据不同项目的要求不断调整国内的政策。

国际援助虽然帮助埃塞的医疗卫生建设取得了进展,但是在援助的过程中也依旧存在着避免不了的问题。国际援助关注的问题为国际社会关注度极高的疾病,而对于地方性的危害较大的疾病则关注较少。如埃塞72%的卫生援助资金流向三大疾病:艾滋病、疟疾和结核病,而对妇幼健康、孕产妇保健和婴幼儿保健等领域的投入严重不足,获得支持的比例不足1%。各国在埃塞援建的医院与治疗中心,有一些医疗设施建设在设计、选址、设备配置和与当地医疗医辅人员能力匹配等方面存在这样或那样的问题。此外,由于埃塞缺乏卫生经费、有资质的医务人员与必要的产品供应,使得这些国际援助的医疗设施有时不能按期投入使用,即使投入使用,由于在设备操作与维护等方面的专业化指导不足,受援医院人员的能力与水平很难得到有效提高,不少医疗设备也因当地基础设施较差,人员使用不当或缺乏维护频出故障而被闲置,使用效果大打折扣,造成了较大浪费。

对于像埃塞俄比亚这样的发展中国家来说,援助是公共支出的一个重要来源。政府有援助收入的目标,并将预期收入纳入财政计划。埃塞俄比亚有计划将其30%以上的收入从外国融资中动员起来。这意味着在收入决定和支出分配时考虑到援助。然而,不稳定和不可预测的外来援助不仅不能带来发展,反而会对埃塞的国家发展计划带来破坏性的影响,“援助流量往往在时间和额度方面的不可预测性正在给埃塞的国家规划带来影响”。2008年金融危机后,西方对非援助发生了较大的调整,不稳定和不可预测的援助带来发展资源的

无效和扭曲使用,并直接损害非洲的增长和发展计划。

结语

尽管埃塞的卫生发展还面临着诸多问题,但是埃塞的医疗卫生改革也一直未停歇。自埃塞总理阿比·艾哈迈德上台后,埃塞便进入了政治与经济的民主化改革中。作为埃塞俄比亚革命阵线(简称“埃革阵”)的主席,阿比呼吁埃塞全体人民与该阵线和政府合作,确保该国的持久和平。阿比总理的民主化改革以及他所坚守的国内和平理念,也无疑为埃塞将来的卫生发展创造一个良好的政治环境。目前在阿比总理的带领下,埃塞的卫生部也开始修订该国的卫生政策,试图扩大该国可持续卫生覆盖的宣传范围,填补过去 25 年来该国现行卫生政策的空白,减少由于饥饿、营养不良和饮食习惯所导致的非传染性疾病的得病率。

如果在埃塞阿比总理的带领下,通过一系列的民主改革使得埃塞的国内局势逐渐平稳,并保证卫生政策的连续性,埃塞俄比亚的医疗卫生发展的前景还是可观的。

Factors and Actors in Ethiopian Muslim Popular Movement (2011-2018)

Nuraddin Aman

Abstract: In contemporary Ethiopia, many popular movements have been taking place by different groups such as the intellectualist movement, ethnic-based movement, youth movement and religion-based movements. Among these, the Ethiopian Muslim movement also known by *Demtsachen Yesema* is a recent movement that mainly takes place from 2011-2018. Taking this into consideration, this study attempts to present the main factors and actors in contemporary Ethiopian Muslim movement from different perspectives. In addition to this, the socio-political impacts of the Ethiopian Muslim movement are treated as well. To do so, both primary and secondary data will be employed in order to bring significant data on the mentioned topic.

I Historical Overview of the Trajectories of Ethiopian Muslim Movements

Islam was introduced into Ethiopia during the arrival of the companions of the Prophet in 615 to find refugee in Ethiopia. However, during this period it was not infiltrated much into the wider regions of Ethiopia until it was exceedingly penetrated in between 685-705 during the period of the fifth Umayyad caliph/dynasty (r.685-705). Following this, Islam in Ethiopia has passed through three major phases namely stages of the establishment and consolidation of the Muslim Sultanates, the stage of the collapses of Muslim Sultanates and the stage of being subjugation under the Abyssinian Christian highland kingdom.

Since the 7th century, in the course of flow and ebb, Islam as an integral part of the different Ethiopian nation and nationalities religion has rejoiced both in secular and non-secular activities and sometimes quarreled with other religions so far. In the modern history of Ethiopia, mainly starting from Emperor Haile Selassie I (1930-1974) regime up to the EPRDF (prior to the 2011 popular protests) the Ethiopian Muslims have been passed through three major stages in the long history of Ethiopian Muslim movements. Accordingly, they have been protested against the government in different periods by bringing three major questions into the wider public such as the quest for citizenship/equal right, public holidays and quest for the establishment of the Ethiopian Supreme Council for Islamic Affairs (Majlis).

The first stage: This stage is mainly characterized that it was a movement for the quest of equal citizenship or simply acquiring equal right as a citizen. For the first time, the Ethiopian Muslims particularly the urban residents have demonstrated their protest against the imperial regime for the alleged assumption of Ethiopia as the island of Christianity in a sea of Islam. Though there have been significant mutual tolerances between the Ethiopian Muslim and Christians, the approach of the Ethiopian imperial regime towards its own fellow citizen mostly for the Muslims were not admirable. This was particularly witnessed during the Emperor Haile Selassie's presentation before the United States Congress in 1954 in which he said "Ethiopia is an island of Christian surrounded by the Muslim". Thus, this alienation strategy of the emperor towards the Muslims had rigorously detached them from legal title to land and access to high-level public jobs and above all relegated them to a second-class status.

Additionally, the emperor's hostility towards the Muslims also follows the adaptation of a pejorative term "Muslims living in Ethiopia" which indicates that Muslims are strange for this country, though the Ethiopian Muslims do not call themselves by this name and they resist being called so. First, the rejection of the identity of the Ethiopian Muslims as an Ethiopian citizen, second the exclusionist system of the Muslim Ethiopian from key government positions and thirdly the limit to obtain equal right to practice the religion alike the followers of Christians were exceedingly instigated the first and well-organized movement in the history of Ethiopian Muslims. This discrimination and inequity subsequently follow an organized demonstration in the city of Addis Ababa in early 1974. In this landmark protest, more than one hundred thousands of Muslim residents of Addis Ababa, students, low-rank clergymen, taxi drivers and public officers of Addis Ababa took the street to show their protests against the injustice system of the imperial rule.

By bringing this into a wider public, the demonstrators holding different banners chanted/denounced that the official designation of "Muslims living in Ethiopia" (which implied that Muslims were aliens) should be changed to "Ethiopian Muslims", religious equality, separation of church and state, the demonstrators also denounced the representation of Ethiopia as a "Christian Island surrounded by an Islamic sea" and thus they chanted "Ethiopia is not a Christian Island; we [Muslims] too are Ethiopians", "Religion is private; the country is common (for all)" and demanded "this saying of the Emperor" to be implemented in practice to the advantage of Muslims in the country, etc. are among the chants of the protesters.

In fact, it was their chant "religion is private; the country is common" and the demand for equal status for their religion that echoed. Shocked by this land-marking demonstration which brought about onto the streets of Addis over 100,000 protesters, members of the aristocracy reacted robustly. The reaction was interpreted as a critical challenge that continued to undermine the historical position of the state. The legitimate rights that Ethiopian Muslims demanded were critical to once again delegitimize the exclusivist discourse that had been reigning for centuries. Characterizing the discourse as unrepresentative to the wider Ethiopian polity, Muslims called for its disempowerment and for setting the state free so that it remains neutral and sable to provide equal status to them. Thus, this kind of organized Muslim movement served as a key positive force that contributed to the 1974 revolution.

The second stage: Aftermaths of the downfall of the imperial regime in September 1974, the Muslims sustained struggling for the right to practice their religious freedom and also demanded for the incorporation of Islamic holidays as national holidays. The demonstrations that erupted in April 1974 had also continued their request for the newly established military government in 1974/1975. Accordingly, Muslims through their representatives submitted a petition to the Derg regime demanding, among others, "the official declaration of the three Islamic festivals i.e. Ed al-Fatir, Ed al-Adha and Mewlid as public holidays.

Next to a movement for the quest of equal citizenship, the second stage is mainly characterized that it was a movement for the right to practice religious freedom and the incorporation of the observation of Muslim holidays as a public holiday. Consequently, the Derg regime has approved the request of Ethiopian Muslims that submitted through their representatives and thus granted religious freedom to Ethiopian Muslims and declared the observation of three Muslim holidays as public holidays on 23 December 1974. Since 1974 the expression "Muslims living in Ethiopia" was officially replaced by "Ethiopian Muslims" and the celebrations of *Ed al-Fatir, Ed al-Adha and Mewlid* as public holidays took place in public places for the first time in the country's history and forms and places of worship recognized officially.

The third stage: During this phase, the Ethiopian Muslims have remarkably struggled for the demand of the establishment of the Ethiopian Supreme Council for Islamic Affairs (Majlis). Even if the demand to establish a national Islamic council was requested before the overthrow of the emperor in early 1974 together with the above mentioned public holidays and others, the request to establish Majlis has again presented rigorously to the Derg regime following the decree of the separation of religion and politics. To do so, Muslims through their representatives submitted a letter that demonstrates the right to establish a nationwide organization that represents Muslims and enables them to lead their own affairs and eloquently participate in the affairs of the country. Accordingly, the Derg regime approved the request of Ethiopian Muslim and thus the Ethiopian Supreme Council for Islamic Affairs (Majlis) was formally established in 1976 "but throughout the period of the Derg regime, it only functioned as a de facto, not dejure, organization."

Following the recognition of the quest for citizenship/equal right, public holidays and quest for the establishment of the Ethiopian Supreme Council for Islamic Affairs (Majlis) under the Derg regime, another demonstration erupted in 1994 under the EPRDF rule demanding the inclusion of Sharia (Islamic law) as one of the bases for the new Ethiopian constitution but abruptly suppressed by the regime. As discussed above, Muslims strived for generations the right to get equal citizenship, practice their religion, to gate the proper public space, and to be visible with their own religious and cultural identity in the face of the country. Post-1991, Muslims under the EPRDF rule has initially relatively enjoyed the freedom of worship and religious plurality that grant them equal rights with the followers of other religion until the fresh protest was erupted in 2011 due to the following factors.

1.1 Factors for the Contemporary Ethiopian Muslim Movement (2011–2018)

The coming of EPRDF into power in 1991 paved the way to practice the religious rights and freedom that subsequently resulted in the revival of religious movements particularly for Islam and Protestant Christianity. Thus, this new political arena has heightened the freedom to propagate religions, allowing the distribution of religious texts both the imported and locally published and relaxation of press freedom allowed for the translation in various vernaculars.These kinds of proceedings have also paved the way for marked interest, produced a new consciousness among the Muslim population generated new religious affiliations and made Islam in Ethiopia more visible compared with the past. The improvement of technological facilities, the movement of the peoples from rural to urban and in recent times social media have all allowed for greater availability and dissemination of information. This consequently has been released an increase for religious revivalism in the vast area of Ethiopia. However, in the late 1990s, the approach of the EPRDF towards Muslim Ethiopia has deteriorated due to the fear of the development of Islamic militant movements in the horn Africa and the context of regional and global geopolitics.Therefore, the religious rights and freedom that boosted the Muslim Ethiopian following the coming of EPRDF in 1991 have retreated firstly because of the 1995 incident at al-Anwar Mosque between the Muslim and government forces. This incident abruptly follows the interference of the government to control the Ethiopian Islamic Affairs Supreme Council, the restriction/close of some Islamic institutions and newspapers. In 2008, the Ministry of Education has decreed a law that enforces a ban on religious symbols’ such as niqab (woman veil) and congregational worship in all educational institutions both in private and public. Following this decree, the Mekela University was the first institution that implements this law and thus dismissed Muslim students that found performing congregational prayers inside the campus. Subsequent to this measure, on December 8th, 2008, Addis Ababa University Muslim students called for an organized wide protest in solidarity with Mekela University Muslim students.In fact, the protest that instigated in different universities resulting in this ban has played a major role in paving the way for the birth of a nationwide Muslim movement that orchestrated in 2011.

As discussed above, the context of regional and global geopolitics has deteriorated the positive approach of the EPRDF government towards the Ethiopia Muslims and thus results from the interference of the government to control the Majlis, restrict/close some Islamic institutions and newspapers, ban on religious symbols and group prayer in the universities. In addition to this, in July 2011 the Ethiopian government together with the then Majlis has invited the Ahbash ideology from Lebanon in order to blend the Ethiopian Muslims by this ideology throughout the country. Therefore, the quest for secularism, reform of the Majlis and imposition of the Al-Ahbash ideology by the government are among the major factors for the Ethiopian Muslim movements that mainly exploded in 2011.

1.2 Quest for the Implementation of Secularism

The ruling party that came to power in 1991 has granted the religious rights and freedom particularly when the 1995 constitution has proclaimed the Separation of State and Religion, and guaranteed freedom of religion (Article 11). In the beginning, Ethiopian Muslims have enjoyed with the newly introduced rules until the government break the rule and interfered in the religions attributable to the pressure of regional and global geopolitics.Since then, the Ethiopian Muslims have been complaining the alleged interference of the government into the religion, particularly when the government was involved in the internal debates and conflicts among the Muslims including in controlling the Majlis in the late 1990s. Even if the instantaneous movement that orchestrated to condemn the government has not made out publicly, soon after the coming of Al-Ahbash in 2011 by the request of the government; Muslims began complaining about government's violation in their religious affairs contrary to the principle of secularism. In the modern history of Ethiopian Muslim, this consequently follows a well-organized movement against what they call "government meddling in purely religious affairs."

1.3 Al-Ahbash, the EPRDF Government and the 2011 Ethiopian Muslim Popular Movements

Al-Ahbash as an ideology was first preceded by a Lebanese based spiritualist movement "Jam‘ ī yah al-Mash ā r ī ‘ al-Khayr ī yah al-ʾIsl ā m ī yah" or "The Association of Islamic Charitable Projects (AICP) founded in the 1930s by Ahmad al-Ajuz. Following the death of Ahmad al-Ajuz, the organization was overtaken in early 1983 by Sheikh Abdullah ibn Muhammad ibn Yusuf Al-Harari, an Ethiopian origin. Soon after Sheikh Abdullah Al-Harari begun led this organization, the ideological movement of this group was named Ahbash, a name derived from the root of Habesha referring to the origin of Sheikh Abdullah Al-Harari. It is said that the movement from its time of establishment has played a major role in Lebanese politics mainly during the 1980s and active member of the parliament in 1989. More willingly than basing its participation on religious fondness, in the sense of in search to Islamize politics, the organization promulgated itself as being part of a "public service within the Lebanese political framework, emphasizing the need to uphold political stability, to promote social and religious pluralism, and to serve Lebanon's national interests".

In July 2011, the Ethiopian government together with the Majlis has invited this ideology with the purpose to combat the Islamic revival groups. To do so, the government has designed the strategy that is supposed to moderate Islam or to form its own version of Islam that certainly derived from the Sufi mythic order. Thus, in July 2011, through the structure of Majlis, a wide program was set by the government that intended to provide extensive training about the ideology of Al-Ahbash for selected religious leaders from different parts of the country. According to Mohammad Dejen, three major actors namely the Majlis, the Ethiopian government and US government are involved in the importing and endorsement of Al-Ahbash ideology in Ethiopia.

Even if the government rejected the allegation that the state interfered in the propagation of Al-Ahbash ideology it was seen that the Ministry of the Federal Affairs and its minister Shiferaw Tekle-Mariam has attended the conference in Harar and the workshop in Ghion Hotel. In addition to this, during the conference at Ghion Hotel Shiferaw Tekle-Mariam has addressed his concern pertaining to the development of Islamic extremism in Ethiopia and thus conveyed his appreciation for the coming of Al-Ahbash ideology as a solution for the Muslim general public that according to the beliefs and doctrines of the politico-religious faction called "Association of Islamic Charitable Projects" also known by Al-Ahbash. By doing so, the government has provided enough security guards for both the trainee and trainers during these periods. However, the conference was not last long due to most of the trainees (mainly Imams, Sheikhs and other prominent religious leaders) were walked out in aversion at when they come to realize that both parties (the *Majlis* and the government) are enforcing them to amalgamate with Al-Ahbash ideology.Following this event, the news about Al-Ahbash campaign and government interfering in religious affairs has reached the wider public that consequently fallout the 2011 Ethiopian Muslim popular movements also called "Demtsachen Yesema" (literally let our voice be heard) against the EPRDF government and Majlis.

The government believes that the developments of religious extremism by the Salafi/Wahabi movement are extremely exacerbating the widespread of political Islam in the Horn Africa. The late Prime Minister Melles Zenawi in his April 2012 parliamentary speech also blamed the widespread of this group in the vast area of Arsi-Bale region of south-east Ethiopia. Accordingly, to combat this group, the government through the office of the *Majlis* has taken action in Awolia College in Addis Ababa in December 2011 by dismissing all the school's Arabic teachers. From then onwards, weekly (each Friday) Muslim demonstrations was first sparked in Awolia College and subsequently widespread into other regions of the country. The protest that erupted in July 2011 that initially protested against the government to stop for its alleged support for expanding the teaching of Al-Ahbash ideology has continued in a broad form, particularly, comprising from demanding for the return of the Awolia college teachers up to the quest for the reform of Islamic Supreme Council also called Majlis.

For a long period, the Islamic Supreme Council has been run by elders who have no enough modern educational backgrounds. To this contrary, the increasing number of young scholars from time to time has played a major role in shaping the Muslim people, especially, the urban jewelers' using mainstream media such as Africa TV, social media, newspaper and magazines such as *Alquds, Bilal, Yemuslimoch Guday, Selafia, Sawtul-Islam*, etc. Due to this, Majlis leaders apparently faced a hard struggle for power and legitimacy from the intellectual Muslim activists. They are criticized for corrupt practices, lack of a legitimate and functional organization and less proficiency in leading the Muslim general public. Most of them are far less educated in both secular and non-secular areas compared with the young, well trained with religious knowledge and conscious Muslims. Moreover, the intellectual Muslim activists also complain that the member of the Islamic Supreme Council is assigned by the EPRDF government and mostly comprised of government-appointed figures that do not represent them instead of through fair, free, democratic and independent election. As a result, by addressing this into the wider Muslim public, an organized Muslim movement by the intellectual class has escalated over issues of religious freedom and secularism. The quest of the movements steadily extended in its scope; both in its demand and enormity. The sizes of the protesters enlarged from time to time and thus demonstrated their complaint in a non-violent way during the 2011-2014 consecutive struggle periods. To accomplish the task of this movement, representatives from the intellectual classes, elders and activists were chosen by the people in order to facilitate the complaints of the Muslims with the then ruling parties.

Following the formation of these representatives, on 20 April 2012, about one million have demonstrated in Aweliya institute and thus the movement that limited inside the compound of Awelia collage has widespread each Friday first in different mosques of Addis Ababa such as the grand Al-Anwar Mesjid, Sheikh Hojale Mesjid, Kera Mesjid, Ayertena Mesjid and further spread in other regions like Dirre Dawa, Harar,Baddessa, Dessie, Shashemenne, Asasa, Asella, Adama, Jimma, Alaba, Gondar, Chagni, etc. Despite the government's announcement to take repressive measures, in the next Friday (5May 2012), the Muslim protests even spread to towns of Somali and Afar regions.In fact, the protesters during their grievance against the government expressed slogans like "We want our right! Stop Ahbashism campaign! The people want to step down the Majlis! Allahu Akbar! (Allah is great), they chant in Arabic "Ash-Sha' ib Yur ī d Isk' ā ṯ Al-Majlis"! (A slogan originally adapted from the Arab spring), denounce the continued government interference in the religious affairs; the right of the public to elect the leaders of the Muslim community have become formal mottos of the public. In addition to this, during the 2011-2014 Ethiopian Muslim popular movement, the protesters carry the white ribbon, yellow card, and other non-verbal modes of expression such as crossing hands above head to expose and oppose the plot of the state.

However, the response of the government towards to porters was harsh, particularly, in one of the protests that took place at Asasa town (Eastern Arsi) on 27 April 2012; the Federal police killed at least seven protesters and wounded many more. Other similar repressive actions have taken by the security forces in Kofale town, Gerba, etc. Thus, the news about the incident of Asasa spread throughout the country and aggravated the tension between the government and the general Muslim public. Having heard the response of the government, the mass of Ethiopian Muslims have increased their opposition on all fronts. Even if the government has facilitated the election of the Ethiopian Islamic Supreme Council on 7th October 2012, the protesters have continued their protests owing to the arrest of the leaders of the movement and the alleged allegation of the government' s interference in this long-awaited election.

2 Actors in Contemporary Ethiopian Muslim Popular Movements

It is inevitable that any movement can be undertaken by different actors be it formal or informal ways. As discussed above, the movements that embarked in 2011 onwards are initially undertaken without well-organized leadership. However, following the increasing number of the movements from time to time and fundamental demands of the Muslim people, the movement requires leadership that has a capability to facilitate the protests, manage meetings with concerned bodies and above all finding ultimate solutions for the Ethiopian Muslim as well. Thus, this study finds out that in contemporary Ethiopian Muslim popular movement different actors are played a pivotal role in this non-violent movement that mainly takes place from 2011-2018. Accordingly, I have categorized them as internal actors namely the committee or representative of the people, *Demtsachen Yesema* secret group and media outlets and; the external actors are mainly Diaspora Muslim based civil organizations and Diaspora based activists are among the key actors in the contemporary Ethiopian Muslim movements.

2.1 Internal Actors

2.1.1 The Committee (Representative of the People)

Prior to the establishment of the 17 representatives of the Muslim people in January 2012 formally, there have been informal intellectual groups that actively engaged in Muslim issues following the political transition in 1991. The majority of the member of this group was mainly based in different universities and international NGOs such as the African Muslim Agency from Kuwait, the Muslim World League and various Sudanese organizations and the Ethiopian Muslim Youth Association (EMYA). Following the 2011 demonstrations, some of the members of this intellectualist movement group who were acted as the de facto leaders and prized for their intellectual capability and knowledge of Islam are begun key actors in the 17 arbitration committee that officially proposed on 19 January 2012 and established on 28 January 2012.

In January 2012 signature papers are distributed in some mosques of Addis Ababa in order to choose the representative that addresses the Muslim Questions for the governments. Within the short days, an approximate of 500,000 signatures were collected from the Muslim community. On 28 January 2012, the arbitration committee that composes 17 members mainly from religious leaders, intellectuals and elders are formed by the name of"Yemuslimoch Meftihie Afelalagi Komitie" literally "Muslims Solution Finding Committee." By doing so, initially, this committee has organizing, managing as well as addressing the Muslim issues to the wider Muslim public first in Awolia compound and other Mosques in Addis Ababa before they presented to the concerned government bodies. In this movement, Ustaz Ahmedin Jebel, Ustaz Abubeker Ahmed and Ustaz Kamil Shamsu were the key actors of this committee that (has) been aptly articulated the demands of the movement of Ethiopian Muslim in a coherent and organized way. In fact, in the subsequent years, this committee has managed to keep the demonstrations that took in different parts of Ethiopia in an outstandingly disciplined and peaceful manner. In the first phase of this organized movement, the government approved the legality of this arbitration committee and invited them to discuss the demands of the Muslim society.

On behalf of the Muslim people, the arbitration committee was presented three major questions to the government. These three questions are: the quest for the implementation of secularism (stop government imposition of the Al-Ahbash ideology), the quest for the reform of the Majlis (the current leadership of "Majlis" doesn't represent Ethiopian Muslims and thus permit free and fair elections to the Ethiopian Islamic Supreme Council), the Aweliya Islamic institute should be administered by an independent board of directors which has no attachment to the "Majlis". During the first conversation with the different government bodies, the arbitrary committees have got positive responses until the security officers barged into the Awoliya compound in one night of July 2012, fired tear gas on the people who took refuge in the mosque, rushed into the mosque shoe clad, and deliberately messed up the praying precinct and hurled the Holy scriptures inside it as well as spoiled the food that prepared for Sadaqa (feast) and unity program.Following this, instead of responding the demands of the Muslim people, the government returned his face against the committee and thus openly rejects the questions of the Muslims and accused the widespread of Wahabiyya/Salafi ideology in Ethiopia. The government also blamed this movement by saying that the Awolia College is serving as a center for the widespread of Wahabiyya/Salafi ideology and as a consequence, the government won't allow this anymore.Consequently, the arbitration committee that initially got legality from the government was arrested on 15 July 2012, and the government labeled them self-appointed terrorists and arrested them under charges of terrorism when negotiations failed.Months after their arrest, before the court passes guilty verdict, *Jihadawi Harakat*- a documentary film broadcasted by the Ethiopian television on 5 February 2013, was aired and thus spontaneously defames this group as a militant terrorist group that linked with Al-Qaeda, Al-Shebab and Boko Haram.

Despite the above three factors for this popular movement, a protest in solidarity with the arrested arbitration committee was also aggravated on 29October 2012, when a federal court in Addis Ababa come to a decision to accuse this committee that arrested on 15 July 2012, with "plotting acts of terrorism" under Ethiopia's Anti-Terrorism Proclamation. A protest was once more continued in public space for a while and whereas in some regions limited within the mosques compound until all of them released following the political transition in Ethiopia in the mid-2018.

2.1.2 Demtsachen Yesema

As discussed above the movement that embarked at the end of 2011 to 15 July 2012, has been publicly run by the arbitration committee in an organized and peaceful manner by formulating three major demands that are: the quest for the implementation of secularism, the quest for the reform of the *Majlis*, and return the Awolia College to the wider Muslim public. Following the arrest of this committee on 15 July 2012, the Ethiopian Muslim movement was begun led by another secret actor known by Demtsachen Yesema (Let our voice be heard!) from July 2012 up to the release of the arbitration committee in the mid-2018. The present researcher has attempted to disclose the real identity of this secret group but none of the informants distinguishes their real identity till nowadays.

*D*emtsachen Yesema was represented the detained Yemuslimoch Meftihie Afelalagi Komi*tie* (Muslims Solution Finding Committee) and become the voice of the Ethiopian Muslim movement. It is also the movement that called for an end to the government's interference in religious affairs of the Muslim community at large. This group has played a significant role in contemporary Ethiopian Muslim movement using a non-violent stratagem. To overtake the protest modestly some of the non-violent strategies are adopted new communication strategies, more or less following the models of the 2011 Arab uprising countries such as Egypt and Yemen. Accordingly, calls for wide demonstration and mottos circulated through SMS messages; news, opinions and criticisms disseminated on internet social media; in-depth analyses of the situation were published on blogs along with comment sections, and videos of the demonstrations posted on platforms like YouTube and Diaspora based Ethiopian media. During this popular protest, Demtsachen Yesema has applied new style of demonstration that has not been used in the past Ethiopian popular movements such as "visual elements, including secular symbols: yellow cards were waved in warning, white ribbons were worn as signs of peace, and mouths were plastered to symbolize the lack of freedom".

By doing so, since it overtakes the position of the arbitration committee, this secret group has also contributed a significant role in unifying and leading the Muslim Umma both in Ethiopia and abroad. In addition to this, from July 2012-2016, the call of this group to the Diaspora Ethiopians irrespective of their religion and ethnicity has also amplified its popularity not only among Muslim Ethiopia but also have reached other suppressed citizens' of the country.

In short, the Ethiopian Muslim movement that took place from 2011 to mid 2018 is widely known by the name Demtsachen Yesema — a name that signifies a symbol of non — violent struggle and demands for the implementation of constitutional rights that grants the right to practice religious freedom and secularism. During these periods, this movement has developed a sagacity of struggling for religious freedom in a peaceful way and as well as enhanced universal consciousness along the lines of Ethiopian Muslims both in informal and formal networks.

2.1.3 Media Outlets

Subsequent to the aftermath of the 2011 protests, almost state media were deficient in presenting the factual information of the movements. Instead of reporting the real factor of the movements, the Ethiopian government using his media outlets has defamed the true nature of the Ethiopian Muslim movements and thus categorizes them as terrorists, anti-peace, extremists endorsing governmental Islam who want to escalate instability and unrest in the country.

However, the widespread of a non-state media outlet such as printing media (newspaper and magazines), broadcast media (TV and radio) and social media has played a significant role in disseminating the actual information, ongoing analysis as well as reporting the true nature of the contemporary Ethiopian Muslim popular movements. In this regard, the introduction of Africa TV, BBN Radio, ESAT TV, Feteh Radio and Raadiyoo Daandii Haqaa in vernacular languages, particularly its coverage on the historiography of Islam and Ethiopian Muslims have played a key role throughout this popular movement. Furthermore, these broadcast media has contributed a major role with alternative narrations of "what it means to be a Muslim and Ethiopian." Even if, the content of some of this media is only limited to Da' wa (mainly a propagation actively encourage fellow Muslims in the pursuance of greater piety in all aspects of their lives), it has been gradually awakening mutual consciousnesses among the Ethiopian Muslim during this critical period in particular.

In addition to the broadcasting media, the role of printing media; weekly newspaper such as *Salafia*, *Sawtul-Islam*, *Ethio-Muslim* and magazines such as *Bilal* and, most notably, *Yemuslimoch Guday* have played a significant role in presenting key demands of Ethiopian Muslim movements that outbreak at the end of 2011 and thus disseminating information's about the non-violent peaceful struggle so that to mobilize the Muslims for the right to practice religious freedom and secularism.

Like that of print and broadcast media, social media has also contributed to the wide mobilization of Ethiopian Muslims, particularly the urban youth with the intention that to struggle for the cause of their religion. In fact, the daily information about the quest of the right to practice religious freedom and fight for the implementation of secularism and as well as the overall panorama of this non-violent movement that circulated on Face Book such as, ድምፃችን ይሰማ-Dimtsachin Yisema, FEZEKER CENTER, Ye Muslimoch Dimts, Anti-Ahbash, Salaten Adera, Awolia School Support Page, etc, Twitter, YouTube mainly Bilal Tube, Pal Talk, Whatsapp, Viber and other websites have awakened the Muslims all through this popular movements. As per my observation, these social media has a large number of followers/subscribers both from Ethiopia and the Diaspora. The followers have received news about the movements, cases of the arbitration committee, programs of the protests in different regions, updates about the response of the governments, etc. Therefore, this follows that similar to the other parts of the world, the spread of social media platform has greatly helped out the Ethiopian Muslims throughout the consecutive struggle against the injustice system of the FDRE government.

2.2 External Actors

Muslim Ethiopians that left the country due to the political suppression or demand for better economic life and thus dispersed into different foreign countries have come together mainly in between the 1980s and early 2000 in order to establish their own organizations that primarily engaged in establishing Da' iwa centers, social organizations, civil and humanitarian rights. A good example for this is the USA-based Foundation of Ethiopian Muslims in North America (FEMNA) first established in 1986 later named First Hijra Foundation in 1995, Badr International Muslims (established in 2002, USA), the Ethiopian Muslims in Europe (2004), Risala International, etc are played a significant role in contemporary Ethio-Muslim movements. Even if their primary goals are intended to improve the spiritual status and the socio-economic life of the members of these organizations in their respective country, but later on when recent demonstrations erupted in Ethiopia they have begun participating in the movements from the distance be it formal or informal ways.

Pertaining to the role of foreign-based Muslim Ethiopian organizations Dereje disclosed that they have established very strong worldwide networks, issued statements on contemporary socio-political events in Ethiopia; held demonstrations criticizing government interference into religious rights; organized joint homeland-Diaspora meetings; and conducted Pal-talks and Tele-conferences, run online radio stations, and sent delegations to Ethiopia. According to this source, the Diaspora based Ethiopian Muslims have been extensively engaged in advocating the right to practice freedom of religion and become influential Islamic voice who speaks for the Muslims rights and articulated the challenges Muslim face in contemporary Ethiopia. It was a time that some of the foreign-based Ethiopian Muslim organizations (mainly the Badr and the Ethiopian Muslims in Europe) have tried to engage with the government and the civil-society in Ethiopia for the realization of inter-religious cooperation, democracy and development in the country.

Following the escalation of government suppression on Ethiopian Muslims global rallies was organized by the above mentioned Diaspora based organizations. For instance, on 21 November 2012, First Hijra Foundation called its members in the US in order to condemn the action of Ethiopian government towards peaceful Ethiopian Muslim protesters' and demanding that the US government cut support through foreign aid to the Ethiopian government that violates human rights. Additionally, subsequent to the release of a documentary film entitled *Jihadawi Harakat,* huge demonstrations were organized on 26 February 2013, by the First Hijra foundations, in the Washington, DC area, in support of the suffering of Ethiopian Muslims back home.

Moreover, the Diaspora based Ethiopian Muslim organizations in their turn has produced several influential activists that later on played a significant role for the success of the struggle that intended for the right to practice religious freedom in a well organized, enhanced and non-violent way. In this regard, the role of Badr International and First Hijra Foundation is enormous, particularly in organizing conferences and inviting influential individuals from different fields such as academicians, religious leaders/scholars, human right activists, civil organizations, etc in order to discuss the suffering of Ethiopian Muslims back home and forward possible solutions as well. A good example of this is an organized conference by First Hijra Foundation held on 26 January 2013, in Washington DC in commemoration of the first year of the Ethiopian Muslim movements for religious rights. In this conference, in-depth analyses on the ongoing protests are presented by different experts and guests from the Christian Ethiopians are also attended and presented their views that assert their solidarity with their fellow Ethiopian Muslims. Among the leading Diaspora based Muslim activists during this popular movement are Sadik Ahmad (based in DC), Akemel Negash (based in Turkey now Toronto), Isaac Eshetu (from Turkey), Abdurahim Ahmed (US), Awol Kassim Allo (UK) and Jawar Mohammed (US), etc. They contributed in giving information, analysis, directions as well as covering the overall phenomenon of the movements on social media and broadcast media. Following the outbreak of the Oromo protest in 2014, the latter two activists (Awol Kassim and Jawar Mohammed) have been engaged in this popular protest too using their prior skills in Ethiopian Muslim movements.

3 The Socio-political Impacts of the Movement

The protest that sparked at the end of 2011-2014 in a public sphere and continued in a silent or mainly on social media campaign up to the release of the committee in the mid-2018 has played a significant role for the raise of community awareness towards the non-violent movement of Ethiopian Muslims. The objective of the movement was initially not clear for non-Muslim citizens of the country and even for some Muslims too. This has mainly happened for two main reasons. First, at the beginning of the protest, the demands of the movements are not addressed in an organized and cohesive way including for the fellow Muslims. Second, the propaganda of the governments using the state media has also misled other Ethiopians about the actual fact of the demands of the movements. Using the narrative of the development of Islamic militant movements in the horn Africa and the context of regional and global geopolitics as a tool, the government at the beginning has able to give the wrong impression about the movements. However, the formation of arbitration committee and the usage of social media platforms for this consecutive movement that demands the implementation of secularism, reform of the *Majlis* and denouncing the imposition of the Al-Ahbash ideology by the government have gradually thrived to reach the heart of the many citizens. Soon after the widespread of the protest in many parts of the country, the Diaspora based Orthodox Church has also addressed their concern on the government's interference on religious affairs and condemned government's action and thus showed their solidarity with their fellow Ethiopian Muslims. As a result, the raise of community awareness by itself has improved the social bond within the wider public during this critical period of the movement regardless of some segregations inline of the ideological/political differences, particularly amongst the elite groups.

In fact, since a long time, the Ethiopian Muslims have been detached from each other due to internal and external factors. Before the outbreak of the protest in 2011, the Muslims are fragmented internally due to the emergence of different sects that resulted for ideological dichotomy within the Muslim, ethnic boundaries, and the lack of technologically advanced facilities that connect the different multi-cultural Muslim groups. The external factor is mainly the nature of regional and global geopolitics that divides the Muslim inline of extremists, radicals, terrorist, alien and indigenous or traditional Islam. Such and other related factors have played a major role for the detachment of the collective honor of Muslim Ethiopians. However, the spark of this movement in

2011 has paved the way for the rapid harmonization and developed synchronization (a sense of *Umma*) among the different multi-ethnic and cultural diversity. In this regard, *Ye Andennet ena Sedeqa Program* (literally the program of unity/solidarity and feast) that take place during the protest period in different parts of Ethiopia and abroad has rigorously contributed for the success of the unity project among the wider Muslim in particular and the country in general. In short, the movement was served as a unifying force among the Ethiopian Muslim and enables them to struggle for the right to practice their religion that guaranteed in the constitution. It furthermore enhances their cohesive power against the EPRDF government and thus at least helps them to hinder the government' s interference in religious affairs. Hand in hand, the movements follows the development of social interactions among the diverse Ethiopians irrespective of religion and ethnic background. Accordingly, this social impact of the movement instantaneously follows for the birth of the well organized social movements of the Oromo protests which first erupted in late April 2014 against the Finfinnee master plan (Addis Ababa Integrated Development Master Plan) projects.

The outbreak of the Ethiopian Muslim movements in 2011 has also entrenched another political impact on the nature and technique of non-violent movement stratagem that has been not applied before. Accordingly, the protesters have introduced a non-violent struggle such as holding the white ribbon, yellow card, and other non-verbal modes of expression of anti-government gesture such as crossing hands above head to expose and oppose government's action. The Oromo and other later protesters are much inspired by these non-violent modes of struggle and in their turn widely adapted it.

By underlining the peaceful nature of their demands, the recent Ethiopian Muslim movements turned to known signs and symbols of peace during the protests which is a new stratagem in the history of the country. In fact, the movement has been consistently demanding for the protection of democratic and constitutional rights and nothing more or less. It has embedded its demands in the most legal and legitimate manner and has staged perfectly nonviolent rallies. This is very significant for the development of an inclusive and non-violent democratic culture, especially in the country where democracy is not well put into practice. There's no doubt that the Ethiopian Muslim community has been radicalized, not in the sense that it has a political agenda, but in the sense that it has attained a higher degree of religious consciousness and hence become aware of it particularistic identity far more than it used to be in the past. The current Ethiopian Muslim popular movement is therefore very significant in affecting the political culture of the country. It has brought about a strong, consistent and yet a moderate peaceful struggle to the government. Most importantly, it has relocated our focus of the paraphernalia for the implementing of secularism and constitutional rights as well as building a democratic state.

Conclusion

Prior to the outbreak of the 2011 Ethiopian Muslim popular movement, three landmark movements have been taken place mainly from the imperial period 1930 up to the EPRDF rule. Accordingly, they have been protested against the government in different periods by bringing three major questions into the wider public such as the quest for citizenship/equal right, public holidays and quest for the establishment of the Ethiopian Supreme Council for Islamic Affairs (Majlis). The legitimate rights that Ethiopian Muslims demanded were critical to once again delegitimize the exclusivist discourse that had been reigning for centuries. Characterizing the discourse as unrepresentative to the wider Ethiopian polity, Muslims called for its disempowerment and for setting the state free so that it remains neutral and able to provide equal status to them. The Muslims served as a key positive force that contributed to the 1974 revolution. Subsequently, the Ethiopian state deposed the monarchic regime and turned a new chapter that parted ways with religion under the socialist military junta, the Derg. As for the question of *equal status,* of becoming a directly recognized organized religious society and a judicial body that Ethiopian Muslims were equally struggling for, they had to wait until late 2011 when a critical juncture recurred in their history of subjugation.

Over the last years mainly from December 2011 up to the political transformation in mid-2018, the Ethiopian Muslims have been demonstrated in different parts of the country, calling for the regime to end its interference in internal religious affairs and demanding for the implementation of secularism, reform of the Majlis and denouncing the imposition of the Al-Ahbash ideology by the government. During these consecutive non-violent movement periods, the regime has responded rather harshly, cracking down on the demonstrations and arresting the arbitration committee and other participants of the movements. This in turn has caused more tense relations between the Muslims and the EPRDF government. With hundreds of thousands holding demonstrations in protest at the government's alleged interference in religious affairs; the government has blamed the protests on a small group of extremists. In December 2011, the state moved to dismiss the administration of the Awoliya religious school in Addis Ababa. In July 2012, police dispersed an overnight meeting at the school for the preparation of Ye Andennet ena Sedeqa Program on the eve of an African Union heads of state summit, and arrested several protesters and organizers of the meeting, which police officials said the meeting did not have any official authorization. Actors behind the meeting, Yemuslimoch Meftihie Afelalagi Komitie (an arbitration committee that composes 17 members mainly from religious leaders, intellectuals and elders) wanted to discuss the overall situations with the government, unfortunately, arrested on 15 July 2012, with "plotting acts of terrorism" under Ethiopia's Anti-Terrorism Proclamation. Following the arrest of the leader of the movement, the Muslims' renewed, but again seriously orchestrated, demand for the release of their leaders and as well as demand the right to practice the religion and implementation of secularism. The movement as a part of the landmark peaceful struggle, from July 2012 continued by another an underground group called Demtsachen Yesema (Let our voice be heard!) up to the release of the arbitration committee in the mid-2018 subsequent to the political transition in the country.

Moreover, some of the demands of this long awaiting movement have become realized when the House of People' s Representatives on 11 June 2020, approved a bill to legally establish the Ethiopian Islamic Affairs Supreme Council (*Majlis*), a move with overarching positive implications for Ethiopian Muslim society. In fact, the proclamation serves as a key instrument for Ethiopian Muslims to reclaim their shared identity as an apolitical community. As an important precedent, the legal gateway also helps Ethiopian Muslims come to a unity centered on their rich history, culture, and, more significantly, their country, Ethiopia.

To sum up, the recent Ethiopian Muslim popular movement is served as a tool of unifying force among the wider Muslim public in particular and the country in general. They have proven that demonstrations by religious groups can be peaceful and that the implementation of secularism can be the aim of these groups. It furthermore entrenched the nature and technique of non-violent symbols of peace during the protests which is a new stratagem in the history of the country that inspires others too.

References

[1] ALEMU T. 2013. The Ethiopian Muslim Civil Rights Movement: implications for democracy in Ethiopia. http://luqmanethiopia.org | info@luqmanethiopia.org.

[2] AWOL K, ABADIR I. 2013. Redefining protest in Ethiopia: what happens to the "Terror" narrative when Muslims call for a secular state? http://luqmanethiopia.org|info@luqmanethiopia.org.

[3] AWOL K. 2013. The "War on Terror" and the Trial of 28 Community Leaders. http://luqmanethiopia.org|info@luqmanethiopia.org.

[4] BAHRU Z. 2001 A modern history of Ethiopia: 1885-1991, 2nd ed. Addis Ababa: Addis Ababa University Press.

[5] FEYISSA D. 2011. The transnational politics of the Ethiopian Muslim diaspora, Ethnic and Racial Studies, 35(11): 1893-1913.

[6] EYISSA D. 2011. Setting a social reform agenda in the homeland: the identity politics of the Ethiopian Muslims in the diaspora. DIASPEACE Working Paper, 9. https://jyx.jyu.fi/bitstream/handle/123456789/36887/DIASPEACE_WP9%5b2%5d.pdf?sequence=1&isAllowed=y.

[7] ÉLOI F. 2015. The Ethiopian Muslims historical processes and ongoing controversies. London: Hurst.

[8] CERULLI E. 1971. Islam yesterday and today. Roma: Instituto per l' Oriente.

[9] HAMZEH A N, Dekmejian R H. 1996. A Sufi response to political Islamism: Al-Ahbash of Lebanon. International Journal of Middle East Studies, (28):19.
[10] NIGUSSIE H. 2013. Audience reception analysis on "Jihadawi Harakat" documentary film among Addis Ababa communities. Addis Ababa: Addis Ababa University.
[11] HUSSEIN A. 2006. Coexistence and/or confrontation? towards a reappraisal of Christian-Muslim encounter in contemporary Ethiopia. Journal of Religion in Africa, 36. http://www.jstor.org/stable/27594361.
[12] JAWAR M. 2013. Growing Muslim activism and the Ethiopian state: accommodation or repression? http://luqmanethiopia.org | info@luqmanethiopia.org, Belgium, 2013).
[13] ABBINK J. 1998. An historical-anthropological approach to Islam in Ethiopia: issues of identity and politics. Journal of African Cultural Studies, 11(2): 109-124.
[14] ABBINK J. 2011. Religion in public spaces: emerging Muslim-Christian polemics in Ethiopia. African Affairs, 110(439): 253–274.
[15] ASSEN M. 2016. Contested secularism in Ethiopia: the contention between Muslims and the government. Addis Ababa: Addis Ababa University.
[16] ASSEN M. 2017. Ethiopia' s Ahbash path to religious moderation and countering extremism: pitfalls and discontents. Journal for the Study of the Religions of Africa and its Diaspora, 3(1): 21.
[17] HASHIMI M. 2012. Ethiopian Muslims and the Ahbash controversy. https://crescent.icit-digital.org/articles/ethiopian-muslims-and-the-ahbash-controversy.
[18] MIFTAH M. 2015. At issue: the "Muslims in Ethiopia complex" and Muslim identity: the trilogy of discourse, policy, and identity. African Studies Quarterly, 16(1): 71-91.
[19] MUSTAFA K, Haghai E. 2006. Al-Ahbash and Wahhabiyya: interpretations of Islam. Cambridge: Cambridge University Press.
[20] ØSTEBØ T. 2008. The Question of becoming: Islamic reform movements in contemporary Ethiopia, Journal of Religion in Africa, (38): 416-446.
[21] ØSTEBØ T. 2010. Islamism in the horn of Africa: assessing ideology, actors, and objectives. https://www.academia.edu/1122520/Islamism_in_the_Horn_of_Africa.
[22] ØSTEBØ T. 2013. Islam and state relations in Ethiopia: from containment to the production of a "governmental Islam". Journal of the American Academy of Religion, 81(4): 1029–1060.
[23] ØSTEBØ T. 2015. Dynamics of religious resurgence in the horn. https://www.africaportal.org/publications/horn-of-africa-bulletin-vol-26-no-2-march-april-2015/.
[24] ØSTEBØ T, SHEMSEDIN W. 2015. The intellectualist movement in Ethiopia, the Muslim brotherhood and the issue of moderation. https://ciaotest.cc.columbia.edu/pbei/noref/0033937/f_0033937_27640.pdf.
[25] ULRICH B. 2004. Islamic history and culture in southern Ethiopia: collected essays. Münster: LIT Verlag.

[26] WUDU T K. 2006. The Ethiopian Orthodox Church, the Ethiopian State and the Alexandrian See: indigenizing the episcopacy and forging national identity, 1926-1991. Urbana-Champaign: University of Illinois.
[27] OMAR A. 2020. The Ethiopian Muslims protest in the era of social media activism. Uppsala: Uppsala University.
[28] LUQMAN ETHIOPIAN-BELGIAN MUSLIMS ASSOCIATION (LEBMA). 2013. The civil rights movement of Ethiopian Muslims context, defining features and implications. Addis Ababa: LEBMA.